THE AFRICAN UNION'S AFRICA

Ruth Simms Hamilton
AFRICAN DIASPORA SERIES

THE AFRICAN UNION'S AFRICA: NEW PAN-AFRICAN INITIATIVES IN GLOBAL GOVERNANCE

RITA KIKI EDOZIE *with* KEITH GOTTSCHALK

MICHIGAN STATE UNIVERSITY PRESS • *East Lansing*

⊗ The paper used in this publication meets the minimum requirements of
ANSI/NISO Z39.48-1992 (R 1997) (Permanence of Paper).

Michigan State University Press
East Lansing, Michigan 48823-5245

Printed and bound in the United States of America.

20 19 18 17 16 15 14   1 2 3 4 5 6 7 8 9 10

LIBRARY OF CONGRESS CONTROL NUMBER: 2013957625

ISBN: 978-1-61186-136-5 (pbk.)
ISBN: 978-1-60917-421-7 (ebook: pdf)
ISBN: 978-1-62895-007-6 (ebook: epub)
ISBN: 978-1-62896-007-5 (ebook: mobi/prc)

Book design by Charlie Sharp, Sharp Des!gns, Lansing, Michigan
Cover design by Erin Kirk New
Cover image of Nkosazana Dlamini-Zuma is used by permission
of the photographer, Elmond Jiyane.

Michigan State University Press is a member of the Green Press Initiative and is committed
to developing and encouraging ecologically responsible publishing practices. For more information about the Green Press Initiative and the use of recycled paper in book
publishing, please visit www.greenpressinitiative.org.

Visit Michigan State University Press at www.msupress.org

Contents

FOREWORD, *Gerald C. Horne* vii

PREFACE xi

ABBREVIATIONS.. xvii

INTRODUCTION: The African Union as Pan-African Method and
as New Study of International Relations.. xix

PART 1. THE AFRICAN UNION IN THEORIES, METHODS, AND INSTITUTIONAL DESIGN
CHAPTER 1
Africa's African Union: Globalization and Global Governance............................ 3

CHAPTER 2
The Evolving "African" Suprastate: Histories, Anatomies,
and Comparisons 29

PART 2. AFRICAN ISSUES AND CONTEXTS: CULTURE, DEMOCRACY, SECURITY, AND DEVELOPMENT
CHAPTER 3
Pan-Africanist Globalization and Cultural Politics: Promoting the
African World View 61

CHAPTER 4
The African Union Democracy: Navigating Indigenous Rights and
Inclusions in Neoliberal Contexts 97

CHAPTER 5

Pax Africana versus International Security: New Routes to
Conflict Resolution 127

CHAPTER 6

Driving the Pan-African Economic Agenda: Ideology
and Institutionalism 153

PART 3. THE PROSPECTIVE AND THE PRESCRIPTIVE
CHAPTER 7

The African Union's *Africa*: Its Prospects and Its Challenges 183

CONCLUSION

The (Pan) African Union Phenomenon: Mali as Exemplar 213

APPENDIX

African Union: Provenance and Derivation of Organs and Institutions
in Comparative Context 241

NOTES 245
BIBLIOGRAPHY 247
INDEX 261

Foreword

Gerald C. Horne

Kwame Nkrumah of Ghana is generally given credit for realizing the Pan-African dream with the creation of the Organization of African Unity (OAU) in 1963 and its recently minted successor, the African Union (AU). This outstanding new book by Rita Kiki Edozie—and her collaborator, Keith Gottschalk—does eminent justice to the fruit of Nkrumah's dream and, in the process, provides a rich and textured analysis of the AU and what it will mean for the all-important global correlation of forces.

Giving Nkrumah his just due for the Pan-African project is not inaccurate, though it must be said that the concept of Pan-Africanism, as traditionally understood, was birthed in the diaspora more than a century ago by such eminent figures as the Trinidadian attorney Henry Sylvester Williams and the US intellectual W. E. B. Du Bois (Walters 1993). Marcus Garvey of Jamaica should be mentioned too in this context (Martin 1976). Even Nkrumah, who attended college in the United States where he was befriended by Du Bois, acknowledged freely the transatlantic orientation of his own brand of Pan-Africanism (Horne 1986).

That Africans torn from the continent were in the vanguard of Pan-Africanism and the need for an organization that eventuated in the AU should come as no surprise. After all, the Africans abroad had an all too familiar understanding of the malign forces that had ripped the continent apart over the centuries—colonialism and its malevolent handmaiden, the unlamented African slave trade in the first place. Consider, if you will, this odious commerce over a period lasting from the 1500s to the 1800s in a vast area stretching from today's Mauritania down the Atlantic coast to southern Angola, stretching widely inland—particularly along the Congo River—then looping its way around the Cape into Madagascar and Mozambique stretching northward.[1] And this only speaks of this dirty business as it populated the Americas and does not include its awful complement that preceded the Atlantic trade and stretched eastward across the Indian Ocean and Red Sea.

Historians ranging from Eric Williams of Trinidad to Walter Rodney of Guyana to the Nigerian-born Joseph Inikori have reminded us over the decades how this malodorous trade fueled the development of Western Europe and North America contributing mightily to the distorting imbalances in global wealth and power that continue to mar this small planet (E. Williams 1994; Rodney 1981; Inikori 2002).

Anthropologists (e.g., Melville Herskovits) and historians (e.g., Michael Gomez) have reminded us that the culture of Africa did not disappear in the diaspora; similarly failing to evaporate—it should be added forcefully—was the comprehension of the negatively transformative aspect of this dirty business on Africa itself and how a stronger continent could have forestalled this grievous tragedy (Herskovits 1941; Gomez 1998). Unsurprisingly, this fueled the Pan-Africanism that Nkrumah detected when he arrived in Pennsylvania in the 1930s to attend Lincoln University.

As Nkrumah was arriving in North America, Pan-Africanism in action was exemplified in the aftermath of fascist Italy's cruel invasion of the lodestar of African independence: Ethiopia. Not only did massive demonstrations erupt throughout the United States in particular, but as well, a number of African-Americans who had acquired only recently the ability to fly airplanes took this skill to Addis Ababa where they helped to develop that besieged nation's air force, then stayed on to develop what is still one of the continent's leading carriers: Ethiopian Airways (Scott 1993; Tucker 2012).

While in the United States, Nkrumah was also a participant in the activities of the Council on African Affairs (CAA), founded by the renowned artist and activist Paul Robeson in 1937 and that too included Du Bois and his eventual spouse, Shirley Graham Du Bois (Horne 2000). Solidarity with Ethiopia and the development of the CAA represent the embryo that was to give birth subsequently to the OAU.

Before and after the 1930s, seafarers from the Americas were in and out of African port cities, particularly Cape Town, where they helped to spread ideas that the authorities deemed to be seditious. The newspaper of the organization founded by the aforementioned Garvey was also circulated in Africa, to the consternation of the colonizers (Vinson 2012). Surely the liberation of South Africa in 1994 after a titanic battle that included the mobilization of African states, the African diaspora, and allies globally has been the most riveting and profoundly important example of Pan-Africanism in action in recent memory. Still, even if the great Nkrumah had never been born and even if Pan-Africanism had not developed in the diaspora, it is highly possible that today there would still be an insistent cry for an AU. Why?

It has been apparent for some time now that powerful political cum economic blocs are being developed making the future problematic for smaller nations that are not part of larger entities. There is the European Union (EU), for example, five hundred million strong with—by some calculations—the largest gross domestic product in the world. There are the Association of Southeast Asian Nations (ASEAN) and Mercado Común del Sur (Mercosur) in South America. There are developing blocs, for example, the BRICS—Brazil, Russia, India, China, and South Africa—that are proceeding formally to a kind of union. That is not to mention the Group of 7, lately the G8, led by the United States. This superpower also has sought to develop the North American Free Trade Association, which includes Canada and Mexico. Even smaller nations have seen the need to unite, as witnessed by the rapid evolution of the Caribbean Community (CARICOM).

These regional groupings were preceded by the formation of the United Nations (UN) itself in 1945 and its powerful Security Council (UNSC), which had been preceded by the League of Nations that emerged from the ashes and embers of World War I. It was within the UN that various blocs began to form, which manifests itself in, for example, African nations deciding who among their grouping should occupy the rotating nonpermanent seats in the UNSC.

In other words, if the powerful band together, as the EU tends to suggest, a fortiori it is incumbent for those not so blessed to do so. It is reminiscent of the illustratively graphic example often deployed by a trade union organizer who holds up a single matchstick before prospective members and breaks it easily in two to demonstrate what happens to those who proceed singly, then holds up a fat bunch of matchsticks and seeks to break it in two and finds that its ample mass will not allow this result. The lesson? In unity there is strength.

No better example of this sobering lesson can be found than the tragic bombing of Libya by the North Atlantic Treaty Organization (NATO) that led to regime change and countless killings. The AU sought to prevent this tragedy from unfolding, but its plaint was ignored as tons of weapons were dropped in northern Africa, many of which leaked into neighboring Mali, which allowed conservative religious radicals to seize a vast region larger than France and led to yet another resolution in the UNSC: this one calling for intervention in Mali, or to put it another way, cleaning up the mess created by the NATO intervention in Libya, a resolution acted upon, as I write, by yet another military intervention in Africa by France.

This latest outside intervention raises yet another troubling matter. There are a number of increasingly influential subregional groupings in Africa, including the Southern Africa Development Community (SADC), the Economic Community of West African States (ECOWAS), the Economic Community of Central African States (ECCAS), the Common Market for Eastern and Southern Africa (COMESA), and other groupings that include powerful African states, such as the Arab League and the Organization of Islamic Cooperation (OIC). The question is this: will the understandable proliferation of subregional groupings allow outside powers to engage in a kind of political arbitrage, playing off one African bloc against another and, thus, undermining the potential of the AU and facilitating external intervention in the internal affairs of African states?

This is a weighty matter, fraught with complication, but it is equally accurate to assert that when heads of state and government seek answers to this complexity, they will turn inevitably to this fact-filled, striking, and thoughtful book that Edozie and her collaborator Gottschalk have produced.

Preface

At the African Union's (AU's) fifty-year jubilee celebratory summit themed "Pan-Africanism and African Renaissance" in May 2013, Africa reaffirmed its commitment to Pan-Africanist ideals and aspiration for "greater unity," its "determination" to build an integrated, prosperous, and peaceful Africa driven by its citizens and representing a dynamic force, including those of equality between men and women and a union of peoples, and their "unflinching belief" in their common destiny, shared values, and commitment to the development of the African identity. On behalf of their citizens, African leaders pledged to the celebration of unity in diversity and the institution of African citizenship. They confirmed the commitment to Africa's political, social, and economic integration agenda, and in this regard speed up the process of realizing the objectives of the African Regional Economic Communities (RECs) and undertake steps toward the construction of a united and integrated Africa, by 2063 (African Union 2013).

We have written *The African Union's Africa: New Pan-African Initiatives in Global Governance* to reveal the complexities of how fifty-five disparate nation-states with close to a billion racially, ethnically, and culturally diverse peoples have embarked on such an ambitious agenda on behalf of Africans. In this regard, our book examines the initiatives of what we refer to as a Pan-African global governance institution and suprastate actor that has emerged on the global politics scene. Our ideological characterization of the AU in this distinctive fashion serves to reveal the institution's efforts to transform the national politics of Africa, on the one hand; and on the other, demonstrating through its own agency in globalizing the practice of African politics, our analysis hopes to unravel the AU's contributions to the emerging global infrastructure of governance. We conceptualize this manner of institutional and ideological behavior that characterizes the institution under study as "the AU phenomenon." Using Pan-Africanist and new constructivist international relations theoretical frameworks to guide and reconstruct our assumptions about the way that globalization occurs, the book will examine the AU as an international governance body of significance that is contributing to the transformation of African national politics in dynamic ways.

With the research data that we have compiled for this book, we hope to support this argument (the AU phenomenon) by illustrating that the AU is gradually achieving regional and global impact. The Union achieves its goals in Africa and the world, we argue, by resuscitating and cultivating a Pan-African vision with an aim of appropriating from the global North the notion that Africa is a global governance issue to be fixed by forces outside of Africa. We examine the AU as a regional and intergovernmental organization as well as an emerging socioeconomically integrated suprastate actor (these institutional statuses many times compete with each other). The book unravels ways that the AU revives Pan-Africanist ideology to wrestle for self-determined control of the continent in a contemporary global governance arena that is controlled by a western-dominated international community.

Throughout the book this notion of the AU phenomenon is illustrated, engaged, and explained in the areas of cultural identity, democracy, security, and economic development; the AU infuses new politics, economics, and cultures into globalization, representing the collective will and imprint of African agency, decisions, ideas, identities, practices, and contexts. Whether the AU employs institutional norms such as Pan-Africanism, African solutions for African problems, hybrid democracy, *Pax Africana*, or the African Economic Community (AEC) to nurture and drive its agenda, with *The African Union's Africa*, we hope to demonstrate that Africa—the world's least developed region—is nevertheless constitutive of crucial values, institutions, agents, actors, and forces that are, through the continent's AU, contributing to the advancement of contemporary global development.

So, what do we think will be the major contribution of *The African Union's Africa*? At this very initial stage of your read, we present the following three-tiered, prospective takeaway. First, the book presents an illuminating case study for the constructivist international relations turn, demonstrating (not merely asserting the need) how through Africa's AU, Africans are contributing to contemporary global development and governance in distinct ways. There is too little in the international relations literature that engages this fact.

Second, however, in illustrating, analyzing, and explaining how the world's least developed continent establishes, evolves, and sustains an international organization second only to the European Union (EU), the book presents the multifaceted and deeply rooted ideational symbol of Pan-Africanism as the key variable that guides African contributionism. Linking Pan-Africanist methodology to international relations this way is also something that we have not seen in the literature of either Africana studies or international relations.

Finally, in presenting a case study of African institutionalism, the book especially rejects dualist theorems that continue to analyze and explain contemporary African affairs and politics in old tropes, in our mind. Neorealist/neoliberal paradigms (both apply their models of Africa from an externalist perspective— outside looking in on Africa) are on one side; and on the other side, there is a simplistic, one-sided, equally externalist application of structuralism and/or neostructuralist, constructivist international relations to Africa (which examines only the socioeconomic, sociocultural, and sociopolitical terrain of African affairs disconnected from the reality of nation-statist politics and tends not to connect bottom-up social and cultural forces to regional collective action, institutionalism, and global governance).

All three international relations theories freeze and reduce Africa to a place that is acted upon by a hegemonic international community that Africa is not part of. The theories tend to carry on an obsolete model of African affairs in colonialist or neocolonialist discourses. In this respect, we feel that the current book alternatively presents Africa's millennial engagement with the world in more complex, nuanced, and dynamic terms. Through the AU, Africans exercise agency (acting in full autonomy from external powers) to conduct a delicate navigation of globalization and a dirigisme engagement with global governance. Such agency allows for the continent's nation-states, subregions, and peoples to forge interdependent relations with global actors in global contexts. The dynamics of such engagement—the struggle by Africans to equalize their continent's asymmetrical relationship with the world—produces for new globalization gains that are progressively, gradually, and mutually reinforcing for both Africa and the globe.

As the book's authors, we are Rita Kiki Edozie, a Pan-African politics and international relations teacher-scholar at Michigan State University, who as first author is responsible for the book's conceptual design and its primary authorship, and Keith Gottschalk, an African continent–based South African scholar of the comparative politics of Africa at the University of Western Cape, South Africa, a coauthor contributor. As Pan-Africanist teacher-scholars committed to the positive transformation of Africa, through the current project, we have pooled our expertise, skills, and talents to present an alternative discourse on African affairs. As college professors and public intellectuals, we target the book's usage for teachers, scholars, and specialists of African affairs, particularly those interested in a vibrant classroom or scholarly conference environment where deliberation and debate of African politics are ripe.

We employ an editorial style that anchors its discussion in the analysis and interpretation of documentary data from primary sources, including participant observations, interviews, archives, and communiqués gathered from the AU headquarter sites, archives, and websites. We apply this data against a diverse array of secondary-sourced scholarly literature written on the AU in books and journal articles. Our writing style and research presentation method strategically uses narratives, argumentation, contextual analysis, and inductive theorization. We also present a considerable amount of descriptive data compiled from statistical sources to support the book's objectives. Readers will have access to editorial support devices to enhance their learning and understanding of this important topic, including illustrations, charts, and document appendices—all that will inform deeply excavated research evidence about the book's topic.

The book is laid out as a three part, seven chapter academic scholarly treatise for multipurpose usage.[1] Each chapter reflects an aspect of the thesis outlined in the introduction and lays out the empirical evidence to support the book's theses in three distinctive parts. There will be a first part that serves to underscore methodological, theoretical, and historical scaffolding for framing the AU as a political and global institution, which will ground the rest of the book. A second part of the book uses issues and events to illustrate the global and national impact of the Union's activities in the areas of political, cultural, and economic globalization. And the third part will draw conclusions and determine future prospects about our thesis regarding the Union's impact on and agency in advancing globalization.

The current book owes tremendous credit and gratitude to our many assistants, unpaid collegial consultants and readers, and family supporters and promoters. To name a few, first, we are indebted to Professor Gerald C. Horne, for—through his Foreword—lending his tremendously powerful voice and intellect in helping to drum up our message about the need for revisionism and reconstructivism in correctly documenting the historical roles of Blacks (broadly conceived) in internationalism. So be it with continental, contemporary Africans!

Of course, we extend the greatest gratitude to Keith's and Kiki's families: Keith's spouse, Kiki's children (especially self-described Africapitalist, Pan-Africanist Goz Anyadiegwu, for his popular and diasporic social media inputs and passionate dialogues with mom about Africa), and our other loved ones have all done their part. Special thanks to the MSU-African-American and African studies doctoral research assistants who have worked on the project: AJ Rice and El Ra Radney. We are grateful to our publishers who demonstrated early confidence and thus commitment to the project: Julie Loehr and Kimberly Simmons of MSU Press. Finally, for access to the AU headquarters in Addis Ababa, Ethiopia, we have enormous gratitude to Adonia Ayebare, Yvette Ngandu, and Wafula Okumu, especially, for opening the door and letting us into their African World time and time again.

Abbreviations

AEC	African Economic Community
AU	African Union
COMESA	Common Market for Eastern and Southern Africa
EAC	East African Community
ECOSOCC	Economic, Social and Cultural Council
ECOWAS	Economic Community of West African States
EU	European Union
NATO	North Atlantic Treaty Organization
NEPAD	New Partnership for Africa's Development
OAU	Organization of African Unity
PAP	Pan-African Parliament
PSC	Peace and Security Council
REC	Regional Economic Community
SADC	Southern African Development Community
UN	United Nations
UNSC	United Nations Security Council

The African Union as Pan-African Method and as New Study of International Relations

A s the plane touched down in Bole International Airport, Addis Ababa, Ethiopia, I began to reflect on the curious questions that my colleagues had asked me about my research travel to Africa this year. Much more familiar with Africanist academics and international researchers traveling to places like Johannesburg, Cape Town, Dakar, Nairobi, Abuja, Lagos, and Accra, many asked "Where is Addis Ababa?" Once I located Addis (short for Addis Ababa) as the capital and foremost commercial city of Ethiopia and informed them that I was headed to Addis for archival and survey/interview field research for the current book on Africa's African Union (AU), in an immediate follow-up, I was asked, "But *why* Addis Ababa, Ethiopia?"

This question stood out to me as I spent my first days in Addis. Of course, the factual and simple response to this question as every Africanist knows is that Addis Ababa, Ethiopia, hosts the headquarters of the AU. In that case, naturally, my visit there was pragmatic—not really about Ethiopia but about the world's largest regional organization (in terms of population and member states), which happened to be located in Ethiopia. It would be as Brussels is to the European Union (EU). What's more, like Brussels has been for Europe and the EU, the cultural geography of Addis has been influenced by hosting the AU, and there are important historical reasons why the AU has chosen Addis as its home.

Along with Liberia (whose case is not as sanguine given its purchase as a lone American colony in Africa and named by the Americans as "liberty area"—land secured for returnee, formerly enslaved African-Americans), in the 1950s and 1960s at the initiation and helm of African independence and pan-nationalism, Ethiopia under the reign of Emperor Haile Selassie was the only African country that had not been colonized by European powers. As a result, the country would serve as the natural seat of the then Organization of African Unity (OAU) as a country symbolizing African self-determination, freedom, and anticolonialism, all objectives folded into the institution that is the now the object and subject of the current study. The Charter of the OAU would be adopted in Addis, following the 1963 Addis Ababa Summit where Emperor Selassie would urge African members with divergent perspectives on African unity (the Casablanca and Monrovia groups) to come together and compromise.

Ethiopianism—a child of and precursor for Pan-Africanism—had become a symbol for the Black world struggle ever since Menelik II defeated the Italian colonialist invasion at the Battle of Adowa in 1896. Despite the Italian comeback and ultimate occupation of Ethiopia for five years under Selassie, the "Lion of Judah" as he is referred to by three thousand years of Ethiopian history that dates to King Solomon, the Ethiopian leader would not accept this conquest as colonization. Using his country's membership in the then League of Nations (now United Nations [UN]), Selassie, also known as Ras (King) Tafari (yes, the roots of the Rastafari "Rasta" global Black culture begun in Jamaica), would again win his country's freedom through geopolitical and international diplomacy, maneuvering in ways achieved by no other African country.

At the inaugural summit of the OAU (from which the AU was born), Ethiopia's Selassie would infuse his international diplomacy skills into an emerging independent Africa and introduce the continent to the world scene.

> We stand today on the stage of world affairs, before the audience of world opinion. We have come together to assert our role in the direction of world affairs and to discharge our duty to the great continent whose two hundred fifty million people we lead. Africa is today at mid-course, in transition from the Africa of yesterday to the Africa of tomorrow. Even as we stand here we move from the past into the future. The task on which we have embarked, the making of Africa, will not wait. We must act, to shape and mould the future and leave our imprint on events as they pass into history. . . . Men on other parts of this Earth occupied themselves with their own concerns and, in their conceit, proclaimed that the world began and ended at their

horizons. All unknown to them, Africa developed in its own pattern, growing in its own life and, in the nineteenth century, finally re-emerged into the world's consciousness. (Nazret 1994–2014)

Of course, in a postimperial revolution (Ethiopians ousted Selassie in a revolution in 1973) and a postcommunist era (Ethiopians again ousted their communist reign of terror regime led by Mengistu Haile Mariam in a third-wave democracy revolution in 1990), Ethiopia's imperial history remains but a coloring of Addis's cultural terrain. One of Selassie's two palaces is a museum, and the monarch's posterity—I am told by the local taxi driver—lives in England.

The other palace is the home of Ethiopia's current postcommunist leaders; while I was there, that leader was President Meles Zenawi, who was Ethiopia's first non-Amharic leader and (sort of) first democratically elected leader, and who held the presidency for twenty-two years. In 2012, Ethiopia has a vibrant and dynamic history of African Abyssinian politics and culture (this country's 60 percent Christian population practiced Christianity before the Italians or the British) that makes it symbolic of the ideals of an Africa that is being sculptured by Africa's AU.

The country is one of too few African countries south of the Sahara (with Tanzanian Kiswahili, Somalia's Somali) whose lingua franca is solely an African language—Amharic. The cultural and linguistic expression of Amharic distinguished this otherwise characteristic modern African city to me. Despite having traveled to several African cities, because of Amharic expression in official discourse, media, and even digital communication (Amharic-lettered keyboards and Google scripts), I formulated a quite admirable impression of Addis as an indigenous African city. Ethiopia's history as an African country at the helm of early international relations is the reason why the country also hosts the UN Economic Commission for Africa (UNECA), a monstrously enormous UN organization itself. It was established in 1958, five years before Africa's OAU (the AU predecessor), and Emperor Selassie would negotiate as one of Africa's two independent nation-states and League of Nations members to host the prestigious UN organization.

Commuting daily through Addis Ababa to the AU headquarters similarly immersed me in the city's everyday character and provided a view to the distinctiveness of the Ethiopianist Pan-Africanist experience evidenced in the city's demography and geography. One had a sense that Ethiopia is an emerging market with Addis sprouting an impressive skyscraper skyline, new dual roadways, roundabouts, and traffic jams in the midst of a panorama of distant hills and plateaus.

The new AU headquarters, donated to the AU by China, contributes to this new modern architecture as the site of the city's tallest building. Postimperial and postcommunist Ethiopians are an emerging middle class and working class going about their business in Addis. Because their country hosts the Union, Ethiopians might be closest in awareness of the AU's goals to create a transnational African citizenship, an integrated cross-continental economy and society, as well as a single African political union—Africa, the suprastate.

At the AU headquarters, most of the service workers are Ethiopian from the country's range of ethnic regions—Amharic, Somali, Tigre, Afar, Oromo, Sudan; the AU likely provides a prestigious employment resource for the country as its late leader, Meles Zenawi, constantly professed to his nation's people. In an early 2012 squabble between the country's opposition and the embattled president, who passed away in office in September 2012, Zenawi defended the AU's erection of a statue of Kwame Nkrumah in front of the new building. Scolding the opposition for its criticism of the impressive statue of Africa's founding Pan-Africanist, "It is only Nkrumah who is remembered whenever we talk about pan-Africanism," Zenawi told local media. "It is a shame not to accept his role" (*Independent* 2012). Of course, the opposition's request to the AU Commission to erect an additional statue of Emperor Haile Selassie alongside Nkrumah was perhaps the Ethiopian people's desire to memorialize their country's own distinctive role in Pan-Africanism as well.

The professional workers of the AU perhaps make up the closest semblance of an African citizenry and collective cultural expression if there ever was one. Walking through the multibuilding headquarters, one recognizes African accents, phenotypes, and cultural profiles from all over the plural continent—north, east, west, central, south, Islands, Anglophone, Francophone, Arabic, Lusophone, Ethiopian, Kenyan, Tanzanian, Senegalese, Egyptian, Nigerian, Congolese, Gambian, South African, Zimbabwean, and a range of others. One of these workers reminded me that through this cohort, Addis houses the largest diplomatic corps in the world outside of New York and Geneva.

It was apparent to me that the AU was also cognizant of this pluralistic African identity that it both represents and convenes. A huge advertising board welcomed visitors to the Union, announcing, "I am an African: I am the African Union." The slogan is accompanied by select photographs of a range of African peoples—a child, a woman, a man—clearly representative of the diversity of the continent. The AU's 2012 campaign's use of "I am an African" has its appropriate roots in former AU President and South African President Thabo Mbeki's 1996 speech "I am African," where he eloquently unraveled both the dynamic and turbulent history of Africa to present the African identity as anyone born of the peoples of the continent of Africa from the Khoi, to the Berbers, to the European migrants. The campaign competes nonetheless with the 2006 Keep a Child Alive ad campaign that featured Gwyneth Paltrow with the slogan "I am African." That controversial ad indicated that modern humans, including wealthy Americans and westerners, are linked genetically to the continent and so should donate to poor Africans today unable to address health crises such as AIDS.

Being in Ethiopia was a poignant reminder of why Africa remains at the heart of global discussions about race and human identity, as the Mbeki speech, the Paltrow ad, and the AU's 2012 branding campaign suggest. Ethiopia is Africa's home for Dinkenesh or Lucy (found in 1974, lived 3.2 million years ago) and Ardi (found in 1994, lived 4.4 million years ago), both touted by skeletal carbon dating and DNA to be evidence of the world's first human ancestors discovered along the continent's long and deep Nile Rift Valley through Ethiopia, Tanzania, Kenya, and Mozambique. Indeed, contemporary modern humans who didn't make the trek out of Africa are today's diverse Africans who have been targeted by Africa's AU for reinvention and revitalization in a continent in dire need of recognition, development, change, and progress.

It is this vision by the AU that has motivated my visit to Addis Ababa, Ethiopia, in connection with the research and development of this book with Keith Gottschalk. The Union's stated objectives have been documented in numerous textual sources that are easily accessible online and in primary- and secondary-sourced materials. Yet, textual and secondary sources do not capture the complex subjectivities of sociocultural behavior, the adeptness of first-discursive observation on my part as author, the close revelation of agentcentric voices, and the appreciation of range, nuance, and other sensibilities that the field visit to the book's main object of study—the AU—provided for the authenticity of the knowledge that Keith and I wished to produce on this subject.

The visit to Addis Ababa is part of our research design that facilitates direct, on-the-ground, empirical fieldwork data-compilation to guide the close observation of what we feel are important political and socioeconomic transformations in Africa today driven by Africa's AU. The research trip to Ethiopia provides the occasion to conduct an ethnographic study of sorts of the AU that allowed for an up close, personal experience with and participant observation of the organization's institutional culture. The trip provided us a ringside view to observe for a short term a detailed description of how the AU organization operates in relation to the Ethiopianist Pan-African history, terrain, and climate that the institution has been immersed in for half a century. Traveling to this site enabled a firsthand observation of the Union's dynamic and intricate, foremost political, Pan-Africanist, and globally relevant function and purpose.

An example of this kind of seeing occurred during the visit, which coincided with the July 19, 2012 Summit incident over the decision of Malawi (the scheduled host of the 2012 Summit) to deny an invitation to the summit to the president of a fellow AU member; I observed the incident as a close bystander in Addis. Joyce Banda, the new president at the time of Malawi and second female president to lead any African country, targeted the Sudan because the country's pariah president, Omar al-Bashir, had previously been issued an arrest warrant from the International Criminal Court (ICC). The ICC arrest warrant of a sitting African president undergoing peace negotiations between warring parties mediated by the AU had been rejected by the Union, who instructed its members to ignore the warrant as unconstitutional and an assault on African sovereignty. In having agreed to host the 2012 Summit, Malawi saw things differently. Arguing that it had an obligation to its international donors who had threatened to withdraw important aid to the country if it did not arrest the Sudanese president in accordance with ICC statutes, a month away from the summit, Malawi withdrew its offer to host.

It was at the eve of my visit that the AU swiftly responded by moving the July summit back to Addis Ababa and reaffirming that member states had an obligation to Africa rather than to the West. The incident was intensely debated by the Ethiopian press and AU employees during the field visit. Dubbed the Malawi Affair, the controversy reignited sentiments of Pan-Africanism among casual African observers, especially among Ethiopian lay workers, who claimed in comparison to Malawi that Ethiopia was a poor country that received international aid, too, even though "their Meles" stood up to Western donors when such donors infringed on Ethiopian sovereignty. Several AU employees saw the incident as a pointer to the glaring challenges that Africa and the AU have in determining their self-reliant political-economic objectives in a contemporary global arena. Each summit brings its own global controversy, as occurred a year later during the AU's fifty-year jubilee celebratory summit dedicated to "Pan-Africanism and African Renaissance." The AU banned some foreign diplomats and noncontinental civil societal organizations who announced that they would protest the then new and controversially elected Kenyan President Uhuru Kenyatta.

As such, in answering my colleagues' question "why Addis Ababa?"—which also became the most frequently asked question raised by the AU employees and Ethiopians interviewed while there—the response is that Keith and I use Ethiopia as a platform to examine the activities of this political institution that we observe as an emerging global governance body and suprastate actor representing the collective action of Africans in the twenty-first century. We have referred to the AU as a Pan-African international organization drawing from its self-proclaimed definition and vision of itself as "An integrated, prosperous and peaceful Africa, driven by its own citizens and representing a dynamic force in [the] global arena" (African Union "AU in a Nutshell").

The AU's first four of its fourteen objectives underscore the role that Pan-Africanism and global governance play in the Union's dynamism. The Union strives "to achieve greater unity and solidarity between the African countries and the peoples of Africa." It seeks "to defend the sovereignty, territorial integrity and independence of its Member States." The Union intends "to accelerate the political and socio-economic integration of the continent"; and it says that it will "promote and defend African common positions on issues of interest to the continent and its peoples" (African Union "AU in a Nutshell").

Ethiopians and AU employees expressed Pan-Africanist aspirations and worldviews during conversations we had with them while in Addis. Discussions on the 2011 Libyan conflict at the time, for example, were still rife among them. Nowhere was evidence of such aspirations more illustrative than in the recent enacting of the AU's alternative political perspectives and policy initiatives on the North Atlantic Treaty Organization (NATO) intervention in Libya. Rather than cooperate as it had done in the past, the AU publically criticized the militarist interventionism of its suprastate counterparts (UN, NATO, ICC) in Africa. The event led to contentious relations between the AU and the West over differences on how to manage conflict on the continent.

As Pan-African political scientists ourselves, we are interested in a number of objectives for the current study. Our questions represent a wide range and scope of African affairs and studies: Why does the AU still stand fifty years after its original emergence as the OAU? How has the organization institutionally evolved, strengthened, and expanded from what later chapters reveal to be the OAU regional to the AU global? Why do all countries in Africa—except one (Morocco)—continue to participate in the organization's collective action? How do African nations and peoples use the AU for their collective interests on behalf of Africa and in the service of Africa *vis-à-vis* the contemporary global governing order?

As such, on one level, we wish to define and describe the AU. However, deciphering the Union's institutional order is not as straightforward as it may seem. Is the AU a regional organization, a suprastate, an international intergovernmental governance body, or all three? As a further matter, we are interested in assessing the role and significance of the AU on contemporary African politics. In this regard, we ask, what are the AU's initiatives in key areas of African affairs—cultural and social identity, democracy and human rights, security and conflict resolution, and economic development—and what impact does the Union make in these areas? These questions prompt us how to understand the AU's political behavior in relation to globalization and global governance. In doing so, we attempt to assess the AU's relevance to African peoples, African nations, African subregions, the African continent, and the international community.

As headquarters to the AU, Ethiopia, with its distinctive history and ideology of Ethiopianism, represents an illustrative preface for grounding the current book's objectives that are illustrated by contemporary incidents like the Malawi affair and the Libyan civil war. Pan-Africanism, Ethiopianism, and the dynamic of the contemporary AU are manifest in W. E. B. Du Bois's *The World and Africa* when he writes,

> The idea of one Africa to unite the thought and ideals of all native peoples of the dark continent belongs to the twentieth century and stems naturally from the West Indies, and the United States . . . where various groups of Africans, quite separate in origin, became so united in experience and so exposed to the impact on new cultures that they began to think of Africa as one idea and one land. . . . It was not, however, until 1900 that a black West Indian barrister called together a conference that would use the word "Pan African" for the first time. (Du Bois 1979)

Curiously, it is the response of a US journalist that coheres together these interrelated themes. That is to say, a *Chicago Tribune* dispatch would refer to Du Bois's Paris conference proposal as an "Ethiopian Utopia," a platform for "the Africans guided by an international organization" (Du Bois 1979, 9). Observations, dialogues, discussions, and debates with Africans in Ethiopia have reinforced for us what has been a historical reality that through political, economic, and cultural globalization, Africans use organizations like the AU to reappropriate and re-represent African affairs in a global context.

The Addis Ababa field visit pushed our research to demonstrate in more succinct ways how the AU is infusing into globalization the collective will and imprint of African agency, decisions, ideas, identities, practices, and contexts. As such, our ethnographic study in relation to the AU in Greater Addis Ababa allowed a space for our subjects to push a more critical, though enthusiastic, elucidation of the book's agenda as stated: as a contribution to enhancing African political change in three interrelated distinct areas that will inform the intellectual bedrock of the current book's subsequent chapters—Pan-Africanism, African agency, and new themes in international relations and globalization studies.

Pan-Africanist Globalism

The field research visit to the AU's Ethiopian headquarters in Addis Ababa marks an important starting point for us in examining what we have referred to as an emerging Pan-African suprastate of regional and global significance in describing Africa's AU. Using theories of continental and diasporic, transactional Pan-Africanism, the book will reveal how the AU is gradually achieving regional and global impact by resuscitating and cultivating a Pan-African vision for Africans by its posture of engagement in contemporary global politics.

Through our analysis of the AU, we see that, as a commitment to African self-determination, to decolonization, and to the revival of African dignity, Pan-Africanist ideals have informed the essence of international politics since the early 1900s when the political movement was founded by Africans in the diaspora and then expanded to the African continent in the decolonizing period of the 1940s and 1950s. Africa's AU has emerged today as a result of the promulgation of the idea embodied in Pan-Africanism that has a deep global history dating back to the Europe-Africa encounter of the early 1500s that produced the transatlantic slave trade and of which Ethiopianism is a close historical relative. Pan-Africanism has a long history in acting as a rallying slogan, a springboard, and an ideological vehicle for cultivating the common efforts of African and African-descendant peoples to advance their political efforts globally. John Gibbs St. Clair Drake's 1968 definition of Pan-Africanism is still the most comprehensive to capture the AU dynamic:

> I begin with a political concept developed by men of action not scholars, by a group of American Negroes and West Indians between 1900 and 1945—Pan-Africanism—the idea that Africans and peoples of African descent in the New World should develop racial solidarity for the purpose of abolishing discrimination, enforced segregation, and political and economic exploitation. (Walters 1993)

A century after the work of Henry Sylvester Williams and W. E. B. Du Bois, the AU phenomenon that we unravel in the current book supports the reality that Pan-Africanism is taking a practical shape albeit in new frames. The Pan-Africanist solidarity that St. Clair Drake refers to is alive and expansive in Africa as it manifests contemporaneously in the local, national, and international political ideologies and processes of Africans and their descendants. It professes its objectives politically, culturally, and economically, particularly in Africa's international relations. Note, for example, the proclamations that emerged from the Pan-Afrikanist Steering Committee of Namibia regarding the 2011 Libyan crisis:

> The Pan Afrikanist Steering Committee of Namibia Against The United Nations Resolution 1973 (PSCNAUNR), notes with deep sadness, the appalling atrocity being committed by NATO's bombardment. . . . We note, with deep regret that there was an Official AU Road Map in place under Article 20 of the United Nations' Charter, wherein the AU Delegation was positioned to meet with the sovereign leader of Libya and the Western sponsored Rebels. Before the AU could carry out its legal and moral duty, The North Atlantic Treaty Organization (NATO), under the guise of the UN deliberately started its bombardment under a hidden agenda for Regime Change, contrary to the principles enshrined within the said Article. (Valiente 2011)

Claims against imperialism, as well as in support of African unity, self-determination, and collective self-resistance, are values that have laced the Pan-Africanist idea and thus guided African affairs for almost two centuries. It is these ideas and their different iterations represented by a range of Pan-African leadership regimes including those of W. E. B. Du Bois, Kwame Nkrumah, and Thabo Mbeki that have cultivated the AU's emergence in 2002, and its institutional growth a decade later, as a torchbearer for Africans' long-standing experience with globalization and geopolitics. Driven by a desire for the solidarity, liberation, and progress of Africa and its descendant peoples, Pan-Africanism guides the political behavior of the AU in dynamic ways.

Scholars of Pan-Africanism have chartered variable Pan-Africanist relationships that they present as models: among African states, among African states and African-origin states in the diaspora, among African states and African-origin peoples and communities in the diaspora, among African-origin states in the diaspora and African-origin communities in the diaspora, and among African-origin communities in the diaspora (Walters 1993). Pan-Africanism also varies according to racialistic, continental, nonstate, state, institutional, top-down, bottom-up, revolutionary, gradualist, instantist, cultural, political, transatlantic, and even trans-Saharan qualifiers (Mazrui 2001). Drawing from all of these variable dimensions, the current book inventively interrogates the AU's political behavior using Pan-Africanism to reveal the Union's *longue-durée* histories and the embedded cultures that it uses to drive its politics. In this regard, the AU is a case study that demonstrates how the Pan-African unity idea has evolved into a forceful ideological vehicle for contemporary African global era politics.

Pan-Africanism arose as one response to five centuries of specifically capitalist slave trade and racism that was part of a world system of merchant capital accumulation—hence its *longue-durée* status. In relation to this, we demonstrate ways that Pan-Africanism drives the contemporary AU political-economic agenda facilitating its emergence as a relevant actor in the contemporary global arena and in global governance. It is the force that underlies the AU's institutional evolution as it contributes to the transformation of African national and global politics in complex and challenging albeit dynamic ways.

Subsequent chapters help us to see the way that the AU resuscitates as well as reinvents Pan-Africanism, using it for cultural and social mobilization to achieve political-economic ends in the contemporary world. With the current book, we argue that, to achieve its ends, the AU is engaged in the reconstruction of a universal African identity among the geographically and socioculturally diverse arena of peoples of Africa and its diaspora who are already linked socially and culturally through complex networks of social relationships and processes (Hamilton 2006). This fact is supported by the AU's 2006 establishment of the sixth region (of five continental regions) or the Diaspora Clause contained in Article 3.c of the AU's Constitutive Act. The clause, which gives African people, communities, and countries born in the African diaspora formal AU membership, indicates to the world that the African world occupies more than a continent. The Pan-African world through which the AU navigates to govern is territorially expanded from the continent throughout the globe.

A hundred years of sustained Pan-Africanism created a global arena in which dispersed Africans and their descendants existed in a multilayered, interactively varied, complex network mediated within an even wider and deeper global social ordering. In establishing the sixth region, the AU sculpts these deep-seated, multidirectional hybrid cultural domains and networks of social relationships and processes to use for its own political ends. The AU's Diaspora Clause has politicized the long-standing historical and sociocultural Pan-African diaspora movement, extending institutionalized continental Pan-Africanism to the diaspora and thereby creating an international network of ideas and practices that, through the AU, can be positioned as a political body (Davis and M'Bow 2007). As an ideology of the AU, Pan-Africanism, we argue, contains the ontology to address the Union's global objectives carrying with it the conscious understanding of African and African-descendant peoples' identity in a larger worldwide activity of continental and diaspora peoples who have obligations and responsibilities to each other (Poe 2003, 50).

The AU congregates Africans on the continent and in the diaspora to collectively reappropriate from the global North the North's undesirable tendency to reduce the entire continent to one of many global governance issues to be fixed by forces outside of Africa based on its own terms and not Africa's. This fact underscores the Union's most important function: to wrestle with external actors for self-determined control of the continent and operate freely in a deeply complex contemporary global governance arena that is dominated by an international community and a global-economic structure that tends to at once exclude, marginalize, and paternalistically control Africa and the African identity.

In 2012 becoming the first woman to lead the AU Commission (the AU's Secretariat), South Africa's Nkosazana Dlamini-Zuma ended her acceptance speech with a quote from Marcus Garvey, a proponent of Pan-Africanism and Black Nationalism: "The history of the movement, the history of the nation, the history of a race is the guidepost of that movement's destiny, that nation's destiny, that race's destiny." Invoking the generational and historical journey that Pan-Africanism has taken to inform the core principle of the AU, in a call for unity Dlamini-Zuma called on the founders of the OAU, saying, "Those heroes and heroines who were pan-Africans held a vision of a united economically and politically emancipated continent at peace with itself and the world" (Jobson 2012).

This is the new Pan-Africanism practiced by the AU: statist, but pluralistic engaging with national state and nonstate actors, culturalist and roots-oriented, but not essentialist, and both continental (and thus regional) and diasporic, as well as internationalist and globalist. In consciously resuscitating and cultivating the Pan-African vision and deploying it in the domains of international politics, new security, and international political economy, the AU infuses into globalization the collective will and imprint of local, national, regional, and global African agency, decision making, ideality shaping, identity formation, policy practices, and the formulation of culturally specific contexts that lend specificity to continental domains and peoples in a global era.

Our Pan-Africanist method employs a goal similar to that articulated by Ronald Walters, who has argued that through a mutual exchange among Africana communities worldwide, the AU can bear the burden of Africa and its descendants and ameliorate their politically, economically, and socioculturally marginalized condition on the globe (Walters 1993). In this regard, the current authors support the AU's viability as a public good for Africa consistent with Pan-Africanist aspirations.

The AU as Case Study of New International Studies: "African Solutions for African Problems"

Our utilization of themes drawn from methodological Pan-Africanism directly relates to our book's analysis of the AU in connection to new theories in globalization studies. This helps to understand the Union's engagement with African politics in a global era. The widely popular phrase—and now core principle of the AU—"African solutions for African problems" reflects this intersectionalism between global-era expression of Pan-Africanism and new international studies reflected as global governance. First coined by former OAU and AU president Olusegun Obasanjo of Nigeria to reflect the core ideology that would justify the necessity of the establishment of a new global AU out of an old regional OAU, African solutions for African problems would refer to African autonomy and the imperative to develop indigenous capacities and public policy solutions for continental affairs (Apuuli 2011).

The exact meaning of the African solutions mantra is interpreted variably along an axis of ideologies supporting a Pan-Africanist framework, on the one hand, and a global governance theoretical framework, on the other. An AU magazine, the *AU Monitor*, reflects on what the phrase really means. It asks whether African solutions for African problems is aimed at mobilizing Africans to solve their problems, or if it is a cop-out to explain inaction toward Africa from the international community, or even a self-serving shield to protect African dictators from international prosecution. In response, Bjorn Møller describes the phenomenon in both Pan-Africanist and global governance contexts that may be integrated.

On the one hand, Møller argues that in Africa African solutions for African problems connotes and invokes a genre of pan-nationalism, a pride and a can-do attitude, and marks a break with the not so distant past when all the continent's problems were justifiably blamed on the European colonialists and their neocolonialist successors. In this regard, we agree with Møller that the phrase in actuality signals a new and more constructive attitude toward African affairs embodied by Africans. In the aftermath of the failure of the international community in the

1990s to decisively deal inter alia with the genocide in Rwanda and state collapse in Somalia, Møller would argue that African countries resolved to craft their own solutions to the problems emerging on the continent (Møller 2009).

At another level, according to Kasaija Phillip Apuuli, African solutions for African problems may suggest evidence of Africa's new global engagement. It would mark a new acceptance of division of labor and sharing of responsibilities with the international community by Africans. It would reflect the complexity of Africa's problems, which requires a collective and collaborative approach premised on a range of partnerships that should seek to establish coordination on both the international and continental levels (Apuuli 2011). Both nationalist and global governance values explain how the notion of African solutions for African problems made its way to become one of the founding principles of the AU by 2002.

The AU's African solutions for African problems mantra, which the current book will argue drives the organization's contemporary political dynamic and behavior, presents an intricate way to examine the Union within an academic theoretical framework that David Held and Anthony McGrew have conceptualized as political, economic, and cultural transformational globalization (Held 2004). The authors' institutional analysis of globalization provides a way to see the AU as a vehicle of complex global convergence and divergence that serves to foster the institutional change of nation-states, local cultures, and economies. With Held and McGrew, our own adoption of a transformationalist perspective of globalization takes the phenomenon (globalization) as an existing reality of international relations that is considered to be amenable to the transformation of worldwide social relations across all its diverse dimensions: the economic, the cultural, the historical, and the contemporaneously internationalist. Through the AU example, we agree with the authors, however, who argue that these processes are dialectical, integrating, fragmenting, uniting and dividing; paradoxically, they both include and exclude select locales while being mediated by domestic and global factors (Held and McGrew 2007).

The pioneering scholarly intervention of Jeffrey Haynes, in his book *Comparative Politics in a Globalizing World* (Haynes 2005), complements this global studies research design by its bridging of the subdisciplines of comparative politics and international relations. The current book serves as an important case study for scholars and students who want to see the closer integration of conceptual formulations and research findings in these two traditionally distinct though overlapping areas of study; *The African Union's Africa* presents theoretical, empirical, as well as methodological evidence that the two go hand in hand in an age of globalization. Presenting a methodology that incorporates new methodological agendas in international relations and comparative politics brings us to the added phenomenon of African agency and by implication new ways of approaching the study of Africa. We agree with classic and pioneer international relations constructivist scholar Alexander Wendt when he argues that anarchy can be a structural fact about the world that states inhabit, but that it is up to politicians (and international relations scholars) to decide how to deal with that anarchy (Wendt 1992).

We feel that for too long the fields of comparative politics and area studies have ostensibly produced for the field of African politics a parochial, subarea study of African politics that has been approached from a skewed, introverted, country-case, bounded terrain. As an example, when the continent is examined in the context of globalization, it is often observed from the positioning and perspectives of global actors in ways that localize African political issues while sidestepping and subverting themes related to African countries' national sovereign foreign policies and especially their Pan-Africanist agency. This approach tends to elide African agency and conceal the required integrated analysis that underscores the intersections among local, national, regional, and global African political processes.

Other special international relations topics such as colonialism, structural adjustment, and trade issues have informed the most recent study of globalization in Africa; but they are single-issue topics that either present Africa as economically marginalized in the global system or present the continent as a collapsed bottom-tier region in the global security system. Not only is it important for political science methodologies to incorporate the reality of global practices into the study of African politics, the study of political science and its subgenre international relations must do more to examine the dynamism, complexity, nuance, and vibrancy of African agent–led practices in transforming national politics comparatively and in contributing to an impact on global affairs.

Our book especially draws from the scholarship of newer scholars of African international relations, such as Tom Tieku, who in developing the concept of African agency in international relations has identified factors and conditions that enable African states to exercise agency defined as the autonomy that Africans have through their lawful representatives (institutions) to define, act, own, control, and lead on issues that affect them (Tieku 2011).

Tieku argues that the Pan-African framework of the AU has enhanced African agency in multiple ways, including making the African voice louder in a crowded international conflict theatre and in turning representatives of the AU African international organization into de facto leaders and key actors in international community conflict-resolution interventions in Africa. Such a framework provides Africans with an institutional capacity to project African voice in prescribing its own self-determined policy solutions on important African affairs, a factor that further facilitates Africans' abilities to exercise independent (from the international community) authority in decision-making regarding issues that affect the continent (Tieku 2011).

A methodological parallel for the emerging concept of African agency is the longer-standing concept of African-centeredness developed by the Afrocentric literature (see Keto 2001, M. Asante 1998) and concerns the approach to writing about Africa by the current authors. Pan-Africanist agency represents a theoretical worldview as well as a methodological prism for writing and researching about Africans on the continent and in the diaspora. Africans should be the subjects of the story, which should be told from their epistemological perspectives and reference points, and such references should demonstrate Africans' self-determined capabilities and preferences.

C. Keto states that the African-centered paradigm places Africans at the center of information construction about Africans and leads to the formulation of a social policy that derives its inspirations from the relocation of knowledge about Africans, people in Africa, and peoples of African descent outside Africa (Keto 2001). In arguing for the inclusion of Africans' self-defined realities into the historiographical study of world history, Keto's African-centered thesis is little different from Tieku's quest for African agency and our own analysis of the AU's contemporary Pan-Africanism. As authors of the current study, given the AU's institutional longevity, since 1963 (as the OAU), and its impact in advancing a certain character of African politics by the twenty-first century, we are surprised that there are few comparative politics, international relations, or even African politics books dedicated to an analysis of the AU for usage in political science and international relations classrooms and scholarship. Exciting new analyses of globalization and comparative politics ignore the entire continent in their analysis. Up until October 2010, Wikipedia's "international relations" entry listed every regional organization on the globe—except for the AU. It was the current lead author who included the AU on the Wikipedia site in its rightful academic citation.

Despite this intellectual slight, our research shows that in terms of institutional development as well as impact on the region, Africa's AU is second only to the EU; Asia's Association of Southeast Asian Nations (ASEAN) and Latin America's Organization of American States (OAS) pale in comparison. None have evolved the elaborate institutional architecture and legal code that the AU has built. Neither can any of these organizations boast of having committed the number of peacekeeping soldiers to conflict zones in their regions. Perhaps the AU's economic union presents the greatest comparative challenge; however, even in this realm, through the Union's regional organizations and its predecessor, the OAU, customs and trade unions, as well as Regional Economic Communities (RECs) and rules, economic integration constitutes a significant component of the complexity and the advancement of the AU.

As such, the current book on the AU hopes to fill the gaps in analysis laid bare by others by applying a different prism through which to tell our story about Africa's AU and the AU's reconstruction of and engagement in Africa. In departing from what seems to be the standard analysis of African politics by several books in the field, our book's trajectory uniquely interjects the discussion of the AU into contemporary international relations debates, discourses, and trends, including constructivism, Pan-Africanism, and postcolonial studies. We employ an interpretive methodology to an analytic induction narrative analysis and cross-national comparative case study discussion to support our thesis about the AU.

We have drawn from both primary and secondary data. In addition to the rich literature and scholarship of knowledge produced on the Union from books and journals, we have gathered, compiled, and analyzed firsthand materials from AU satellite sites, institutions, and websites, as well as conducted field research at the AU's Addis headquarters and firsthand survey-interviews with AU officials. We examined archival documents, communiqués, reports, and meeting and conference minutes, as well as articles about the AU from continental news sources. In addition, as readers of the current book advance through parts and chapters, they will encounter a chronological sequence time and again. First, African governments sign a treaty for a structure that remains dormant, or is not actually set up. Second, within a decade or two, they create a new mechanism for the same purpose, and this mechanism functions intermittently. Third, a decade later, they inaugurate a new entity for the same purpose, which this time becomes operational.

The constructivist underpinning of our book, and its associative Pan-African discourse, covers space and time on scales vast by those usual in political studies. This is about not a country, but a continent. We discuss not the four years between elections, but over a century. Only China and India match the one billion people of Africa. Only Russia approaches the territorial size of Africa. One consequence of this is that we will be discussing an unusual kind of political leader of the AU organization. To advance their political career, politicians need something that will reap benefits within the four or eight years before the following election. In bureaucratic politics, military officers seeking a rank promotion and civil servants wanting advancement prefer projects that will show results within three to five years.

But for political leaders to devote a major share of their time and energy, and to use up valuable political capital, on a project that will only show significant benefits after the end of their political careers, and whose major rewards cannot arrive until after the end of their lifetimes, requires a rare kind of visionary. Europe had such a special politician in Jean Monnet. Africa has had several such rare political leaders with this commitment to the long perspective: Kwame Nkrumah, Thabo Mbeki, and Olusegun Obasanjo were prominent among them. Equally important were their back office administrators, who strove to wrest success from the reluctant: Diallo Telli, Salim Ahmed Salim, Adebayo Adedeji, Alpha Oumar Konaré, and Jean Ping. Of them, Telli paid with his life.

It is six score years since the Congress on Africa in Chicago led to a journalist coining the term "Pan-Africanism." Between the first proposal for an African Court of Justice and Human Rights (ACJHR) and for an African High Command and their eventual operationalization lay a half century of lobbying. From the founding of the OAU in 1963 until the completion of the last scheduled phase of the AU's Treaty of Abuja stretch seventy-one years. Our methodology is rooted in ground truth. This book starts the clock running, not from when a treaty is signed, but from when it came into effect, or from when a supranational court issued its first judgment, or from when the entity concerned started operations. For example, the Abuja Treaty, signed in 1991, came into effect in 1994. With this span of time as the warp and Africa and its diaspora as the weft, we shall explore the weaving of the fabric of Pan-Africanism.

The construction of social identities already foregrounded in our discussion of Ethiopia is an important dimension of the AU project and Africa agenda in this regard. The western construct of the concept "sub-Saharan Africa" often carries problematic baggage of a covert racial classification. Africa itself prefers different concepts and usages. There are a few African intellectuals who focus on historic conflicts between Arab and Black kingdoms and communities, but these are not the social identities that African institutions choose to organize around. The alternative division into central, east, north, south, and west regions is of UNECA and OAU vintage. Importantly, we should note that the choice of borders between such regions is not purely geographical but is a political decision and is not static but dynamic. For example, the Rwandan government chose to move from the central to the east region and was joined by Burundi in prioritizing membership of the East African Community (EAC). The Democratic Republic of Congo government moved from the central region by its choice to join the Southern African Development Community (SADC), becoming the largest member of the south region, reflecting historic rail and other economic linkages.

Sudan from the start affiliated not to the north region, but to the Common Market for Eastern and Southern Africa (COMESA), where it was later joined by Egypt and Libya. In short, the states of the north region construct identities of themselves as Maghreb or Nile Valley states, rather than privileging identities such as north Africa versus sub-Saharan Africa. Such a conceptual division carries an implicit racial partition based on skin color. It cannot be based upon religion, for a majority of African Muslims live south of the Sahara. Similarly the definition of an "Arab state" is political, rather than one of language or color. Three current members of the Arab League are states of black nations that have Arabic as their second, not home, language: Comoros (Kiswahili), Djibouti (Somali and Afar), and Somalia (Somali).

In short, the preference of many western institutions to dismember the continent—even for purposes of publishing statistics—between a sub-Saharan Africa and a north Africa and the Middle East is as infelicitous and obscurantist as it would be to conceive of a sub-Alpine Europe versus a north Europe and Eurasia. It will not be used in our book; our book follows African usages. Most African countries have multiple identities, and their AU membership is for the great majority alongside their membership in four international organizations that include them with their former imperialist conquerors and other non-African countries.

These organizations run along historical and linguistic lines and are currently titled the Commonwealth, Comunidade dos Paises de Lingua Portuguesa (CPLP), League of Arab States, and the Organisation Internationale de la Francophonie (OIF). And there are many political organizations that are Pan-Africanist and diasporic as they convene African and African-descendant peoples worldwide. One example is the Pan-African Liberation Organization (PALO) whose objective is to build revolutionary political and economic relationships between the diaspora and the continent to improve the material conditions of Africans on and off the continent. As reflected in the US-based Organization of Pan African Unity (OOPAU) website, the reality that the African identity and thus AU agenda is globally, culturally, and racially diasporic will not go unreported by the current project.

> Let it be known that we will reach out to all the African Nation's so we are
> allowed as African American's be allowed to join the African Union, we are
> a nation within a nation, so we must be allowed to join our brothers and

sisters in unity. We need the affirmation of our brothers and sisters in the Motherland, so that we are not still looked upon as ex-slaves or illegitimate children of the world. We need our brothers and sisters at home, to welcome us back into the family. We also need to dispel any and all differences between us, so that we may show our children how to be a good family member. (OOPAU)

To the many naysayers (and there are many—inside and outside of the AU), we agree that there is a lot to criticize about the AU; the organization has many challenges and limitations and continues to make many mistakes while failures no doubt abound. Nonetheless, to address these issues, we are not pessimistic; rather, we combine our global studies methodology with the Pan-Africanist method to present a prescriptive agenda for the current project—as is the constructivist style. That is to say, our analysis of what we refer to as the AU's transformationalist globalization presumes proactively by us as scholars that globalization is and can continue to produce public goods for contemporary states and societies as long as such goods are ethical and humane, combining economic efficiency with equity and social justice (Held 2004).

BOOK OVERVIEW

Our ideological characterization of the AU in the distinctive fashion described above serves to reveal the institution's efforts to transform the national politics of Africa, reformulating and reconstructing national politics pan-nationally, on the one hand; and on the other, demonstrating through its own agency in globalizing the practice of African politics, our analysis hopes to unravel the AU's contributions to the emerging global infrastructure of governance. Each chapter of *The African Union's Africa* is developed strategically to reflect an aspect of the thesis and scope outlined above while laying out the empirical evidence to support the book's objective in seven chapters, three distinctive parts, and hundreds of pages.

A first part serves as methodological and theoretical grounding for the rest of the book while, by using empirical issues and events to illustrate the global and national impact of the Union's activities, a second illustrates the way that the AU engages with four main issues of African affairs—security, African identity, democracy, and political economy—to realize its goals. Drawing its core evidence from primary-sourced interviews of AU officials, a third part serves to draw conclusions and determine future prospects about the book's thesis regarding the Union's impact on and agency in advancing Pan-African globalization and transforming while formulating a contemporary genre of African politics.

Part 1 introduces the theoretical and methodological lenses through which to provide an intellectual and scholarly premise and a comparative institutional context required for examining the book's objectives and thesis, as well as for following the qualitative and empirical data laid out in rest of the book. Chapter 1, "Africa's African Union: Globalization and Global Governance," establishes the book's key object of study, the AU, and our key arguments about the AU, and then goes on to present our theoretical and methodological framework about this thesis objective: Africans' role in advancing a contemporary genre of Pan-Africanist, transformational globalization through the AU. In this chapter, we employ theories of global governance and political, economic, and cultural globalization to inform hermeneutical lenses through which subsequent chapters will examine the impact that the AU is having on the reconfiguration of African politics and affairs and its prospects for realizing the organization's own self-defined goals and objectives.

Chapter 2, "The Evolving 'African' Suprastate: Histories, Anatomies, and Comparisons," introduces the structure of the AU as a regional and global organization and institution. In this chapter, we establish the AU as nascent suprastate. In answering the questions "What is the AU?" and "How does it compare to other like-institutions?" we describe the AU's institutional strength in relation to other international organizations—the EU, for example. We also illustrate the AU's architectural evolution comparatively as an evolution of its predecessor, the OAU, as well as from Africa's RECs. Here, we spell out our claim that, despite Africa's status as least developed and most globally marginalized in terms of institutional advancement, the AU stands second only to the EU.

That is to say, in terms of its scope, depth, impact, and institutional evolution, the AU appears to be a formidable international institution with significant regional legitimacy and growing global impact. In this regard, we will define the AU constitutively, historically, subregionally, and comparatively, showing how these elements have fostered the Union's emerging suprastate and global governance actor status and identity. To do this, we dissect the political and institutional elements that support our definitional analysis of the AU's structure and architecture. For example, we will see how the AU's Constitutive Act is key to this architecture; it is the social contract and legal code that underlies the AU's political profile and Africans' will for collective action.

In relation to this, the chapter introduces the AU's most important structures of governance through which it exercises its powers, including the Assembly, the AU Commission, the Executive Council, the Pan-African Parliament (PAP), the Peace and Security Council (PSC), the Economic, Social and Cultural Council (ECOSOCC, a civil societal body), and the ACJHR (continental court).The advanced evolution of AU institutions, governance bodies, and policies are at stark contradiction when imagining Africa's underdevelopment and global marginalization. Our key query here is to demonstrate the AU's capacity to achieve its institutional status at this juncture in global politics.

We use the chapters in Part 2 to interrogate and assess the impact that the AU has had on African politics on the one hand; and on the other, the impact that this organization's collective action has had on globalization in relation to the four big AU Africa issues: cultural identity, democracy and politics, security, and the political economy of development. Part 2's chapters tell stories about internationally topical events and provide our readers with a more rigorous interpretive deduction of the AU's political actions. Chapter 3, "Pan-Africanist Globalization and Cultural Politics: Promoting the African World View," introduces the first African issue through which the AU practices its politics: cultural identity. The chapter examines the principles, values, and norms that undergird the AU's contemporary global, collective action.

Given our thesis that the AU exists, functions, and acts today as one of two global emerging suprastates that has embodied the collective will of Africans, this chapter establishes the rationale behind the AU and demonstrates ways that the AU spreads its own African world view. We are guided by this question: How does an AU come about in light of Africa's deep pluralism, the historically global dispersal of its peoples, its underdevelopment, and its hegemonic marginalization? Arguing that the AU is a product of the *longue-durée* globalization of Africa fostered by the power of the Pan-Africanist idea, in this chapter we see the role that cultural transformative globalization has played in fostering the emergence of the AU.

That is to say, we demonstrate how the AU has emerged from the promulgation of the Pan-Africanist idea, identity, and ideology, which we show to have had a global and circular history and future derived from a desire for the solidarity and liberation of Africa and its descendant peoples. Characterized as the notion of a Pan-Africa or Global Africa, the AU has emerged from—and acts within—a globalization that consists of an unbounded geographical and sociocultural space made up of the diverse peoples of Africa and its diaspora. In this chapter, we see how these peoples are linked through complex historical and transgenerational networks of social relationships and processes that the AU reconstructs and utilizes to continue the historical role that Pan-Africanism has played in mobilizing shared, collective political action to achieve global goals.

This chapter will trace this global circularity that both shapes and is shaped by the AU. We trace its initial first-stage Pan-Africanist roots developed by African-descendant nonstate actors as early as 1893, its continental Pan-Africanism or second-stage Pan-Africanism in the 1963 creation of the OAU during African independence, and its third-stage iteration signified by the historic emergence of the AU. In doing so, throughout this chapter we see the origins of the idea of Pan-Africanism, the diversely dispersed identities that it encapsulates, and the ideology that it imbibes to have succeeded in becoming the cultural marker that the AU uses to advance its contemporary globalization.

Significantly, the chapter examines the activities of the AU's ECOSOCC, an organ that is used to increase African citizens' participation—as well as other sociocultural arenas through which the AU directly pools its ideas from, engages with, and impacts African peoples. The chapter analyzes the AU's efforts at reconstructing the African identity. Our main goal is to determine whether the AU is really relevant to ordinary African masses, organized as individuals, civil societal movements, business and professional interest groups, ethnic groups, and the like. African nationalism, culturalism, and liberalism are all important vehicles through which the AU attempts to mobilize African masses in the advancement of local-national and global change.

We will examine the ways in which these societal elements interact and engage with liberal and Pan-Africanist ideals by interpreting the dialogues, deliberations, and events conducted by select AU suborganizations such as ECOSOCC, the African Academy of Languages (ACALAN), the African Commission on Human and Peoples' Rights, the African Court of Justice and Human Rights (ACJHR), and the numerous AU quangos to demonstrate the intricate relations among Africa's national regimes, communities, and peoples and the way that a complex cultural globalization that negotiates Africa's deeply plural values, identities, and ideologies is invoked by the AU to advance the institution's global objectives.

The chapter reveals the AU's capacity to socially construct from above Africa's shared cultural values and norms throughout the continent; we refer to this as "cultivating Pan-Africanism." Additionally, the AU also "glocalizes"; that is to say, it draws from the values and norms of diverse local African communities and peoples, appropriates these microcultures, and projects them as the plural African identity. Like chapter 4 on the topic of democracy, chapter 3 provides evidence of the AU's attempt to grapple with the continent's complex pluralism and diversity in negotiating what Mazrui has dubbed Africa's triple heritage: African indigeneity, Islam, and Westernism (Mazrui 1987).

For example, as we look at the African Commission on Human and Peoples' Rights based in Banjul, Gambia, and its court based in Arusha, Tanzania, and we examine some cases brought to the court, we see how the global-local nexus that brings together global liberal and contextual local and national values in Africa comes to bear in fostering the AU's hybrid Pan-African identity. Culturalism—understood as Africans' attempts to resuscitate colonially suppressed precolonial identities in the continent—is also an important project of the AU that will be examined in this chapter. AU culturalism is evidenced, for example, by the year 2000 establishment of ACALAN in Bamako, Mali. ACALAN has been committed to trying to get many of Africa's languages made official around the continent.

As well, there are numerous professional organizations from those that are as modest as the African regional electrical power grids to the more populous Africa Cup of Nations (CAN— Coupe d'Afrique des Nations). We call these quangos; they are loosely affiliated with the AU and certainly utilized in ways that seek to enlarge while deepening the notion of an African.

Democracy, human rights, and pluralism are also values and identities around which the AU organizes and advances its political agenda. The topic also deals with a genre and style of political practice: democratic politics. Democracy and human rights are also very much part of the modern values held by Africans that are imbibed and promoted by the AU. In providing an analytical framework for interpreting the AU's democratic behavior and performance since 2002, chapter 4, "The African Union Democracy: Navigating Indigenous Rights and Inclusions in Neoliberal Contexts," examines the political-economic context from which the AU emerges and operates in the twenty-first century; we refer to this context as the 1990s third wave of democratic capitalism and global democracy.

To complicate the analysis, we ask the following questions: What political-economic factors constitute the underbelly of the Union that caused it to have controversially elected President Obiang Nguema Mbagoso as its president in 2011, for example? Was Benghazi's 2011 uprising an Arab democratic spring that required the AU's democratic intervention to restore democracy? Is the AU a democratic institution? Why and how have Africans—through the AU—imbibed the values of democracy as important principles that guide the continent's unity vision? How does the AU's democratic profile influence both the continent and the Union's internal, domestic (among African nations) as well as its international legitimacy to contribute to political and democratic change among its member states and in positioning Africa to the world in a global democratic era?

In addressing these questions, the chapter will show how fifty-four African countries undergoing various dimensions of democratic transition, transitional democracy, democratic consolidation, democratic reversals and setbacks, and especially democratic capitalism voluntarily evolve an AU in 2002 and participate in it with the goal to collectively advance democracy, improve governance, reverse economic decline, and evolve a culture of human rights for their nations and peoples in observance of global standards. International political economy issues are important at this time in explaining the AU's rise as we see the devastating impact that the International Monetary Fund (IMF)/World Bank's structural adjustment policies have had on African economies and African governments' sustained attempts to offer alternative and self-defined initiatives for the continent's development. Several African countries became exclusionary democracies (Abrahamsen 2000) or choiceless democracies (Mkandawire 1994) where substantive democratic sovereignty was constrained by the imposition of neoliberal economic and their associated good governance policies and conditionalities by international finance institutions (IFIs): the IMF, World Bank, and World Trade Organization (WTO).

We use these conditions to interrogate the democraticness of the AU. We contend that the AU's notions of democracy and human rights are ideas that have evolved from earlier struggles of African self-determination and democratic renewal, and they have been combined with conventional ideas of liberal democracy, good governance, and human rights to guide the Union's political behavior with respect to democratization. We will analyze the key democracy organs (Assembly, PAP, ACHPR, African Peer Review Mechanism [APRM], ECOSOCC), initiatives (the AU Democracy Charter), and events that the AU uses to achieve internal democracy and regional democratic integration as well as assess these ideas and structures against prominent AU democracy interventions, ranging from Zimbabwe to Libya; we conclude by assessing the AU's role in advancing global democracy.

The chapter will support our thesis that the AU is a democratic institution that is gradually contributing to the democratic attainment of its member states and is advancing global democratic goals. We will examine the influence that the OAU-AU-RECs policy interventions have had in deepening democracy in transitional democracies such as Ethiopia, Ghana, South Africa, Nigeria, Libya, Senegal, Tanzania, Liberia, and Lesotho, which are all African national states that are uniquely structurally linked to the shaping and social construction of the AU, but are also states that have been transformed by the Union's actions. We also see how these policies are fostering regime change in nondemocracies such as Central African Republic, Togo, Mauritania, Niger, and Guinea-Bissau and prevented democracy from being overthrown in Lesotho.

Chapter 5, "*Pax Africana* versus International Security: New Routes to Conflict Resolution," continues Part 2's deeper analysis in discerning the global-national relationship traversed by the AU, its member states, Africa's societies, and the global governance architecture. Segueing from Part 1's chapter 2, in chapter 5, we expand our thesis inquiry regarding the AU's institutional luster to consider whether the institutional savvy of the AU's governance structures necessarily translates into real regional and global power for the institution. In this chapter, we ask what capacity the institution has to achieve its goals. In this regard, the chapter is used to present the tenuousness of the AU's geopolitical hegemony in relation to the institution's architectural prowess. The reality is that the AU has difficulty in navigating global hierarchies in which it finds itself at the bottom. The AU's weak global capacity and hegemonic influence was demonstrated during the Libyan conflict of 2011 where the organization unsuccessfully wrestled with the UN and NATO to implement its own intervention policy to end the crisis.

Chapter 5 extends and elaborates our hypothesis about the suprastate capacity of the AU by examining further the body's capacity and legitimacy to achieve its Pan-Africanist international goals, particularly in the global security arena. Does the international community view the Union to be a suprastate global actor partner legitimately responsible for addressing international conflict in the global arena—even on the African continent? Implying a negative answer to this question, in 2011 the then chairperson of the AU Commission, Jean Ping, proclaimed that there were lingering disagreements between the AU and the UN over the Libyan crisis. The UN claimed that its charter gave the UN Security Council (UNSC) universal jurisdiction over global conflict, including Libya's, and that the AU's jurisdiction in global affairs was subsumed under the UN's. The UN claimed that this fact had been codified in the UN Charter's Chapter 8, which classifies the AU as a regional organization that must seek permission to act from the UNSC (African Union 2011).

The chapter will reveal how, in 2002, the AU established a new and strengthened mandate to establish its own security norms that contradicts the UN's minimalized view of its role. Premised on earlier Pan-Africanist aspirations to address conflict in Africa, in the 1960s Kwame Nkrumah first proposed the establishment of a unified defense strategy for the continent based on an African

Military High Command and a unified foreign policy. Leveraging Nkrumah's idea, later scholar Ali Mazrui would introduce the notion of *Pax Africana*—the notion that the peace of Africa is to be assured by the exertions of Africans themselves (Mazrui 1967); Africa would police its own continent.

Using Mazrui's underlying thesis, throughout this chapter we will see how the AU's Constitutive Act adopted the principle of *Pax Africana* in its Nonindifference Clause—Africa's "responsibility to protect" (R2P) doctrine—an AU rule that allows Africans (the AU) to intervene into the political affairs of sovereign African nations undergoing conflict when certain criteria are met. In unraveling these themes, in many ways the chapter serves to establish our book's core thesis with respect to the AU's quest for hegemonic power *vis-à-vis* global powers, including the West (EU, NATO, US) and the UN, in relation to new security issues. The chapter will demonstrate how the AU competes for the power to represent the continent in global institutions and arenas in order to circumvent what it deems as international rules deployed by the UN and NATO that Africans perceive as unfairly targeting the continent and restricting their sovereignty.

We will see in this chapter how nowhere did the criticality and diverse dynamics of Africa's geopolitical security relations with the West and the international community crystallize more as evidence for the importance of our thesis than the 2011 civil war in Libya and the UN's R2P resolution, described by former South African president Thabo Mbeki as a setback for African self-determination initiatives brokered by the AU (Mbeki 2011a; *Guardian* 2011). The chapter outlines the way that these kinds of encounters underlay and serve to drive the AU's political and global capacity, behavior, and profile.

Also in this chapter, we examine some AU peacekeeping and conflict-resolution case studies to illustrate the impact that the decision by African countries to allow for infringements on their sovereignty are having on conflict resolution in what continues to be a conflict-prone continent. We examine the AU's conflict-resolution bodies, its rules, decisions, and codes as they have become particularly manifest in the PSC to determine the significance of the AU's security interventions in regional, national, and local conflicts on the continent. The AU and the international community's contests over Libya, Somalia, Sudan, Chad, and Kenya illuminate these complexities and provide an opportunity to illustrate the national-global tussles for power between the AU and the international community. We use this chapter to demonstrate the way that incidents such as these impact on issues of country-level justice and peace. We also see ways that externalist, international community, global governance interventions are beginning to clash with African nations' notions of collective sovereignty and independence. We examine how these contentions have begun to inform important global debates in international relations of which the AU is at the center.

Chapter 6, "Driving the Pan-African Economic Agenda: Ideology and Institutionalism," examines what some would consider Africa's—and by extension the AU's—most important objective, which is to achieve self-determined economic development and freedom from global economic marginalization and dependence. We refer to this objective as "owned and operated" development (Edozie 2004). In this chapter, we examine the economic and social-integration development agenda that the AU carries forth across the continent, using the political economy sectors of economic integration, international trade, and foreign direct investment, aid, and development, as lenses through which the organization carries forth this agenda. The chapter serves to illustrate the AU's new leadership agency in this respect by examining the institution's brokering of new economic principles, strategies, and suborgans and subinstitutions that would better navigate the complexities of the global economy in the new millennium to achieve economic public goods for Africans.

In this chapter, we will see how a foremost goal for Pan-African unity has been to reverse Africa's elusive attempts to achieve economic development that will place Africa on par with the rest of the world. The AU's Constitutive Act enshrines these objectives and posits them as African values when it resolves to use collective action to reverse economic marginalization in production, trade, and investment and to maintain control of African self-determined economies. Since 2002, the AU's economic agenda has built on its predecessor's African Economic Community (AEC) 1991 Abuja Treaty whereby Pan-Africanist member states resolved to fully erase intra-African trade barriers and create a single African economy of scale to compete in the global economy and achieve a 2034 vision for Africa to become a suprapolitical institution that governs such an economy.

We demonstrate how the AU uses four important institutions to achieve its economic goals: the ideology of the AEC, the AU's suborgans, ministerial Specialized Technical Committees (STCs) and especially its proposed financial institutions (African Central Bank, the African Investment Bank, the African Monetary Fund), as well as the New Partnership for Africa's Development (NEPAD) and Africa's RECs. The AEC has acted as a programmatic bedrock and a vehicle for integration that the AU uses to aspire to a continent-wide economic community. The AU Commission's suborgans and the Assembly's ministerial STCs imbibe the AEC ideology to carry forth the AEC's objectives; while the AU's financial institutions are innovations that it will create to more comprehensively implement its economic agenda, they are not yet operational.

On the other hand, the continent's RECs—the Economic Community of West African States (ECOWAS), SADC, COMESA, EAC—continue to present mesolevel models and experiments of what a continent-wide economic union would look like, and which the AU engages in to achieve its economic goals. Since it was formed controversially as a partnership product between the West and Africa, once the AU's NEPAD had wrestled control from the G8 to promote and implement an African-owned development agenda, the institution became the Union's foremost economic organization.

As the title suggests, in chapter 6, we analyze the act's economic resolutions for African processes as an ideological lens of African owned and operated development. In this regard, the chapter examines the AU's attempts and goals to achieve its regional economic integration, development, and greater inclusion and production in a new global economy. In doing so, we assess the AU's institutional economic organs, activities, trajectories, and accomplishments in the context of economic globalization while asking several important questions: What are Africans' economic aspirations in this era, and what role is the AU playing in addressing such aspirations? How and why do African member states participate in AU economic development initiatives? What measurable gains has the AU achieved in eradicating African underdevelopment, in achieving regional integration, and in integrating the continent into the global economy?

We use this thesis and our research questions to assess the AU's progress in making impact on Africans' economic agenda and developmental prospects. We conclude that the AU's economic initiatives are making progress in the areas of strengthening the ideology of self-reliance and self-determination, increasing and deepening cross- and intraregional institutional relationships among member states, and proliferating the number of development initiatives and projects, while consolidating development operations across the continent. It is unclear, however, whether the AU has made much impact on measurable development outcomes for Africa, or made substantial enough progress toward economic integration and union.

Part 3 concludes the book with two important final chapters that make proscriptive and prescriptive inferences, inductions, deductions, and conclusions about the AU's challenges and opportunities with respect to its performance and continued impact on the politics of Africa. Chapter 7, "The African Union's *Africa*: Its Prospects and Its Challenges," examines the AU's and Africa's future as determined by the challenges and thereby the prospects of the AU to accomplish its goals in three important areas: resources, organizational capacity, and legitimacy. Regarding resources, the AU is a product of and seeks to develop the poorest continent in the world. As such, poor, fragile, and weak member states of the AU cannot fund its agenda. The result is that the AU has also gone down the road of relying on external foreign aid to support its activities. This has also resulted in a muting if not perversion of the self-determined Pan-African agenda.

While resources do affect the organization's capacity to perform, so does the AU's institutional, technological, and human resource prowess and leadership. The AU is loosely and contradictorily structured in three institutional parameters: a regional organization, an international intergovernmental organization, and an emerging suprastate. As a result, many of the AU's Constitutive Act pronouncements remain aspirational pronouncements and do not have the institutional authority to move beyond rhetoric to action.

The challenge of AU legitimacy follows from the organization's limitations in resources and organizational capacity, although its core issue—political will and support for the Union's authority and power—stands alone. The AU is challenged by legitimacy in two areas, international and national. International legitimacy refers to the AU's interactions and engagement with a hegemonic international community whose goal is to maintain political-economic stability and order on its own terms. As evidenced by the lukewarm response from Western powers to AU proposals to reform the UNSC, the reconfiguration of the United States as a sole superpower since the end of the Cold War, and the consolidation of Africa's former colonial powers in the all-powerful EU, without shaking off the perception that the continent is of a lesser civilization, the AU has an uphill battle in both governing itself and, what's more, governing the world.

Achieving national legitimacy is an even bigger boogey man for the AU. The truth is that since the heyday of the continental Pan-African congresses, Pan-African unity has always been aspirational among national environments. One could argue that the current OAU-AU configurations of African unity are indeed products of the failure of Nkrumah's and, later, Gaddafi's visions to unify Africa. Are African nations committed to the AU agenda in this regard? As member states celebrate the many annual meetings, projects, programs, policies, and laws that they create for Africa in the AU's name, they nonetheless cherish their national sovereignties no matter how tiny the country.

Be that as it may, laying bare this contradictory terrain upon which the AU attempts to achieve its goals for Africa, chapter 7 makes a closer assessment of the Union's impact on the security, democracy, and sociocultural and economic dimensions of African politics. We argue that the AU's impact and thereby necessity for Africa is gradual, nuanced, varied, and continually challenged by regional and global realpolitik. In doing so, while continuing our analytical induction method of thoroughly interpreting and analyzing secondary-sourced materials and archival data, for this chapter we complement this method with our supplemental quasi-ethnographic study of the institution's organizational culture, which includes an interview survey of AU employees. We use their responses to us on a range of topics on the organization that they work for to provide conclusive evidence of our thesis and objectives.

Dedicated to the crisis in Mali in 2013, the AU's Twentieth Ordinary Session, held in Addis Ababa, Ethiopia, on January 27 and 28, 2013, began its session with the adoption of the Resolution on Mali. The resolution claimed that on behalf of Africa, the AU reiterated its firm commitment to the national unity and territorial integrity of the Republic of Mali, noting that the continued occupation of the northern part of Mali by various armed, criminal, and terrorist groups was a serious threat to peace, security, and stability in Mali, in the region, and beyond. Strategically titled "The (Pan) African Union Phenomenon: Mali as Exemplar," our book's conclusion reaffirms the book's research objective using the AU's 2013 Mali Resolution as a vehicle to summarize key elements of the current book's major research questions, core thesis, and key themes about Africa's AU—and the AU's Africa.

The chapter functions as an applied analysis and conclusive discussion of our AU phenomenon thesis that sought to reveal and assess how it is that in reinventing Pan-Africanism Africa's AU is increasingly sculpting a prominent place for itself and for Africans in today's global era. It does so by advancing Africa's political, security, cultural, and economic integration and development in global governance. In addressing the manner that the AU manifests the AU phenomenon to address the problems of one of its members and the impact that such action has on the continent and in the world, the AU's 2013 Mali Resolution is used as a guide to conclusively answer our book's major questions: Is the AU relevant to Africa and to the global governance of Africa? Does it matter to African politics? Is it making change in key areas of African affairs: cultural and social identity, democracy and human rights, security and conflict resolution, and economic development?

We conclude that the AU is relevant to Africa and makes a difference to African politics; in this chapter, we demonstrate how Mali 2012–13 is an exemplar of the affirmation of this thesis by showing how, through Mali, the AU delicately navigates global power hierarchies and negotiates with powerful global institutions in order to attain its own ends in Africa. The AU's intervention in the Malian crisis reflects the new genre of African politics that is manifest in the AU's style of governance that our book seeks to unravel as it core objective. The

AU's significance is drawn from its collective agency representative of a geopolitical dirigisme used to continually evolve its institutional structure and deploy its codes, public policies, projects, programs, human capital, and initiatives to assert its supremacy over Africa and on behalf of it in a global world. The conclusion reviews the previous chapters with subsections presenting the Malian crisis and the AU response in "The Malian Crisis: A Historical, Regional, and Global Survey" and "Greater Pan-Africanism with African Solutions." We conclude our book thesis about the AU's impact on the continent and in the world in a final subsection entitled, "Neocolonialism versus Asymmetrical Dependency." In the chapter's "Finale," we restate our book's key objectives and themes.

By the conclusion of *The African Union's Africa*, we will have hoped to demonstrate that Africa—the world's least developed region—is also constitutive of crucial agents, actors, and forces that are contributing to the advancement of contemporary global development; that Pan-Africanism lives and, with its core practices in diasporas and transnational cultural and political cross-migrations, must be viewed as a significant practice for the study and understanding of international relations given the reality of globalization processes; and that constructivist international relations needs to be expanded to connect and interlink social movements and forces with political regime action especially in the relatively (to the rest of the world) marginalized region that is the continent of Africa.

PART 1

The African Union in Theories, Methods, and Institutional Design

Africa's African Union: Globalization and Global Governance

In September 2005 on behalf of Chadian victims, a Belgian judge charged former Chadian President Hissène Habré with crimes against humanity, war crimes in Chad, and torture while he was president from 1982 to 1990. Habré sought political refuge in Senegal. Subsequently, on March 17, 2006, the European Parliament demanded that Senegal turn over Habré to Belgium to be tried. Senegal did not comply. Instead, Senegalese authorities—where the former Chadian president had now been exiled for almost twenty years—arrested Hissène Habré and asked the African Union (AU) to recommend how to try Habré. On July 2, 2006, the AU called on Senegal to prosecute Habré in the name of Africa.

The international incident described above underscores the core themes of the current book on Africa's AU in relation to new trends and theoretical perspectives in Pan-Africanism and global governance. The Hissène Habré saga underscores the core elements of the ensuing discussion about the AU and its current imprint on African politics and international relations. The case demonstrates the multiple and overlapping layers that the AU navigates among Africans' local—individual citizens, local African communities, national African states—as well as regional and global political processes. For example, the July 6 decision by the AU to delegate authority to the nation of Senegal to prosecute African human rights crimes on behalf of Africa, which had initially been taken up by the European Union (EU), provides a framework for the thrust of our book's core argument. The AU has emerged as a facilitative agent of global governance (for and of Africa) that is at once negotiating, countering, and weaving together these complex elements of the twenty-first-century global architecture.

Be that as it may, more than five years after the AU's decision to try Hissène Habré, the former Chadian leader still lives freely in Senegal as the case remains embroiled in the aforementioned international tussle over control of the trial. Even among relatively more progressive democratic regimes in the country, Senegal still invokes sovereignty over the Habré case, making it difficult for even the AU to impose its political will. While both Senegal and the AU are united in rejecting an international donor aid package to have Habré tried in Belgium, without adequate resources of their own, the prosecution process remains stalemated. In 2011, the AU presented Senegal with a hybrid plan: an AU Extraordinary African Chamber would be created within the Senegalese justice system with the presidents of the trial court and the appeals court appointed by the AU (Human Rights Watch 2011).

In this regard, the Habré case demonstrates the AU's limitations, and challenges, and perhaps legitimizes the criticism that the institution may sometimes be a toothless bulldog. The argument insinuates that, despite its bold rhetorical assertions, the AU's capacity to make real impact on African politics and affairs is severely constrained by sovereign national interest, by international community interests, by its own rather incremental developmentalism, and by the dearth of resources that it has to run its operations. All of these factors affect the institution's ability to have immediate and more consequential influence in transforming the continent in ways consistent with the institution's aspirational goals.

New globalization theories attempt to explain the Habré-EU-AU–Chadian individual's rights nexus laid out above. One news magazine's announcement of the AU's entry into the global lexicon in 2002, titled *First Europe, Now Africa*, states, "For the . . . world, especially the nations of the Western Hemisphere— whom the one-worlders can't wait to shoehorn into another regional superstate, as prelude to a global merger under the UN—the African Union is but another ominous precedent" (American Opinion Publishing 2002). Those who advocate the abolition of nations' sovereignty to hand over power to a single world government similar in structure to the United Nations (UN) and the EU—and now the AU—are ideologically referred to as "one-worlders"; they are the intellectual advocates and policy practitioners of a phenomenon currently referred to as global governance (Rosenau et al. 2006). The global governance debate emerges from a post–Cold War environment begun in 1989, in which national politics everywhere has undergone significant transformations as a result of globalization.

According to the view of the proponents of globalism, we live in an increasingly global age in which states are being subjected to huge political, economic, and cultural processes of change that are causing their power to diminish (Held 2004). Globalization according to this view is creating new economic, political, and sociocultural circumstances that are serving to transform state powers.

It was this global context that ushered in Africa's AU in 2002 on the heels of the new millennium. Based in Addis Ababa, Ethiopia, the AU illustrates the continent's symbolic response to globalization in this regard. Originally formed to succeed the Organization of African Unity (OAU), which had been founded in 1963, on July 9, 2002, Africa's union of (then) fifty-three (minus Morocco) national states aims to foster unity and development through the economic, political, and sociocultural integration of African nation-states and peoples. The AU is structured as a regional institution that is loosely constituted similarly to the EU. In addition to its complex, though much advanced, architectural evolution compared to its predecessor, from the OAU, which had been established during Africa's decolonizing era of the 1960s, emerged the continent-wide AU, which would be founded on new principles to advance new African interests thrown up by globalization.

For example, with decolonization virtually complete with the first free and fair elections in South Africa in 1994, Africans would now be ready to relax a little on the strongly held position around state sovereignty and thereby adopt a *Pax Africana* Nonindifference Clause derived from Nkrumah's idea to establish a collective African security agenda. In doing so, the AU became the only regional organization—or international institution—to incorporate as law into its Constitutive Act the override of noninterference and sovereignty in its member states' national affairs when humanitarian conflict is rife.

Globalization and global governance form important contexts for understanding Africa's AU whose political-economic initiatives, processes, practices, decisions, actions, and interactions in and on behalf of Africa forge a lens for examining the integrative study of African comparative politics and international relations. It also reveals the varying effects that political, economic, and cultural globalization have on actually existing contemporary African politics. In this context, the current study underscores a unique and distinctive thesis about the AU in relation to globalization and global governance. We argue that Africa's AU engages in *transformationalist globalization*, a perspective on globalization formulated by global studies scholar David Held. Held (2004) examines globalization as a complex set of interconnecting relationships through which political power is exercised indirectly. This is the way that we see the AU as primarily possessing a political role where Africa's states, peoples, and communities utilize the institution through collective action.

Such an introspective analysis of the AU lays bare the cultural, political, and economic processes that are transforming African politics in local, national, regional, and global domains. Our framework provides critical reflection on the way that the AU utilizes the suprastatist governance and pan-national state-building authority that has been partially delegated to it by African member states to push forward a supranational integrationist agenda. It opens up a way to see how African national governments are increasingly becoming compelled to resolve their socioeconomic development agendas and security conflicts by conceding to a wider scope of authority in the AU beyond the narrow national. What's more, the politics of the AU seek to penetrate its authority and scope beyond member states into subnational communities, interests, and arenas within which African citizens are beginning to shift their expectations toward the AU's enlarged Pan-African vision.

Understanding the political dimensions of globalization in relation to the study of the AU also reveals the reality that the organization is foremost a political institution made up of legal codes, bureaucratic operations, political processes, public policies, and authoritative decision-making dynamics. In establishing a complex democratic political system and security mechanism through its Constitutive Act, an AU Commission (secretariat), an Assembly of Heads of State and Government, an Executive Council, a Pan-African Parliament (PAP), the Peace and Security Council (PSC), and a range of other organs, the AU is gradually establishing its own internal political institutions and mechanisms through which to enact its supranational politics. The institution uses these mechanisms and a transnational sociopolitical mobilization strategy to gradually actualize its vision to achieve economic integration and political union—the Union Government—in 2063 whose objectives have been identified and summarized as follows:

> A united and integrated Africa; an Africa imbued with the ideals of justice and peace; an inter-dependent and virile Africa determined to map for itself an ambitious strategy; an Africa underpinned by political, economic, social and cultural integration which would restore to Pan-Africanism its full meaning; an Africa able to make the best of its human and material resources, and keen to ensure the progress and prosperity of its citizens by taking advantage of the opportunities offered by a globalised world; an Africa engaged in promoting its values in a world rich in its disparities. (Constitutive Act of the African Union 2000)

Not too long after the AU's enactment of its Constitutive Act proclaiming continental integration and unity, to further complete its vision of what some have referred to as an explicit irredentist, global-political objective to extend its territorial boundaries to African-descendant peoples in, especially, the United States, the Caribbean, and the Americas, in 2006 the AU established the Sixth Region Diaspora Clause. Through this act, the AU would invite Africans resident outside of the continent and African heritage peoples to participate in the AU's Constitutive Act to establish African unity and achieve economic development.

As such, like other international governmental bodies—the UN and the EU—Africa's AU has entered the controversial fray of a globalization debate that deliberates about these kinds of institutions' prospects, opportunities, and challenges in becoming or simply being a suprastate—defined as an international state that seeks to partner with while also superseding the regional, national, and subnational layers of political society (Held 2004). Tom Tieku's thesis on African agency in international relations is relevant in relating the discussion of collective-action institutional bodies like the AU to African constructivism in international relations (2011). Tieku guides us beyond the binary constructs and thinking about African agency, where some have argued that in a globalized world all structural constraints that limit African agency in a global system have fallen away while others have argued that the big structures of global inequality continue to treat the continent as a victim of globalization.

A complex and nuanced approach to agency would be to examine, as Tieku does, the factors and conditions that are fostering Africans' mitigation and excavation of global structures that limit their freedom. The AU's neofunctionalism presents an important example. Neofunctionalism provides African states with agency to employ the Union's institutional organs and mechanisms to enhance the African voice in a hierarchical international arena in which Africa is normally marginalized. The AU provides political backing to the African players on the ground, and in the process, through partnerships, makes African actors leaders of external actors who attempt to govern Africa. The AU allows African governments to deploy their own actors to support African initiatives.

We contend that whether the AU is or is not indeed a suprastate with agency, it at least can be seen to strive to behave like a significant international institutional actor in both global governance and the governance of Africa in strident ways. The AU advances the tenets of a common African culture through the resuscitation of Pan-Africanism and attempts to construct a shared African personality and identity to use as a basis for political mobilization. It is evolving an economic community of Africa as it embarks upon formulating and directing new development plans, such as the African Economic Community (AEC) and the New Partnership for Africa's Development (NEPAD), as it consolidates and increases African development gains and interjects Africa's competitive edge into a global economy. Additionally, using as its adherents these conditions created by dimensions in cultural and economic globalization, perhaps the AU's most compelling suprastate function is political globalization where it attempts to exercise its emerging institutional architecture, used as it claims to socially construct and re-represent for Africans a self-determined and agentcentric route and negotiation through the complex throes of globalization.

First Europe, now goes Africa? Perhaps not! Even current crises in the EU suggest that the proscriptions of one-worlders, regionalists, or supranationalists are pervaded with challenges. What's more, integration theorists are circumspect about the accuracy of neofunctionalist theory anyway. The assumptions of the theory have always taken for granted that regional integration is an intrinsically sporadic and conflictual process. And the hope that, eventually, member states' citizens will begin shifting more and more of their expectations to the region, a process that will increase the likelihood that economic-social integration will spill over into political integration, has certainly not been proven true—in the European case to say the least (Schmitter 2004). And our book will show that in spite of the AU's bold claims to establish a Union Government by 2063, the neofunctionalist spillover to integration is severely challenged in Africa as well.

Be that as it may, the current study of AU integrationist and union politics does not seek to explain African integration. Contrarily, its more minimal goal is to reveal alternative ways that the world's least developed region is also constitutive of an impacting, dynamic politics manifest by agents, actors, and forces that are contributing to the advancement of contemporary global trends. Emerging theories, debates, and practices about globalization illustrated by the Habré case provide a theoretical lens through which we seek to understand what we define in this book as the AU phenomenon. The theoretical starting point for examining the topic is the dizzying empirical context and the emergence of the diversely complex intellectual discipline known as globalization and global governance.

The current chapter presents a more in-depth intellectual exploration of globalization and global governance, presenting them as core theoretical building blocks that guide our study of the AU. The chapter examines emerging theories that explain political globalization's role in the creation of suprastates as well as the role that constructivism plays in advancing cultural and economic globalization. Through this chapter, we will see how these theoretical prisms ground our thesis about the provenance, emergence, and national, regional, and global geo-political transformations, challenges, and opportunities occurring within African politics using the AU as our vehicle.

TRANSFORMATIONAL GLOBALIZATION AND AU GLOBAL GOVERNANCE

Globalization theory offers a more curious terrain for our study as we are interested in the sociopolitical, socioeconomic, and sociocultural context that shapes the AU's institutional behavior. Having been attributed to many an event and issue occurring in contemporary international relations, globalization, according to Anthony Giddens (2002), produces opportunity, prosperity, and development, or else inequality, poverty, and underdevelopment, according to Manfred Steger (2003). Globalization can be understood by examining three discrete though intersectional domains of disciplinary methodology: political, economic, and sociocultural. David Held (2004) further characterizes globalization by social relations that are stretching beyond national territorial boundaries and fostering an intensification of flows and networks of interaction and interconnection that are further conditioned by an increasing interpenetration of economic and social practices that bring distant societies and cultures together.

Defined this way, globalization can be seen to produce a global institutional infrastructure of policy operations that challenges national structures of political organization. Held (2004) particularly articulates the dynamism of globalization by demonstrating ways in which the cultural, economic, and political lives of ordinary people everywhere in the world seem increasingly shaped by events, decisions, and actions that take place far away from where they live and work.

Three distinct theoretical perspectives for understanding globalization's impact on national state power include the globalist, the traditionalist, and the transformationalist approaches (Held 2004). Of these three theories, the transformationalist perspective elucidates the political behavior and impact of Africa's AU. Transformationalists are neither celebratory (globalists) like the one-worlders who believe that national power has become subsumed by a new global architecture; nor, however, are they skeptical (traditionalists) of globalization thereby believing that the phenomenon has been exaggerated and therefore has little impact on state power. Traditionalists are apt to see the increased importance of regionalism over globalization.

A transformationalist perspective of globalization will see supranational regional organizations like the AU as reconfiguring national power but not replacing it. In this view, transformational globalization provides regional organizations a premise for the evolution and practice of new forms of politics. As such, organizations like the AU and its satellite organs are at once regional, transnational, and global; they create innovative responses to globalization to both take advantage of and allay its consequential impact on the national arena. In a transformative global world, these new dynamics of political power in turn facilitate the agentcentric development of new and progressive structures of democratic accountability and foster a global system of governance where national and local politics are potentially pluralized, democratized, and empowered, but where nation-states continue to retain a key role (Held 2004).

A transformationalist globalization theoretical framework presents for our analysis of African politics a way to view more clearly a scaffolding of the historic power shift from national governments to evolving systems of regional and global governance within the continent. These evolving systems reconfigure the political architecture using a process of political coordination in which the tasks of making and implementing global or transnational rules and of managing transborder issues are shared among governments and international and transnational organizations. These are the conditions that Held and his contributors (2004) argue create the suprastate—international governmental organizations brought into being by formal agreements among governments. As these organizations increasingly become more entrenched features of the global political landscape, they become distinguished by their autonomous legal personality, their relative universal membership, and their functional responsibility in a range of political, social, cultural, and economic sectors (McGrew 2004).

Of the varying dimensions of globalization—political, economic, and cultural—political globalization is of foremost salience for the current study to understand the ways that national governments have come to adapt their roles and functions in this genre of a new global neighborhood. That is why Anthony McGrew argues that political globalization extends the analysis of the globalization phenomenon to issues of power, authority, legitimacy, and the processes involved in governing (McGrew 2004). Globalization's political shell of this kind is increasingly referred to as global governance, a phenomenon that Adil Najam has defined as the management of global processes in the absence of a global government (Najam 2002).

Francis Kornegay connects the AU's acclaimed suprastate politics to Najam's definition by referring to a concept that he calls polycentric sovereignty (Genge,

Kornegay, and Rule 2000). Polycentric sovereigns enjoy multiple power bases through which to exercise their politics. While the AU may have been originally founded as a regional body that serves to interconnect geographically contiguous African states, examining the institution as a suprastate with at least emerging polycentric sovereignty reveals distinctive aspects of the AU's dirigisme in fostering a genre of regional cooperation whose power bases are drawn from national and local domains that are in turn projected onto global politics.

G. Aforka Nweke has used similar international relations theories of functionalism and neofunctionalism to explain the political behavior of the OAU—and thus implicitly, of the AU, which is its successor. In that organization, very similarly to the AU, Nweke suggests that cooperation in economic, social, cultural, technical, and defense spheres by member nation-states served to transition the continent to the more integrated political community in which supranationality or the supremacy of its policies desired by the current AU is assured (Nweke 1987). In explaining EU integration theory, Philippe Schmitter tells us that neofunctionalism places major emphasis on the role of nonstate actors, especially the secretariat of a regional organization, in providing the dynamic for further integration. While member states remain important actors in the process as they set the terms of the initial agreement, they do not exclusively determine the direction and extent of subsequent change.

Instead, argues Schmitter, regional bureaucrats seek to exploit the inevitable spillovers and unintended consequences that occur when states agree to assign some degree of supranational responsibility for accomplishing a limited task, and then discover that satisfying that function has external effects upon other of their interdependent activities (Schmitter 2004). In this regard, J. A. Scholte (1997) would argue that the AU is an institution in which national state members have voluntarily interjected themselves into collective foreign policy networks of regional cooperation that help them pursue new challenges emanating from globalization.

Theories of international organization go a long way in appropriately explaining the AU's institutional dynamics that influence the Union's political behavior. With its near universal continental membership (all but Morocco), African nation member states have through the AU evolved for their respective nations foreign policy organs such as the Assembly of Heads of State and Government, the PAP, the PSC, and the Economic, Social and Cultural Council (ECOSOCC) to assist in the achievement of their political-economic and sociocultural goals. Especially, the AU Constitutive Act (the AU's legal code) provides opportunities for African nation-states to remain as important primary institutions that have set rules and norms for Africa. Neofunctionalism, whereby nation-states create and control the organization for their own ends while delegating the heavy lifting of governance to external institutions, is at work in this regard in fostering the AU's emerging supranationalism, but this may be limited. This is because while states use the AU as a function and extension of their politics and governance, these same nation-states have not been able to exclusively determine the direction and extent of the AU's subsequent attempts to reconfigure their own national authority and power.

As well, in advocating the criticality of global governance's ability to advance contemporary global issues in the absence of a legitimate global political authority, many scholars now speak of global governance in the context of the emergence of an entirely new field of scholarly study and practice in global public policy. Thomas G. Weiss describes global governance as the concrete cooperative problem-solving arrangements that increasingly involve another amorphous concept, the international community made up of the UN, G8 countries, the EU, the United States, international secretariats, and other nonstate actors, such as the International Monetary Fund (IMF), the World Bank, the World Trade Organization (WTO), and leading nongovernmental organizations (NGOs) (Weiss et al. 2007).

Note that the AU is rarely seen in this light as an agent of globalization in the global governance industry. Instead, the continent is spoken about, to, or on behalf of by the more legitimately perceived multilateral global actors noted in Weiss's definition. In the 1990s, William Pfaff called for the EU to resuscitate an ideology of "disinterested neocolonialism" in its foreign policy engagement with Africa. This ideology, Pfaff claimed, would take the shape of the establishment of an EU trusteeship of the African continent where African governments would delegate their sovereignty for half a century so that Europe would effectively govern what Europeans considered a disintegrating region (Pfaff 1995).

One way that Africans have responded to this neocolonial threat is to come up with the slogan "African solutions for African problems" (former Nigerian President Obasanjo). The sentiment is reflective of AU member states' desire to govern themselves in a supposedly postcolonial era. Perhaps the AU is the continent's fulfillment of Ali Mazrui's *Pax Africana* where, in a 1967 book, the author asserted that the peace of Africa needed to be assured by the exertions of Africans. Inter-African intervention to resolve Africa's problems was more legitimate than intervention by outsiders (Adebajo 2010). This is why the accelerated pace by which the OAU was to transition to the AU, within a year in the early twenty-first century (2001–2), was one important response by Africans to an external global governance of the continent that before its appearance on the scene appeared to subvert the continent's delicate fifty-year independence from colonialism.

The AU's structure conforms to global governance and political globalization theories. When globalization is seen as the internationalization of government activity and the transnationalization of cultures and societies, it provides a vehicle for the ways that power and politics have become stretched across frontiers. Through the collective activities of African governments, African politics is creating a distinctive form of global politics from terrains and arenas that have nurtured institutions like Africa's AU. Yet, while the AU's global activities do have the potential to constrain the autonomy of African's national powers, the continent's nation-states accede to the power of the Union in order to become part of a complex set of interconnecting global relationships through which they may exercise their power collectively in new ways.

Within global governance and political globalization theory, the AU operates as an institution and schema of continent-wide integration established to achieve unity, self-reliance, and economic independence in the global system.

CONSTRUCTIVISM AND CULTURAL GLOBALIZATION IN THE AU

While political globalization serves as an important way to examine the AU, theories of cultural and economic globalization offer additional methodological prisms through which we can discern the Union's political behavior. That is to say that new theories of cultural politics and political economy present more nuanced, comprehensive, and diverse ways to interrogate the AU's emergence, impact, and practice on contemporary African state-society national politics in a global era. Because globalization entails sociological, cultural, and economic aspects, its significance penetrates far more deeply than the political to inform and formulate a distinctive practice politics.

We have already explained how transformationalist globalization offers an important key through which to interpret the AU's emergence and practices in cultural and economic realms as it assumes a given underlying methodology that leans toward constructivist approaches to international relations. Differently from realist, liberal, or structuralist explanations of world politics, constructivism is a theory of international relations that shows how power politics and social relations, rather than being constitutive of nature (realist school), elite/institutional cooperation (liberal school), or materialist interest (structuralist school), is in actuality constitutive of human agency and practice. In this view, politics and economics are otherwise socially constructed, as Alexander Wendt famously stated. Constructivist theories of international relations reveal ways that the structures of human association are determined primarily by shared ideas and by the mobilization of identities and the interests of purposive actors (Wendt 1999).

Martha Finnemore's scholarship has done a lot to deepen our understanding of the relationship between national state behavior in the international arena using a constructivist model. In *National Interests in International Society* (1996), Finnemore argues that the international structure is embedded with meanings and social values from and by which states construct and devise their interests through sociopolitical interaction with each other. Significantly, as well, constructivists like Finnemore and Wendt believe that ideas and processes that have been constructed form a structure, considered as institutions, of their own that in turn impact upon international actors. Finnemore's own study of the World Bank and the organization's influence on national and global attitudes to world poverty underscores her thesis about a constructivist theory of globalization.

Kathleen R. McNamara's (1999) study of the European Monetary Union is another important case study in this area. McNamara identifies changing ideas about governments' proper role in monetary policy-making as critical to forging a neoliberal consensus among the European states. When international organization theorists such as John Mearsheimer argue that an international institution is a set of rules that stipulate the ways in which states should cooperate, he refers to the cultural lacing of politics. Mearsheimer goes on to argue that these stable sets of norms, rules and principles are formalized in international agreements and embodied in organizations (Mearsheimer 1994/95; Makinda and Okumu 2007).

While constructivist theory has now emerged as a mainline theory of international relations, constituting what the International Studies Association refers to as the third debate, the theoretical framework has not been applied frequently enough to illuminate the study of African international relations. Indeed, the notion that an African international relations exists is also controversial as much of the study of African politics remains trapped in parochial frames. Nonetheless, where constructivism paved the way for a new genre of international relations scholars to introduce neohistoricism, social movements, gender issues, and environmental issues into an understanding of international relations, few scholars have been able to apply this framework to Africa.

In a statement indicting this fact and the continued inattention to race in international relations, Robert Vitalis reinvoked classic constructivist Stanley Hoffman's appeal to move away "from the perspective of a superpower . . . toward that of the weak and the revolutionary" (Vitalis 2000, 331). Indeed, constructivist international relations pioneer Alex Wendt himself, rather than apply the constructivist prism to understand Africa, concluded that "African IR is just one or two steps behind Europe, but will eventually get there just like everyone else" (Wendt 2008). One of the few books on African international relations that attempts to apply the constructivist turn to the continent's international relations is Kevin Dunn and Timothy M. Shaw's *Africa's Challenge to International Relations Theory* (2001), which Dunn, a constructivist Africanist international relations scholar, claims attempts to place Africa and African experiences as a starting point for analysis and theorizing. Dunn argues that in troubling the Western-centric international relations theory that has created a system of dispositions that posits their historical experiences and cultural values as the norm for the international community—and that, we add, historically and contemporarily misrepresent Africa—the value of using a constructivist methodology serves to place African experiences at the forefront, rather than as aberrant footnotes to the discipline's theories (Dunn 2008).

Constructivism pushes to the forefront social—and especially national—identities that have been formed by being located within the narratives that we use to know, understand, and make sense of the social world. Dunn demonstrates how narratives of national identities are formed by a gradual layering on and connecting of events and meanings through the selection of events themselves, the linking of these events to each other in causal and associational ways (plotting), and the interpreting of what the events and plots signify (Dunn 2008). Yet, as Dunn implicitly acknowledges, much of this new constructivism in African international relations is still caught up in a Western-centric prism. What is more valuable to us in the current study is how to apply constructivist international relations to a study of African international relations. In a 2008 Theory Talk interview, Dunn asks,

> Which actors, practices, mechanisms, institutions, and so forth are implicated in the social construction of a given identity, at a given historical moment? Can we isolate a range of constitutive practices and agents? How does one engage in an empirical investigation of the discursive construction of identities? That is, what types and forms of discourses "count" and which ones do not? How much weight should be put on specific discourses and narratives? How can we understand the discursive commonalities and disjunctures in identity construction? How are material practices and forces related to these discursive constructions? How does one grapple with social contestation and intentional agency? (Dunn 2008)

Underscoring the cultural elements of constructivist international politics, we examine the AU through a constructivist international relations theoretical framework. In responding to Dunn's quest for methodological precision and nuance in applying the constructivist frame—which actors, practices, mechanisms, institutions, and so forth are implicated in the social construction of a given identity, at a given historical moment?—our own study herein examines Africa's AU in its reconstruction of the African identity. In Africa, the norms of Pan-Africanism, self-determined development, African sovereignty, and hybrid-liberal democracy undergird primary institutions that embed and drive the AU's political behavior.

There is just no reason why one shouldn't examine organizations like the AU as primary institutions like Finnemore's World Bank and McNamara's EU that are mobilizing global governance and that are underlaid by social identities and cultural politics. Like these institutions, the AU also embodies a stable set of norms, rules, and principles who become actors as knowledgeable social agents (Makinda and Okumu 2007, 8). Makinda and Okumu's study of the AU implicitly examines the AU's Constitutive Act (as a practice of constitutionalism) as an example of an institution that shapes the identities and interests of Africans and their AU.

Constructivism provides an important and valuable way to examine Africans' own role and contributions in socially constructing globalization in this respect. While its suprastate structure sees the AU primarily as a political body emerging from the polyarchic and multiple-complex set of networks that are reshaping the global governance architecture, the AU's interactions and actions with its member states and international actors are more substantively understood by examining the role that cultural globalization plays in constructing the meaning, values, interests, and identities of diverse and plural African actors in the advancement of globalist political objectives.

The role that cultural globalization plays in situating the assemblage of social traits, practices, and goods utilized to construct meaning symbolically and to nurture the identity of shared goals among disparate cultures and societies presents an important methodological variable to examine the AU's political behavior. A closer analysis demonstrates how cultural globalization acts as a facilitative building block for the AU's sustenance as a political global institution making its mark in contemporary global governance.

Walter Anderson has noted that "Symbols of all kinds have detached themselves from their original roots and float freely like dandelion seeds around the world" (Anderson 2001, 145). David Held adds that whatever globalization has achieved, it has done so as a result of the significance of the power of culture (Held

2004). Similarly, an emerging school of constructivist international relations argues that it is through an understanding of sociocultural identities (ethnicities, racialisms, nationalisms, religions, regionalisms, and diasporas) that politics ends up where it is. Differently from the political realists, liberals, and structuralists, these postmodern constructivist scholars are more inclined to demonstrate ways that powerful interests are embedded in the social constructions of identities in ways that further subsume these interests to outer cultural claims.

In this regard, a transformationalist, agentcentric view of globalization sees globalization as a complex set of interconnecting relationships through which political power is indirectly exerted culturally (Held 2004). Transformative globalization fosters the transnationalization of cultures and societies in ways that stretch power and politics across frontiers. As such, we would not see cultural globalization as imperialism, where a singular homogeneous flow travels from the West to Africa, which merely tells only one story of globalization regarding Africa. Globalization is a two-way street in which cultural flows also travel from Africa (the so-called periphery) to other parts of the globe in significant ways. Transformationalists also acknowledge a cultural element in the definition of globalization that views globalization as a process emerging from a *longue-durée*, hybridized mélange where both symmetrical and asymmetrical cultural mixing and pluralistic and alternative modernities have all structured the evolution of contemporary globalization (Pieterse 2003). Hugh Mackay (2000) argues that culture is a crucial component of globalization because it is through culture that common understanding is developed and connections between places and nations are made.

Timothy Murithi's analysis of the AU further supports the role that culture and constructivism play in advancing globalization. Through the narrative of Pan-Africanism, the AU seeks to construct and reconstruct the African identity in a millennial world. Murithi (2005) has stated that by 2002, the AU had emerged as the third stage of the institutionalization of the idea, ideology, and identity of Pan-Africanism. In this respect, the AU becomes a twenty-first-century reexpression of the nineteenth-century idea of Pan-Africanism. This is a global idea that emerged from a resistance movement initiated by diaspora Africans in response to the transatlantic enslavement and displacement of Africans, to the colonization of the continent, and to the structuring of the modern world around racism against Africans.

In 1963, Pan-Africanist Kwame Nkrumah told the All-Africa Peoples' Congress in Accra, Ghana, that Pan-Africanism had four main components: national independence, national consolidation, transnational unity and community, and economic and social reconstruction (Makinda and Okumu 2007). Nkrumah—considered Africa's father of Pan-Africanism—underscored the cultural undercurrents and antecedents of the AU when he pronounced, "For too long in our history, Africa has spoken through the voices of others. Now, what I have called the African personality in institutional affairs will have a chance of making its proper impact and will let the world know through the voices of Africa's own sons" (Makinda and Okumu 2007). In the twenty-first century, the AU has been established in an ideological context that serves to resuscitate the late Dr. Nkrumah's 1960s Pan-Africanism and bring it forth into the new millennium through a new genre of African leadership including the late Muammar Gaddafi, the former South African president Thabo Mbeki, and Senegal's former president Abdoulaye Wade. All used the cultural discourse points of African pan-nationalism and African renaissance to recultivate the notion of an African personality and identity among fifty-five disparate postcolonial states. In this regard, the AU emerged and continues to act as a mechanism through which a shared African voice, collective political agency based on a shared history, and a self-determined will to sustain an African identity could be mobilized in a culturally plural and diverse continent.

Cultural context and constructivism of this sort would facilitate the AU's political action where the institution would draw from and manipulate culture to exercise its political power to inject the African identity and collective will into the complex reality of globalization and global governance. Nkrumah viewed the Pan-Africanist personality and identity as the route to global power that would unite Africa to become one of the greatest forces for good in the world (Nkrumah 1965). The cultural politics method helps us to see that the AU's policy acts and decisions are discourse representations, its political processes are formulated through sociocultural identity mobilizations, and its contemporary political behavior and profile are informed by historical culminations and shared cultural contexts.

The AU's construction of meaning about what it is and the diverse domains from which it draws the norms and values that it invokes in Africa's name is integral to the analysis of the AU's establishment in 2002 and the way that it has operated as a global institutional actor since then. Understanding processes of cultural globalization underscores an important part of this book's main thesis whereby we posit the AU as a constructivist institutional actor that fosters African agency in international relations. The AU resuscitates and reconstructs the idea of Pan-Africanism to enact new *dirigiste* statecraft sometimes through, on behalf of, or upon African nation-states, communities, and peoples in a globalized political terrain.

Economic Globalization and Africa in the New International Political Economy

While political globalization provides an institutional bedrock for the AU, and cultural globalization facilitates common ideas, identities, and ideologies through which it directs its political acts, economics completes the trinity of roles that globalization plays in understanding the AU's regional and geopolitics. As such, economic globalization formulates an important third variable complementing politics and culture in our thesis about the AU's globalization. Incidentally, the AU is primarily driven by economic interests, while it engages directly with explicit elements of economic globalization to reverse Africa's marginalization and foster the continent's greater global integration and development.

What's more, our methodology views economic ideas as being closely part and parcel of new international relations theories of constructivism that have extended constructivist international relations to the economic realm by embedding them in ideas, norms, and the organizational culture of international organizations. Viewing economics this way is to see how economic practices are closely connected to social norms and are used by political practices. In *Cultural Political Economy* (2010), Jacqueline Best and Matthew Paterson expand on the relationship between culture and economics by examining economic impact on societies and cultures, examining the role of economic habits and practices as well as the cultural constitution of the economy more broadly. The authors' cultural-political economy methodology therefore emphasizes ways in which culture is implicated in everyday economic practices and thereby contributes to the growing literature on the everyday politics of the international political economy.

Economic globalization occurs when forms of intense interdependence and integration of international economic relations in production, trade, and financial investment all influence, both positively and negatively, national economic policies and compel them to participate in integrated cosmopolitan transnational economic relations (Thompson 2000). Grahame Thompson has argued that economic globalization can take the form of enmeshment—complex patterns of reciprocal interdependence and integration among economies—or it can take the form of marginalization where the unevenness of economic development pushes certain economic actors out of the heart of economic development and into subsidiary and peripheral positions (Thompson 2000).

Cultural political economy and constructivism provide a framework for our understanding of the AU's core economic constitution, construction of its narrative, and its impact on African state-societies. Through its economic programs such as the AEC and its NEPAD, we see how the AU uses a transformationalist economic globalization to reconfigure Africa's marginalized circumstance in the global economy toward a status of greater enmeshment and integration as described by Thompson. The AU's global economic goals reflect Africa's attempts to replace what it views as the hegemonic external (and sometimes considered neocolonial) interventionist policy prescriptions of the G8 and now G20, international finance institutions (IMF, World Bank), and Washington Consensus with its own self-determined agenda to reverse the continent's economic marginalization and underdevelopment. This agenda is an African owned and operated agenda whereby the AU's numerous economic organs are attempting to achieve continent-wide socioeconomic integration that would serve to cultivate the consolidation and pooling of the continent's national economic resources so that Africa's small, underdeveloped, and poor economies will be able to reap development benefits from maximal economies of scale in the global economy (Edozie 2004).

Decolonizing and postcolonial Africans have always used collective-action bodies to attempt to reverse their bottom-tier status in the global social hierarchy. Nkrumah and other African nationalists in the 1960s understood that colonialism contributed to the continent's loss of development opportunity and contributed to its current underdevelopment (Murithi 2005). Despite relative—though uneven—development gains in the immediate postcolonial period from the 1960s to the 1980s, the African economic crisis by the mid-1980s and early 1990s saw the advent of control of African nations' economic policies by international finance institutions such as the IMF and World Bank, and the deepened erosion of the continent's economic sovereignty.

This is how Africa entered the global era of the new millennium—as a crisis spot that the *Economist* magazine described in its headline feature as a "Hopeless Continent" (*Economist* 2000). The contemporary global governance agenda with its economic fulcrum in the Washington Consensus appropriated this crisis representation of Africa and presented Africa as an issue among other global problems to be solved, including climate change, the global financial crisis, free trade, and global security. However, considered a paternalistic international public policy posture toward the continent, this approach to Africa in global affairs has been referred to negatively by Bill Ashcroft (1997) as the "New Internationalism."

In this style of international relations practice and policy prescription toward Africa, the continent is absorbed into—and in many ways subsumed under—a global, transnational, cultural, and economic reality in a way that resuscitates colonial misrepresentations of Africa that lie behind the advanced industrial world's hegemonic control and marginalization of the continent (Ashcroft 1997). Hence, the flurry of representations of Africa since the 1990s—former British prime minister Tony Blair's reference to Africa as a "scar," for example—had by the turn of the millennium ushered in a humanitarian interventionist global governance public policy posture toward the continent that elided the diversity, complexity, and self-determined agency of the continent's political-economic affairs.

The international community's inclination to control much of Africa's national economic sovereignty—and increasingly its security relations—through global governance institutions like the IMF, World Bank, and nowadays the UN, as well as its tendency to symbolically characterize Africa's underdevelopment in negative labels shrouded in Western economic interests and to engage with Africans in a paternalistic stance, has not gone unnoticed by Africans who know too well how structures of meaning about it continue to be associated with the hegemonic practices of international powers (Edozie and Soyinka-Airewele 2010).

In 2002, leading what he referred to as the African renaissance in response to the continent's economic, cultural, and political marginalization in contemporary global affairs, former South African president Thabo Mbeki called for the AU's NEPAD to be considered as "A balance between our rights and duties as Africans to protest against an unjust world order and our need to practically engage our development partners with a partnership that breaks the old relationship between hapless African recipients of aid and benevolent donors [that] must be created" (Mbeki 2002a). The subtext of Mbeki's remarks suggests that, without collective voice (cultural globalization) and collective economic power (economic globalization) projected and exercised through an organization like the AU, Africa would remain discursively represented as well as governed by international policy makers, scholars, journalists, and others in the world in ways that subvert the potential vibrancy of a self-determined practice of African affairs in the new millennium.

In celebrating ten years of the AU, reflecting on the organization's achievements, Mbeki reaffirmed the AU's rationale when he stated that Africa had a duty to exercise her right to self-determination free from foreign interference and neocolonial dependence. Mbeki saw the Union's economic goals as serving to accelerate the process toward the political and economic integration and unity of Africa providing Africans with the right to control their natural resources, as well as the ability to eradicate poverty and underdevelopment and to repudiate theft of national wealth by a corrupt and predatory elite (Jere 2012). The role that economic globalization plays as a core element that explains the emergence and behavior of the AU is again represented in these words spoken by former AU president Mbeki in remarking on the same ten-year anniversary of the institution in 2012:

> We saw in the AU the transformation and modernization of the African economies to end their status as producers and exporters of raw materials, thus also to end the unequal and exploitative economic relations between ourselves and the north and [the desire] for Africa to assume her rightful place within the global governance, to end her marginalization, as well as her grossly unequal access to the claimed benefits of the process of globalization. (Mbeki 2012)

By implication, Mbeki's words suggest that at its core the AU is an economic organization, but one that we add is embedded in history, culture, society, and political organization.

GLOBAL, REGIONAL, NATIONAL, LOCAL COMMUNITY IMPACT—AND VICE VERSA

A final way to examine the AU, particularly to discern the institution's impact on African politics and thereby present a methodology employed by our book to assess this impact, will require the organization's analysis as a vehicle through which globalization influences politics at the nation-state, community, and individual levels. In turn, we need to see how nation-state and community-interest politics shape AU political action from a bottom-up perspective. That is to say, we need to see the role that AU-led globalization performs in transforming African states and societies in their national environments, as well as the role that African peoples in these contexts play in fostering, adapting to, or otherwise circumventing globalization.

Excluding Morocco, African nation-state membership with the AU is universal, thereby allowing the AU to have comprehensive impact on African peoples. With the emergence of democratization thrusts globally, including in Africa, nation-states are increasingly (certainly this process is not complete) more representative of their populaces; as a result, institutions like the AU have developed mechanisms and organs to represent peoples and communities directly. In this regard, for a continent so diverse in ethnicity, nationality, race, religion, and economic ranking, understanding why the prospect of a suprastate political union by 2034 remains so prominent in African politics is an important heuristic research inquiry for this book.

The current study would not be the first to examine the impact that globalization in this vein is having in reshaping national politics at the macro level. In arguing that globalization is the great bridge for two traditionally separate disciplines—comparative politics and international relations—Jeffrey Haynes presents a suitable theoretical prism to examine the AU's impact in transforming African politics in a global era. In *Comparative Politics in a Globalizing World*, Haynes's main thesis is that a key effect of globalization is to increase the porousness of state borders, which enhances the significance of external actors in the implementation of many domestic outcomes. The thesis acts as a valuable framework for examining the effects of globalization comparatively on national politics, as well as for observing the divergent ways in which nation-states are structurally incorporating new external globalizing issues into their domains (Haynes 2005). The way that globalization contributes to a given shift and adaptation to new political behaviors and cultures is an important start for assessing our objective to examine and illustrate the AU's impact as a global actor on behalf of African nation-states and societies.

Classifying contemporary national political regimes into established democracies, transitional democracies, and nondemocracies, Haynes identifies a range of issues associated with globalization at the comparative national political arena and demonstrates how states with different types of political regimes adjust and adapt to various aspects of globalization. Four major issues dominate African politics and affairs in the contemporary global era: security, political change and democracy, economy and social development, and socioculture and identity. Examining global impact on the national political system along the lines of these four issue areas, Haynes's global-national formula captures the ways that globalization affects domestic political structures and processes in these various kinds of states. This model analyzes globalization's influence in three arenas: political structures (fostering democratization and regime change, managing and reducing political conflict), economic structures (facilitating regionalization and development), and cultural structures (expanding human rights) (Haynes 2005).

These globalization variables influence the domestic national structures and induce political change. First, through the international diffusion of democracy and human rights, democratic ideas are transforming nations in a two-way external–internal snowballing process that characterized the 1990s snowballing of third-wave democratic transition processes during the end of the Cold War (Jowitt 1993, 22; Haynes 2005). Demonstrating the impact that the global human rights paradigm has had on the national arena since the turn of the millennium, Haynes chides countries who claim that the way they treat their subjects is no one else's business and argues that these countries are relics of the past (Haynes 2005). A third area of globalization impact examined by Haynes is in security relations in ways that political violence in the domestic arenas have become globalized and post–Cold War conflicts have fostered an insecure global environment.

While Haynes's methodology helps us to scaffold the complexity and nuance of global-national and national-global impact in this respect, his epistemological assumptions are Eurocentric. Haynes's analysis infers that the global human rights domain is a Western-originated idea and that the global or globalization interventions are the preserve of Western-originated international organizations, especially the UN and the EU. Haynes's study presumes that it is the international community and its organizations that represent the external global forces that are influencing change in developing world national contexts.

Our own study revises Haynes's model for the purpose of seeing a different relationship between globalization and the national politics of Africa. We interject the role and agency that continental processes play in national level African politics, contending that it would be valuable to examine the AU's relationship with its member states and African peoples through a revision of Haynes's taxonomy. Doing so reveals the imprint that the AU is having on the continent's national regimes and political systems. For example, the AU commits African states to the institutionalization of democratic governance individually and collectively through the actions of its regional and continental intergovernmental bodies. In article 4 of its Constitutive Act, the AU commits member states to the following principle, among others: "respect for democratic principles, human rights, the rule of law and good governance." The AU-NEPAD's African Peer Review Mechanism (APRM) is a country-level bilateral democracy peer review program that cultivates democratic cultures among regimes. Also, the AU's interventions in the name of democracy into several African countries signify the impact that the AU's political culture of democracy mobilization is having on distinct African states and regimes.

Moreover, regarding human rights in Africa, Western liberalism is many times contested in culturally specific localities that produce alternative interpretations of rights and democracy based on African historical and situational contexts. Through its ideational regime of Pan-Africanism, the AU's Diaspora Clause embodies globalization drivers by stressing Africans' self-determined human rights derived consensually and born of a resuscitation of the African personality and identity that has been suppressed by centuries of slavery, colonialism, and neocolonialism. By establishing institutions such as the African Commission on Human and Peoples' Rights, the AU Commission's African Citizens Directorate and Diaspora Organizations (CIDO), the PAP, and the PSC, the AU navigates the interweaving meanders of Africa's precolonial, colonial, and postcolonial experiences in relation to its contemporarily constructed national and subnational cultures as building blocks to cultivate the complex hybrid panregional culture from which African constructs of human rights are formulated.

In the security realm, as well, the AU has become an important transnational globalizing force through which to tackle the violence and conflict that has gripped Africa since the 1990s. The institution's intervention charter and its fifteen-member PSC are just two vehicles through which the AU attempts to have national impact in countries like the Sudan, Somalia, and the Congo. Indeed, through the AU, Africans are also evolving values that can provide significant lessons for the globe. Significantly, for example, the AU is the only regional or international organization—indeed superseding even the UN—to have at least legally permitted internal intervention into the sovereign affairs of its member nations through its Nonindifference Clause (art. 4.h of the Constitutive Act).

As a policy and rule, by adopting the Nonindifference Clause, the AU's PSC can now legally assess a potential crisis situation on the continent, send fact-finding missions to trouble spots, and authorize and legitimize intervention into sovereign African nations that are undergoing internal violence and conflict. As a value, nonindifference represents a unique achievement for the AU and for African peoples, states, and societies; it allows for collective security and the integrity of protecting African peoples in times of heinous conflict and war.

Article 4.h emerged as a result of many contentious deliberations and discussions between the AU, its member states, and its many citizens' organizations, whose deliberations on African security issues continue; the rule provides but one of many examples of the AU's global impact on African states and societies.

Conclusion: The AU Phenomenon

Together with our revised Haynes impact model, which methodologically unravels the ontological parameters required to examine the Union's impact on transformations in African politics, transformational globalization of Africa in its political, economic, and sociocultural manifestations explains the AU's raison d'être in the new millennium. Drawing from the theoretical threads of cultural and economic globalization, as well as from sociopolitical events and contexts occurring in African politics and global affairs in the current global era, our objective in *The African Union's Africa* seeks to illustrate ways that political, cultural, and economic globalization intersect to facilitate the emergence and behavior of suprastates like the AU. *project rather than an event*

The theoretical and methodological framework that we have employed to examine what we refer to as the AU phenomenon reveals how such institutions are fostering participation in and advancement of the complex project called globalization. This scenario is played out in Africa when the AU uses the underlying structures of globalization—culture and economics—politically (constitutional and legal might and decision-making capacity) to construct an African-world context for participating in globalization and for striving to globally govern the continent and its diaspora. Political, economic, and cultural globalizations are employed as intersecting precipitators of transformation for the African continent's political schema in this regard.

From this scenario, we posit a thesis for the book in which we contend that it is in this globalized context that the AU represents African regions, nation-states, societies, and peoples and fosters their agency in a global arena. The institution achieves its objectives by cultivating the mutual intraregional interaction and integration of Africa's state-societies so as to facilitate and project their collective political will globally as pluralistic agents involved in social construction and reconstruction, postnationalism, and complex transnational integration. In this thesis framework, we demonstrate how the AU's contemporary actions and behavior have originated in the legacy of an African Pan-Africanist decolonization era from the 1940s to the 1960s, that in the postcolonial period the AU has been developed and cultivated by a predecessor regional organization (the functionalist, concentric, gradualist OAU), and that the AU's actions, policies, and ideas have more recently crystallized in an African renaissance, post–Cold War global era, in which the AU has emerged and finds its primary playing field.

In reformulating Haynes's framework to infuse our African-centered methodology and applying it to the AU, our own study of the AU thus provides an important case study by which we illustrate why and how nations give up elements of their sovereignty to participate in collective action. The extent and diversity by which as a globalizing force the AU is changing political, social, and economic relations within and between African national environments constitutes an important hypothesis through which to assess this organization's impact.

Political, economic, and cultural globalization remain as undercurrents that determine the AU's sustainability, growth, and realization of its goals for Africa in its tenth-year anniversary as its members highlight areas in which the Union remains severely challenged. Of concern is the Union's snail pace toward political and economic integration and its inclination toward a top-down statist governance style. As well, Côte d'Ivoire, Libya, and Mali signify disunity among members to foster *Pax Africana* collective security, while the G8's abandonment of the Union's economic action plan (G8 Africa Action Plan 2002) illustrates that global partnerships of which it claims to lead are still very much hierarchical to Africa's disfavor.

The African Union's Africa will reveal how it is that Africa's AU is increasingly sculpting a prominent place for itself and for Africans in today's global era. The rest of our book will demonstrate how the AU advances Africa's political, security, cultural, and economic integration and development; sets continent-wide political-economic and social public policy standards; mobilizes and lobbies the African bloc at the UN and the WTO; carries out many African peacekeeping operations and policy prescriptions in African conflicts ranging from Somalia to the Sudan; and advances a continent-wide, as well as cross-continental, global, diaspora Pan-Africanism.

As each subsequent section and chapter examines the initiatives of Africa's AU as a global governance institution and actor in light of the aforementioned activities, we critically analyze and assess the AU's practices in transforming the national politics of Africa on the one hand, and on the other, the impact of this African institution on global governance with respect to African political and economic development and in using cultural politics to advance the collective foreign policies of Africans as well as African descendants in a global era.

The Evolving "African" Suprastate: Histories, Anatomies, and Comparisons

Perhaps world history and current global politics would be different: if the thirteen US colonies had failed to agree on federation in 1789, and broken up into thirteen independent countries; if India had remained divided between fifty-five princely states; if China was now divided between fifty-five warlords; and most significantly, if Africa's fifty-five states were one country under one government. This last hypothetical would have become reality had Kwame Nkrumah had his way at the 1963 foundation of the Organization of African Unity (OAU) to which Africa's African Union (AU) is a sequel. In his own prescient book *Africa Must Unite*, first published in 1963 (with nine reprints and editions since), Nkrumah, Africa's founding Pan-Africanist, advocated "The ultimate goal is a United African States" with "a continental parliament":

> In my view . . . a united Africa—that is, the political and economic unification of the African continent—should seek three objectives: firstly, we should have an overall economic planning on a continental basis. This would increase the industrial and economic power of Africa. . . . The lesson of the South American republics *vis-à-vis* the strength and solidarity of the United States of America is there for all to see. . . . We should therefore be thinking seriously now of ways and means of building up a Common Market of a United Africa. . . . Such a [continental] Government will need to maintain a common currency, a monetary zone and a central bank of issue. . . . Secondly, we

should aim at the establishment of a unified military and defence strategy.
. . . For young African States, who are in great need of capital for internal
development, it is ridiculous—indeed suicidal—for each State separately and
individually to assume such a heavy burden of self-defence, when the weight
of this burden could be easily lightened by sharing it amongst themselves. . . .

The third objective we should have in Africa stems from the first two
which I have just described. If we in Africa set up a unified economic planning organization and a unified military and defence strategy, it will be
necessary for us to adopt a unified foreign policy and diplomacy. . . . The
burden of separate diplomatic representation by each State on the Continent
of Africa alone would be crushing, not to mention representation outside
Africa. The desirability of a common foreign policy which will enable us to
speak with one voice in the councils of the world, is so obvious, vital and
imperative that comment is hardly necessary. (Nkrumah 1970, 221)

Nkrumah would call his supranation the United African States (UAS) and
would justify this different turn for the continent during the decolonizing era
of the 1950s and 1960s by arguing that unity rather than balkanization into
separate nation-states would foster Africans' greater and faster achievement of
global power through political, economic, and social consolidation. UAS would be
a federated single nation-state little different from the United States of America.
It would harmonize the then existing political institutions among Africa's sovereign former colonies and seek to reintegrate the continent's economies and
cultures in a way that fostered the development of a viable and strong African
nation that would take its place in the global arena.

We know that in the 1960s, Nkrumah was not to realize his vision for Africa;
nonetheless, the founding continental Pan-Africanist's idea for African unity was
replaced with an alternative vision that would hope to achieve the same ends
eventually—the OAU. The idea of gradualism, institutionalism, and functionalism en route to African integration and unity implied that African decolonizing
nation-states would cooperate as sovereigns in slowly developing the structures,
elements, and institutions required to evolve unity and integration in the future,
and turned out not to be such a bad idea. After all, in an era of globalization,
as the OAU became Africa's AU, the 1990s saw a flurry of institution building
among existing regional organizations, and a host of new ones founded. The AU
Constitutive Act of 2000, its structure, and its subsequent performance must
be examined in light of these twentieth-century contemporaries—the League
of Arab States, the Organization of American States (OAS), the Association of

Southeast Asian Nations (ASEAN), the European Union (EU), and the United Nations (UN).

None of these regional organizations, however, except for the EU (with three orders of magnitude more budget than the AU), approach the solid maturity of the AU. The North American Free Trade Agreement (NAFTA) would not contemplate a parliament or free movement of labour; ASEAN and Mercado Común del Sur (Mercosur) do not deploy peacekeeping armies; the Unión de Naciones Suramericanas (UNASUR) is yet to be operationalized. Perhaps Africa's weak states have a greater need for strong institutions and so tend to build a sturdy and complex architecture for collective action (Schmidt 2010, 30). To fob off neocolonial inclinations from an increasingly predatory international community, the AU would evolve collective governance administered by a single authority to address and embark upon Africa's wide array of diverse and complex state-building needs in a global arena.

Inspired by the question of how to promote stronger political and economic integration in Africa, the 1999 Sirte Declaration established the premise for a need for a newly improved Pan-African institution that would replace the OAU club with one endowed with supranational competencies to enact common policies and compliance mechanisms among African member states to achieve the continent's Pan-African goals. In the previous chapter we presented functionalism and neofunctionalism as frameworks to explain the Union's dynamic dirigisme among and of African nation-states to facilitate cooperation in economic, social, cultural, technical, and defense spheres so that Africa would achieve political community and a single supranational authority.

Further, chapter 5 critically examines this supranational authority by taking a closer look at the AU's architectural institutional structure evolved to achieve its governance objectives from the perspective of international security. That chapter will apply contested practices of the AU's emerging supranationality to the notion of *Pax Africana*, Ali Mazrui's coinage of Kwame Nkrumah's Pan-African call for an Africa High Command and Army, to address the encroaching neocolonial interventionist proxy wars during Africa's decolonizing period (Mazrui 1967).

Nonetheless, the current chapter is guided by the following questions that help to expand upon by way of deepening (in the case of chapter 1) and foregrounding (in the case of chapter 5) these issues: How is the AU organized? What institutional elements make up its architecture? What normative codes, rules, and agreements drive the AU's national, regional, and global behavior? Is it a suprastate? In responding to these questions, the chapter thematically defines the AU constitutively, historically, subregionally, comparatively, and universally.

In this regard, the chapter has two related objectives. Firstly, even the casual observer of international affairs will see that, decades after Nkrumah published *Africa Must Unite* proposing his vision for a United Africa, through the OAU-AU, Africans have rolled out an elaborate institutional architecture to use to achieve his Pan-African unity goals: In thirty-one years, they created the Treaty of Abuja for an African Economic Community (AEC); and the Constitutive Act of the AU was established ten years later. In forty-one years of the dream, the Pan-African Parliament (PAP) held its ceremonial inauguration. Forty-six years later, the New Partnership for Africa's Development (NEPAD) Planning and Coordination Agency (NPCA) was formed to address continental infrastructure, development, and broad macroeconomic policy. Forty-eight years later, the five brigades of the African Standby Force (ASF) are ready prior to their formal launch. And the technical steering committee for the African Central Bank (ACB) has started meetings in Abuja, preparatory to its intended opening in 2021, which would be fifty-eight years after Nkrumah's advocacy. In its fiftieth year, at its 2013–14 AU Commission stakeholders meeting, the AU launched the Pan-African University, a continental institution that is the culmination of the union's efforts to revitalize higher education and research in Africa and to establish an African university at the core of Africa's development.

In a new contemporary global era, a new cadre of African leadership has taken up Nkrumah's union mantra, and South Africa's Thabo Mbeki stands out in underscoring the significance of the AU project to the architectural reconfiguration of African politics. As first president of the AU, at its 2002 inauguration in Durban, South Africa, Mbeki would simulcast his own country's historic transition with Africa's. In explaining the importance of the AU's Constitutive Act, Mbeki stated, "The Constitutive Act is the supreme law of the Continent which has been approved by all of our parliaments . . . to meet the challenges facing Africa today. In its [Constitutive Act] spirit, we must work for a continent characterized by democratic principles, institutions and . . . the rule of law" (2002b). The depth of complication involved in understanding the practicality of Mbeki's institutional vision for Africa through the Constitutive Act suggests the complexity of the AU project in terms of constitutionalism, governance, and leadership. As such, a first objective of the current chapter is to navigate this complexity in terms of understanding the institutional structure of the Union. We examine the historical depth from which the AU has evolved, as well as the Union's universal and regional scope, and assess its institutional variety and degree of strength, power, and authority as an emerging suprastate to govern Africa in a global context.

Compared to the EU, in institutional and organizational advancement and in its expansiveness and encroachment throughout the region in forging an integral network and movement toward integration, Africa's AU may justifiably be described as an emerging suprastate organization. The AU's most active and prominent institutions are the Assembly and the AU Commission, which constitutes eight departments and nine bureaus, including Women and Gender, Civil Society and Diaspora (CIDO), and NEPAD. Its most emergent and promising institutions are the Peace and Security Council (PSC), the Economic, Social and Cultural Council (ECOSOCC), the PAP and its parastatal intergovernmental organization (IGO), NEPAD. The AU's architecture represents wide reach and has evolved from a deep scope. Between the first proposal for an African Court of Justice and Human Rights (ACJHR) and the demand for an African High Command and their eventual operationalization lay a half century of lobbying. From the founding of the OAU in 1963 until the completion of the last scheduled phase of the Treaty of Abuja in 2034—the journey toward political union and economic integration—stretch seventy-one years; we have currently reached fifty years in this journey.

The AU's institutional structure is a continuation, though also an expansion, as well as an innovation of its predecessor, the OAU, which in turn fostered the birth of an ever-proliferating range of other regional and subregional organizations known as Regional Economic Communities (RECs) such as the Southern African Development Community (SADC), the Common Market for Eastern and Southern Africa (COMESA), the Economic Community of West African States (ECOWAS), and the East African Community (EAC). These organizations mesh with, and also reinforce, both the AU and the Pan-African project. What's more, too much of the current literature on the Pan-African union project offers the narrowest possible conceptualization of Pan-Africanism as only IGOs. Yet outside the suprastate's formal suborganizations, there grows a veritable forest of continental and subregional civil society organizations, quangos, business and professional associations, and nongovernmental organizations (NGOs). Even within the IGOs, articles or books typically consider either the AU or the RECs, but rarely consider them together. Yet the AU, like the EU, must be understood as built upon a sandwich of IGO partnerships and treaties, each heavily overlapping the membership of others, but legally separate. A host of treaties explicitly stitches the continental and subregional organizations together as the warp and weft of the AU project: the AU architecture spans historical time as the warp, with Africa, its diaspora, and the global community as the weft; in this regard, to understand the AU's capacity as a regional and international actor is to explore its *longue-durée* as well as contemporaneous and comparative functionalist architectural development. Thus, our second goal for this chapter serves as our first attempt to analyze the book's thesis about the organization's regional and global agency and behavior and its impact on African politics. In this chapter we identify and reveal the organization's bureaucratic structure that informs the underpinnings of the AU's neofunctionalism, including its global governance infrastructure structured as partnerships.

In relation to its global governance, the significant question is whether the AU's whole (its institutional architecture) is significantly weightier than the sum of its parts (its capacity). Thus, while in this chapter we illustrate the AU's leviathan (apparently all-powerful) superstructure similar in organizational savvy to the EU, at the same time, the chapter merely posits the question of the AU's lameness characterized by its incapacity to make significant impact. Subsequent chapters will more fully interrogate the Union's capacity to act decisively as a hegemonic institution driving local, national, regional, and global change for Africans.

Evolving Architecture and Influences: Historical OAU, Comparative IGOs, and RECs

Despite its formal establishment in 2002, we know in 2013 that the AU is actually a fifty-year organization rather than a ten-year one. As such, to understand the Union's institutional anatomy, one must understand the historical evolution of its predecessor—the 1963-established OAU—from which the AU was born. As well, to discern the AU's institutional structure as a modicum of its contemporary behavior, it is important to compare its historical evolution with similarly structured international organizations—of course the EU (evolved from the European Coal and Steel Community [ECSC] and later the European Economic Community [EEC]), but also the OAS, ASEAN, and the Arab League—all correlatively established in a post–World War II international environment. Differently from these international organizations, however, a distinctive element of the AU is its correlate formation with Africa's RECs. The AU-REC (and other intra-African organizations referred to as quangos) institutional relationship may be described as a historically evolved love affair: sometimes autonomously, as distinct international bodies of their own competing with the AU; and other times interactively, forging structural integrative alliances with the AU.

The appendix illustrates this broad and deep array of the AU anatomy's multiple influences required for understanding its institutional form: comparative IGOs, the historical precedents of the AU; and the correlative, parallel, interactive evolution of Africa's RECs. The table classifies IGOs, taskforces, and structures, as well as its associated NGOs and loosely affiliated subregional organizations (RECs) that make up the institutional network that the AU uses to exercise its functionalism. These influencing elements are interwoven among each other with each criterion informing the other to build the AU's institutional architecture.

The AU's architecture amounts to a neofunctionalist organization similar to the EU. Whereas the EEC of 1957 grew out of the ECSC of 1952, in the same way, we see that the AU grew out of the OAU. The OAU was the second institutionalization of Pan-Africanism, representing Pan-Africanism's first permanent organizational structure; the AU has been described as the third institutionalization of Pan-Africanism.

The OAU forms part of the AU architecture as it symbolically traces the historical evolution and the on-the-ground context of regionalism from which AU institutions were built. The decade-old AU's structure is in reality a fifty-year one when its structural precedent, the OAU, is factored in. The AU's institutions may also be seen to predate the OAU and reach back to 1893 when the Congress on Africa in Chicago led to a journalist coining the term "Pan-Africanism," the Union's cultural driver. The notion of a congress—the political convening of Africans and African-descendant nonstate actors around a desire to achieve collective political freedom—continues to inform the AU's structure in the form of institutions like ECOSOCC and the more formal PAP.

The turning of the circle for a return to people-centered congresses in an age of statecentric Pan-Africanism of the OAU and AU started in 2004, with the AU's ECOSOCC statute making provision for African citizens: twenty diaspora organizations to be represented alongside 130 unions, professional groups, NGOs, faith-based organizations, and civil society organizations from Africa (Statutes of the ECOSOCC of the AU, art. 4). Episodic Pan-African congresses of the twentieth century are now replaced by a permanent council with annual and quarterly sessions and conferences convened by the AU CIDO directorate.

The quantum jump of the OAU into the AU was presaged by the OAU putting down roots in various organizational ways. Upon independence, each African state was admitted to the UN, so all founding OAU-AU members were also UN members. The UN's structure would inform an important benchmark for the eventual OAU and later AU structure. For example, the UN aims at maintaining peace and security, developing friendly relations, achieving international cooperation, and harmonizing international relations.

The Charter of the UN includes article 2.7 that stipulates noninterference in the domestic affairs of member states (United Nations 2011). Only on a case-by-case basis could the Security Council (UNSC) issue a "chapter seven" order to enact military force against a state that was a grave threat to international peace though not for reasons of domestic repression and dictatorship. Like the OAU, UN membership was founded on an all-in universality principle, including all dictatorships. (The only exclusions were two of the defeated former Axis powers being delayed in admission—although they were already democracies—until 1956 for Japan, and until 1973 for Germany.)

The very name Organization of African Unity evoked the name of the Organization of American States. This was founded by a charter in 1948, with a lineage going back to 1890 (Avalon Project 2008). Like the OAU, the OAS's mandate was "to promote their solidarity, to strengthen their collaboration, and to defend their sovereignty, their territorial integrity and their independence" (art. 1). Article 15 of the Bogota Charter specified no interference in the internal or external affairs of a member state. This ensured that military dictators and juntas were the great majority of members in good standing for decades.

The OAU would be based on "respect for the sovereignty and territorial integrity of each State and for its inalienable right to independent existence" (Charter of the OAU, art. III.3). The 1963 Charter of the OAU starts, in fact, with more progressive rhetoric than its contemporaries, ASEAN, the Arab League, and the OAS. Its preamble includes these clauses:

> Conscious of the fact that freedom, equality, justice and dignity are essential objectives for the achievement of the legitimate aspirations of the African peoples, . . .

> Persuaded that the Charter of the United Nations and the Universal Declaration of Human Rights, to the Principles of which we reaffirm our adherence, provide a solid foundation for peaceful and positive cooperation among States.

However, this is soon followed, as in the ASEAN, Arab League, and OAS charters, by article III:

> Member States . . . solemnly affirm and declare their adherence to the following principles: . . . Non-interference in the internal affairs of States.

This ensures that the preamble's rhetoric remains nonjuridical and is only aspirational or inspirational. The charter reiterates defense of the "hard-won independence as well as the sovereignty and territorial integrity of our states" in its preamble, in article II.1.c, and in article III.3. Also, compared to both the US and South African constitutions starting with the words "We the People," the OAU 1963 Charter has the more elitist formulation "We, the Heads of African States and Governments" and "the High Contracting Parties."

Thus while functionalism manifest through the Noninterference Clause defined the OAU like its contemporaries of the time—the UN, Arab League, OAS, et al.—neofunctionalism defined by the AU's Nonindifference Clause distinguished the AU as a global institution emerging in the new millennium. Nonindifference would drive the AU's structural change toward Pan-African unity, underscoring a more aggressive functionalism and assertion of supranational authority over the organization. The OAU Charter set out its functionalist agenda in a mandate analogous to its contemporary regional organizations. Article II.1 specifies its purposes: "(a) To promote the unity and solidarity of the African states; (b) To coordinate and intensify their cooperation . . .; (c) To defend their sovereignty, territorial integrity and independence; (d) To eradicate all forms of colonialism from Africa," as well as cooperation across the whole range of government policies. It is based on the equality of states, meaning one vote to each member state regardless of size, as with all its contemporary regional organizations. The OAU's institutions were similar to those of ASEAN, Arab League, and OAS, but slightly more elaborate.

Comparing the OAU-AU with other regional organizations, we can recognize generic similarities. First, their founding document affirms high ideals rhetorically, followed by a commitment never to intervene in the domestic affairs of another member state. Second, the apex organ is regular conferences of heads of government. Third, between such summits, the secretary-general has only administrative, not executive authority. Fourth, there are a number of committees seeking cooperation or sharing of information over a range of usually noncontentious issues from public health to transport and communications.

Interesting differences between the OAU and its contemporaries include the commitment "to eradicate all forms of colonialism," which reflects that one-third of African countries were then still under imperialist or settler rule, a situation that remained for a far smaller proportion of countries in Asia and the Americas at the time of the forming of the Arab League, OAS, and ASEAN. The Commission of Mediation, Conciliation and Arbitration and the Defence Commission were African innovations that had almost no precedent in contemporary regional organizations. Moreover, while not included in its charter, the OAU's founding meeting also established a permanent Liberation Committee, which in turn had three standing committees: for Information, for Finance, and for Defence (Esedebe 1982, 202–3). This committee had its head-quarters in Dar-es-Salaam, at the time Tanganyika's capital, its own budget, and vastly more financial and other autonomy than any other OAU organ (Wolfers 1976, 177).

The OAU had some major achievements during its thirty-nine years. It unremittingly sustained and orchestrated for three decades diplomatic lobbying and pressure against apartheid until South Africans won democracy. This was difficult during the Cold War era, as the then dominant world powers, the West, considered the apartheid South African regime as an anticommunist ally of us against them and almost always vetoed sanctions against apartheid. The same resistance also applied to the OAU's lobbying against the Portuguese Empire (a North Atlantic Treaty Organization [NATO] member) and also the anticommunist Rhodesian (Zimbabwe) settler minority regime.

As well, the "strictly confidential" *Adu Review* of the OAU offered an analysis in 1972 that remains as true four decades later:

> The future economic and social advancement of member states of the OAU depends to a very large extent on decisions and actions taken outside Africa. It is recognized therefore that African states and the OAU, which is the principal organ of the African states, should increasingly play a dynamic role in those international organs which attempt to influence the framework within which global policies in the economic and social fields are ordered. (Wolfers 1976, 101–2)

So the OAU Economic and Social Affairs Department's strategy was to coordinate the pressure of African states within international forums, to work toward a unified policy in negotiating treaties with the EU such as Lomé in 1975 and others. The negotiating team from African countries were sometimes serviced by the OAU.

Another major achievement was to negotiate with UN Secretary-General U Thant in 1965 permanent cooperation between the OAU and the UN Economic Commission for Africa (UNECA), also based in Addis Ababa, Ethiopia. This significantly augmented the OAU capacity and capability as "UN staff and money were contributed to the preparation of working papers essential to OAU decisions" (Wolfers 1976, 99). It is relevant to record that UNECA employed many Africans in sensitive policy posts. As well, UNECA convened a meeting of African finance ministers in the year of the OAU's founding to set up the African Development Bank (AfDB). The AfDB then cooperated with UNECA and the OAU to jointly host various meetings aimed at seeking common economic bargaining positions in negotiations (Wolfers 1976, 102). This partnership of the OAU with UNECA and the AfDB also increased the capacity of the OAU.

Significantly, as Nkrumah had also pointed out in the very year of the OAU's founding, it was an impossibly huge burden for African countries, on average smaller and poorer than the average ASEAN, Arab League, or OAS member, to pay the salaries and foreign exchange costs of embassies abroad (Nkrumah 1965). Consequently, the average African state could afford less than ten foreign embassies and consulates. Typically, these would be in its neighboring states, in its former imperial power, and in the two contemporary world powers.

There were only two cities in the world where they were all represented: their UN missions in New York, and their OAU representatives in Addis Ababa. So a majority of any African country's bilateral negotiations, and all its multilateral negotiations, would of necessity occur on the fringes of the OAU and also the UN. The OAU opened a bureau in New York in 1970 to coordinate African voting in line with OAU resolutions (Cervenka 1977, 34). In 1972 it opened a Geneva office to interact with the UN specialized agencies headquartered there. The OAU strengthened, at least among governmental elites, the construction of a social identity as African, as opposed to citizenship of a ministate or microstate. The benefit was to socialize the political elite of a continent into acceptance of, and often preference for, multilateral ways of thinking and acting, a point noted by Bayart: "Although the performance of African multi-national organizations is usually derided as pitiful, the institutional dimension of continental integration is significant and decisive. This is because the economic communities and customs agreements, the central banks . . . have more value as systems of sociability and creators of a real political domain than in their economic efficiency" (2009, 200). Summits were not merely pomp and extravagance. This point was recognized from the start by President Gamal Nasser: summits were attended "in order to strengthen the contacts, in order to be acquainted with each other, and in order to strengthen the brotherhood in Africa" (Wolfers 1976, 36).

The OAU facilitated or encouraged the founding of a veritable host of subregional organizations, which served as cornerstones toward constructing regionalisms and continentalism and reciprocally strengthened each other. From the year of its founding, it also set up numerous ad hoc mediation committees to peacefully resolve border disputes where possible, and where not to negotiate ceasefires: in 1963, Morocco-Algeria; in 1964, Somalia-Ethiopia; in 1965, Somalia-Kenya; in 1966, Rwanda-Burundi; in 1974, Mali-Upper Volta. "There is hardly an African conflict or dispute in which the OAU has not played a role" (Kouassi 1984, 49).

Learning from missteps made during these unilateral and multilateral conflict-resolution interventions, the OAU founded in 1993 its Mechanism on Conflict Prevention, Management and Resolution. This was in all but name the Commission on Conciliation, Mediation and Arbitration that had been proposed in its 1963 charter: a team of diplomats and negotiators who would attempt to negotiate ceasefires. Culminating all else, the gruesome genocide in Rwanda in 1994 revealed that neither the OAU nor the UN had the political will nor military capability to intervene. Immediately afterwards, in 1995 the OAU proposed setting up a peacekeeping brigade in each of its five geographic regions, a proposal that was achieved in the first decade of its successor, the AU.

As far as the AU's historical evolution goes, four decades of the OAU have also seen the organization facilitate and encourage the birth of an ever-proliferating range of other regional organizations known as RECs. These organizations mesh with, and also reinforce, both the AU and the Pan-African project. The Constitutive Act of the AU in 2000 commits African states to "coordinate and harmonize the policies between . . . Regional Economic Communities for the gradual attainment of the objectives of the Union" (art. 3.l). The AU's Protocol Relating to the Establishment of the Peace and Security Council of the African Union of 2002, for example, bluntly states that "the Regional Mechanisms are part of the overall security architecture of the Union" (art. 16.1). The 2007 Memorandum of Understanding on Cooperation in the Area of Peace and Security, which includes ECOWAS, SADC, the Eastern Africa Standby Brigade Coordinating Mechanism (EASBRICOM), and the North African Regional Capacity (NARC), institutionalizes them within the AU. The regional organizations agree to submit reports every six months to the AU Commission chair; the AU Commission chair will have annual meetings with the regional organizations' chief executives and open liaison offices in the regional organizations' headquarters, with reciprocal arrangements also encouraged.

In parallel with the OAU, the closing decades of the twentieth century saw the founding of these continental and subregional organizations. They covered the range of IGOs, qungos, and business and civil society associations with a continental mandate. This makes Africa's RECs the geographic cornerstones for continental integration. Indisputably, Africa's four leading RECs today are COMESA, EAC, ECOWAS, and SADC.

Adebayo Adedeji played an outstanding role in founding three of Africa's regional economic organizations, an unparalleled achievement. He spent three years of tireless shuttle diplomacy across West Africa to persuade sixteen presidents to found ECOWAS in 1975. He then moved to Addis Ababa to head UNECA: "His sixteen year tenure became the ECA's longest and most dynamic: he skillfully converted the organization into a pan-African platform to continue his efforts to promote economic integration, and his efforts led to the creation of COMESA and ECCAS in 1981 and 1983 respectively" (Adebajo 2011, 11). The 1991 Treaty of Abuja, which paved the way for the AU as the penultimate fruition of political African union, proposed that Africa's RECs strengthen themselves and advance toward becoming free trade areas. This did occur for three of the existing RECs: EAC, SADC, and COMESA. ECCAS and the Arab Maghreb Union (AMU) are mostly dormant.

The AU has adapted ECOWAS peacekeeping and conflict-resolution organs in a process in which Nigeria and other ECOWAS members of the AU drew upon their own experiences to shape an AU evolution that adapted ECOWAS precedents. Table 2.1 illustrates the diffusion of norms from ECOWAS to the AU, down to even the nomenclature. Unlike the UN, but like ECOWAS, the AU's PSC may order military intervention by a two-thirds majority, so minimizing paralysis, and no country can exercise a veto. Moreover, the UN has no equivalent to the Panel of the Wise, but ECOWAS does have a precedent.

TABLE 2.1.   PEACEKEEPING INSTITUTIONAL COMPARISON: ECOWAS AND THE AFRICAN UNION

ECOWAS	AFRICAN UNION
Mediation and Conciliation Council	Peace and Security Council (PSC)
Ecowarn	Continental Early Warning System (CEWS)
Council of Elders	Panel of the Wise
Economic Community of West African States Monitoring Group (ECOMOG), later ECOWAS Standby Force	African Standby Force (ASF)
Defence Council and Defence Commission	Military Staff Committee
Decisions by Two-Thirds Majority	Decisions by Two-Thirds Majority

On the economic front, as early as 1976, the OAU established the institutional premises for the AU with the later Treaty of Abuja as the key driver of the AU's ultimate emergence in 2002. In 1976 the Kinshasa Summit endorsed Mobutu's revival of Nkrumah's call to establish a Common African Market. This led in 1980 to the Second Extraordinary Session of OAU Heads of State and Government adopting the Lagos Plan of Action to establish an AEC. These efforts would foster the achievement of the economic, social and cultural integration of Africa.

This leisurely pace sped up with the ending of the Cold War and the acceleration of globalization, bringing pressures for global free trade as the new World Trade Organization (WTO) became a General Agreement on Tariffs and Trade (GATT) with teeth. Ripples went around the world, leading to a host of regional organizations strengthening themselves and revising their founding charters, from the EEC to ASEAN to ECOWAS, COMESA, and SADC. New institutions sprang up, such as NAFTA and Mercosur. The OAU members signed the ambitious Abuja Treaty of 1991, which came into effect in 1994, to establish the AEC.

The OAU represented a deliberate choice with the OAS format of organization instead of the EEC, as argued above. This dramatically changed with the Treaty of Abuja, which proposed to import lock, stock, and barrel all the institutions of the EU over a time frame matching the thirty-five years of its deepening integration between the Treaty of Rome and the Maastricht Treaty. The signatories of the Abuja Treaty agreed to establish a Pan-African Parliament, an African Court of Justice, an Economic and Social Council, and a Community Solidarity, Development and Compensation Fund. Chapter 6 covers its detailed phases for the economic integration of Africa; this section analyzes a shift in rhetoric since the OAU Charter of 1963.

The Treaty Establishing the African Economic Community did not reiterate the 1963 OAU Charter emphasis on the sovereign independence of each state. Instead, article 3.a referred to the "*inter*-dependence of Member States" (emphasis added) plus the EU principle that is the diametric opposite of the doctrine of nonintervention in others' domestic affairs: "harmonisation of policies" (art. 3.c). Article 6.2.f.ii commits the fifty governments to "integration of all the sectors namely economic, political, social and cultural."

None of the nondemocratic African members among those signing the treaty objected to article 3.g—"Recognition, promotion and protection of human and peoples' rights in accordance with the provisions of the African Charter on Human and Peoples' Rights"—or 3.h: "Accountability, economic justice and popular participation in development." As well, article 5.3 addressed the lack in the

OAU Charter of any provision to enforce decisions: any state defying decisions may be subject to sanctions including the suspension of membership. Article 6.5 specified a maximum of forty years to implement all provisions of the treaty.

While the treaty obtained sufficient ratifications to come into force within three years of its signing, five years elapsed before any action. This finally occurred with the 2002 founding of the AU starting in Sirte, Libya, further discussed and deliberated in Lomé, Togo, and finally debouched in Durban. In Sirte, the late Muammar Gaddafi of Libya revived the essence of Nkrumah's vision of a federal UAS with one unified military force. Before this Pan-African proposal could suffer the same fate as thirty-six years earlier, President Thabo Mbeki and his diplomats leapt into lobbying the continent's governments, helped by Nigerian support. As a compromise on a US-style federation, Mbeki advanced the EU model of neofunctionalism, an incremental progress toward an eventual confederation; on paper this had already been agreed to in 1991 by the signatories to the Treaty of Abuja.

The Sirte Declaration of September 9, 1999 agreed to symbolize this qualitative change by renaming the OAU the AU. The governments adopted the elaborate Constitutive Act of the AU at the Lomé Summit on July 11, 2000, which achieved enough ratifications to enter into force on May 7, 2001. The AU was inaugurated in Durban on July 8, 2002. The reengineering of the OAU into the AU has two major dimensions. First, the AU completely took over the personnel and institutions of the OAU in Addis Ababa. The secretariat was retitled on EU lines as the AU Commission; the Council of Ministers was retitled the Executive Council. Second, there were dramatic expansions in its mandate, plus the founding of the institutions promised in the Abuja Treaty.

THE AU GOVERNMENTAL AUTHORITY: THE CONSTITUTIVE ACT, THE AU COMMISSION, THE EXECUTIVE COUNCIL, THE ASSEMBLY, THE PSC, AND NEPAD

The quantitative differences between the OAU and the AU are big enough to become qualitative, starting with the very name of its founding document. Any organization may have a charter. But the term "act" in Constitutive Act implies the weight of a statute promulgated by a parliament; "constitutive" evokes a constitution, as in the founding of a new state. African member states consciously and strategically directed this change, thereby suggesting their desire for the new organization to achieve supranational authority on behalf of their collective interests in a new global arena.

The AU's new mandate enacted in the Constitutive Act is contrasted with the OAU's 1963 Pan-African nationalist narrative privileging sovereignty while also adjusting to a new genre of twenty-first-century Pan-Africanist unity, democracy, and human rights assertiveness. That the conflicting clauses are deliberately adjacent in the act appears to reflect the power balance between the Mbeki-Obasanjo thrust and the less democratic rulers, where neither side could exclude the wording of the other. Compare the following articles:

> 3.b, defend sovereignty and independence
> versus
> 3.c, accelerate the political integration of Africa
> 3.h, promote and protect human rights and peoples' rights
> 5.c, founding the Pan-African Parliament (with implications for sovereignty)
> 4.g, noninterference in internal affairs
> versus
> 4.h, right to intervene in genocide, crimes against humanity, and other grave circumstances
> 3.g, "promote democratic principles and institutions, popular participation and good governance."

Indeed, the AU Constitutive Act is a world first for international organizations in recognizing a right of humanitarian intervention in a sovereign independent state. The PAP Protocol was the first in the world to prescribe a minimum quota for women members of parliament (MPs): one-fifth, though the PAP has not yet refused to accredit national slates of MPs who arrive without one women MP (Protocol to the Treaty Establishing the AEC Relating to the PAP, art. 4.2). The protocol also explicitly defends multiparty democracy (art. 4.3).

The wording in the Constitutive Act's article 3 is key. Political *integration* is conceding far more than cooperation; likewise, use of the name "parliament" implies the ultimate grant of law-making powers and supranational authority over at least certain agreed areas. Clearly, the other diametrical confrontations will be decided by a power struggle on a case-by-case basis each time conflict comes to a climax in Mauritania or Zimbabwe, Comoros, Congo, or Côte d'Ivoire, Madagascar or the Sudan. Diplomats and other lobbyists will battle to accumulate a majority of votes on their side.

Like the Abuja Treaty, the Constitutive Act sought to remedy the OAU Charter's omission of any way to enforce OAU decisions upon members. Article 23, titled

"Imposition of Sanctions," empowered the AU to suspend the benefits of membership to all states defaulting on paying their annual membership dues, then specified,

> any Member State that fails to comply with the decisions and policies of the Union may be subjected to other sanctions, such as the denial of transport and communications links with other Member States, and other measures of a political and economic nature to be determined by the Assembly. (art. 23.2)

Article 30 demands the suspension of "governments which shall come to power through unconstitutional means."

Illustrated by table 2.2 (AU Organogram), the AU's Constitutive Act provides for an elaborate institutional architecture showing the relationships among the AU's functions and organizations underscoring the way the institution functions. The organogram maps out the wide scope of the AU's governance authority whose power to enact decisions is concentrated in the AU's diplomatic core, which constitutes the AU Commission, the Assembly of Heads of State and Government (Assembly), and the Executive Council. Nonetheless, the AU's governance functions and scope cover key areas of African affairs, including security, parliamentary, judiciary, culture and society, and economics. The AU has established organs, secretariat departments, commissions and directorates, and quasi-governmental affiliates in each of these areas.

As an intergovernmental body, the AU Commission is the organ that has the most authority to achieve the Union's governance objectives. The Commission is extremely powerful and virtually controls the entire AU organization. The precedent Commission, the OAU-General Secretariat, had grown by 1965 to seven posts and sixty-eight contracts, reaching 252 personnel by 1970, including eight political appointees at the top. The staff came from twenty-eight member countries. The establishment rose to 346 persons by 1974 including the first person from a state not yet a member—Angola. However, the upgrading of the OAU into the AU saw the General Secretariat restyled as the Commission, as in the EU, but it was not yet accorded supranational authority. President Thabo Mbeki got the principle accepted that future secretaries-general should be chosen from retired heads of government, to increase the stature and authority they could assert in behind-the-scenes negotiations. The AU's first secretary-general was retired Malian president Alpha Oumar Konaré, followed by Gabon's Deputy Prime Minister and Foreign Minister Jean Ping. In 2012, South Africa's Dr. Nkosazana Dlamini-Zuma was elected as the Commission's first female chairperson.

TABLE 2.2. AFRICAN UNION ORGANOGRAM AND EXTENDED FAMILY (FOCUSING ON ACTUALLY FUNCTIONING ENTITIES)

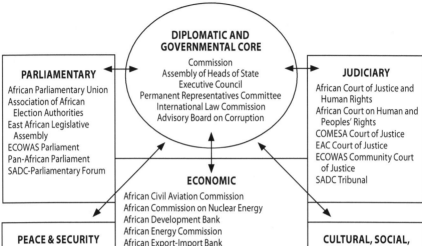

DIPLOMATIC AND GOVERNMENTAL CORE

Commission
Assembly of Heads of State
Executive Council
Permanent Representatives Committee
International Law Commission
Advisory Board on Corruption

PARLIAMENTARY

African Parliamentary Union
Association of African
  Election Authorities
East African Legislative
  Assembly
ECOWAS Parliament
Pan-African Parliament
SADC-Parliamentary Forum

JUDICIARY

African Court of Justice and
  Human Rights
African Court on Human and
  Peoples' Rights
COMESA Court of Justice
EAC Court of Justice
ECOWAS Community Court
  of Justice
SADC Tribunal

ECONOMIC

African Civil Aviation Commission
African Commission on Nuclear Energy
African Development Bank
African Energy Commission
African Export-Import Bank
African Peer Review Mechanism
African Petroleum Fund
African Regional Intellectual Property
  Organization
African Organization for Standardisation
African Tax Administration Forum
African Telecommunications Union
Association of African Central Banks
Banque Centrale des États de l'Afrique de l'Ouest
Banque des États de l'Afrique Centrale
Common Monetary Area
Communauté Économique et Monétaire de
  l'Afrique Centrale
EAC
ECOWAS
Interafrican Bureau for Animal Resources
Inter-African Phytosanitary Council
NEPAD Planning and Coordinating Agency
Organisation Africaine de la Propriété
  Intellectuelle
Pan-African Infrastructure Development Fund
Pan-African Postal Union
Pan African Veterinary Vaccine Centre
Regional African Satellite Communications
  Organisation
Scientific and Technical Research Centre
Semi-Arid Food Grain Research and Development
Southern African Customs Union
SADC
Southern African Power Pool
Union Économique et Monétaire Ouest-Africaine
Union of African Railways
Union of Producers, Transporters and Distributors
  of Electric Power in Africa
West African Power Pool

PEACE & SECURITY

Africa Forum
African Centre for Studies
  and Research on Terrorism
African Policing Civilian
  Oversight Forum
African Standby Force
CEMOC
Continental Early Warning
  System
Committee of Intelligence
  and Security Services
  of Africa
Military Staff Committee
Peace and Security Council
Panel of the Wise

CULTURAL, SOCIAL, AND CIVIL SOCIETY

Citizens and Diaspora
  Organizations
African Academy of
  Languages
Afro-Arab Institute for
  Culture and Strategic
  Studies
CELHTO
Economic, Social & Cultural
  Council
Pan-African News Agency
Supreme Council for Sport
  in Africa

The Commission's most prominent tussle for power is that between the Commission's Peace and Security Department and the PSC. The Commission has drawn up agendas for PSC meetings, and on occasion taken decisions that should have been made by the PSC. The latest additions to the Commission are the Advisory Board on Corruption and the Commission on International Law (AUCIL), with eight departments headed by regionally representative commissioners, elected on the basis of a gender quota (50 percent of the commissioners must be women), and department directors. There are also nine directorates reporting to the Bureau of the Chairperson, which significantly include directorates on Gender, and on Citizens and Civil Society. Headed by an elected chairperson and deputy chairperson, the AU Commission is supposedly the motor of the AU. The Commission develops common policy frameworks for member state ratification and supposedly coordinates the African developmental, integration, and unification effort.

The Commission is challenged by its absence of truly supranational powers to implement and enforce decisions and to lead the unification agenda, whereby its strength is in leading the AU as an intergovernmental body. Making decisions, ratifying them collectively, and implementing them in the form of actually existing policy analysis and enforcement are the preserve of two its twelve organs: the Assembly, which functions through the Executive Council (composed of ministers or authorities designated by the governments of member states); and its advisory board, the Permanent Representatives Committee, composed of permanent representatives of member states accredited to the Union and other duly accredited plenipotentiaries of member states resident at the headquarters of the Union.

The Assembly is the supreme organ of the Union and its key functions are to

(a) Determine the common policies of the Union, establish its priorities, and adopt its annual programme;

(b) Monitor the implementation of policies and decisions of the Union as well ensure compliance by all Member States through appropriate mechanisms;

(c) Accelerate the political and socio-economic integration of the continent;

(d) Give directives to the Executive Council, the PSC of the Commission on the management of conflicts, war, acts of terrorism, emergency situations and the restoration of peace;

(e) Decide on intervention in a Member State in respect of grave circumstances namely, war crimes, genocide, and crimes against humanity;

(f) Decide on intervention in a Member State at the request of that Member State in order to restore peace and security;

(g) Determine the sanctions to be imposed on any Member State for non payment of assessed contributions, violation of the principles enshrined in the Constitutive Act and the rules, and non-compliance with the decision of the Union and unconditional changes of government. (AU Organs, Constitutive Act)

Another important organ working closely in decision making with the AU Assembly, Executive Council, and Permanent Representatives Committee, is the PSC, which held its inauguration in Addis Ababa in 2004. It comprises ten members elected for two years and five elected for three years, who have capacity for peacekeeping, including financial contributions. Election selects states to give regional representation. The PSC has strong emphasis on mediation and conflict prevention, with a Panel of the Wise, a Situation Room, and Continental Early Warning System (CEWS). To ensure that the AU is not hindered like the OAU by lack of budget, the PSC has its own Peace Fund, raising donations in addition to the AU's own allocation. Also, states participating in its ASF may be required to bear their own costs for the first three months of deployment.

The preamble to the PSC's Protocol states it is building on the precedent of the OAU's Mechanism of Conflict Prevention, Mediation, and Resolution. But it is also clear that this marks the start of the AU's shift from adoption of EU institutions to adaptation of ECOWAS organs. We have already seen how Nigeria and other ECOWAS states shaped an AU evolution that adapted ECOWAS precedents, down to even the nomenclature. Each of the five permanent members of the UNSC may veto any intervention. By contrast, the PSC may order even military intervention by a two-thirds majority, so minimizing paralysis.

To date, peacekeeping is arguably the AU's major activity. There have been over 360 meetings of the PSC, compared to the average two dozen meetings of other organs. Boots on the ground in Sudan, Somalia, and elsewhere grew to over twenty-five thousand, equalling the five brigades of soldiers and police envisaged for the formal start-up of the ASF in 2010. More than that, the ASF is already de facto an African *Standing* Force—the ASF has been in continuous action for over seven years, now with a permanent Military Staff Committee. PSC operations will be analyzed in our chapter 5 on the AU Peace and Security Architecture and on responsibility to protect.

The Panel of the Wise was constituted in Addis Ababa in 2007. It is interesting that the first institutionalization of linkages between the AU and the RECs, pledged in the Abuja Treaty, occurred not in economic matters, but with the chair of the AU Commission opening liaison offices in each of the regional mechanisms for peacekeeping. The first such AU office opened in the ECOWAS headquarters during 2010, with the AU Commission chair now hosting regular meetings with the regional heads. Other components of a continental security architecture included founding the African Centre for Studies and Research on Terrorism (ACSRT), headquartered in Algiers, Algeria. This offered counterterrorism training and shared intelligence between member states. The Committee of Intelligence and Security Services of Africa (CISSA) also started in 2004, processing covert intelligence.

The PAP inauguration came into being in 2004, with Midrand, South Africa, designated as the permanent site. How does the PAP compare with other regional parliaments? Only the European Parliament (EP), the Parlamento Centroamericano, and the ECOWAS Community Parliament are older. The EP first met in 1958, but only upgraded to direct elections in 1979 and has only been able to assert power since 1998. Currently the EP consists of 751 MEPs from 27 member states. Seats are allocated between countries on the principle of degressive proportionality (Schmidt 2010, 30). Countries with larger populations elect more MPs than smaller countries, but smaller countries are overrepresented. Between Malta and Germany, the value of an individual's vote is 10:1. The ECOWAS Parliament is discussed in the next chapter. All other regional parliaments proposed, such as the UNASUR Parliament and the Arab League Parliament, are not yet operationalized.

The PAP intends to move from indirect to direct elections within a shorter period than the two decades this took the EP. Currently, countries are represented on the senate principle of equal representation per state, five MPs (Protocol to the Treaty Establishing the AEC Relating to the PAP, art. 4.2). This results in a 1000:1 ratio in the value of a voter between Nigeria and the Seychelles; the PAP will presumably evolve in the direction of the EP's and the ECOWAS Parliament's degressive proportionality formulas. The PAP started determined lobbying to acquire authority and increase its budget and other resources. The PAP has set up ten portfolio committees, including one for Cooperation, International Relations, and Conflict Resolution (PAP 2006). The 2005 AU budgetary reform enabled the AU for the first time to pay not half but the full PAP allocation in its budget. Simultaneously, retired South African president Mandela lent his stature to the launch of the Pan-African Trust Fund in 2006, which started with German and UN donations. By 2010 the PAP budget rose to $14 million, the second largest item in the AU budget.[1] In addition, individual countries are responsible for their own MPs' remuneration and per diem expenses, while the host country (South Africa) covers all capital and some operational costs of the PAP.

PAP MPs gave priority to objecting to their marginalization, by both the Assembly and the PSC, in negotiations over Darfur and other peacekeeping operations including their right to be involved in all future peace negotiations. The PAP has the right to receive annual reports from the PSC and to ask for interim reports (Protocol Relating to the Establishment of the PSC of the AU, art. 18). The PAP is also lobbying for codecision over the AU budget, oversight over all AU Commission directorates, and the ability to send monitoring teams to all national elections in AU member states. While the AU adopted Kiswahili as its fourth official language in 1986, the PAP website can claim the first actual use of Kiswahili since 2004. One remarkable aspect is that the Abuja Treaty anticipated that founding a PAP would be among the toughest achievements to accomplish and scheduled it for the final stage forty years ahead, ending in 2034 (Treaty Establishing the AEC, art. 6.2.f.iv), but the PAP started three decades ahead of schedule.

Civil society was swift to use the space opened up by the PAP. The first demonstration outside the PAP came from over one hundred Ethiopians protesting on December 9, 2005, against the killing of women and children in Ogaden. Fifty Ugandans followed this on December 30, 2005, with a demonstration against the detention of their leader back home and the banning of their meetings (PAP 2006).

Analysis of the PAP must point out that its intrinsic importance is far more than the terrain it opens up for oversight of the AU executive, and later legislative authority. First, the AU is constituted as an IGO, comprised of elite heads of government, cabinet ministers, diplomats, and civil servants. Nowhere in the world may civil servants publicly criticize their own governments. The PAP and ECOSOCC are the first AU institutions that broaden participation to include civil society. MPs have freedom of speech to publicly criticize undemocratic regimes. As part of this, the PAP has the potential to take the lead toward the democratization of both the AU itself and the continent. Second, the majority of African countries are classified as either democracies or as partly free. Their parliamentarians can bring soft power to bear upon the minority of repressive regimes, such as those in Equatorial Guinea, the Gambia, Swaziland, and Zimbabwe.

How does the PAP compare with other regional parliaments? The Parlacen and ECOWAS Parliament websites are basic. The ASEAN Interparliamentary Assembly drops all matters on which it cannot reach consensus; that is, any one MP can veto a resolution, so blocking it on every contentious issue (AIPA 2013, art. 7.3). The other regional parliaments have merely announcements about them. Only the EP (European Parliament 2011) and the PAP have advanced to the point of running an online Hansard of their debates, in addition to publishing their resolutions, and demonstrate substantive activities such as election observer missions and significant input into their regional organizations.

When ECOSOCC was inaugurated in 2005, it showed a world-first innovation subsequent to the Abuja Treaty and the Constitutive Act. As mentioned above, its statute-making provision for civil society included twenty diaspora organizations to be represented alongside 130 civil society organizations from Africa (Statutes of the ECOSOCC of the AU, art. 4). While several countries facilitate members of their diasporas in obtaining visas or naturalization, they do not take kindly to advice and criticism from their diaspora, still less institutionalize their representation.[2] Another world first is that ECOSOCC institutionalizes representation by the diaspora of not one country, but one continent. Its tasks started with selecting and accrediting civil society organizations.

The African Court of Human and Peoples' Rights was inaugurated in Banjul in 2006 (African Court of Human and Peoples' Rights 2011), followed by the African Court of Justice inaugurated in 2008. These courts are now being unified as the ACJHR in Arusha, Tanzania (Protocol on the Statute of the ACJHR). The court has jurisdiction to decide cases brought by AU member governments against each other or concerning AU-related treaties. Individual governments may give consent to persons or NGOs bringing cases against them. The African Commission on Human and People's Rights may also initiate litigation. The court operates on the principle of subsidiarity. In 2011 the court ordered the Libyan regime to "immediately refrain from any action that would result in loss of life or violation of physical integrity of persons."[3] While the AU lacked the hard policing power to enforce this, such judgments add their soft power to one side in the competition for public support and in the negotiations that usually end such conflicts.

The AU's organs also consist of eight Specialized Technical Committees made up of "senior officials" and by 2013 must be attended by the relevant national cabinet ministers biennially, and annually for those on Defence, Finance, and Gender (Constitutive Act, arts. 14 and 21). Last but not least is the permanent establishment of Pan-African administrators. At the OAU's start, Ethiopian Emperor Haile Selassie generously seconded personnel "full of energy and innovation," paid from the Ethiopian budget (Wolfers 1976, 51–52).[4] A tough challenge in attracting and retaining staff was that the OAU could never match UN salaries for UNECA, also housed in Addis Ababa. During its founding year, Ethiopian sponsorship of $400,000 paid for a provisional secretariat of eighteen professional staff, while the emperor also donated a building intended for a police academy to become Africa Unity House, plus a residence for the secretary-general, and title deeds to 85,000 square metres of land (Wolfers 1976, 85–87).

As well, the AU's budgetary formula revision ranks equally in importance with any institutional consolidation. In 2005 the countries with the largest gross domestic products agreed to collectively pay 75 percent of the AU's annual budget on top of their national dues. This action of Algeria, Egypt, Libya, Nigeria, and South Africa underwrote the viability of the AU, marking another qualitative advance on the OAU.

AU-Style Global Governance and Partners

The AU's elaborate intraregional institutional architecture has also fostered the institution's development of an equally elaborate global governance structural mechanism—referred to as international partnerships—to deal exclusively and strategically with the world on its own terms with important consequences. The AU uses its institutional structure deployed strategically to establish the continent as a dynamic force in the international arena. The Union is acutely aware of the power embedded in an international community whose own global governance agenda is to manage Africa's problems. There is an important philosophy under-pinning these partnerships that are based on the goal to obliterate the age-long pattern of donor-recipient relationship and move toward one founded on recipro-cal obligations and responsibilities. By establishing strategic partnerships, the AU places itself and Africa in front of the global agenda mobilizing resources, knowledge, and political will for the continent on its own terms.

The Union achieves this agenda through four distinct partnership genres: continent to continent partnerships, continent to country partnerships, AU part-nerships with other international and regional institutions, and partnerships in demand as new states or regions request additional partnerships. Examples of these partnerships are as follows:

Continent to Continent Partnerships

Partnership between Africa and the Arab World
Africa-Europe (EU) Partnership
Africa-South America (ASA) Summit
Asian-African Sub-Regional Organisations Conference (AASROC)

CONTINENT TO COUNTRY PARTNERSHIPS

Africa-India Forum Summit
Africa-Turkey Partnership
Africa-China: Forum on China-Africa Cooperation (FOCAC)
Africa-United States: African Growth and Opportunity Act (AGOA;
    a relationship, not a partnership)
Africa-Japan: Tokyo International Conference on African
    Development (TICAD)
Africa-France Partnership
Africa-Korea Partnership

INSTITUTION TO INSTITUTION PARTNERSHIPS

Organization of American States (OAS)
Organization of Islamic Cooperation (OIC)
the Commonwealth
Organisation Internationale de la Francophonie (OIF)

What makes the institutionalization of such global engagements more important for Africa than is the case for other continents and countries is that intra-African trade is far lower than is the case for the EU or other continents and global trade far higher. Through these partnership genres, the AU is consciously establishing itself as a vehicle for Africans' strategic cooperation in the world. The Union's strategy is to use these global relationships to market Africa's position, acquire support to achieve its objectives, and increase Africa's international standing and global leverage. As a consequence, the AU's budget was raised by 2010 to US$250 million, half of it coming from international donors.

In the diplomatic realm, for example, the growing stature of the AU as a global governance institution, compared to the earlier OAU, saw new inroads for African foreign policies in the realm of global affairs when in 2006 the United States became the first of fifty-three states to formally accredit ambassadors to the AU. Alongside these, regional organizations such as the EU, Arab League, and the OIF followed suit. No state had contemplated accrediting diplomats to the former OAU, but they clearly decided that the AU carries more weight in international affairs and global governance. Two regional communities have recently also shown enhanced standing. China, Saudi Arabia, and Turkey have now accredited special representatives to COMESA, with China additionally posting a diplomat accredited to ECOWAS. These diplomatic postings are in the nature of consular-level representation.

Nine AU members are also members of the Arab League, and these two regional organizations held joint summits in 1977 and 2010 to mediate tensions. Accompanying this has been a flurry of serial international conferences, where the AU speaks on behalf of Africa. These started with TICAD, first held in 1993 and four times subsequently. In chronological order, the next to follow was FOCAC in 2000, with the China-Africa Development Fund (CAD Fund) opening offices in Johannesburg and Addis Ababa. Further such conferences include the ASA Summit, first held in 2007, which set up the Africa-South America Cooperation Forum (ASACOF); the Africa-India Forum in 2008; the Korea-Africa Forum in 2009; and the AU-US Summit in 2010. Africa-Turkey relations are also expanding, as is AASROC. All the above diplomatic activity was buttressed by major business contacts and corporate panel sessions.

The AU-EU mission provides an important illustration of how the AU's institutional partnerships impact global governance as it perhaps exemplifies the symbiotic relationship and the mutual value that the global governance strategy yields for Africans in the world. The mission monitors AU-EU cooperation and works closely with all the EU institutions—in particular its Commission, Council of Ministers, and EP. The mission also prepares and coordinates regular working meetings of the EU and AU Commissions in Brussels and Addis Ababa and the ministerial troika meetings that have been institutionalized since the first EU-Africa Summit in Cairo in 2000.

The mission coordinates the group of African ambassadors in Brussels and monitors the implementation of the Cotonou Agreement between the EU and the African, Caribbean, and Pacific (ACP) states. The AU-EU mission coordinates the activities of the African countries (forty-eight of the seventy-nine ACP countries) and harmonizes them with the development and international cooperation strategies of the AU. It also acts as secretariat to the group of African ambassadors and representatives of the fifty-four of fifty-five AU countries—including South Sudan and Somali, and excluding Morocco—in Brussels. The mission also coordinates the activities of other regional communities with representatives in Brussels, like ECOWAS and COMESA. Finally, in representing the AU in the twenty-seven member countries of the EU, the mission pays particular attention to the African communities throughout the EU, helping them strengthen and rationalize their structures and explaining to them the important role that the African diaspora worldwide plays in contributing to African development and building the AU.

The FOCAC (AU-China) and TICAD (AU-Japan) forums represent the most developed examples of sites where the AU itself, alongside national heads of state, shares sovereignty in negotiating African interests in global governance. FOCAC delivered the impressive new AU Conference and Office Complex built free of charge to the AU by the Chinese government and Ethiopian workers, and commissioned in January 2012. These partnerships are analogous to the EU opening embassies and accrediting ambassadors, about which the right-wing British newspaper the *Telegraph* grumbled: "Embassies in the key capitals of Beijing, Kabul, and Addis Ababa, the seat of the African Union, are regarded as marking a major shift to giving the EU a role as a global player" (Waterfield 2010). The same naturally applies to the AU diplomatic missions to New York, Washington, Geneva, Brussels, and Cairo. One milestone to watch for is when these missions will be formally upgraded to the title of embassies, as the EU did, in its case in 2010. This is yet another example of the AU asserting supranational authority in a way not contemplated by or for the OAS or ASEAN, still less by or for NAFTA or Mercosur.

More precisely, AU global partnerships represent a transforming hybridity, in which the AU—like the EU—demonstrates both intergovernmental and supranational characteristics during a half-century of *longue-durée* evolution from an IGO toward becoming a supranational authority. What we might conceive of as shared sovereignty is clearly a long-term feature, as is even true of a confederal constitution, which still lies far in the future for both the AU and EU, after they merge their military and diplomatic establishments. Already, however, the AU and ECOWAS, and the SADC on its behalf, have asserted the ultimate supranational power in the name of exercising their authority of international security by deploying peacemaking armies in civil wars from Liberia to Lesotho—and more recently, Mali.

A permanent part of the AU's diplomatic foreign policy will be its sixth region, the diaspora. The latest Global African Diaspora Summit, held in Johannesburg in May 2012, agreed to set up a Diaspora Advisory Board to address issues such as the right to return and five legacy projects. It would set up a skills database of diaspora African professionals, an African Diaspora Volunteers Corps, and an African Diaspora Investment Fund. It would develop a marketplace to facilitate innovation and entrepreneurship among Africans and the diaspora, as well as establish an African Remittances Institute to mitigate the exploitative bank fees charged to transnational workers sending money home across borders.

The work of the AU always uses diplomacy as its first resort and military deployment as the last. This necessitated what we may conceive of as an embryonic diplomatic corps. As OAU, the AU set up a New York bureau in 1970 to service its coordination of African delegates to the UN. Next followed its mission to UN specialized agencies in Geneva in 1972. Third came the OAU mission to the EEC in Brussels, which the AU upgraded to a permanent mission, followed by its mission to the Arab League.

The Permanent Observer Mission of the AU to the UN in New York illustrates the manner in which the Union has strategically deployed and extended its institutional structure to engage in corridors of global power. The AU office at the UN states several objectives, including developing and maintaining constructive and productive institutional relationships between the AU and UN as well as promoting a common view within the African group in international negotiations. The office's core functions are enumerated as follows: to assist in coordinating the activities of the African group at the UN, to advise the AU headquarters on strategies for addressing emerging issues at the UN, to assist AU member states to adopt common positions in the UN, to maintain contacts with UN agencies based in New York, including the UN Development Programme and UN Children's Fund (UNICEF), to assist with procurement for the commission and other organs, and to facilitate the exchange of information between the AU and the UN.

Yet, in 2011, two of the AU's key members of the nonpermanent UNSC—Nigeria and South Africa—voted in support of a UN resolution to establish a no-fly zone in Libya paving the way for NATO military intervention and violent regime change despite the AU's collective defiance of the UN resolution and NATO intervention. The institution deliberated on what went wrong at the AU mission at the UN. The office had failed in its objective to assist member states to adopt AU common and harmonized positions on key UN votes.

One of the first actions of the postwar appointment of the new chairperson, Dr. Dlamini-Zuma, was to address this blatant failure of the AU institutionally. She has strengthened the quality of staffing and appointed a professional higher-level ambassador who will enliven the liaison and global lobby functions of the AU to avoid future debacles that the Libyan crisis brought upon the Union.

Conclusion

Despite the fact that it did not alter the intergovernmental structural capabilities of the OAU Pan-African project, the AU can be seen to have been established as an institutional reform platform to replace the institutionally bottle-necked bureaucratic OAU. Through the AU Commission, for example, the AU's biggest structural accomplishment compared to the OAU has been to create legal and political openings for advancing the process of African integration. The AU Commission would encourage gradual continental integration and strengthen the architecture of the Union; and through the illustrious and visionary leadership of three Commission chairpersons since 2002 (Alpha Konaré, Jean Ping, and Nkosazana Dlamini-Zuma), the AU Commission's heightened profile in Addis Ababa has contributed to the organization's having become now more widely recognized as an actor and partner in political matters on the global scene (Laporte and Mackie 2010).

Nonetheless, continuous challenges to the AU's institutional design followed by demands for institutional reform have dominated discussions of the Union's capacity and future. For instance, dissatisfied with the pace of African economic integration and political union ten years later, member states have sought to reform the AU architecture to enforce greater governance. Again in Sirte in 2009, the Assembly decided on the establishment of a strengthened AU Commission, reestablishing it as an African Union Authority. The AU Authority would be the body that would govern pragmatic, progressive, and transitory political arrangements toward a United States of Africa. During the July 2009 Summit in Sirte, the Assembly requested the Commission to take all the necessary steps to prepare the required legal revisions (including of the Constitutive Act), the structure of the new Authority, and the financial implications of the transformation of the Commission into the AU Authority. The Authority would promote integration more aggressively, test out new forms of partnerships between it, RECS, and member states, and explore how member states could progressively transfer elements of sovereignty to the Pan-African level AU.

In illustrating and dissecting the AU institutional anatomy, we have merely scratched the surface of whether or not the AU's institutional architecture provides the international/regional organization with the capacity to act as a supranational entity in the global era. How the organization calls up its new complex architecture to exercise supranational authority and power to enact political impact and change on national, regional, and global politics is the subject of Part 2 and subsequent chapters that will expand upon this thematic and apply it to political processes and practices.

PART 2

African Issues and Contexts: Culture, Democracy, Security, and Development

Pan-Africanist Globalization and Cultural Politics: Promoting the African World View

Marcus Garvey, Dr. Martin Luther King, Malcolm X and a host of other Black legends all acknowledged that in order for Blacks worldwide to change the paradigm of disrespect and exploitation we face daily, Africans in the Diaspora and the continent had to find effective ways to re-connect and work toward the unification of the continent into a giant country. That Union of African States would have the leverage in international relations to change for the better how Africans see themselves and how Africans are seen.

The African Union, the current all-African body that is establishing itself to speak for, negotiate for and work for such African unification, has invited the Diaspora to join that process as voting members with 53 continental African countries in order to move as quickly as possible toward that future. We, in the Diaspora, must organize ourselves in an unprecedented way in order to accept that invitation. (*Report on the New York Town Hall Meeting* 2007)

The extract is cited from a 2007 New York City town hall gathering organized by African Americans in the New York area to respond to the historic Sixth Region Diaspora Clause policy enactment of the African Union (AU). In 1976, the Organization of African Unity (OAU) had divided Africa into five regions: West Africa, Central Africa, East Africa, Southern Africa, and North Africa. In 2002, more than twenty years later, the fifty-three countries that signed the founding AU Constitutive Act proclaimed that they were "inspired by the noble ideals, which guided the founding fathers of our Continental Organization and generations of Pan-Africanists in their determination to promote unity, solidarity, cohesion and cooperation among the peoples of Africa and African States" (Zahorka 2002).

Again, four years on, in 2006, the Constitutive Act expanded its vision to achieve a united African suprastate to a sixth region, which would be located outside of the bounds of continental Africa—in the African diaspora. If, as Valentine Mudimbe once proclaimed (1994), Africa was invented by Western European enlightenment explorers, in the twenty-first century Africa's AU is reinventing the idea of Africa while reconstructing the African identity and positing the notion of being African as a shared continental and unified global political entity.

As reflected in the spirit of the New York City town hall organizers' communiqué, the establishment of the AU Diaspora Clause invokes an important academic discussion about the way that the AU is engaged in a particular genre of social constructivism and cultural globalization. In this chapter, we demonstrate ways that the AU participates in fostering the universality of the idea of Africa and the notion of an African nation while tracing by way of illustration and documentation Mammo Muchie's claim that the African nation is not based on territoriality but on an African consciousness premised in a prolonged history and culture of resistance against dehumanizing beliefs, prejudices, and practices (Muchie 2003).

The establishment of the historic Sixth Region in 2006, popularly referred to as the Diaspora Clause, typifies the AU's boldest attempt to illustrate the complex scaffolding involved in Africans' contribution to and the advancement of globalization in this regard. In the introduction, we theoretically introduced the argument that an important implication of the AU's Diaspora Clause has been the AU's resuscitation and appropriation of a brand of Pan-Africanism, using it to develop a common understanding and connection among African nations and African-descendant peoples cross-continentally and globally. In that chapter, we underscored the way that the AU uses culture and history to expand its reach to plural and diverse African peoples of the five distinct regions of the continent as well. This is how the AU promotes to the world the way that Africans make sense of their lived experiences drawn from narratives based in their own histories, cultures, and philosophies, hence the African world view. How else would the organization drive its agenda? Bringing elite heads of states, bureaucrats, and professional employees from member states together in an AU congregation is certainly not enough.

The current chapter invokes a range of heuristic questions that underscore the importance of a cultural analysis of globalization in relation to our study of the AU. How are Africans contributing to the advancement of norms, values, institutions, and mechanisms for action in the contemporary global order? What role has the AU played in constructing meaning, values, interests, and identities of diverse and plural actors in the advancement of its globalist political objectives? What assemblage of cultural traits, practices, and goods has been used to construct meaning symbolically in order to nurture the identity of shared goals among disparate cultures and societies in Africa and its diaspora? Why and how does an AU emerge as a privileged idea and identity in relation to the nationally bounded identity—an Ethiopian, Senegalese, Ghanaian, or Nigerian, or African-American, or Jamaican—in the twenty-first century? And in what ways is the AU's cultural globalization bringing Africans on the continent and their descendants closer to political union and citizenship?

Responding to these questions reveals a way to examine how the AU utilizes a new hybrid brand of Pan-Africanism to advance a diverse and complex genre of globalization that we argue is primarily sociocultural. We see how the AU achieves this feat by redeploying Pan-Africanism and using it as a vehicle for cultivating cultural flows. Pan-Africanism functions as the AU's marker and symbol that is used to foster greater political recognition and integration among historically, geographically, ethnically, nationally, and linguistically plural and diverse African peoples in both the continent and what is defined now as the African diaspora.

Additionally, in illustrating and demonstrating the AU's impact in reconstructing Africa, in this chapter we show how individual Africans, through their participation as nonstate actors and quangos, have played, and continue to play, a vital and vibrant role in complementing the AU intergovernmental machinery. A plethora of organizations in energy, telecommunication, transport, sports, culture, and other fields helps construct the AU's efforts to achieve integration. In practicing cultural politics and cultural globalization, civil society associations, community-based organizations, social movements, and nongovernmental organizations (NGOs) bring a critical mass of participatory activities to the AU's effort to achieve continental and diasporic integration and in constructing a continental identity. These in turn provide the framework for growing corporate business activities on a continental and global scale.

Drawing on this theoretical framework, in this chapter we demonstrate how forging relationships, fostering mutual communication and exchange of ideas and sharing of practices, and representing and interpreting the nuances and complexities of diverse communities of identity and interest constitute a foremost objective for the Union to achieve its Pan-Africanist goals. Chapter 3 illustrates the ways in which the AU uses Pan-Africanist ideas, ideology, and identities as bases for its political mobilization; this is a process that is consistent with the AU's self-proclaimed objective to position Africa's local and national community impact as well as global engagement in promoting its own values in a world rich in disparities (Daniels 2009).

In underscoring the aforementioned revelations about the role that culture plays in the AU's regional and global engagement, subsequent subsections will examine Pan-Africanism's various historical, ideological, institutional, and geographical iterations as these variables relate to the AU's contemporary functions and goals. We then take a closer look at the six geographical zones of global Pan-Africa. Looking at case studies of the AU's interactions with nonstate actors, quangos, and civil society groups in communities, regions, and countries all over the span of the African world, we conclude by demonstrating the AU's impact on globalization in this regard as its own fashioning of a continent-led, pluralist, global-era Pan-Africanism.

PAN-AFRICANIST GLOBALIZATION: A HISTORY OF AN IDEA, 1893–2013

When in her election victory speech, Dr. Nkosazana Dlamini-Zuma invoked Pan-Africanists in the line of Marcus Garvey and Kwame Nkrumah, she strategically profiled what would be an ideological strain of her regime that would revitalize the Pan-African idea to regenerate and unify Africa and promote a feeling of oneness among the people of the African world (Esedebe 1982). She would not be the first African politician to use Pan-Africanism as a rallying slogan, a springboard, and an ideological vehicle for cultivating the common efforts of African and African-descendant peoples to advance their political efforts globally. Pan-Africanist ideas have shaped the AU's *longue-durée* as well as its broad vision for global African unity.

African-descendant diasporas of W. E. B. Du Bois's genre first forged the idea in response to enslavement, racism, colonialism, and imperialism; these events further facilitated the transcontinental movement against racism and in support for Black liberation and African nationalism, ideas that continue to inform core elements of the unity vision. In a speech to the Second All-African People's Congress in 1960 pioneer Pan-Africanist Kwame Nkrumah predicted this future for African unity when he proclaimed that the third stage of institutionalizing Pan-Africanism would achieve continental consolidation, community, and economic-social reconstruction and transnational unity (Poe 2003). In the late 1990s, recently ousted Libyan leader Muammar Gaddafi resuscitated Nkrumah's ambition to realize this goal in a United African States (UAS), an idea that slowly gained ground among the then fifty-three African nation-states in the form of the AU.

Pan-Africanism has had a long, deep, and broad ideational history in which differences have manifest according to the varied geographical, ideological, and institutional contexts from which the idea has been thrown up. It was concerned with two elements: oneness of all African people and their descendants, and a commitment to improve their lot (Poe 2003, 51). The range of Pan-African ideas has been drawn from these various sources and contexts. Most agree, however, that Pan-Africanist thought begins with diaspora communities in the late 1800s, who as African descendants who had become citizens in the New World lived within a racial climate in which they were constantly denigrated because of their African identity. These diasporas responded to the legacy of slavery, racism, and the dissemination of negative stereotypes about black people with Pan-Africanism. For the diasporas, Pan-Africanism was to be considered in the following terms:

> Africa was the homeland of Africans and persons of African origin, solidarity among people of African descent, belief in a distinct African personality, rehabilitation of Africa's past, pride in African culture, Africa for Africans in church and state, and the hope for a united and glorious future Africa (Esedebe 1982, 20).

And, according to Daryl Zizwe Poe:

> Racial identity and the concept of the global "African World" became an important driving force for this genre of Pan-Africanism. The practice of Pan-Africanism has always involved African descendants and Africans in an array of local struggles that are part of a larger worldwide activity involving Africans and African descendants everywhere whose various segments have obligations and responsibilities to reach each other. (2003, 47)

The first political cultivation of the Pan-Africanist idea began in the late 1800s, after the 1893 Chicago Congress on Africa, with the Pan-African Congress of 1900 held in London under the auspices of the activities of pioneer diaspora Pan-Africanists like Henry Sylvester Williams. The idea had been founded by freed Africans like Williams in the diaspora who began the intellectual and civil societal agitations against slavery, colonialism, and racism toward African peoples. A Trinidadian lawyer resident in London, Williams himself began his sociopolitical movement against British colonialism in Trinidad, which he described as a "synonym of racial contempt" (Muchie 2003). Williams was also dissatisfied with the conditions of Africans in South Africa, which resulted in the formation of the world's first Pan-African Association (PAA) in 1897. PAA's goal was to foster friendly relations between the Caucasian and African races (Muchie 2003, 28). Williams went on to become the first African descendant to speak in the House of Commons, and during his one-year residence in Cape Town, South Africa, became the only Black lawyer in the city. He would later organize the Pan-African Congress as an occasion upon which black men—and women—worldwide would speak for themselves and influence public opinion in their favor (Sherwood 2010).

Several other important diaspora personalities founded the inspiration for this movement, which included both men and woman. Anna Julia Cooper, for example, was one of only a few African-American female representatives to participate in and address the first Pan-African Congress that Williams established (May 2007). Like Williams, Cooper's brand of Black radicalism was international and progressive in incorporating the struggles of both diaspora African-Americans in the United States, and also Haitians and Africans in the continent. Another notable diaspora Pan-Africanist icon in this struggle was W. E. B. Du Bois. Du Bois viewed the Pan-African movement as aiming at an intellectual understanding and cooperation among all groups of African descent in order to bring about the industrial and spiritual emancipation of the Negro people (Esedebe 1982). Du Bois was the first African-American man to earn a PhD, and having founded the Paris Pan-African Congress, he presided over four of the five preindependence congresses from 1919 to 1945.

Du Bois's early brand of Pan-Africanism uniquely underscored the global historical importance of Africa (Karenga 1982). A second Pan-African Congress that Du Bois helped to organize set the preliminary stages for the African self-determination and unity principles that would inform the AU's Constitutive Act a century later. In the immediate aftermath of World War I, the Congress demanded from the League of Nations "that the natives of Africa and the peoples of African descent be governed according to land, capital, labor, education and state (*democracy*)" (authors' emphasis) (Du Bois 1979).

The Pan-African Congresses (manifest in a series of conferences in 1919, 1921, 1923, 1927, and 1945) represented the Pan-African movement of the time (see table 3.1). It was already a transatlantic political and cultural mobilization network of African-descendant diasporas and the early African nationalists. The early movement would lay the foundations of the African independence movement after World War II and transition the style and substance of Pan-Africanism from what St. Clair Drake referred to as racialistic Pan-Africanism to statecentric or institutional Pan-Africanism. The 1945 Manchester Pan-African Congress, whose attendees included Du Bois, George Padmore, Kwame Nkrumah, Jomo Kenyatta, and Kamuzu Banda, would provide a platform for this transition. At this conference, the previous meetings' accommodationist policy with colonial rule would be replaced with the demand for colonial freedom and independence (Muchie 2003).

TABLE 3.1. TIMELINE OF PAN-AFRICAN CONGRESSES 1893–2014

1893:	Congress on Africa, Chicago
1900:	Pan-African Congress, London
1919:	First Pan-African Congress, Paris
1921:	Second Pan-African Congress, London, Paris, and Brussels
1920s:	"African for the Africans": zenith years of UNIA branches in Africa
1923:	Third Pan-African Congress, London and Lisbon
1927:	Fourth Pan-African Congress, New York
1945:	Fifth Pan-African Congress, Manchester
1958:	First All-Africa People's Conference, Accra
1960:	Second All-Africa People's Conference, Tunis
1961:	Third All-Africa People's Conference, Cairo
1974:	Sixth Pan-African Congress, Dar es Salaam
1994:	Seventh Pan-African Congress, Kampala
2004:	AU inaugurates Economic, Social and Cultural Council
2014:	Eighth Pan-African Congress, Johannesburg

Three significant brands of African nationalism could be observed at the 1945 Manchester congress: an indigenous strand represented by Jomo Kenyatta;

the Black diaspora strand of Garvey and Du Bois's "Africa for Africans"; and the socialist strands of Leopold Senghor, Félix Houphouet-Boigny, and Nkrumah (Mazrui and Tidy 1984). The Manchester congress triggered the age of Kwame Nkrumah's thought from 1945 to 1965. His speech at the conference would trigger a new direction in the Pan-African movement toward African independence. Nkrumah would assert that the goal of the Congress should be the "liquidation of colonialism and imperialism from Africa." The shift was reflected in Nkrumah's speech as he stated, "Those of us from Africa, more numerous at this assembly than on the earlier ones, had decided that reformism offered at best a delaying strategy. At worst, it could be met just as sharply as outright demand for complete and absolute independence" (Padmore, 1947).

The Manchester conference was considered the zenith of the Pan-Africanist movement as it shifted to mass action in Africa rather than in Europe (S. Asante 1997). The struggle would be achieved in the African homelands. With Kwame Nkrumah's friendship and partnership with Trinidadian Pan-Africanist George Padmore, transatlantic diaspora Pan-Africanism would be integrated with the foremost elements of African nationalism as the shift to continental Pan-Africanism championed by Nkrumah resulted in Ghana's independence in 1957. Under Nkrumah's leadership, Ghana would become the base for the development and organization of Pan-African thought and activities. The country would convene the first Conference of Independent African States (CIAS) in April 1958 and the First All Africa People's Conference in Accra in December 1958. CIAS would establish a diplomatic framework for the political union of Africa, while the December conference would provide a haven for African liberation movements in their struggle to end colonialism.

Kwame Nkrumah's genre of Pan-Africanism has been referred to as the second phase of Pan-Africanism (Murithi 2005). Revered as the father of continental Pan-Africanism, Nkrumah would nonetheless incorporate diaspora racialist and transatlantic Pan-Africanism into his political thought. Nkrumah noted that "all peoples of African descent" were African and belonged to the "African nation" (Poe 2003, 5). The ideology of Nkrumahism was used as the vehicle to synthesize a range of Pan-African ideals, including revolutionary, racialistic, integrationist, and continental. Nkrumahism's Pan-Africanism would begin the journey of institutionalizing Pan-Africanism as Nkrumah aggressively began its promotion among independent African nations during the era of decolonization.

Pan-African nationalism would foster the second stage of Pan-Africanism in the 1963 establishment of the OAU in Addis Ababa, Ethiopia. The second stage of Pan-Africanism represented many shifts in the ideational assumptions and premises of the Pan-Africanist movement. This genre of Pan-Africanism would be dominated by the continental and statecentric as well as gradualist strains. The earlier racialist brand of Pan-Africanism advanced by Williams and Du Bois would be displaced in international significance by the new continental and institutional manifestations of Pan-Africanism, though racialist, transatlantic Pan-Africanism continued as a nonstate, culturalist movement in the diaspora, especially in the United States (Walters 1993).

The newer cultural premises of continental Pan-Africanism spearheaded by Nkrumah are best understood by the diverse ideas imbibed by two factions of African nationalism whose compromise pact would ultimately found the OAU. These groups were Nkrumah's Casablanca group, and the Brazzaville group that expanded to become the Monrovia group. The 1960 Congo crisis, in today's Democratic Republic of the Congo (DRC), sparked the intellectual formations of these groups. Whether the meeting in Morocco attended by Ghana, Guinea, Mali, and Egypt was spearheaded by Nkrumah to salvage what would then be his almost two-decade ideological aspirations for a UAS against the earlier formation of the moderate Brazzaville group or whether the meeting was simply a call for the few independent African progressive states to debate the Congo as a case by which African union had to be achieved is not important.

The fact is that the Casablanca meeting underscored the ideological parameters of Nkrumah's brand of Pan-Africanism—integrationist, revolutionary, and socialist. Dominated by Nkrumah and the Egyptian nationalist leader Gamal Abdel Nasser, the Casablanca meeting developed the Casablanca Charter that would enshrine Nkrumah's United States of Africa vision within a socialist agenda. The Casablanca Charter called for the establishment of a number of committees that would underscore some of the institutional elements of today's AU. These included the African Political Committee, the African Economic Committee, the African Cultural Committee, the African Consultative Committee, and the Joint African High Command (Poe 2003).

The less progressive Francophone African countries, including Congo-Brazzaville and Côte-d'Ivoire, held a meeting with Ethiopia, Nigeria, Sierra Leone, and Liberia around a more moderate African response to the Congo crisis and a rejection of socialism; they would forge the Brazzaville group. An extended version of Brazzaville, including the attendance of twenty African nations at a meeting in Liberia, and subsequently in Lagos, Nigeria, would constitute the Monrovia group. This brand of Pan-Africanism would stand for a more gradualist posture toward African unity that would not alienate the West from the future economic development of the continent. Ethiopia's Haile Selassie characterized the ideological Pan-Africanist visions at the second Monrovia group conference in Lagos.

> We are told that Africa has been split into competing groups and that this is inhibiting cooperation among the African states and severely retarding African progress. One hears of the Casablanca group and the Monrovia group, of the Conakry and Dakar Declarations, and we are warned that the views and policies of these so-called groups are so antithetical as to make it impossible for them to work together as partners in an enterprise to which all are mutually devoted. But do such hard-and-fast groupings really exist? And if certain nations sharing similar views have taken measures to coordinate their policies, does this mean that, as between these nations and others, there is no possibility of free and mutual cooperation? . . .
>
> Ethiopia considers herself a member of one group only—the African group. When we Africans have been misled into pigeonholing one another, into attributing rigid and inflexible views to States which were present at one conference but not at another, then we shall, without reason or justification, have limited our freedom of action and rendered immeasurably more difficult the task of joining our efforts, in harmony and brotherhood, in the common cause of Africa. . . . No wide and unbridgeable gulf exists between the various groupings which have been created. . . . We urge that this conference use this as its starting point, that we emphasize and lay stress on the areas of similarity and agreement rather than upon whatever disagreements and differences may exist among us. (Ajala 1973, 10)

In 1963, at an African Heads of State and Governments meeting in Addis Ababa, Selassie's speech would foster the reconciliation of the two visions for African unity. Thirty of the thirty-two independent African nations were represented and presented four distinct charters for African unity, including Nkrumah's call for instantaneous unity and integration. Sékou Touré called for a reconciled Casablanca and Monrovia charter under a United Africa and Senegal's gradual economic integration. Touré insisted that the Addis Ababa conference not close until a charter had been adopted. Selassie's wish came true; hence a compromise charter established the OAU.

Pro-Nkrumahist scholars and followers viewed the OAU Charter compromise as a mere continental association whereby African unity would be promoted, the sovereign equality of all member states would be upheld, and the principle of noninterference would be maintained. This charter was a far cry from the vision for Pan-Africanism that had begun with Williams, DuBois, and Nkrumah. Nonetheless, with its objectives to promote the unity and solidarity of African states, to defend their sovereignty, territorial integrity, and independence, and to eradicate all forms of colonialism and finally to promote human rights, the OAU would represent yet another transition and iteration of the Pan-Africanist movement. Adejumobi and Olukoshi (2008) would refer to the OAU as a statist intergovernmental organization with an overarching mandate for liberation of the continent.

Despite its reputation as a dictators club, the OAU accomplished its foremost goals. The OAU's thirty-nine-year legacy cultivated among member countries shared norms and principles regarding African unity. Yet, by 2002, with the post-apartheid transition of South Africa, twenty-two newly independent states had joined the Union, thereby completing for the OAU the elimination of colonialism on the continent and at least the realization of member state unity (Adejumobi and Olukoshi 2008). In the new millennium, despite South African decolonization and the end of proxy cold wars fought on African soil, new challenges exposed Africa's economic underdevelopment as parts of the continent were afflicted with HIV-AIDS and new brutal conflicts in Sierra Leone, Liberia, Rwanda, the DRC, Burundi, Somalia, and the Sudan, to name a few. The OAU needed a new ideational boost, an energizer that would accelerate Pan-African integration to make faster progress in advancing Africa's self-determined development vision. The 2002 formation of the AU out of the OAU represented the third institution-alization of Pan-Africanism.

Two continental leaders—the former president of South Africa Thabo Mbeki, and the late leader of Libya Muammar Gaddafi—personified the Pan-Africanism that drove the emergence of the AU; each reappropriated the idea of Pan-Africanism in different ways. Mbeki would invoke the idea of an African renaissance, an idea that complements rather than substitutes Pan-Africanism. On the other hand, promoting a form of neo-Pan-Africanism (Muchie 2003), Gaddafi promoted Arab-African relations around a geographical consideration of African unity that would present an African bloc to compete with other world blocs. The Pan-Africanism that gave birth to the AU would contend with, complement, as well as reconcile these two ideological strains within a new context of Africa and globalization. While taking on a controversial role, at the 1999 OAU Summit in Sirte, Libya, Gaddafi reintroduced a Nkrumah model of African integration and resuscitated notions of the racial unity of Africa.

South Africa's renaissance philosophy combined with Gaddafi's resuscitation of Nkrumah's Casablanca Charter once again mobilized Africans to forge greater unity and integration to combat these challenges. In doing so, Gaddafi reignited another strain of Pan-Africanism—trans-Saharan Pan-Africanism. At the 1999 OAU Summit in Sirte, Libya, Gaddafi offered the resuscitation of Nkrumah's vision as an alternative to the continent's possible disintegration as a result of its challenges. Gaddafi would proclaim: "We do not deny that we are Arabs. But politically and geographically we are Africans for thousands of years until the last migration. . . . our forefathers emigrated over land; that is why they are called 'Bir' [Berber]"(Muchie 2003).

In 2001, presenting the more moderate version of African unity as a replica of Nigeria's 1960s opposition to Nkrumah's Casablanca integration model, Nigeria's Olusegun Obasanjo ratified the formation of an AU that would embody a version of African solutions for African problems. In 2002, in Durban, South Africa, the AU was officially launched and South Africa's President Thabo Mbeki became its first chair.

The elimination of apartheid in South Africa instigated the renaissance philosophy of Pan-Africanism as yet another cultural shift and iteration that would advance cultural globalization in Africa. Mbeki's invocation of an African renaissance fits comfortably with the sustained renascent pulses that had dominated the Pan-Africanist movement. Pan-African renaissance would string together the philosophical strains of a country that had only recently been freed from centuries of racial oppression and colonialism and a Pan-Africanist vision for a united and developed Africa (Muchie 2003, 47).

The AU's 2006 enactment of the Diaspora Clause (sixth region) represented yet another expansion of Pan-Africanism. The clause has reignited transatlantic Pan-Africanism while perhaps serving to reunite it with continental Pan-Africanism. What's more, the AU's institutional and statecentric brand of Pan-Africanism is recultivating global relations with nonstate and cultural Pan-Africanist forces including an array of African heritage peoples and governments, African civil societal groups, African-American civil rights social movements, Pan-African identity activists, and movements in the Caribbean and Central and South America. In doing so, the AU's Pan-Africanism seeks to reconstruct shared symbolic meanings among Africans and African descendants in ways that broach a renewed common understanding among and between peoples and nations of the Black world.

THE UNITED STATES OF PAN-AFRICA: A VISION

If indeed the next stage of Pan-Africanism is the construction of the African nation and the African citizen (Muchie 2003) in a country envisioned as Pan-Africa (Du Bois 1979), to what extent are Africans through the contemporary manifestation of Pan-Africanism constructing it? Rather than the fifty-four independent territorial countries that make up the continent today (including the two with partial recognition), the ideal of an African nation would be defined by the consciousness that has been cultivated by Pan-African predecessors and that is based on the continent's and people's history and culture of resistance against dehumanizing beliefs, prejudices, and practices. It would represent the logo of that consciousness and the living resistance that has defined Pan-Africanism since 1900 (Muchie 2003).

Nonetheless, we also see from the history of Pan-Africanism that the idea is also deeply contested from ideational, ideological, identity, and organizational platforms. Pan-Africanism contains complex and diverse characteristics as an institution that seeks to cross, as well as transcend, a multiplicity of identity borders locally, nationally, regionally, and globally. Pan-Africa's pluralism has been a bedrock as well as a challenge for African unity. In December 1958, at the All-Africa Peoples' Conference convened in Accra, Ghana, Shirley Du Bois (W. E. B. Du Bois's wife) delivered an address on behalf of the then ninety-one-year-old Pan-Africanist veteran entitled "The Future of Africa." Du Bois stated, "If Africa unites, it will be because each part, each nation, each tribe gives up a part of the heritage for the good of the whole. That is what union means; that is what Pan-Africa means" (Esedebe 1982).

By the 1963 establishment of the OAU, its thirty-one founding states had already demonstrated the perils of diversity—factionalism, stalemate, compromise—that had the potential to foster disunity and breakdown. Nkrumah recognized this challenge when he pleaded with his colleagues in the 1960s in a speech that was reminiscent of Du Bois's 1958 call for Pan-Africa:

> Our freedom stands open to danger just as long as the independent states of Africa remain apart. . . . It is for us to . . . surmount the separatist tendencies in sovereign nationhood by coming together speedily into a Union of African states . . . territorial boundaries are the relics of colonialism that divide us. (Nkrumah 1965 xvii in Muchie 2003, 42–43)

the gradualists of the Monrovia group—and not Nkrumah's Casablanca on the day, in laying the foundation of African unity in the postcolonial era, Nkrumah's ideals and Pan-Africanist visions continued to underlie Africa's postcolonial unity endeavor. The foremost challenge for the early OAU was to ground African nationalism and racial Pan-Africanism in the new context of a postcolonial independent Africa consisting of sovereign territorial nation-states shrouded further in ethnic, linguistic, ideological, and national differences. How would the experience of Africa be universalized in such a context? How would unity be established in such diversity?

The gradualist approach of the Monrovia group would adopt a statecentric approach based on absolute equality of sovereign, national African states, the right that each state would not be involuntarily annexed to another state, but rather, there would be voluntary union of one state with another. Nonetheless, the OAU also adopted a liberal cooperation framework whereby the organization would support solidarity among states. Regular and consistent cooperation among member states would cultivate shared norms and multilateral decision making and action among Africans in ways that would foster an organic consciousness among Africans and their descendants. These events fostered the emergence of the contemporary AU.

The Union's diversity challenges have been exhibited in different iterations of African leadership as well. By the time that the AU was established in 2002, four generations of activist African leaders had emerged: the Pan-Africanist generation, the nationalist generation, the globalist generation, and the renascent or new Pan-Africanist generation (Akokpari, Ndinga-Muvumba, and Murithi 2008). Pan-Africanist leaders dominated the first stage of Pan-Africanism up to 1945 (from Williams to Du Bois), while the nationalist leaders who focused on nation building and national identity in their respective nation-states dominated the second-stage, statecentric Pan-Africanism of the OAU era. A third group of leaders is the globalist generation, usually consisting of opposition leaders who favor global identity claims of democracy, pluralism, human rights, and a liberalized market economy. However, the new Pan-Africanists, who are also of the global era, privilege Africans' self-determined efforts to transform the continent's own social, economic, and political conditions (Akokpari, Ndinga-Muvumba, and Murithi 2008).

The OAU began to embark upon the recognition of the vast diversity of the continent by zoning. Thirteen years after its founding at the Twenty-Sixth Ordinary Session held in Addis Ababa (1976), the organization divided the continent into five regional zones. The resolution established the five zones on the premise that there would be an equitable geographical distribution of representa-tion, on a regional basis, of all OAU member states in the United Nations (UN), at the UN specialized agencies, with other international organizations, and within OAU institutions. Zoning would become a first step in constituting a diverse yet democratically inclusive, federated multiregional continental union. The five regions were northern, western, central, eastern, and southern.[1]

The deep and broad scope of diversity of Africa is reflected in the five regions. Linguistic diversity, for example, which is a reflection of Africa's precolonial ethnic and subnational cultural diversity, is merely one level illustrating the continent's pluralism. While the current AU has adopted four languages for its official opera-tions—English, French, Arabic, and Portuguese—as many as two thousand languages are spoken on the continent. As well, the continent's national identi-ties are primarily manifest through a former colonial culture, including English, French, Portuguese, and Spanish, with Northern Africa's Arabic, Ethiopia's Amharic, and Tanzania's Kiswahili being the only official indigenous, national, lingua franca cultures represented. The continent is religiously diverse with most countries containing within them sizable majority and minority affiliations to African religions, Islam, and Christianity.

Africa's five regions are microcosms of the diversity that is representative of the whole continent. Like the whole continent, it is difficult to find regional cultural universality; shared identity is based on historical experiences by peoples and communities who have traversed and resided in common territorial and spatial neighborhoods. Regional Economic Communities (RECs) such as the Economic Community of West African States (ECOWAS), the Southern African Development Community (SADC), the East African Community (EAC), Arab Maghreb Union (AMU), the Economic Community of Central African States (ECCAS), and the Common Market for Eastern and Southern Africa (COMESA) have also fostered regional cultures and contexts for shared identities. Political cultures vary from region to region as well. As early as 1962, the Casablanca and Monrovia groupings grew out of a combination of both ideological and regional factors. While still exhibiting their early nationalist cultural legacies, Africa's 1976 regions differ according to several variables, including decolonization experience and independence wave (1, 2, 3), charismatic leadership, and national country prominence in pan-regional and global contexts (see table 3.2).

Like the continent, the diversity of the global diaspora implies that this process will be a challenge for the AU. While Africans, African-Americans, and Afro-Caribbeans are united by their common ancestry and their history of oppres-sion and suffering under their European conquerors, these peoples also share

TABLE 3.2. PAN-AFRICAN AFRICA

	FORMER COLONIAL POWER/LINGUA FRANCA	INDEPENDENCE	PAN-AFRICANIST POSITION	CHARISMATIC LEADERSHIP	GOVERNMENT TYPE	ETHNIC STRUCTURE
REGION AND COUNTRY PROFILES	French	1st wave	Monrovia	Pan-Africanist New Pan-Africanist	Socialist	Highly plural (more than 10)
	British	2nd wave	Casablanca	Pan-Arabist Radical Marxist	Marxist-Leninist	Moderate (less than 10)
	Dutch	3rd wave	Brazzaville	Cultural Nationalist Liberal Nationalist	Capitalist	Relatively homogeneous (less than 3)
	German		Neutral			
	Arabic		Casablanca	Radical Marxist	Socialist Marxist	Relatively homogeneous

NORTH AFRICA

Egypt	Arabic/British	1st wave	Casablanca	Nasser Pan-Arabist	Capitalist	Relatively homogeneous
Libya	Arabic/Italian	2nd wave	Casablanca/Monrovia	Gaddafi Pan-Arabist/Pan-Africanist	Socialist	Relatively homogeneous
Algeria	Arabic/French	2nd wave	Casablanca	Bella Pan-Arabist/Pan-Africanist	Socialist	Relatively homogeneous

WEST AFRICA

Ghana	British	2nd wave	Casablanca	Nkrumah Pan-Africanist	Capitalist	Moderate
Guinea	French	2nd wave	Casablanca	Touré Radical Marxist	Capitalist	Moderate
Senegal	French	2nd wave	Monrovia	Senghor Cultural Nationalist	Capitalist	Moderate
Nigeria	British	2nd wave	Monrovia	Balewa Liberal Nationalist	Capitalist	Highly plural

EAST AFRICA

Ethiopia	Italian	2nd wave	Monrovia	Selassie Cultural Nationalism (Ethiopianism)	Capitalist	Highly plural
Tanzania	Germany/British	2nd wave	Neutral/Monrovia	Nyerere Cultural Nationalist	Socialist	Relatively homogeneous

	FORMER COLONIAL POWER/LINGUA FRANCA	INDEPENDENCE	PAN-AFRICANIST POSITION	CHARISMATIC LEADERSHIP	GOVERNMENT TYPE	ETHNIC STRUCTURE
CENTRAL AFRICA						
Congo-Brazzaville	French	2nd wave	Brazzaville/ Monrovia	N/A	Capitalist	Moderate
DRC	Belgian	2nd wave	Casablanca	Lumumba Pan-Africanist	Capitalist	Highly plural
SOUTHERN AFRICA						
South Africa	Dutch/British	3rd wave	N/A	Mbeki New Pan-Africanist	Capitalist	Relatively homogeneous

conflict perceptions of each other that have emerged as a result of their separate historical experiences, as well as by the practice of colonialism and neocolonialism (Mwakikagile 2007). The notion of Pan-Africanism cannot be assumed and must be cultivated (Appiah 1993). In both regards, as a result, the AU's sixth region and its African diaspora consensus definition may be too broad, too bland, and do not recognize the diverse configurations of African-descendant peoples, nations, and communities in the diaspora. This problem may have caused the AU to miss the strategic and specific bounded units of global Africa where the Diaspora Clause hasn't always appreciated the range of ideological strains, and the geocultural versus state versus nonstate manifestations of Pan-Africanisms practiced around the globe (Kornegay 2008).

Mapping a Diverse Continent and Diaspora: Regions 1–6

West Africa is one of the most vibrant regions in Africa as well as the most formidable designer of and contributor to the Pan-Africanist forces that underlay today's AU. The region's tragic and historic location for the European transatlantic slave trade of Africans to the New World; Liberia and Sierra Leone, its location for the Back to Africa and Returnee movements from the United States, Brazil, and the Caribbean; Nkrumah's Ghana; most West African countries' first-wave independence (1957–61); Francophone African Negritude and the revolutionary socialism of Senegal and Guinea; and Nigeria's economic, political, and culturally hegemonic status as the Giant of Africa inform the contributing factors that make it a foremost region.

We have already seen how, as a quasi-independent colony purchased by the American Colonization Society, Liberia in West Africa became an early hub for the Pan-Africanist activities of W. E. B. Du Bois as well as Marcus Garvey's Back to Africa movement in the 1920s. In 1923, Du Bois was appointed by the US State Department to represent the US government in the inauguration of Charles King to a second term in office as president of Liberia (M'bayo 2007). Du Bois used the occasion to promote Liberia (albeit a pro-America Liberia) as an important intellectual reservoir for the Pan-Africanist ideas of the likes of Edward Blyden. In another West African country, Ghana, there is little doubt that the charismatic personality of a single individual, Kwame Nkrumah, has made the difference in fostering the country and the region's political culture. In 1957, Nkrumah remarked that the independence of Ghana would be meaningless unless it was linked with the total liberation of Africa. Nkrumah inspired the ideological posture of the Casablanca group and, by creating the Bureau of African Affairs, caused Accra, Ghana, to become the focal point of activity in support of African liberation struggles for those who would become Africa's greatest nationalist leaders: Joshua Nkomo, Agostinho Neto, Eduardo Mondlane, Milton Obote, Sékou Touré, and Modibo Keita (Muchie 2003).

Throughout the 1930s through to the 1970s, the charismatic personality and Pan-Africanist leadership of Leopold Senghor would place Senegal at the helm of the mobilization of cultural Pan-Africanism. Senghor's Negritudist ideas encountered and complemented the political Pan-Africanism fostered by Du Bois in the 1930s. While a socialist, like Nkrumah, Senghor's deep affiliation with Francophone Africa and his allegiance to a transnational cultural nationalism whose borders spanned Dakar, Paris, and Harlem would land Senegal among the Brazzaville and ultimately the Monrovia Pan-Africanist groupings. Guinea and Mali, which were Francophone West African nations affiliated with the Nkrumahist Pan-Africanist philosophies, under Sékou Touré and Modibo Keita would also symbolize the ideological and cultural vibrancy of this region. Guinea and Ghana in 1958 announced to the world that their two countries would constitute themselves as the nucleus of a union of West African states that had been inspired by the thirteen American colonies. The leader of the only Francophone African country to organize Guineans into a successful "non" vote in a referendum that would choose to remain part of the French colonial empire, Touré would claim that his decision had blazed a trail for African independence and solidarity that would realize a United States of Africa (Esedebe 1982).

West Africa's regional diversity would not be complete without the role that Nigeria has played in both ideological and cultural Pan-Africanist formation. In the formation of the OAU, the country's tripartite nationalist movement (Hausa, Yoruba, and Igbo) culminated in a moderate, functionalist Pan-Africanism. Affiliating to the Monrovia group whose Charter for African Unity would ultimately be ratified in Lagos, Nigeria, at the group's second meeting, Nigeria's prime minister at the time, Tafawa Balewa, emerged as a dominating personality. Balewa's moderation is said to have contributed to the gradualist-functionalist approach that underlies the AU Pan-Africanist principles today (Kloman 1962).

Nigeria's middle-of-the-road moderate Pan-Africanism remains a consistent philosophy that the country uses to facilitate the culture of West Africa. The country's hegemonic stature fostered its prominent role in founding ECOWAS, in hosting the OAU's Lagos Plan of Action, the African Economic Community (AEC), and New Partnership for Africa's Development (NEPAD), in promoting the "African Calabash Approach" to conflict resolution under its leader and former OAU chairman, Olusegun Obasanjo, and in once again recommending a gradualist-functionalist AU in 2001 over Libya's quest for an Nkrumahist AU vision.

While East Africa records less of an active role in first- and second-stage Pan-Africanism, Ethiopia hosted the headquarters of the continental Pan-Africanist unions under the OAU and its successor organization the AU. Consisting of the Horn of Africa countries and the former EAC, the region is diverse in both precolonial and colonial histories and cultures. Nonetheless, two countries in the region—Ethiopia and Tanzania—are distinctive in their representation as the only African countries whose national cultures are indigenously African and not reflective of a former colonial power. As a result, both countries represent, for the East African region, an important contribution to the idea of the universal African. Mazrui has noted that the Ethiopian's spirited and determined resistance to Italian invasions (the Battle of Adowa, 1896, and the Ethiopian War of 1935–36) inspired anticolonial Pan-Africanism all over the world (Mazrui 2001). Most agree that Emperor Haile Selassie's Pan-Africanism evolved from a conservative, feudal leader of Ethiopia who referenced the country's roots in the Solomonic Middle East instead of in the cultures of East Africa. Selassie would eventually become a stalwart Pan-Africanist who used his symbol of radical and revolutionary Pan-Africanism abroad to broker the establishment of the OAU in 1963. Selassie would implore his nationalist colleagues when he proclaimed: "This conference cannot close without adopting a single African charter. We cannot leave here without having created a single African organization. . . . If we fail in this, we will have shirked our responsibility to Africa and to the peoples we lead. If we succeed, then, and only then, we will have justified our presence here" (Poe 2003).

Ethiopianism thus developed as both a form of early Pan-Africanism associated sometimes with the emergence of independent African churches that would follow in the tradition of Ethiopia's two-thousand-year history of African, independent Christianity, and a global political Pan-Africanist movement worldwide symbolizing Black resistance to western imperialism. Ethiopia's historic capital city, Addis Ababa, became a befitting headquarters for institutional and state-centric Pan-Africanism in the OAU and the AU.

There are divergent symbols of Ghana's Nkrumah brand of Pan-Africanism compared to that practiced by Tanzania's Julius Nyerere. Mwalimu Nyerere was an ardent and militant African nationalist and an equally convincing and persuasive Pan-Africanist. However, differently, Nyerere saw a tension between nationalism and Pan-Africanism (Shivji 2011). While Nyerere understood the role that anticolonialism played in inventing and thus universalizing an African identity, the nationalist known as Mwalimu (teacher) was renowned for his successful nurturing of an African-styled sovereign, territorial nationalism in the name of Ujaama (the African family). C. L. R. James would state that Nyerere's greatest accomplishment was in laying the basis of an African state while the Arusha Declaration in which Nyerere laid down his principles is one of the great documents of the post–World War II era (James 1963, cited in Shivji 2011). In 1974, Julius Nyerere's African national identity would attract the venue for the sixth Pan-African Congress, almost thirty years after the fifth Pan-African Congress held in Manchester, UK. C. L. R. James, a Trinidadian Pan-Africanist scholar, had requested Tanzania as the venue because of the country's model of self-reliance.

Africans have legitimately been reluctant to adhere to the normative sub-Saharan Africa / North Africa-Middle East divide. This is particularly true because of both regions' shared experiences with nationalism and Pan-Africanism. Mazrui notes a significant strain of Pan-Africanism—trans-Saharan Pan-Africanism—that represents the solidarity of the peoples of Northern and sub-Saharan Africa (Mazrui and Tidy 1984). Egypt's own revolutionary nationalist, Gamal Abdel Nasser, is credited with having begun the process of re-Africanizing Egypt in ways that recultivated historic Arab-African solidarity on the continent. Nasser worked with many African leaders, including Nkrumah (despite their later competitive rift), to stand up against imperialism (Muchie 2003). Committing Egypt to support African liberation movements, Nasser would write: "We cannot in any way stand aside even if we wish to, from the sanguinary and dreadful struggle now raging in the heart of the continent between five million whites and two hundred million Africans. We cannot do so for one principal and clear reason—we ourselves are in Africa" (Mazrui and Tidy 1984, 52).

Morocco and Algeria, also Maghreb countries, played pioneering Pan-Africanist roles during the second phase. The Casablanca group gets its name from the North African country Morocco, whose King Hassan II called for and hosted the historic meeting in his country. Algeria's Ben Bella also played an influential role in fostering Pan-African unity. Given the country's historic role in forging the OAU-AU, Morocco's singular absence as a contemporary AU member is significant. Morocco left the OAU in 1984, when many of the other member states supported the Sahrawi nationalist Polisario Front's Sahrawi Arab Democratic Republic.

During the third phase of Pan-Africanism—the formation of the AU—it was North Africa's Libya that would launch a rekindling of trans-Saharan Pan-Africanism. We have seen already how ousted leader Muammar Gaddafi's 1999 Sirte Declaration called for Africa's resuscitation of Nkrumah's United States of Africa vision, which in principle launched the AU in 2002. Apparently, Gaddafi turned back to Africa in the 1990s during Libya's period of isolation from the West and alienation from other Arab rulers. Gaddafi maintained that Africa existed as a geographical entity that historically included Arabs. Yet North and sub-Saharan Africans alike have been cautious of the personalist ("King of Kings of Africa") motivations behind Gaddafi's Pan-Africanist intentions. Additionally, there had always been concern by some members as to whether Gaddafi's brand of Pan-Africanism was a reactionary anti-Western rant that could serve to foster hostile Africa-West relations (Akram Hawas in Muchie 2003, 293). Needless to say, no North African leader would foster greater integration between North Africa and the rest of the continent.

Hosting the Brazzaville Pan-Africanist group (in the Congo-Brazzaville) and the home country (Gabon) of the illustrious AU Commission Chairperson Jean Ping, Central Africa, a region of mostly Francophone, small African states, has received little attention as a region of Africa. Underrepresentation of the region was one reason why, in 2011, President Obiang Nguema Mbagoso of Equatorial Guinea was elected AU chair despite his controversial democratic leadership credentials. Africa's largest and richest (in mineral resources), though most troubled, nation, the DRC, is part of this region. The home of Patrice Lumumba, the DRC has historically existed in Africa's Pan-Africanist imagination. The Congo-Brazzaville Pan-Africanist grouping would be the first to convene to deliberate on critical issues regarding the sovereignty and security of Africa in light of the DRC-Congo crisis in 1960. The Brazzaville meeting debated whether or not to invite UN and African troops into the Congo, and its moderate conclusions to support international intervention through the formation of the Casablanca group would spur the security principle behind the AU—that Africa will police itself (Mazrui 1967).

Aside from Malawi (Nyasaland), Zambia (Northern Rhodesia), and Botswana (Bechuanaland), much of Southern Africa was still under colonialism during the early stages of the second phase of Pan-Africanism that would establish the OAU in 1963. Dr. Hastings Banda, Malawi's charismatic, nationalist leader, however, had attended the 1945 Fifth Pan-Africanist Congress in Manchester. Notwithstanding Portuguese colonialism in Angola and Mozambique and apartheid/settler colonization in South Africa, Southern Rhodesia (Zimbabwe), and South-West Africa (Namibia), Pan-Africanism would target Africa's southernmost region for its raison d'être. Targeting this region was tantamount to the goals of African unity and would require another three-decade struggle to remove the last bastions of colonialism from the continent.

There is no wonder that this region hosts some of Pan-Africa's most charismatic and celebrated liberation leaders—Mondlane, Samora Machel, Neto, Robert Mugabe (controversially)—and a host of South African nationalists ranging from Robert Sobukwe, Walter Sisulu, and Nelson Mandela to Thabo Mbeki. The 1994 historic dismantling of apartheid in South Africa marked a historic turn in the Pan-Africanist movement; representing the Southern African region and the continent, South Africa would take on the new Pan-Africanist leadership. In what some suggest was a rescuing of the Pan-Africanist vision away from Gaddafi's ultraradical vision, South Africa's Thabo Mbeki would rationalize change to the AU.

The OAU engaged in four decades of struggle, aiming to realize the goals of the continent's modern-day founding fathers. The OAU lived up to its mandate to eradicate all forms of colonialism from Africa. In his "I am African" speech, Mbeki would exhibit both the diversity and solidarity of struggle that embodied southern Africa's, and now continues to embody continental Africa's, struggle for the African personality. In May 1996, as deputy president, Mbeki proclaimed that it felt good to be an African in a postapartheid Africa.

> I am born of the peoples of the continent of Africa. The pain of the violent conflict that the peoples of Liberia, Somalia, the Sudan, Burundi and Algeria is a pain I also bear. The dismal shame of poverty, suffering and human

degradation of my continent is a blight that we share. The blight on our happiness that derives from this and from our drift to the periphery of the ordering of human affairs leaves us in a persistent shadow of despair. This is a savage road to which nobody should be condemned. This thing that we have done today, in this small corner of a great continent that has contributed so decisively to the evolution of humanity says that Africa reaffirms that she is continuing her rise from the ashes. Whatever the difficulties, Africa shall be at peace! However improbable it may sound to the skeptics, Africa will prosper! (Ndlovu-Gatsheni and Ndhlovu 2013, 71)

The last region to fully decolonize, led by Africa's most industrious economy and multiracial culture, South Africa and the SADC may indeed spearhead the Pan-Africanism required to cultivate the African universal identity that the AU's first president, Thabo Mbeki, refers to.

The sixth region—the contemporary African diaspora—is a highly plural space that consists of a number of historical and geospatial experiential African-descendant cultures. There is the historical diaspora community with its hegemonic concentration of African-Americans in the United States, as well as the less powerful, though hugely populous Afro-Brazilian community. There are also African-descendant nation-states such as Jamaica, Haiti, Trinidad, Guyana, Grenada, Barbados, and other Caribbean states with African-descendant major-ity or minority populations. The diaspora also consists of a new constituent of postcolonial African immigrants who reside in the United States and in other formerly colonizing, advanced industrial nations such as the United Kingdom, France, Belgium, Spain, and Germany.

The idea and practice of Pan-Africanism is as contested as it is cultivated in this global space. Multiple interpretations, iterations, and manifestations of Pan-Africanism have dispersed all over the global terrain. As the AU attempts to reconstruct its own philosophical strain and political brand of Pan-Africanism, it is not surprising that it encounters several roadblocks that challenge the full real-ization of global African unity. The challenges are myriad with those stemming from political and epistemological discourse differences between Afrocentrists and Eurocentrists, Black nationalists and African nationalists, and diaspora nationalists and continental nationalists (Poe 2003, 2).

The Atlanticist diaspora paradigm (Gilroy 1993) is critical of the Asante-style, African-centered genre of Pan-Africanism (S. Asante 1998), describing it as an unwarrantedly purist, retrograde, essentialist, racialist, and an unrealistic transnational identity choice for African heritage communities in the diaspora.

African-descendant peoples resident in the Americas and Europe would best claim Western civilization as integral to their global heritage. Atlanticist diasporas emphasize the mixed cultural attributes and formations that have shaped African descendant identities in the West, suggesting that it cannot be assumed that Africans on the continent necessarily adhere to a shared sense of a Pan-African identity.

However, in positing Afrocentric Pan-Africanism as an essentialist, monolithic identity, the Atlanticists simplify and misrepresent the concept of Pan-Africanism, relying on dualist binaries to formulate their theses themselves. The Atlanticist analysis omits the complex pluralisms that are embedded in Pan-Africanism's multiple strains evidenced by Pan-Africa's six global regions. Pan-Africanism, especially the AU's current institutionalization, emphasizes an ontological pluralism, mixing, and syncretism required for traversing, negotiating, absorbing, and complementing local-global cultural encounters and contexts. The AU's historical Pan-Africanist focus need not be seen as foundationalist but instead demonstrates that historical rendering is capable of producing knowledge about current conditions of African and African-descendant peoples in ways that have important contemporary political implications (Okpewho, Davies, and Mazrui 2001).

By mobilizing a composite, rather than essentialist, Pan-African identity, the AU is merely engaging in global cultural coalition politics: bringing together peoples with shared histories, heritages, and cultures and contemporary common political-economic goals that have been derived from such histories. This fact reveals another tension dividing diaspora, the Afrocentric, and the Africanist understandings of the Pan-Africanist terrain that focuses on differences between the nature of its study, institutional practices (Patterson and Kelley 2000), and orientation—continent-led versus diaspora-led. Political scientists tend to examine Pan-Africanism through the study of nationalisms while historians, sociologists, and cultural studies tend to focus on the study of diaspora through nonstate actors and sociocultural forces (Johnson 1998). The truth is that during the long history of Pan-Africanism, both practices—statecentric and nonstatist—have occurred. Caribbean and African-American diaspora social movements initiated transatlantic Pan-Africanism and dominated the process for its first five decades of the global movement.

THE AU'S GLOBAL-ERA PAN-AFRICANIST CULTURAL POLITICS: COLLABORATING WITH CONTINENTAL AND DIASPORA NONSTATE ACTORS

Phase 2 (OAU) and 3 (AU) Pan-Africanisms have been shaped by continental, nationalist, statecentric, and institutional forces advanced by African sovereign nations embarking upon collective nation-state action. Current AU Pan-Africanism attempts to utilize and engage in all forms of Pan-Africanist practice—phase 1's Diaspora civil society movements and phase 2 and 3's state-centered institutionalism. Despite the Union's challenges in achieving a more concrete political and transnational unity, the emerging suprastate's practices in specific continental and diaspora locales around the world are evidence of its contribution to the advancement of cultural globalization. These events that may be characterized as the AU's global-era Pan-Africanism are worth illuminating and examining. In local, national, regional, and global contexts, the AU is both exemplifying and fostering its cultural and sociopolitical agency.

In these diverse contexts throughout global Africa, the suprastate can be seen to be creating, adapting, and reinventing cultural identities in congregates of global political power (see table 3.3). This is how we see the AU's global-era Pan-Africanism whereby the international organization navigates its six regions scenario to enact its cultural global politics in the twenty-first century. All over continental Africa and in the diaspora, the AU utilizes a wide range of activities through which to achieve its goals in this regard, including the convening of annual meetings, sponsoring of academic conferences, holding continent-wide and transnational events, enacting numerous policies disseminated by communiqués and press releases, and devolving its committee and subcommittee activities down to nations, localities, and civil societal organizations.

Pan-Africanism began with nonstate actors whose contemporary existence has become a vast inventory of all continental and subregional NGOs and civil society organizations in Africa. While AU institutions appear to lean toward a corpus of statecentric presidents, cabinet ministers, and diplomats, indisputably the dimension of Pan-Africanism that exceeds even the mass following of Garveyism at its zenith are these sociocultural reservoirs such as sports, language, development, and the activism of civil society organizations and groups convened in a continental format of quangos that the AU affiliates with to deliver its Pan-African message.[2] These organizations include the African Airlines Association, founded in Accra in 1968 (AFRAA 2011), the

TABLE 3.3. GLOBAL PAN-AFRICA, 1906–2011

	Prominent Pan-Africanist Leaders	Pan-Africanist Activity	Relations/Contacts with the African Union
AFRICA			
Liberia	Edward Blyden	Sent delegates to Pan-African Congresses 1–5	Convene through AU General Meetings
Ghana	Kwame Nkrumah	Conference of Independent African States (1958); All-Africa People's Conference (1958)	Convene through AU General Meetings
Ethiopia	Haile Selassie	Battle of Adowa inspires Ethiopianism (1896); established headquarters of Organization of African Unity (1963); remains headquarters of the African Union	Convene through AU General Meetings
Libya	Muammar Gaddafi	Resuscitated Nkrumah's African Integration (1999)	Convene through AU General Meetings
Nigeria	Olusegun Obasanjo	Helped found ECOWAS and integral in developing African Economic Community, NEPAD, and African Calabash Approach; 2001 ratified formation of the African Union	Convene through AU General Meetings
Uganda		7th Pan-African Congress (1994)	Convene through AU General Meetings
Tanzania	Julius Nyerere	Arusha Declaration (1967); 6th Pan-African Congress (1974)	Convene through AU General Meetings
South Africa	Thabo Mbeki	1st president of the African Union	Convene through AU General Meetings
CARIBBEAN		**CARICOM**	
Haiti	Louis Bellegarde	Sent delegate to 2nd Pan-African Congress	
Jamaica	Marcus Garvey	Established United Negro Improvement Association and African Communities League	Government of Jamaica represented at Salvador AU-sponsored Diaspora Conference (2006); convene through CARICOM-AU Joint Meetings
Trinidad and Tobago	Henry Sylvester Williams	Established the Pan African Association; helped organize 1st Pan-African Congress (1900)	Hosted AU-Diaspora Conference (June 2004); convene through CARICOM-AU Joint Meetings
	George Padmore	Helped organize 5th Pan-African Congress (1945)	

	Prominent Pan-Africanist Leaders	Pan-Africanist Activity	Relations/Contacts with the African Union
LATIN AMERICA			
Guyana (LA)	Walter Rodney	Prominent Pan-Africanist and Liberation Fighter	Convene through CARICOM-AU Joint Meetings
Brazil			Hosted AU-Diaspora Conference in Salvador (2006)
THE WEST			
United States	W. E. B. Du Bois	Helped organize Pan-African Congresses 1–5	New York Town Hall Diaspora Meeting (2007); CIDO-RCC NYC/Manhattan October 2010- Building Bridges Conference-invited; African Unity of Harlem
	St. Claire Drake	Influential Pan-Africanist writer	
	Malcolm X	Established Organization of Afro-American Unity (1965)	
	Asante/ Karenga	Afrocentrism/Kwanzaa	
Great Britain		Site of Pan African Congresses 1–5	
France	Léopold Senghor (1920s)	Negritude movement	

African Union of Architects, founded in 1981 in Lagos, the Association of African Universities, founded in Accra in 1967 (AAU 2011), the African Association of Zoos and Aquaria, founded in 1989 in Pretoria (PAAZAB 2006), the All Africa Council of Churches, founded in 1963 in Nairobi (AACC 2012), the African Medical Association, founded in 2006 in Johannesburg (AfMA 2011), and the African Women Lawyers' Association, founded in 1998 in Accra. In addition, the most vibrant continental academic association is the Council for Development of Social Research in Africa, based in Dakar (CODESRIA 2011). The African Publishers' Network was convened in 1992 in Abidjan. Abidjan is also headquarters for the African Parliamentary Union, founded 1976. The Organization of African Trade Union Unity (OATUU), founded by merger in 1973 in Accra, appears to be run by a few underresourced individuals, as it still lacks a website in 2012. More active is the African Stock Exchange Association, founded in 1993 in Nairobi (ASEA 2011). Some of these NGOs are hybrid associations that comprise both civil servants, academics, and other individuals from civil society. The African Policing Civilian Oversight Forum (APCOF), founded in 2004, includes a member of Nigeria's Police Service Commission, Rwanda's ombudsman, and a member of South Africa's Independent Complaints Directorate, as well as university-based hers (APCOF 2013). This cross-section above demonstrates the comprehensive range of these civil society organizations that the AU uses to achieve its integration objectives. That is to say that all of these social organizations develop a continental perspective for their profession, business sector, class, or institutional base. They deepen multilateral ways of thinking and acting. The Internet era facilitates strengthening their organization and founding other NGOs and quangos.

In the area of sports, for example, Francophone African countries held the first Friendship Games in 1960 in Madagascar, which grew by 1965 into the All Africa Games held in Brazzaville, involving 2,500 athletes from thirty countries. They were organized by the Supreme Council for Sport in Africa, which from 1977 affiliated itself as a specialized agency of the OAU. By the 2011 continental games held in Maputo, competitors had doubled to five thousand players covering twenty sports from fifty-three participating nations (AAG 1998). An interesting variant are the ECOWAS Games started in 2011, as the first to popularize a mass identity based around a regional community. The televised African Cup of Nations (CAN—Coupe d'Afrique des Nations) soccer tournaments draw in tens of millions of players, fans, and spectators. Founded in 1957 by Egypt, Sudan, and Ethiopia, it is today staged every second year, in odd-number years, to alternate with Fédération Internationale de Football Association (FIFA) world cup years.

Resuscitating and promoting African languages is also an important cultural politics for the AU. The African Academy of Languages (ACALAN) was founded in Bamako and affiliated to the AU in 2006. Typical projects include the Vernacular Cross-Border Language Commission and encouraging use of African languages in cyberspace (ACALAN 2012). One major challenge for the AU is that almost all linguistic funding in Africa is from only former colonial powers to sponsor the languages of their vanished empires, such as French and, to a lesser extent, English. This means that Kiswahili, for example, as the most multinational and transstate of indigenous African languages, enjoys no such sponsors.

While the OAU formally added Kiswahili onto its list of official languages in 1984—a year ahead of Portuguese—it in practice lacked the budget to ever hire translators to use it for the remaining two decades of its existence. Even today, the AU website is limited to mirrors in Arabic, English, French, and Portuguese; sometimes media releases are limited to only English and French. It was only the Pan-African Parliament (PAP), in 2004, who for the first time actually translated documents into Kiswahili and used it on an official website. Even now, this remains limited to the PAP, and even there is limited to only a symbolic number of documents. Kiswahili's main progress so far is at the national and east African regional level, where a number of states use it to varying degrees as an official language or a lingua franca.

The international NGO Congrès Mondial Amazigh (CMA), the World Amazigh Congress, lobbies for the Tamazight language (Berber and Tuareg) in six countries. Tamazight speakers won concessions during the Arab Spring of 2011. Tamazight gained recognition as an official language in Morocco; the Algerian government recognized it as a national language that may be chosen as a subject in schools and used in broadcasting; the Nafusa communities in west Libya started broadcasts in it and also using it in schools.

Another dimension of culture and politics where change is measured over generational timescales is among gender relations in the AU and on the continent. The OAU's Assembly of Heads of State and Government remained an all-male entity throughout the twentieth century. The reengineering of the OAU into the AU started the change when Liberia's President Ellen Johnson Sirleaf became its first woman head of state. The protocol founding the PAP, article 4.2, specified that at least one of the five members of parliament representing each country must be a woman. This was a world first for the foundational treaties of any of the regional parliaments. The first PAP president elected was a woman, Gertrude Mongella.

Other first instances of a woman being elected the head of AU institutions occurred, symbolically enough, in the African Commission on Human and Peoples' Rights (ACHPR). Salimata Sawadogo was elected its president in 2003, with another woman, Reine Alapini-Gansou, becoming ACHPR president in 2009. That year also saw Nana Awa Daboye become the first woman judge to be elected president of the ECOWAS Community Court of Justice. Most recently, Dr. Nkosazana Dlamini-Zuma became the first woman to be elected chair of the AU Commission. Among other gender reforms, the AU condemned the practice of female genital mutilation in 2006, reiterating the 2005 Maputo protocol. Sixteen AU member countries have outlawed the custom, but in practice rural educational and political campaigns will be far more important and effective. Equal access to education and employment are clearly crucial to equal rights and opportunities for the majority of Africa's women.

The AU's cultural politics is transnational, diasporic, and thereby global. Like much of its Constitutive Act laws and policies, the Diaspora Clause itself has emerged as a result of a number of meetings and conferences held in various countries on the continent as well as in the diaspora. New York City, Brazil, and Trinidad and Tobago have been hosts to some of these conferences that have been convened in the same fashion as the twentieth-century Pan-Africanist congresses.

However, these twenty-first-century congresses are organized and attended by state and nonstate actors, including state representatives, community-based organizations, civil society organizations, and scholars from the continent and from the diaspora.

There are numerous evidences documented of these kinds of activities. For example, in its attempt to recognize the diaspora in the Caribbean, the AU participates in state-to-state multilateral relations. It invited the secretary-general of the Caribbean Community (CARICOM) as a special guest to its Fifth Ordinary Session of Assembly to address the Opening Session. The CARICOM secretary-general's designate affirmed the Caribbean's approval to involve the representatives of the Caribbean Diaspora in deliberations in the Economic, Social and Cultural Council, the civil society advisory group. Meetings between CARICOM representatives and AU members have also taken place in Mozambique and Nigeria aimed at deepening connections between the regions through exploring and developing approaches to common challenges and issues.

While CARICOM has been an important institution representing the diaspora in the Caribbean, the United States has seen similar relations emerging between the AU and the country's African diaspora especially through nonstate actors. Author and activist Herb Boyd emphasized the importance of unity between the diaspora and the AU in the African-American New York–based newspaper *New York Amsterdam News*. In December 2010 at the City College of New York, the College's Black Studies Department and the AU Diaspora Task Team held a town hall meeting. This meeting served as a forum for civil society groups to engage with the ambassador of the AU to the United States to develop a framework for better organization of the diaspora, enhancing relations between them and the AU. Key speakers at the meeting spoke of the importance of the AU's initiative, referencing the intellectual influences of Kwame Nkrumah, Marcus Garvey, and W. E. B. Du Bois.

These AU-Diaspora meetings constitute sites of analysis for examining the AU's cultural global politics in a more introspective manner; the meetings operate as encounters that provide us with representations of cultural tropes where discourses and dialogues among a diverse range of Africans and African-descendant peoples and sociopolitical movements are involved with the construction and reconstruction of ideas that become the essential impetus of political decision-making. For example, in 2005 the AU posted a first round of its minutes concerning the deliberations on the Diaspora Clause as follows:

DECISION ON THE DEFINITION OF THE AFRICAN DIASPORA
Doc. EX.CL/164 (VI)

The Executive Council:

1. TAKES NOTE of the Definition of the African Diaspora as proposed by the Commission;
2. REQUESTS the Commission to refer the issue to a meeting of Experts from Member States for a more suitable definition;
3. FURTHER REQUESTS the Chairperson of the Commission, in consultation with the Chairperson of the Union, to determine the appropriate date for launching ECOSOCC taking into account the request in paragraph 2 above. (African Union "Organs")

Decision 164 had evolved from earlier AU deliberations on this topic in Trinidad and Tobago by experts from the continent and from the diaspora in June 2004. A previous recommendation of the definition of diaspora had been rejected by the AU Executive Council's Permanent Representatives Committee (PRC): because it had not included the so-called modern diaspora, the committee felt that it was not inclusive. Another reason that it was not accepted was the clause's failure to include the notion of what later became known as the "African cause" in its narrative. Here, the PRC emphasized that the diaspora should include African-descendant people who were willing to be part of the continent.

The final derivation of the Diaspora Clause emerges from this series of deeply engaging discussions and exchange of views similar to the one that had occurred in Trinidad and Tobago on a range of interpretations of Pan-Africanism. The report records the following broad definitions by delegates present:

The African Diaspora includes:

- The peoples of African origin whose ancestors within historical memory came from Africa, but who are currently domiciled in other countries outside the continent and claim citizenship of those countries;
- The Africans who, for various reasons, have settled outside the continent, whether or not they have kept the citizenship of an African country;
- Within the context of a and b above, the Diaspora, in their relations with Africa, should also express their common will to contribute side by side with other citizens of Africa to the building of the African Union. (African Union 2005)

These early definitions were still metamorphosed by subsequent deliberations that synthesized the Addis Ababa definitions into the current consensus
definition that now represents the Diaspora Clause or article 3.c of the AU's
Constitutive Act: "To invite and encourage the full participation of the Diaspora as
an important part of our continent to build the African Union." The definitional
changes that emerged as a result of sustained and diverse participant deliberations reveal that Africans and African descendants understand the complex and
divergent historical trajectories that inform the diversity of the African diaspora.
What's more, while it is assumed that the AU's Diaspora Clause has an instrumental goal to capitalize on remittance investments from new African diasporas,
the diaspora deliberations tell us that the inclusion of the modern diaspora was
in fact an afterthought. The Diaspora Clause emerges as a result of the AU's sustained cultivation of long-standing social capital relations with historic diaspora
communities, with descendant communities as the main target. As well, the final
consensus decision has been a shared formulation by diaspora participants.

The same process is occurring in other diaspora contexts. In 2006, the AU
and the government of Brazil hosted an international conference of Africans and
Africans in the diaspora in Salvador, Brazil. The meeting was attended by the then
chairperson of the AU, six African heads of states, the prime minister of Jamaica,
Lula (Luiz Inácio Lula da Silva, a former president of Brazil), a number of AU governmental officials, representatives of civil societal groups, and especially notable
scholars from the diaspora and from the continent. Scores of Afro-Brazilians
attended the conference whose goal sought to facilitate a partnership between
Africans and Africans in the diaspora. Some participants saw the meeting as the
third stage of an African Diaspora partnership, which would focus on the institutionalization of discussions, debates, and negotiations between Africans and its
descendant peoples. Institutionalization was seen to be a vehicle that would foster
strengthened partnerships among these heritage peoples in ways that culminated
in what many participants at the conference proclaimed would be a mutual goal to
unite Africa. One of the conference respondents commended the AU's conferences
and meetings, especially when they are held in Latin America, where diaspora
contributions to the histories of these societies are only just beginning to be
unearthed (Akukwe 2006).

Finally, ensuring that a diaspora policy includes only those committed to the
African cause demonstrates that there exists a sustained Pan-African political
consciousness evident in the AU's deliberations regarding its global outreach to
the diaspora. The insistence of including only those who are committed to the
African cause suggests that including the diaspora in the building of a united and

developed Africa is the Diaspora Clause's ultimate goal as declared in the AU's Constitutive Act of 2002. The enactment of the Diaspora Clause as AU policy and the discourse tropes that have contributed to this reality represent merely one strain that demonstrates the process of the AU's practice of global cultural politics. It is the AU's implementation of the Diaspora Clause and its institutionalization of the clause broadly and deeply in scope that will measure the African impact on globalization.

In this regard, the AU uses two of its institutional bodies to achieve its goal to shape global African unity: the Economic, Social and Cultural Council (ECOSOCC) and the Civil Society and Diaspora Department (CIDO). ECOSOCC was established in 2005 to foster the building of partnerships between African states and African civil societies. Article 3.3 of the Statutes of the Economic, Social and Cultural Council of the African Union states that "ECOSOCC shall also include social and professional groups in the African Diaspora organizations." Twenty diaspora organizations will be part of the AU's ECOSOCC, the advisory civil society body of the AU.

The AU Commission's CIDO is an institutional body where the AU manifests its diaspora initiatives. CIDO's goal is to hold regular dialogues with diaspora communities around the world. The committee holds annual consultative forums with African-descendant communities in the United States, the Caribbean, South America, and the Middle East through the regular convening of Regional Consultative Conferences (RCCs) in various regions of the world with diaspora populations. The goal of the conferences is to formulate a road map for effective diaspora participation in engaging an agenda for the integration and development of Africa.

A mixture of old and new diaspora civil societal groups was reported to have attended the meetings; some of them were Afrikan Unity of Harlem, Youth Icons, African Cultural Exchange Club, the December 12 Movement, African Sun Times, Falou Foundation, the Drammeh Institute, African Poetry Theatre Inc., Cameroon Organization, World African Diaspora Union, Gulla Geechee Nation, the Africa Channel, Saga Africa, and the Sixth Region Diaspora Caucus (SRDC), to name a few. The AU initiated its First Consultation of the African Diaspora of the African Union at its headquarters in downtown New York. Entitled "Building Bridges across the Atlantic," the two-day conference, held on October 21–22, brought together over fifty diaspora-based civil society organizations with representatives from the AU.

Discussions about common interests and organization globally animated this meeting as it did the Second Consultation of the African Diaspora of the

African Union in 2011. One group—the civil society organization Afrikan Unity of Harlem, Inc.—stated the importance of the diaspora standing in solidarity with the African continent.

> No longer will we accept a developed country or otherwise rights to call for regime change in Africa. We as the Sixth Region of Africa must stand with the Union in its efforts of pervading in its authority, its peace and stability in Africa and overall, it's structural unification of the entire continent. (Afrikanunityofharlem 2011)

Conclusion: The Value of AU-State-Nonstate Linkages and Interactions

The AU's engagement with Africa's quangos and its establishment of the Diaspora Clause provide evidence and illustrate a significant way that the AU participates in, shapes, and advances the project of cultural globalization through Pan-Africanism. Through its state-nonstate linkages—which constitute political actions—the AU proceeds to utilize cultural politics to achieve its means. It does so by cultivating state, regional, and civil societal partnerships throughout Africa and the diaspora; and it uses Pan-Africanism as a cultural artifact to shape perceptions and forge identities among the inhabitants of these regions. The events and activities that the AU organizes constitute examples of the international institution's deep immersion and the full enactment of its goals to reinvent Africa.

The AU's statecentric Pan-Africanism is shaping sociocultural processes in regions one through six to serve its own global ends as it strategically interweaves among several sociopolitical layers and negotiates an assemblage of symbolic traits, practices, cultural markers, and goods that embody African ideas, identities, and ideologies. This way the intergovernmental organization meets its greatest challenges in attempting to establish and build a global nation out of deeply diverse, continental sub regions and an—albeit sometimes divided—complexly structured Africana world.

Using Pan-Africanism to redistrict Africa into five regions and to enact the diasporan sixth region in a complex global space are actions that support the reality that African continental initiatives are contributing to globalization using cultural politics. As it cultivates six regions out of an entire globe of multiply constituted and hybrid sociocultural and political diaspora domains, the AU's

Pan-Africanism strategically excavates the long-standing, deeply historical, and broadly global roots that precede its current organizational manifestation. In using Pan-Africanism as a symbolic marker to reinvent outward notions of place for Africans and her descendants in the global arena, the Diaspora Clause supports a notion that continental Africans not only possess a deeply seated public memory of a diaspora cultural consciousness, but they continue to participate in the reintegration and transposition of what have historically been cultural Pan-Africanist initiatives into direct global political action.

The AU's statecentric, global diasporic initiatives may or may not turn out to be more consequential than the cultural surges and informal ebbs and flows of nonstate actors of the past, who while certainly having legitimately kept shared identities alive over time, have been unable to use the power of the state, political institutions, and global governance bodies to enact a lasting and broadly penetrating institutionalization of Pan-Africanism in ways that the AU is attempting to achieve. Be that as it may, so is the AU's institutional cultural Pan-Africanism limited in terms of achieving concrete political reconfiguration and reunification of a global or even continental African personality as Nkrumah envisioned. After all, the AU has not achieved a continental or a global African world citizenship. Black peoples worldwide remain divided by a range of national sovereignties and citizenships that are not explicitly adhered to a notion of an Africa.

Then again, the value of the AU may indeed be its cultural politics rather than a rigid form of formal sovereign politics. Universal involvement and participation in the AU may remain configured in a transnational nonlegal construct where states and particularly nonstate actors on the continent and in the diaspora play a voluntary role based on their shared cultural experiences. Perhaps it will be the onus of continental African and African-descendant states, peoples, and nonstate forces to respond to the AU's Constitutive Act proactively in the diversity of manners that they may choose to contribute while maintaining national sovereign citizenships. For now, we see the positive value of the AU where it utilizes Pan-Africanism to mediate and direct the continental and diasporic sociopolitical context, thereby both cultivating and promoting an African world view.

The African Union Democracy: Navigating Indigenous Rights and Inclusions in Neoliberal Contexts

T his is how a news press story announced the African Union's (AU's) election as chairperson for the year of President Obiang Nguema Mbagoso of Equatorial Guinea in 2011:

> Nothing here should come as a shock, but the AU's credibility and relevancy took another nose dive when the organization elected President of Equatorial Guinea as the new chairman. . . . He assumes the AU mantle when myriads of recent [democracy] crises in Egypt, Tunisia, and Ivory Coast require exemplary leadership from the continental mother body. President Obiang, a dictator himself who took over in a bloody military coup in 1979, presided over several waves of political repression and corruption. . . . Can a dictator tell another dictator to step down or point a finger at another dictator claiming "you rigged the election, so step down"? Clearly the AU's overt embrace of dictators in its organizational structure as well as its double standard in dealing with dictators is undermining its efforts. (*Africa Village* 2011)

A few months after Obiang's controversial emergence to the helm of African leadership, in March 2011, the Libyan crisis blew up, and the discourse over the AU's status as a democratic body became increasingly debated and contested from within the organization's membership as well as among its diaspora and the international community. Debates about Gaddafi's status and profile as a dictator, whether the Benghazi rebellion within Libya was a prodemocratic spring or a violent, secessionist militia, and whether the AU is a dictator's club that under the leadership of the likes of Equatorial Guinea's Nguema had any kind of legitimacy to resolve conflicts arising from democratic insurgencies like the one in Libya will be the subject of the current chapter as a way to assess Africa's and the AU's democratization trends.

Democracy and democratization represent important political regime norms that inform the AU agenda for Africa. To be seen as a credible international actor in the global era, attaining the status of liberal democracy is the foremost assessment criterion. What's more, to achieve its continent-wide development and conflict-resolution goals, democracy is an important mechanism. Africa is often misleadingly labeled in blanket authoritarian narratives, such as the reference to the AU dictator's club. Nonetheless, the reality is that African individuals, groups, and nation-states all aspire for democratic ideals; the AU's own aspirations for the same are collective reflections of the democracy phenomenon. In its aspirations to attain democratic governance for its own internal operations, for its nation-state members, and for individual Africans asserting rights from the continent's political regimes, the AU partakes in a form of social and cultural constructivism. In doing so, the AU's democracy promotion represents in itself an institutional norm and value that it uses to engage in the ideational (the idea of democracy), in citizens' rights and participation, and in its norm modeling and peer review of African nation-states.

In 2013 approximately 59 percent of African countries are classified as either democratic or partly democratic by Freedom House, the international nongovernmental organization (NGO) that rates the democraticness (presence and extent of democracy measured by the attainment of political rights and civil liberties) of countries around the world (see table 4.1). While not a fully democratic profile, this statistic still gives the African continent a mixed record. This is no doubt demonstrative of the unevenness of democratic attainment among the Union's fifty-four member states. Nevertheless, while it is a fact that President Obiang and the late Colonel Gaddafi—the former elected controversially, and the latter never having been subjected to democratic elections at all—have played prominent roles in AU governance, so have leaders who come from Africa's democratic countries, including South Africa's President Thabo Mbeki and the late President Bingu wa Mutharika of Malawi. In fact, the AU's first chairperson (2002–3), Thabo Mbeki, used his renaissance philosophy to position democratic renewal as the hallmark of the AU's agenda.

TABLE 4.1. AFRICAN UNION MEMBER STATES FREEDOM RATING 2013

	African Country	Free	Partially Free	Not Free
1	Algeria			X
2	Angola			X
3	Benin	X		
4	Botswana	X		
5	Burkina Faso		X	
6	Burundi		X	
7	Cameroon			X
8	Cape Verde	X		
9	Central African Republic		X	
10	Chad			X
11	Comoros		X	
12	Côte d'Ivoire			X
13	Democratic Republic of the Congo			X
14	Djibouti			X
15	Egypt			X
16	Equatorial Guinea			X
17	Eritrea			X
18	Ethiopia			X
19	Gabon			X
20	The Gambia			X
21	Ghana	X		
22	Guinea		X	
23	Guinea-Bissau		X	
24	Kenya		X	
25	Lesotho	X		
26	Liberia		X	
27	Libya			X
28	Madagascar		X	
29	Malawi		X	
30	Mali			X
31	Mauritania			X
32	Mauritius	X		
33	Morocco		X	
34	Mozambique		X	
35	Namibia	X		
36	Niger		X	
37	Nigeria		X	
38	Republic of Congo (Brazzaville)			X
39	Rwanda			X
40	São Tomé and Principe	X		
41	Senegal	X		
42	Seychelles		X	
43	Sierra Leone	X		
44	Somalia			X

African Country	Free	Partially Free	Not Free
45 South Africa	X		
46 South Sudan (N/A)			
47 Sudan			X
48 Swaziland			X
49 Tanzania		X	
50 Togo		X	
51 Tunisia		X	
52 Uganda		X	
53 Zambia		X	
54 Zimbabwe			X
Total	11	20	22

Source: Freedom House, *Freedom in the World 2013*.

This chapter examines the AU's democratic profile, character, performance, and aspirations in the context of the immediate post–Cold War period of the early 1990s through to the beginning of the millennium, when the AU was established. This era is appropriately defined as one of democratic capitalism where both liberal democratic transitions and neoliberal economic policies became fused processes promoted to developing world regions by both international finance institutions as well as G8 and United Nations (UN) development foreign policy organs. It is an era that scholars referred to as global democracy where globalization and democracy have become associated with a single process of international governance; democratic change has been integrated into the world economy, information technologies, and the growing desire for a place in the larger regional economic and political communities (McColm 1992, 572–73). In the 1990s, most African nations struggled amid enduring conflict, chronic budget deficits, and an inability to catch up in the global economic rat race (Walraven 2004).

Referred to then as the African crisis, the period also ushered in an era in which democratic development—with neoliberal ideology, human rights discourse, and the good governance mantra as its anchors—became the discourse tropes used by an international community external to Africa to govern Africa from outside and within. Following the global wave of democratization, various African countries also underwent a redemocratization process while also implementing neoliberal structural adjustment programs during this period. In light of its reappropriation tendency to wrestle from the international community an African self-determined path to development, the AU would integrate global democracy and democratic capitalism principles into its Constitutive Act and internal governance organs, particularly as African countries experienced protracted transitions to democracy themselves. As an example, the AU Constitutive Act Preamble states: "We [are] . . . determined to promote and protect human and peoples' rights, consolidate democratic institutions and culture, and to ensure good governance and rule of law." These objectives are repeated in article 3.g, which states that the Union will "promote democratic principles and institutions, popular participation and good governance." And again, article 4.m states that the AU will be guided by "respect for democratic principles, human rights, the rule of law and good governance".

Nonetheless, the act's rhetorical assertions with regard to democratic principles in its rules are only part of the story of democracy and the AU. Of significance is how the AU uses its suprastate authority in a way that gives the institution the powers to build and cultivate democracy among its members through structural and physical intervention and enforcement or otherwise through peer review and modeling (evaluation, exposure, recommendation, and sanctions) (Adejumobi and Olukoshi 2008). While the AU's many Constitutive Act articles may serve to advance and deepen democratic consciousness and awareness on the continent, it is the sway and quality of the AU's democratic leadership and structures that will direct democracy's more impactful function and deeper penetration to facilitate the democratic change of its members.

For example, with regard to democratization, the AU's suprastate authority is tested in article 4.p, which states that the AU condemns and rejects unconstitutional changes of governments. Yet, while this clause may have guided AU diplomatic interventions in Zimbabwe, Togo, Niger, Madagascar, Guinea, and Mauritania and more recently in Côte d'Ivoire and Libya, and thus may have constituted the AU's political solution to promote and protect democracy and governance, the AU's interventions present no simple solutions to the structural contradictions that are associated with democracy and development. What's more, for the 2011 Libyan case and other nondemocratic members of the Union, the Constitutive Act doesn't address how and when these members will become democracies or even if the Union desires them to be.

The AU's internal institutional structure also presents an important way to assess the organization's democratic behavior. Doing so presents insights into the manner in which fifty-five independent nation-states participate in collective governance in a democratic way. The Constitutive Act has evolved a number of internal governance organs, including its commission, its one year rotational leadership of the Assembly, the Pan-African Parliament (PAP), and the Economic, Social and Cultural Council (ECOSOCC), to ensure that the AU is governed democratically. AU internal democratic governance has as its objective the achievement of equality of participation for member countries, regions, and African peoples constituted in the continent's numerous civil societies, communities, and other nonstate actors. Electing Obiang, for example, as president in 2011 resulted from this democratic process. Obiang was nominated by the AU's Central African region to the one year presidency through a General Assembly vote whose decisions would be based on consensus or a two-thirds majority.

The AU's emergence in a democratic era invokes several questions that will hope to clarify Africa's record of democracy with respect to the mandate of the AU in relation to Nguema, Gaddafi, and other high-profile democracy scenarios such as Zimbabwe. Why and how have Africans—through the AU—imbibed the values of democratic capitalism as important values that guide the continent's Unity vision? How does the AU's democratic profile influence the Union's internal, domestic (African nations) and international legitimacy to contribute to democratic change among its member states that will serve to position Africa appropriately in a global democratic era? Examining the implications of the 1990s decade of democratization in Africa referred to as the third wave of democracy helps to reveal the democratic status of the AU.

Additionally, however, with this chapter, we draw an important conclusion about the AU's democracy impact and performance. To continue to classify Africa as failed at democracy and largely dictatorial suggests the continuation of an unwarranted discourse of Afro-pessimism in the analysis of African affairs. The reality is that the continent's fifty-five (and the AU's fifty-four) countries' democratic attainments vary. Yet there is no doubt that democracy in Africa, like in other developing world regions, is tenuous, transitional, and thus developmental. Democratization in Africa has gone through at least two epochal iterations, the first in the decolonizing period when, for a short time between 1960 and 1965, African countries underwent a period of nationalist democracy where Africans struggled for self-determination and self-governance with the end result being the emergence of new independent states with borrowed Western democratic forms ranging from British Westminster parliamentary, to French hybrid, to American presidential systems. Since most of these systems broke down by the late sixties through to the eighties, a second wave of democratization in Africa would not occur until the late eighties to the nineties in the global context of what Samuel Huntington has called the third wave of democratization (Huntington 1991).

If Africa's Organization of African Unity (OAU) presided over a largely nondemocratic continent in the late 1960s, the AU would preside over a largely democratizing one whose values both fostered the AU's emergence while also directing the institution to complete the job of democratic transition. Nonetheless, herein lies the conundrum in which the AU finds itself as a democratic body by 2013: half free and half unfree. Yet, through their collective visioning in the AU, free and unfree Africans pool their aspirations for self-determination, which in itself derives from democratic struggles in Africa that we refer to as an African-centered democracy (Edozie 2008), with global democratic ideals embedded in liberal democracy. From this ideational alliance are forged the Union's democratic goals, objectives, attainment, and impact. In this respect, the AU's democratic profile reflects Africans' historical, gradualist, developmentalist democratic goals.

In this regard, the AU's democratic profile may be described as a hybrid democracy as well. That is to say that through the AU's predecessor, the OAU, Africans advocated strongly for the inclusion of culture and self-determination into the formulation of a human rights discourse for a UN Declaration of Human Rights. As well, during the 1960s to the 1980s, in touting one-party, palaver-style democracies, several African countries posited alternatives to liberal democracy. By incorporation into its acts, institutional organs, initiatives, and policy prescriptions, particularly evidenced by the AU's 2005 Democracy Charter, we see how the AU has imbibed the Africanized values of democracy that were at once based on Pan-African self-determination, an alternative human rights turn of the 1980s, and the liberal democratic capitalism of the 1990s third wave that had become the dominant regime for global democratic politics by the time that the AU came onto the scene. Some African scholars have defined Pan-Africanism broadly as an ideology of democracy and human rights where in an African federal framework, the purpose is a government of Africans by Africans (Tigroudja 2012).

As such, as seen by this history, by its structural circumstance, and by its constituent values, organization, and policy rules, the AU is a hybrid democratic institution whose democraticness is syncretic and experimental while also strategically and consistently aspiring to foster the democratization of its members. Africa's hybrid cultural context of Pan-Africanism and liberalism provides a vehicle for the AU's democratic performance. The AU achieves democratization for the continent by governing the Union's activities in a democratic manner; it fosters both horizontal and vertical representative inclusion among equal member states as well as attempts to cultivate direct engagement with African peoples and communities. Moreover, the AU's developmental political economy also guides its action. The Union recognizes the poverty and underdevelopment of its members as factors that inhibit democratization and that cause insecurity.

As such, rather than prescribe policies that exclude member states that were not democratic at the AU's founding or prescribe military interventions targeting regime change to effect democratic change on the continent, through its peer-review mechanism, the AU instead uses its democratic principles and policies to encourage democratization among such members.

That is to say, the AU has no qualms in exercising its supranational authority regarding democracy when it comes to maintaining democracies that have already transitioned. In such cases, it enforces its Constitutive Act policy of unconstitutional removal of a government by intervening to restore the status quo. AU enforcement of this policy has ranged from suspension from the Union (Togo, Niger, and Madagascar) to aggressive diplomatic intervention (Côte d'Ivoire and Libya). In the global arena as well, by embarking on global partnerships with the European Union (EU), the United States, and the UN, and in cultivating opportunities for collective African representation in international bodies, we see how the Union advances the global democracy movement as well as Africans' democratic inclusion in that movement.

Subsequent sections of this chapter will examine Africa's democratic ideas and processes in the context of a post–Cold War era of democratic capitalism and global democracy in relation to the AU's emergence and behavior, demonstrating ways that these ideas are ensconced in notions of self-determined democracy and reconfigured in the hybrid ideas of a Pan-African renaissance and resuscitated developmentalism. Other sections identify and analyze the key democracy organs that the AU uses to achieve internal democracy and regional democratic integration, and proceeds to assess these ideas and structures against prominent AU democracy interventions, ranging from Togo to Libya. The chapter concludes with a section that traces the AU's role in advancing global democracy. The subsections support the thesis that the AU is a democratic institution that is gradually contributing to the democratic attainments of its member states as well as advancing global democratic goals.

From African Rights to African Renaissance: Promoting Hybrid-Developmental Democracy

The 2005 AU's African Charter on Democracy, Elections and Governance preamble lists twelve principles and motivations that its members will adhere to with regards to their goal to democratize Africa. The four declarations below extracted from the charter's narrative embody the continent's collective values, goals, and achievements regarding democracy. The Preamble reads that AU members will be,

> Inspired by the objectives and principles enshrined in the Constitutive Act of the African Union . . . which emphasises the significance of good governance, popular participation, the rule of law and human rights. . . .

> Committed to promote the universal values and principles of democracy, good governance, human rights and the right to development;

> Cognizant of the historical and cultural conditions in Africa;

> Seeking to entrench in the Continent a political culture of change of power based on the holding of regular, free, fair and transparent elections conducted by competent, independent and impartial national electoral bodies. (African Union 2010)

Good governance, popular participation, human rights, rule of law, African cultural context, and regular free and fair elections all constitute an important thread that ties together the AU democracy profile whose character we argue reflects the hybrid and developmental experience of democracy in Africa. This is to say that while the Democracy Charter adopts the universal liberal democratic norms of its period (elections, participation, good governance, rule of law, human rights), its commitment to developmentalism and African invention inclines its authors to link democracy to African cultures, to the continent's economic development, and to peace building on the continent.

This hybridity has emerged from several factors: the self-determination democratic struggles that Africans experienced during the continent's nationalist and Pan-Africanist era, the OAU's formulation during the 1980s of a human rights regime that incorporates Africans' collective values, the modern adaptation—through decolonialism and globalization (third wave of democracy)—of liberal democratic institutions, and the constant experimentation, adaptation, and innovation of the liberal democracy, a factor symbolized by Thabo Mbeki's notion of the African renaissance. The AU's developmentalism has emerged due to the recognition that the AU's house is half free. Through the institution's collective power, the AU's democracies adopt subtle, diplomatic, soft-power peer-review mechanisms, policies, and initiatives to nudge their unfree members toward democratic change and to consolidate and deepen democracy among the democracies.

The 1990s represented a global context whereby democracy and democratization in Africa would be underscored and resuscitated by the characteristics that hybridity and developmentalism threw up for the continent. The democratic change around the world that occurred at the end of the Cold War in 1989 has been characterized as the third wave of democracy (Huntington 1991, Fukuyama 1992, Diamond and Plattner 2010); countries in the former Soviet Union and the developing world, including in Africa, underwent political-economic reconfigurations that have been described as "democratic capitalism" (Berger 1992). Developing world and transitional countries would undergo dual transitions—to democracy and to neoliberal laissez-faire economics. Scholars of the day and international finance institutions argued the mutuality of both transitions as the most viable route to wealth, growth, and development. Democracy would foster growth and development, and neoliberal economies were judged as genres of democratization.

Good governance, human rights, and the rule of law became the mantra for this era of third wave democratic capitalism, which was characterized by both political and economic variables. Politically, third wave democracy was fashioned after the American liberal democracy with its core elements in the minimalist state. The role of the thin state would be to institute good governance by mediating civil societal interests and ensuring the political, civil, and human rights of its citizens. Economically, the minimalist state would institute the rule of law by protecting private property and providing an infrastructure for global economic activity including free trade and entrepreneurial investment and employment opportunities. For developing world countries, the transitional nature by which countries would adopt democratic capitalism from their previous statuses as nonliberal democratic, welfare socialist, or communitarian state societies caused the decade of the nineties to be one of much flux, chaos, uncertainty, resistance, unrest, and social volatility. These conditions led to what Guillermo O'Donnell (1996) would refer to as the emergence of developmental democracies in the developing world.

Democratization in Africa reemerged in this context. Several symbolic democratic transitions in the continent in the early 1990s demonstrated that Africa was following the global trend. These were Benin, Senegal, Zambia, Mozambique, Namibia, and South Africa. Later democratic transitions in Mali, Tanzania, Ghana, Nigeria, Kenya, and Malawi would propel a critical mass of democratic African states to forge an AU with democratic ideals. Economics would determine the direction of the Union's values as well. By the end of the 1990s, most African countries had implemented some form of neoliberal structural adjustment with various outcomes. Growing at a rate of 12 percent a year in the nineties, for example, Mozambique was reported to be the fastest growing economy in the world in 2000 (Muchie 2003). Notwithstanding, by 2004, Africa still garnered less than 2 percent of the world's gross domestic product and was the region with the largest poverty ratings (Adejumobi and Olukoshi 2008).

Embodying the dual transitional processes of a postapartheid South Africa, and interjecting them to a vision for democratic and economic renewal for the whole of Africa, in 1995 at an OAU Heads of State and Government meeting in Tunisia, Nelson Mandela first coined the ideal of Africa's "new renaissance" that would seek to unite Africa economically and politically (Akokpari, Ndinga-Muvumba, and Murithi 2008). Forged not too long after this, the new AU would be different from the old OAU. The AU would instead encapsulate Africa's political-economic and democratic transformations to offer a political, economic, and social project aimed at creating a democratic space across Africa. The AU would use democracy as a way to promote economic development, reflect a common African identity (Akokpari, Ndinga-Muvumba, and Murithi 2008, 33), as well as enhance Africa's place in the global economy.

The AU would be the response to Africa's new path toward institution building in which Africa's peoples would be represented to embark upon continental change and renewal. No longer able to ignore their domestic opposition forces, strategic African democratic states successfully canvassed the AU idea that would provide a common platform for African peoples and their grassroots organizations to be involved in the continent's discussions and decision making. Africa's new democratic values would embed the AU's Constitutive Act as African leaders and peoples pledged to use the institution to foster relations among African governments; especially, the AU would cultivate relations among all segments of African civil society, including women, youth, and the private sector, while determining to promote and protect human and people's rights, democratic institutions, good governance, and the rule of law (Walraven 2004).

Nonetheless, despite the global context that fostered Africa's and the AU's democratic principles, such values had also evolved, and thus been informed by, earlier political-economic configurations on the continent, particularly during the decolonization and immediate postcolonial sixties, seventies, and eighties. The African context facilitated a world by which Africans have encountered and reformulated democracy around their own cultural and economic milieu. The AU imbibed these values through its predecessor's (the OAU's) establishment of the African Charter for Human and People's Rights in Banjul, Gambia, in 1986. The charter is an example of the continent's attempt to construct and reconstruct democratic values in a way that is grounded in African indigenous, historical, and cultural norms in spite of the plurality of such norms. The African charter reflects African values of human rights by its conferral of rights to peoples and not just to individuals as the Western human rights discourse does. The African charter also underscores the importance of duties in the consideration of rights; it reaffirmed the anticolonial stance with its emphasis on self-determination and gave as much weight to economic and cultural rights as had been given to political and civil rights (Viljoen 2007).

As well, by emphasizing the communal aspect of rights and in recognizing that the family is the natural unit of society, the charter injected the importance of African peoples and communities as important elements of democracy and human rights. The charter reflects Africa's long-standing struggle for cultural determination and freedom from all forms of colonialism through its reconciliation of political and civil rights with economic and cultural rights. The charter represents an African adaptation to democratic ideas and recognizes the rights of Africans to healthcare and welfare (Viljoen 2007, 483–535).

The AU has adopted the charter's values to reflect the hybrid posture of Africans toward democratization. While the Union's Constitutive Act does not directly refer to the OAU's human rights' charter for its democratic referencing, its Democracy Charter does refer to the rights of development and pledges its democracy principles in cognizance of Africa's histories and cultures. What's more, the AU has established a new human rights organ in the form of the African Court of Justice and Human Rights to promote its rule-of-law democracy objectives. In article 2 of the Protocol to the African Charter on Human and Peoples' Rights on the Establishment of an African Court on Human and Peoples' Rights, the AU has made provisions to complement its values with the 1986 African charter when it declares that the court shall complement the protective mandate of the African Commission on Human and Peoples' Rights (ACHPR; Akokpari, Ndinga-Muvumba, and Murithi 2008).

Postapartheid South Africa first promoted the idea of an African renaissance to mobilize Africans in support of a renewed and strengthened integration that resulted in the AU's 2002 establishment. Former President Mbeki did so by reconciling African values, democratic principles, and African renewal with the universal democratic capitalist ideas of the millennial era. In re-presenting Nkrumah's idea of a United States of Africa, the African renaissance became a cross-continental dialogue between the postmillennium-termed Afro-optimists (supporters of African renewal) and Afro-pessimists (pessimistic about African capacities). For Mbeki, an AU African renaissance would foster continental development and forge a new transnational, transcultural, and transhistorical African identity through which innovation and economic progress would occur (Tomaselli 2003).

In underscoring new trends in the global nature of democratization, the AU would also need to consider the meaning of democracy in the context of a world system that is based on the progressive integration of states and societies into regional and global political-economic networks (Held 1995). Global democracy would refer to the way in which national democracies everywhere would be aggressively influenced by the global economy, by the hegemony of regional and global organizations, and by the increasing legitimacy of international law and security alliances (Held 2004). It is this regional and global context that would influence the AU's independent action to determine its future as a continent of democracy, peace, stability, and shared development and prosperity.

INSTITUTIONAL VEHICLES OF DEVELOPMENTAL DEMOCRACY

Hybrid and developmental values also lace the AU's internal democratic processes and procedures. Equal country representation and peer review, peoples' participation, and civil societal and interest representation are the building blocks for the Union's attempts to govern democratically. The institution's internal democratic aspirations affect its democratic legitimacy and profile on the continent and outside of it. Three important organs stand out as vehicles for driving the Union's internal governance democratically. The Assembly and the African Peer Review Mechanism (APRM) represent democratic values of country representation and state-to-state mutual consultation and exchange. The PAP reflects the AU's attempt to engage its activities, decisions, and outcomes directly with African peoples through citizen participation and representation. ECOSOCC is an organ that reflects the AU's democratic ideals in engaging Africa's civil societies and other targeted citizens' groups and issues, such as women, youth, and private sector interests.

The AU's Assembly is the supreme organ of the AU and comprises the African heads of states and governments or their representatives (Makinda and Okumu 2007). Because of the importance of this body in AU policy enactment and decision making, the democratic credentials of the heads of states/governments are an important prism for assessing the democratic nature of the Union. The reality is that in 2011, 60 percent of the leaders that represent the assembly were elected in democratic elections, while the remaining 40 percent were not. Be that as it may, whether the body functions and operates democratically and the extent to which the body is democratically inclusive of all of its members represents a more effective assessment to understand the AU's democratic behavior in this regard. The rotational chair, the body's extraordinary meetings, its voting mechanisms, and its control over the Constitutive Act are all procedural criteria used by the Assembly that may determine its institutional democratic functions.

The first organ to consider is the body's leadership through its chair as this position represents the face of the Union continentally and globally. The Assembly's chair is elected by the heads of government, and the position serves for one year. The foundation body elected as its first chair former president of South Africa Thabo Mbeki in 2002. Mbeki, a democratically elected and charismatic leader, embodied the democratic ideals of the Assembly using the leadership to profile a New South Africa in order to mobilize democratic renewal throughout the continent as well as broker new engagements and partnerships for Africa abroad. Serving two consecutive terms from 2004 to 2006 (each one-year term was renewed) was former Nigerian president Olusegun Obasanjo. While Obasanjo had served a leadership role in the OAU as Nigeria's military head of state in the 1970s, the general's democratic credentials in the new millennium reflected Nigeria's democratic transition in 1999 and Obasanjo's election as the country's Third Republic democratic leader. Tanzania and Malawi's democratically elected leaders, Presidents Jakaya Kikwete and Bingu wa Mutharika, both held the Assembly chair.

However, Libya's late head of state, Colonel Gaddafi, was also an elected chair of the Assembly in 2009. Despite Gaddafi's nondemocratic credentials, the Libyan leader represented the North African region's turn to lead in a system that attempts to rotate leadership equally across the diverse continent. While many members were uneasy about Gaddafi's rise to the helm of the AU and the reputation of the new institution as a result, Gaddafi's unity vision similar to Nkrumah's (a single African military, economy, and citizenship) was compelling to the majority of members that supported his nomination.

The Assembly's extraordinary summits held twice a year reflect the democratic nature of the AU through the style and substance of topics deliberated and decided upon as well as through the voting mechanisms through which binding decisions are made. The Assembly reaches its decisions by consensus, although in the absence of consensus it does accept majoritarian voting by at least two-thirds of the members and a simple majority on procedural matters (Makinda and Okumu 2007). Preference for consensus decision making in a democracy over majoritarian vote reflects African democratic values. Kwasi Wiredu (1996) argues that arriving at a consensus has been drawn from Africa's precolonial palaver political systems whose main principle is to arrive at justice only when everyone agrees. Of course, the AU strives to become an enlarged federalist democracy with many complex layers of decision making and accountability that is representative of diverse constituencies too. Thus, employing modern democratic procedural voting mechanisms like the two-thirds majority vote serves to augment the Union's internal democratization processes.

The Assembly is the architect of the AU's Constitutive Act that, among other important functions, decides on intervention into member states. This function gives the Assembly considerable power to direct and advance democratization on the continent. Extraordinary sessions of the Assembly have recorded heated debates, deliberations, and contested votes among members on decisions over interventions into member states experiencing democratic breakdown and conflicts. Moreover, the range and reach of the Union's decisions will influence the quality of its impact. An Assembly decision may be binding or merely a recommendation, resolution, or opinion that is not binding but whose intention is to guide and harmonize the viewpoints of member states (Makinda and Okumu 2007).

The AU has been criticized for the Assembly's nonprovision of checks to its power or accountability mechanisms by African people (Makinda and Okumu 2007). Not including this provision suggests s dictatorial structural inclination of the AU organ. The AU's PAP serves to complement the Assembly's limitation in this regard. It is believed that the PAP holds out the hope of reflecting the democratic aspirations of all the peoples of Africa in realizing a dream held by generations of Pan-Africanists and African democrats (Adejumobi and Olukoshi 2008, 75). In conceiving the PAP, the AU declared it should evolve to be an African parliament that would be elected by direct universal suffrage, with full legislative powers, that would override national legislation, so that it could respond directly to democratic constituencies of people and communities in Africa rather than to nation-states (Walraven 2004).

Nonetheless, in its formative years, since its establishment in March 2004, the PAP has remained an advisory and consultative body with headquarters in Midrand, South Africa. AU member states will appoint members of parliament (MPs) from their national parliaments or delegative organs with at least one member appointed being a woman. The gender quota has been successful in fostering greater participation and representation by African women as 20 percent of the PAP's legislative offices are held by women. Each country is represented by an equal number of MP slots thereby underscoring the AU's principle of equal representation rather than proportional representation. Nigeria, Africa's most populous country, gets the same number of MPs as Botswana, one of the continent's smallest countries in population size. MPs are no-party representatives as the protocol restricts party formation while privileging member state legislative representation. The PAP's protocol provides for direct elections eventually, while in the meantime the PAP is involved in peer reviews of elections among member states.

The PAP's current impact on democracy in Africa is not exclusive to the internal democracy domain. It has broader functions as the subinstitution also participates in discussions of the range of political, economic, social, military, and other issues with which Africa is confronted. Be that as it may, the PAP's mere advisory and evaluative role in its probationary period on matters related to democracy, human rights, and good governance, while fostering peer review among members, does not have suprastate capacity to effect substantive democratic impact on member states and African communities as of yet (Walraven 2004). Another concern regarding the democratic capacity of the PAP is its lack of independence from the AU, though the PAP's external powers in relating to the matters of member states and other non-AU bodies and institutions does provide an important function for the AU's role in fostering developmental democracy.

It has already been determined that the PAP is a gradually evolving institution whose full legislative powers will be a function of the future. Meanwhile, however, the parliament's impact on the Union's policymaking is in its broad deliberative powers in advising and consulting with other AU bodies on important decisions. In this regard, the PAP is represented at the Assembly meeting sessions. Furthermore, the composition of the MP structure is another avenue for the PAP's democratic impact on member states. Because national delegates must reflect the diversity of political opinion from their home states, opposition representatives are likely to be represented at the AU in a way that positions the parliament to throw up more fruitfully deliberated advisory decisions (Walraven).

If nothing else, the PAP has been relatively successful in creating a forum for the voice of African peoples. Since its inception in 2004, it has convened 265 legislators with a president and four vice presidents represented by each region. PAP has held regular sessions and has passed numerous resolutions and recommendations. The parliament has assigned election-monitoring observer teams and also deployed missions to conflict zones including Darfur, Côte d'Ivoire, Mauritania, Chad, and more recently Libya requiring governance and human rights interventions. In its Eighth Sitting of the Fourth Ordinary Session, for example, in May 2011, of its seventy members, forty-three members voted in favor of a motion on Libya condemning the North Atlantic Treaty Organization (NATO) bombing, calling for solidarity with Libyans in their time of need, and endorsing the notion of finding African solutions to the situation. On October 28, 2009, the second legislature of the PAP opened its First Ordinary Session and began a new five-year mandate with many still calling for the PAP to be given full legislative powers and for its members to be elected by universal suffrage.

Another organ that facilitates AU democracy is ECOSOCC. At its inauguration in 2005, the then AU Commission chairperson Alpha Konaré stated that ECOSOCC would serve as a tool against authoritarian regimes, hostile external efforts, and the negative waves of globalization (Makinda and Okumu 2007). With the objective of giving civil society organizations an institutional platform—including professional groups, NGOs, social groups, community-based organizations, and labor, religious and cultural groups—ECOSOCC is expected to provide an additional forum for democracy across Africa. The organ distinguishes its role from the PAP in providing a forum for the interests of nongovernmental groupings and not individual and community representation.

Like other AU organs, ECOSOCC has emerged from a history of social movement mobilization, democratic struggle, and agitation by pluralistic nonstate actor initiatives across the continent. Examples include the 1990 Charter on Popular Participation that has been described as a testimony to the renewed determination of the OAU to place the African citizen at the center of development and decision making. Again, in 2001, the OAU hosted a civil society conference in Addis Ababa to assist in the promotion of a homegrown African civil society and contribution to the fulfillment of a future AU mission. As its principal channel for civil society, ECOSOCC would be the AU's major consultative body to support Pan-African civil society organizations and networks; it would provide them with financial support and observer status and host meetings before each AU summit (Adejumobi and Olukoshi 2008). ECOSOCC civil societal representation can be national, regional, continental, and from the African diaspora.

ECOSOCC's impact on country-level processes and vice versa presents an important way to examine the democratization processes of the AU. ECOSOCC mandated the setting up of chapters within AU member states that had the purpose of strengthening the role of civil society in respective countries on the continent. The respective chapters ensure that the objectives of the AU are practiced in member states, and they encouraged further participation by civil society in global, continental, and national political arenas. South Africa's chapter is organized around several sectors; for example, women, youth, arts, culture, heritage, labor, professionals, faith, business, media, and NGOs, including community-based organizations, are all eligible to be elected to serve on ECOSOCC's South African National Council. The national structures further participate within ECOSOCC activities in provincial and local branches of their organizations.

The South African ECOSOCC chapter credits itself with having influenced policy positions during AU presummits, for having adapted their programs to declarations emanating from the AU Assemblies, for having commemorated AU holidays, and for having formulated their own decisions to the AU for ratification and adoption. In this regard, ECOSOCC-South Africa spearheaded the participation of civil society organizations in the APRM process in South Africa and has participated in Election Observer Missions at regional levels through the Southern African Development Community (SADC) (ECOSOCC-SA).

The AU mobilizes continental democratic development through the gradual change in norms and standard-setting of its justice organs, including the founding charters of its predecessor OAU organs and Africa's Regional Economic Communities (RECs), which the AU continues to borrow from as well as engage and interact with. The African Charter on Human and Peoples' Rights preamble affirms that "civil and political rights cannot be dissociated from economic, social and cultural rights." The signatory states are committed by its first article to recognize the human rights it specifies and to take measures to give them effect. This implies a concession from sovereignty. The charter gives its ACHPR a mandate to pronounce upon human rights violations at the request of a state, an institution of the AU, or an African organization recognized by the AU (art. 45.3).

Following the principle of subsidiarity, article 50 specifies that all national remedies must first be exhausted or would be unreasonably prolonged. Further, the AU Commission issues a ruling and reports unrepentant violating regimes to AU summits. This soft law, a naming and shaming, provides an example of how the AU establishes a legal system to generate norms and to secure compliance without either legislature or sovereign enforcer (Álvarez 2006, xvi–xvii).

The AU-OAU and its affiliated RECs have a long tradition of using its courts to deepen democratic ideas and ensure that Africans' rights are protected. The most recent judicial authority being established is the African Court of Justice and Human Rights (ACJHR), with its seat in Arusha. Within two years of its establishment, the court's antecedent, the African Court of Human and Peoples' Rights, accepted a high-profile case concerning human rights violations: in the matter of the African Commission of Human and Peoples' Rights v. the Great Socialist Libyan People's Arab Jamahiriya (Order 004/2011), the court issued an injunction attempting to prevent further human rights violations. So far, the ACJHR has acted as a court of the first instance, but its continental jurisdiction implies that it will evolve to become an apex court of appeals, when regional courts cover between them all African countries and the SADC Tribunal is reestablished.

One of Africa's most impressive developments has been the judicial activism of its continental and regional courts. The courts often entertained cases that are well beyond their treaty-defined jurisdictional bases. This showed courage and their decisions expressed a boldness given the relative newness of these institutions. It is also impressive that these bold decisions are made in a context in which adherence to notions of national sovereignty is very strong (Gathii 2011). The Economic Community of West African States (ECOWAS) Community Court has shown remarkable judicial activism in extending its jurisdiction into human rights cases within three years—not four decades—of deciding its first case. Landmark judgements include the case of Chief Ebrahim Manneh v. Republic of the Gambia (ECW/CCJ/APP/04/07). This was a habeas corpus ruling for a journalist illegally detained and held incommunicado to be released and paid $100,000 in compensation. That this violation occurred in the state that is the seat of the ACHPR makes this a significant case of contested norms between a national sovereign and a continental commission and regional court. The case of Hadijatou Mani Koraou v. Republic of Niger (ECW/CCJ/JUD/06/08) confirmed a government's responsibility to protect a woman from forced marriage and forced labour on the unwanted husband's farm, ordering that she be paid $100,000 compensation. The case of Socio-Economic Rights and Accountability Project (SERAP) v. the President of the Federal Republic of Nigeria (ECW/CCJ/APP/08/08) upheld the right to universal free education for children whose families could not afford to pay fees.

The Common Market for Eastern and Southern Africa (COMESA) Court of Justice, seated in Khartoum, has not yet accepted cases concerning human rights violations by member governments, but the East African Court of Justice did so merely one year after hearing its first case. James Katabazi and 21 Others v. Secretary General of the East African Community and Others (Judgement Ref. No.1 of 2007) ruled illegal those police and military actions that overruled the granting of bail by a Ugandan court.

The SADC Tribunal became record-setting among its global peers when it asserted jurisdiction over human rights cases right from its first hearings. The SADC Tribunal also successfully adjudicated Campbell and Another v. Republic of Zimbabwe (SADC [T] 03/2009) and Mike Campbell (Pvt) Ltd and 78 Others v.

The Republic of Zimbabwe (SADC [T] 02/2007). These, the first two in a sequence of cases, concerned farm owners receiving no compensation when their farms were redistributed during an agrarian reform program. With a politicized and racialized background, President Robert Mugabe denounced this series of SADC Tribunal rulings, including subsequent ones holding the Zimbabwe government to be in contempt of court. Mugabe has derided attempts by the SADC Tribunal, often insinuating that the body lacked power to do more than refer this series of cases to the SADC Summit. After lobbying by the Zimbabwe delegates, the SADC Ministerial Council terminated the SADC Tribunal. Its pending and current cases were suspended. A letter from four judges protested that they were not even able to collect their personal belongings (*Cape Times* 2011). While the rule of law lobby lost this battle, they will win the war over the long duration, as judicial activists renew their confrontations with authoritarians.

Avoiding Democratic Reversal: National Impact and Case Studies

The AU's democratic policy enactments, values, principles, ideas, and institutional structures come together in the institution's capacity to physically act, by way of supranational intervention into member states, in regard to the advancement or support of democracy on the continent. Democracy interventions by the AU have been conducted as a result of Assembly resolutions to the AU Commission in relation to the observation of the Constitutive Act's article 4.p where members reject unconstitutional changes of governments. Zimbabwe, Mauritania, Togo, Madagascar, Niger, Côte d'Ivoire, and Libya all inform important prisms through which to examine the complications involved in the Union's hybrid and developmental democratic principles.

AU interventions have ranged from a conscious resolution not to intervene (Zimbabwe 2002), to assertive, conflict-resolution, diplomatic mission intervention (Zimbabwe 2007, Madagascar 2009, Côte d'Ivoire 2010), to condemnation, suspension, and nonrecognition of coup regime (Mauritania 2005, Madagascar 2009) as well as sanctions (Togo 2005, Guinea 2009, Niger 2010; see table 4.2). As exemplified by one of the OAU-AU's first test cases for democracy intervention, Zimbabwe's 2002 and 2008 electoral crises provided a testing ground. In the way that the AU approached the issue, Zimbabwe interventions also underscored Africans' hybrid and developmental approach toward democracy, especially in

TABLE 4.2. AU DEMOCRACY INTERVENTIONS

	DEMOCRATIC REVERSAL TYPE/DATE	AU INTERVENTION STYLE	INTERVENTION OBJECTIVE	OUTCOME
Zimbabwe	Disputed Elections Mugabe and Tsvangirai / 2002 and 2008	Support (2002); Diplomatic mission (2007)	Reconcile conflicted political parties/groupings	Government of National Unity – Mugabe and Tsvangirai
Madagascar	Militant opposition and power take-over Ravalomanana and Rajoelina 2001 and 2009	Sanctions, Suspension, and Diplomatic Mission (2002, 2008)	Reconcile conflicted political parties/groupings	No democratic outcome as of July 2011
Togo	Military imposition of unelected leader – Gnassingbé/2005	Sanctions	Hold elections	Elections in 2005 and 2007, Faure Gnassingbé elected in multiparty poll
Mauritania	Military coup d'etat—President Taya (ousted in 2005) and President Abdhallahi (ousted in 2008)	Sanctions, Suspension	Restore elections	Elections in 2007 elected Abdallahi, and in 2009 elected military coup leader, Abdel Aziz
Guinea	Bloodless military coup by captain groups 2008	Suspension	Restore elections	Election in 2010, longtime opposition leader Alpha Condé elected in multiparty poll
Niger	Bloodless military coup against Tandja 2010	Suspension	Restore elections	Election in 2011, longtime opposition leader Issoufou elected in multiparty poll
Côte d'Ivoire	Disputed elections between Gbagbo and Ouattara 2010–11	High-level diplomatic mission intervention	End conflict	No new election, Ouattara installed through a military rebel action supported by France and UN
Libya	Militant prodemocracy movement 2011	High-level diplomatic mission intervention	End conflict	Ongoing

contradistinction to liberal Western democratic values. A transitional OAU-AU representative was critical of what it considered was European zeal to have Africans oust Robert Mugabe claiming that

> We reaffirm our adherence to the decisions and resolutions of the 2001 Lusaka OAU/AU Summit which expressed full support for Zimbabwe in her quest to redress the wrongs of the colonial era which among other things include institutionalized, skewed development and unbalanced distribution of the country's wealth, resources and means of production. (*Herald* 2002b)

Africa's inclination has been to assess the Zimbabwean democracy crisis through structural rather than liberal lenses. The AU's position reflected Africans' preference to construct democratic systems that have been adapted to their own historical and sociocultural contexts, including colonialism, anti- and postcolonialism, global dependency and inequality, late economic development and poverty, late nation-state formation and regime stability, and cultural pluralism. These are structures that influence a divergent Western, liberal trajectory toward democratization for Africa.

Compared to Zimbabwe, Madagascar's similarly chronic democratic crisis has also presented several challenges for the AU's intervention and impact for change. In 2002, Marc Ravalomanana assumed the country's presidency in what could have been considered a democratic spring, a people's revolution. Like the Zimbabwean election, Madagascar's results were disputed between his opposition party and the then incumbent president, Didier Ratsiraka. On account of Ravalomanana's unilateral declaration as the winner of the disputed poll and his assumption to power through the support of the country's high court and despite a militant opposition, the AU was criticized for its duplicity in suspending Madagascar on the basis of article 4's unconstitutional change in government clause while not doing the same for Zimbabwe. Nonetheless, the AU maintained its exclusion of Madagascar, noting the obvious differences between the two countries' disputed polls.

Ravalomanana went on to lead the country into a second-term election victory in 2006 where he received 56 percent of the vote without a need for a run-off election. It was the 2010 vote that once again illustrated the difficulty of enacting democratic consolidation in Madagascar. This time, with Ravalomanana as incumbent, a democratic movement against Ravalomanana by former mayor Andry Rajoelina propelled the country into an ongoing democratic crisis with Rajoelina assuming the role of the presidency in what the AU denounced as

Rajoelina's unconstitutional assumption of the Madagascar presidency supported by the country's de facto authorities. After the AU's failed attempts to persuade the Rajoelina regime to implement an agreed power-sharing deal that would create a transitional coalition with Madagascar's four rival political parties, the AU slapped sanctions on Madagascar for failing to implement accords to end a long democratic crisis.

The 2005 democratic reversals in Togo and in Mauritania presented less ambiguity and therefore led to action by the AU. In Togo, with the death of long-time nondemocratic leader General Gnassingbé Eyadéma, the Togolese army appointed Faure Gnassingbé, Eyadéma's son, to succeed him instead of allowing Mr. Fambaré Natchaba, president of the National Assembly at the time, to assume the position of acting president pursuant to the Togolese constitution. In this case, the AU acted swiftly, immediately warning Togo that it would not accept the unconstitutional transfer of power and calling for the immediate restoration of constitutional legality in Togo. The AU called for a suspension of Togo from participating AU activities, imposed sanctions, and encouraged a democratic solution to the country's crisis. AU pressure worked as Gnassingbé agreed to step down and participate in a nationwide multiparty election, which he won. Since 2005, Gnassingbé and his party have entered into coalition governments with the opposition. Even here, the AU's swift position was contrasted by the Western media as hypocritical. The AU, however, invoked the violation of article 4 for its actions in Togo, which did not apply to Zimbabwe.

The AU suspended Mauritania twice since its equally rocky democratic transition in 1992 when coup leader, President Maaouya Ould Taya, was officially elected in a multiparty poll. In 2005, however, the AU was forced to suspend Mauritania's membership after a military coup ousted Taya. The AU Peace and Security Council (PSC) resolved that the suspension would remain in place until constitutional order was returned to the West African state. The AU sent a mission to Mauritania to dialogue with the junta in a plan to restore the country to democratic normalcy. While a subsequent poll in 2007 did restore democracy temporarily to Mauritania with the election of President Sidi Ould Cheikh Abdallahi, nevertheless, in 2008 the AU would again suspend Mauritania from the bloc following a coup against Abdallahi. The pressure would force General Mohamed Ould Abdel Aziz—leader of the August 2008 military coup—to organize, stand for, and win the presidential elections in 2009. The AU rescinded Mauritania's suspension and has been forced to deal with the contradictory, suboptimal, and tenuous democratic trajectory of some of its members.

In 2008 and 2010, Guinea and Niger would similarly constitute difficult cases of democratic transition for the AU, although both cases represented the Union's maturity in applying its hybrid and developmental democratization intervention policies to reverse democratic reversals. The AU would suspend member countries who changed regimes unconstitutionally while also working diplomatically with the regime to facilitate a transition to democracy through either recommendations for power sharing or organizing new elections. In 2008, the AU suspended Guinea after Captain Moussa Dadis Camara seized power following the death of long-serving President Lansana Conté. The AU announced that Guinea would remain suspended until the return of constitutional order in that country. However, because many in Guinea supported the coup, the AU decided not to apply sanctions against Guinea, pledging instead to work closely with the coup plotters to try to bring Guinea back to constitutionality.

In a 2010 multiparty election, Alpha Condé, a longtime Guinean opposition leader won the election pledging national unity through democracy, food self-sufficiency in three years, universal education and health access, economic development, and the encouragement of foreign investment and regional integration. Moreover, the AU decided to reward General Sékouba Konaté, the former interim head of state of Guinea for successfully moving Guinea into a democratic state by appointing him as the high representative of the AU for the operationalization of the African Standby Force—and possibly keeping him away from Guinean politics.

Again in 2010, the AU would suspend yet another of its members following a military coup—Niger. In this coup the increasingly unpopular President Mamadou Tandja was deposed and the government was dissolved. In this case, the AU did impose sanctions on the county and demanded that Niger return to immediate democratic rule. But the coup came with mixed blessing from the Niger populace as thousands of people took to the streets in support of the coup d'état. Calling themselves the Supreme Council for the Restoration of Democracy (CSRD—Conseil suprême pour la Restauration de la Démocratie), the coup leaders promised to turn Niger into an example of democracy.

An AU special envoy for Niger expressed satisfaction with the body's mission to Niger after having met with the ruling junta. The mission's report stated that the AU was satisfied with the CSRD's reiteration and willingness to move toward a constitutional and democratic regime immediately and that the military regime members had agreed not to contest for any post in the new elected government. In April 2011, longtime opposition leader Mahamadou Issoufou's Nigerien Party for Democracy and Socialism won a presidential runoff with 58 percent of the vote in his third attempt to contest elections in Niger.

Recent democracy conflicts in Côte d'Ivoire and Libya (2011) perhaps drew some of the sorest challenges for the AU. This is because both cases emerged from and resorted to violent civil wars, and the numerous conflict-resolution policies presented were integrated with various iterations and layers of hegemonic power jockeying for influence, interests, and stakes in both countries, especially by the UN, France, the United Kingdom, and the United States.

In Côte d'Ivoire, the AU and ECOWAS took many ambivalent positions, ending up abandoning their mediator role and propositions to facilitate a union government and to establish an international inquiry into the disputed elections, and instead supporting Alassane Ouattara as the rightful winner. Failure to resolve the conflict diplomatically culminated in a bloody civil war with Ouattara's UN-French imposition, the humiliation and capture of Laurent Gbagbo, many deaths and displacements, and the exacerbation of the north–south divisions in the country. Former South African president Thabo Mbeki was appointed as AU ambassador to the African Mission in Côte d'Ivoire in 2010 to mediate the disputed electoral outcome between former President Gbagbo and now incumbent President Outtara.

Mbeki highlighted the challenges of the AU and the Union's future direction with regard to Africans' long struggle to determine their own routes to peace and democracy. He argued that structural faults including transnational tensions affecting especially Côte d'Ivoire and Burkina Faso, Ivorian ethnic and religious antagonisms, sharing of political power, and access to economic and social power and opportunities underpinned the ten-year conflict in Côte d'Ivoire culminating in the fully blown civil war in 2010–11 over the disputed 2010 election (Mbeki 2011b). The country had been divided into two parts with two governments, administrations, armies, and national leaders, with the north controlled by the rebel Forces Nouvelles, which supported Alassane Ouattara, and the south in the hands of the Gbagbo-led government.

The AU mission noted that elections held under these circumstances would entrench the divisions and animosities exacerbated by the 2002 rebellion stating that,

> In this regard, the international community has assiduously suppressed proper appreciation of various explosive allegations which, rightly or wrongly, have informed and will continue to inform the views of the Gbagbo-supporting population in southern Côte d'Ivoire—and much of Francophone Africa! These are that Ouattara is a foreigner born in Burkina Faso, that together with Burkinabè President Blaise Compaoré he was

responsible for the 2002 rebellion, that his accession to power would result in the takeover of the country especially by Burkinabè foreigners, and that historically, to date, he has been ready to advance French interests in Côte d'Ivoire. (Mbeki 2011b)

The AU seemed to understand that a lasting solution of the Ivorian crisis required a negotiated agreement between the two belligerent Ivorian factions, focused on the interdependent issues of democracy, peace, national reconciliation, and unity. This required the reunification of the country, the restoration of the national administration to all parts of the Ivorian territory, and the disarmament of the rebels and all militia and their integration in the national security machinery. Yet the UN allowed the elections to proceed despite the fact that none of these conditions had been met. By allowing the major powers to intervene to resolve these challenges, using their various capacities to legitimize their actions in using the UN to authorize their self-interests, the events in Côte d'Ivoire reified the marginalization of the Union in its ability to resolve Africa's most important challenges.

The 2011 Libyan democracy spring fostered an intensive debate within the Union about dictatorship and imperialism. Was Benghazi a prodemocracy movement that should have been supported by the Union's democracy clause? Should the AU continue to support Gaddafi, a nondemocratic leader? Despite the contestations over deciding how to intervene in Libya, the AU enacted an intervention policy similar to its previous democracy cases. Again, Mbeki would ask, "The stark choice we faced was—should we side with the demonstrators or with the governments they demanded should resign!" (Mbeki, 2011b). Unlike the Arab League, the AU unequivocally rejected UN Resolution 1973 and the ultimate NATO attack on Libya in the form of Operation Odyssey. The Union enacted a number of immediate actions including condemnation of Gaddafi's suppression of the uprising by the AU's PSC. "We condemn . . . the indiscriminate and excessive use of force and lethal weapons against peaceful protestors, in violation of human rights and International Humanitarian Law . . . and affirm the aspirations of the people of Libya for democracy, political reform, justice and socio-economic development are legitimate"(African Union 2011).

The AU convened a high-level meeting on March 26 calling for a cease-fire, dialogue between the parties, and a road map to resolve the crisis, including the formation of a transitional government, the holding of elections, and the building of democratic institutions to meet the aspirations of all Libyans. The AU also met with the UN Security Council (UNSC), where the representative called for dialogue with all parties without precondition and the acceptance by Gaddafi of competitive democracy and reforms. As the Libyan conflict became protracted, the AU's intervention grew in moral international legitimacy with NATO countries, the United States, France, and the UN, with the AU's commitment to a political solution toward a democratic transition in the country that would meet the legitimate aspirations of all Libyan people to preserve the unity and territorial integrity of their country.

At the close of the Seventeenth Summit in July 2011, the chairperson of the AU, President Obiang Nguema Mbagoso of Equatorial Guinea, noted the concerns of the continent's body to defend all of the people involved in the crisis in Libya as well as to defend the integrity of the African continent. He added that the members' declaration had strengthened the unity of Africa as the majority of delegations at the summit had reaffirmed their commitment to the road map prepared by the AU in resolving the Libyan crisis. President Obiang said that the message to the international community was that the AU was garnering greater respect in regard to issues concerning the continent (African Press Organization 2011).

THE AU AND GLOBAL DEMOCRACY

In light of the Côte d'Ivoire and Libyan democracy conflicts, where the AU as an international organization may have felt that it had little freedom to embark upon the implementation of its own public policy solutions vis-à-vis more powerful intergovernmental organizations and suprastates, its status in a notion of a global democracy is an important consideration to use to assess the AU's democracy profile. The manner in which the AU has the freedom to navigate among local, national, and global domains and contexts with the objective of delivering positive democratic goods for its citizens requires a global democratic arena. It is in this arena that perceptions of Africans' identity come to the fore, and the AU either is or is not perceived as a legitimate democracy broker. Nevertheless, representation of Africans as a bloc is an important value for globalization and democracy. Africans and Africa are underrepresented in international organizations. In promoting its inclusion into an arena that is still hierarchized and dominated by the West, the AU is contributing to global democracy.

The ideas, principles, structures, initiatives, and interventions with regard to Africa's hybrid and developmental democratization profile and practices embodied by the AU illustrate the cumulative effect of the Union's dynamic engagement with third wave democratization. The AU's activities in this respect have been twofold. On the one hand, many of the organization's initiatives are conducted in conjunction and collaboration with international bodies such as the UN, the EU, and the United States. For example, in June 2011, despite the AU's disagreement with NATO on Libya, the AU Commission and the EU Commission pledged to "pursue and deepen . . . cooperation in support of peace, security and democratic governance in Africa to further build on [their] intense and successful political dialogue . . . [to] promote national reconciliation and economic recovery in Ivory Coast, and work jointly to foster good-neighborly relations between North and South Sudan" (European Commission 2011). As well, during the Guinea democracy crisis, the AU and the UN sent a joint mission to compel a democratic transition.

Moreover, in April 2011, a US State Department website would underscore the importance of the United States Agency for International Development's (USAID's) collaborations with the AU's Democracy and Electoral Assistance Unit to improve election processes across Africa assisting the AU to promote the African Charter on Democracy, Elections, and Governance. The communiqué went out of its way to note that the US government viewed the AU as a respected voice on the continent that builds consensus on African issues among member states and stakeholders. The United States expressed its pleasure that the two international entities (the US and the AU) had been engaged in substantive and frank dialogue about how to address such issues as unconstitutional changes in government in Africa (IIP Digital 2011).

Yet, while cultivating partnerships with other international bodies, especially with counterpart suprastates, the AU recognizes the importance of structural forces in the global arena that inhibit Africa's full representation in the global governance network of power. That is why the AU has offered strategic suggestions to the international community on how to deepen African representation in international organizations such as the UNSC. As an example, events in Côte d'Ivoire and Libya underscored the importance of the AU serving as a vehicle for Africans' voices and perspectives in the governance of the continent. In arguing that the UN severely undermined its role as a neutral force in the resolution of internal conflicts in Africa through the Côte d'Ivoire and Libyan cases, Africans raised concerns about the role of the UN as a mere instrument in the hands of the world's major powers. Mbeki noted, "This has confirmed the urgency of the need to restructure the organization, based on the view that as presently structured the United Nations has no ability to act as a truly democratic representative of its member states" (Mbeki 2011b).

In 2005, the AU submitted a proposal to the UN recommending UNSC reform in ways that would contribute to African inclusion and representation in a global democracy. The AU's Ezulwini Report stated that, through the foundation of the AU, the turn of the millennium had positioned Africa to influence reforms of the UN in a united way. The report's key points called for Africa to be fully represented in all the decision-making organs of the UN, particularly in the UNSC, which is the principal decision-making organ of the UN in matters relating to international peace and security. The AU requested not less than two permanent seats with all the prerogatives and privileges of permanent membership including the right of veto and that the AU should be responsible for the selection of Africa's representatives in the UNSC.

Significantly, countering the arguments emerging from advanced industrial countries over whether Africa's nondemocracies could be selected for UNSC permanent representation, the AU asserted that the question of the criteria for the selection of African members of the UNSC should be a matter for the AU to determine. The AU would base its selection on a member's representative nature and capacity. This position indicated that Africans would invoke African democratic values typified by the Union: self-determination, consensus, and equitable representation of the continent's diversity.

CONCLUSION

To date, neither the Ezulwini Report nor any other proposal to reform the UNSC has been adopted. However, the proposal in itself formulated and consistently presented by Africans serves to provide a forum for African voices, desires, and interests, if not decision-making authority—aka democracy—at the highest levels of global power. Implementation of the proposal would, needless to say, represent a bold impact for the AU with respect to globalization, democratizing global governance processes.

Meanwhile, the Union's consistent actions and attempts to foster the incremental democratization of its members through its hybrid and developmental democracy rules and policies, its initiatives in engaging with African peoples directly and democratically, and its penchant and commitment to self-govern internally using democratic procedures have all enhanced the AU's global democratic legitimacy to more effectively advance the democracy of its national members and local constituencies, while also cultivating global democratic relations on behalf of Africans.

Incidentally, on July 4, 2013, one of the AU's biggest donors, Egypt, became the latest country suspended from the AU due to the country's unconstitutional transfer of power that resulted in the overthrow of elected President Morsi's government. Citing that the Constitutive Act prohibits any member state in which there is an unconstitutional transfer of power from participating in the activities of the AU as its reason for Egypt's suspension, the AU reminded the world that it would unambiguously uphold its democratic mandate to prohibit military coups, ostracize putschists, and compel those putschists to hand over power to elected governments as soon as possible.

Pax Africana versus International Security: New Routes to Conflict Resolution

E xamine the following scenarios that occurred in 2013 to illustrate the dire challenges of the African continent in the areas of security, conflict, and conflict resolution. First, there were events in Somalia:

> The UN, a merchant of death and a satanic force of evil, has a long, inglorious record of spreading nothing but poverty, dependency and disbelief.[1]

This was the rationale given by Somalia's al-Shabaab on June 19, 2013, for its deadly attack on the United Nations (UN) compound in Mogadishu that killed twenty-two including six UN staff, seven civilians, and seven al-Shabaab insurgent fighters. Significantly, however, it was Africans that came to the rescue as saviors to keep the peace in Somalia and protect the UN as African Union Mission in Somalia (AMISOM) forces regained control of the UN compound in the ensuing gun battle that ended the conflict. Similar to the role of the North Atlantic Treaty Organization (NATO) in Afghanistan, the African Union (AU)—more specifically the AU's peace and security apparatus—has been the foremost institution to bring a semblance of peace, shaky as it is, to the over two- decade- old conflict in Somalia.

Second, at its May 2013 Summit, the AU accused the International Criminal Court (ICC) at the Hague of "hunting Africans because of their race" and opposed the UN's affiliate institution for indicting and trying its member Kenyan President

Uhuru Kenyatta and his Vice President William Ruto for crimes against humanity. AU Commission chairperson Nkosazana Dlamini-Zuma said the ICC should be a court of "last resort" and that Kenya's newly reformed judiciary was capable of trying the case. With the April 2013 election of the ICC-arrest-warranted Kenyan president and vice president for their role in a previous election's violence (2007), Kenya becomes the second country whose sitting leaders are wanted for war crimes by the international organization to which the three core UN Security Council (UNSC) permanent members—the United States, Russia, and China—have not subscribed. In a resolution drafted by the AU Assembly at the same May 2013 Summit, African leaders threatened a mass withdrawal from the organization that they deemed singularly "targets Africans" for international injustice. The incident shows that Africans—through the AU— and the international community continue to be at loggerheads over the administration of security and justice issues on the African continent (Fortin 2013).

Third, despite the fact that from 1992 to March 2012, Mali was considered quite a blossoming democracy by international freedom ratings, Mali's democracy broke down as the country resorted to civil war and became the site for French military intervention and international conflict resolution. The country had suffered a military coup when mutinying Malian soldiers led by coup leader Amadou Sanogo attacked the presidential palace, state television, and military barracks in Bamako, and formed the National Committee for the Restoration of Democracy and State in declaring the overthrow of the government of Amadou Toumani Touré.

From then on, reversal of democracy was the least of Mali's challenges as the country plunged into a deep political crisis and war, which the putschist military officers lost immediately. Tuareg militants seceded the country's northern region renaming it the independent state of Azawad, which became a haven for warring Islamic extremist militants and other secessionists. Mali's transition from democracy to conflict-prone, collapsed state is a familiar story for Africa—even (or perhaps, especially) in the post 9/11 global era. Between 2010 and 2012, war, conflict, and violence engulfed African member states: revolution in Tunisia and Egypt, outright civil war and international intervention in Libya, coups in Guinea and Mali, militia violence in Mali and Nigeria, more recently the prospects of interstate war between the Sudan and the newly minted South Sudan, chronic violence in the Democratic Republic of the Congo, and portending guerrilla takeover in the Central African Republic, while Somalia sustains a more than two- decade-old state of conflict and conflict resolution, remaining perhaps the world's only real collapsed state.

All three scenarios underscore the priority that achieving security and keeping the peace in Africa play in the challenge that the AU has assumed on behalf of Africans. Given pervasive conflict on the continent, can Africa achieve its goals of integration and political union? Or will the continent's weak states and regions need to unify into a single supranation- state as a means to address the continent's challenges with war and peace? What's more, who keeps the peace in Africa? Africans (the AU) or the international community (the UN, NATO, the ICC, France)? Ali Mazrui's classic 1967 article and subsequent book, *Towards a Pax Africana*, favored the latter scenario and argued that the foremost rationale for African union is to be found in Africa's chronic insecurity situation. Mazrui's book leveraged Kwame Nkrumah's Pan-Africanist vision of an African suprastate that would possess its own army (the African High Command); *Pax Africana* would refer to the notion that the peace of Africa must be assured by the exertions of Africans themselves, and in Ali Mazrui's words, a call for Africans to police their own continent (Mazrui 1969).

The AU's security architecture, an elaborate and sophisticated institutional framework for the operation of its conflict resolution and collective security agenda for Africa, represents a partial fulfilment, perhaps more accurately viewed as a trajectory, for Nkrumah's *Pax Africana*. Manifest in the AU's African Peace and Security Architecture (APSA) and security organ Peace and Security Council (PSC) and its protocol, AU *Pax Africana* is guided by a policy framework referred to as the Common African Defence and Security Policy (CADSP). CADSP is a strategy based on a set of principles, objectives, and instruments that aims at promoting and consolidating peace and security on the continent as well as at releasing energies and resources for development (Touray 2005).

This architecture and CADSP policy assures that the promotion of peace, security, and stability in Africa is higher on the Union's agenda than is economic integration and perhaps political union as it will be difficult to achieve the latter without the former. If Africa does not achieve the former, in an era where war and peace has become internationalized, the continent remains vulnerable to external militarized intervention from former colonial and current super powers in ways reminiscent of colonialism and imperialism. Designing, establishing, and implementing its own security mechanism collectively through the AU, Africa's millennium-era *Pax Africana* struggles to emerge as envisioned by Nkrumah while its structural and ideological attributes certainly have evolved to forge an intricate love-hate relationship with the global power structure.

Resolving conflict collectively in Africa and by Africans in an international era and arena where domestic war and peace matters have become globalized under the quasi-authority of the UN and NATO presents a special challenge for Africa's AU. This fact underscores an important thesis for the current chapter—and indeed, our book. We find that the AU's most dynamic representations in global governance occur in the security domain. Originally, Nkrumah presented his rationale for *Pax Africana* as Africa's solution to the 1963 crisis in the Congo. Dissatisfied with the UN's lip service support (and ultimate betrayal) of Pan-Africanist nationalist leader Patrice Lumumba during the crisis, Nkrumah advanced the idea of a strategic, institutionalized African support for African conflicts. Yet, the Congo crisis and other conflicts, including those in his own native Ghana, continued. These wars erupt for a number of reasons; they are motivated by resource interest, neocolonial control, and a lack of confidence in African self-determination. In Africa, local and national wars easily became international ones. As such, *Pax Africana*—even if the principle seeks jurisdictional authority over just Africa—always competes with *Pax Americana* and *Pax Europa*, whose scope of control is the world.

Former South African president, once AU chairperson, and African elder statesman and AU ambassador, Thabo Mbeki underscored the criticality of the issue in 2011 when he lamented that the casualties of both the 2011 NATO intervention in Libya and French intervention into Côte d'Ivoire were indeed the AU and the continent's self-determined efforts to determine its own path. Commenting on the AU's failure to prevent the NATO bombing of Libya despite its immediate diplomatic maneuvers in deploying, for example, an emergency meeting of the Assembly, its PSC, and the Commission's diplomatic initiatives toward the UN, Mbeki stated,

> The AU and therefore African message withered on the vine, making no impact whatsoever on African and world opinion of what might be done to resolve the conflict in Libya. Western countries have also underlined this marginalisation of Africa by insisting, to this day, that what is important for them is the support of the League of Arab States, with absolutely no mention of the AU. . . . acting through the UN Security Council, [Western countries] have used their preponderant power to communicate the message to Africa that they are as determined as ever to decide the future of Africa, regardless of the views of the Africans, much like what they did during the years of the colonial domination of our continent.
>
> It should not come as a surprise if, over the years, the people of Africa lose confidence in the will of multilateral institutions, such as the UN, to help them change their condition for the better. This will happen

because we will have come to understand that powerful countries beyond the oceans reserve the right and have the capacity ultimately to decide the future of Africa, with no regard for our views and aspirations as Africans. History will record that the moment of the reassertion of this deadly malaise was when the West, acting through the UN Security Council, dismissed the notion and practice of finding African solutions to African problems. (Mbeki 2011b)

The current chapter examines the AU's objectives and institutional behavior in relation to the continent's security domain while analyzing the AU's supra-state capacity and impact in securing Africa and fostering peace throughout the continent. We define capacity by examining both the institution's architectural strength in evolving rules and organs that enable it to implement its security agenda and base it on an assessment of the AU's impact on conflict resolution at the national level and its initiatives in evolving common security policies for its member states. In examining capacity, however, we also look at the AU's legitimacy among the continent's national and subregional domains, as well as its relations with the international arena in being perceived as the lawful authority to enact such rules.

In analyzing and assessing the status of *Pax Africana* in an AU regime, the chapter is guided by several interrelated questions. Does the AU have the capacity and the legitimacy to reduce African conflict? Can the AU's evolving APSA do the job? Is the AU a viable security alternative for continental national governments and for the international community's security governance of Africa (or what we will refer to as super-power suprastates—UNSC, ICC, NATO, US Africa Command [USAFRICOM])? Does the AU's impact on conflict and security on the continent depend on the resolution of North–South geopolitical tensions? Does Africa need the superpower suprastates? Should/can Africa go it alone to achieve *Pax Africana* in a self-determined way?

In first unravelling the AU's security principles, policies, and architecture, subsequent sections of this chapter will simultaneously consider Mbeki's dire warnings to the AU in relation to our thesis about the AU's suprastate neofunctionalism using the global security domain as case study. We attempt to unravel the contradiction of an AU emergent suprastate so elaborately structured, yet that still remains one of the least known and marginalized international actors in international relations theory and practice. We argue that the AU rolls out its APSA, which has been inspired by Nkrumah's principle of *Pax Africana*, to strive to achieve collective continental security, solve and prevent Africa's conflicts by Africans, and rebalance the North–South security hierarchy as it pertains to achieving self-determination for the continent.

Somalia and the Sudan, on the one hand, and Libya and by implication Côte d'Ivoire, on the other, represent case studies for examining the AU-PSC-APSA-CADSP matrix's *Pax Africana* peace keeping and peacemaking initiatives in a global governance context in this regard. Having presented the AU security structure with successes, failures, challenges, and opportunities to continuously improve and expand upon, each case represents significant although divergent impacts that the Union is having on local, national, and global environments in the security domain. Somalia demonstrates a successful PSC case where the AU acts alone but requests support from the international community (UN) on its own terms. In the Sudan, the AU delicately cooperates with the UN in a joint mission. In Libya and Côte d'Ivoire, countries with longstanding imperial interests (British, French, and US oil interests in Libya, and French investment interests in Côte d'Ivoire), the AU's PSC achieved minimal outcomes except for strengthening Africa's voice and posture in the global security architecture.

The potentiality of the tripartite hybrid cross-regional and global institutional collaboration among the AU, the Economic Community of West African States (ECOWAS), and the UN reflects an alternative vision for *Pax Africana* in which Africa (carried forth by the AU's PSC underlaid by its security architecture, the APSA) is in the driving seat in inviting assistance from the global community to resolve the continent's security challenges. In this regard, rather than neocolonialism, postcolonialism explains new trends in African affairs, where even in the security realm, Africa asserts its symbolic supremacy albeit in partnership with the real political economic powers of global governance. Or, especially given that UN Resolution 2085 comes with no funding but a lot of authority and power dispensed by the UNSC, does *Pax Africana* exemplified by the AU's resolution of the Mali crisis represent not a *Pax Africana* at all, or a severely weakened, compromised, and dependent state of African attempts to control the continent's security affairs? The AU's global governance manifestation of *Pax Africana* may also assume a codependent or an interdependent relationship with global governance institutions like the UN with each mutually reinforcing each other to address the messy matrix that has presented the equally uncertain challenges of global security in an era of globalization.

In elaborating and analyzing this thesis, the rest of the chapter will provide a brief history and theory of the AU's evolving *Pax Africana* and an illustration of the architecture of the AU's security organs, and using contrasting cases of the Union's conflict resolution interventions—Côte d'Ivoire and Libya on the one hand, and Somalia and the Sudan on the other—we will conclude by analyzing the prospects of the AU's security architecture achieving *Pax Africana* in an arena of global governance.

PRINCIPLES AND VALUES: *PAX AFRICANA*, COLLECTIVE SECURITY, AND INTERVENTIONISM

Omar Touray situates *Pax Africana* as belonging to a shift in the post–Cold War environment from realism to idealism. Internationalist idealism (an ideology of international relations), he argued, would surmount the world's renewed interest in African institutions and "African solutions to African problems" (Touray 2005). In "The African Union's New Security Agenda: Is Africa Closer to a Pax Pan-Africana?," Kristiana Powell and Thomas Kwasi Tieku cite Congo-Brazzaville President Denis Sassou Nguesso who appropriately articulates the aspirations of the new African security architecture. Nguesso proclaimed that a strengthened and capacitated security architecture will help African people to conquer war (Powell and Tieku 2005). The authors argue further that the principles underlying the AU's security agenda are hybrid—derived from the principles embodied in both a Pan-African *Pax Africana*, as well as from prevailing postmodern international security norms documented in the International Commission on Intervention and State Sovereignty (ICISS) 2001 Report on "Responsibility to Protect."

The principle of *Pax Africana* undergirds the AU's vision to achieve socioeconomic integration and penultimate political union by establishing the AU Non-Aggression and Common Defence Pact, which is part of the vision of building a strong and united Africa that will collectively defend itself. The Defence Pact (art. 4. d) requires that African member states "undertake to establish an African Army at the final stage of the political and economic integration of the Continent." In establishing what they have titled a "Solemn Declaration on a Common African Defence and Security Policy" (CADSP) in February 2004, AU member states would agree to fourteen distinct measures in the areas of determining their own version of *Pax Africana*.

CADSP is guided by the principles enshrined in the Constitutive Act of the AU and in the UN Charter. The agreement calls for a common vision of a united and strong Africa based on scrupulous respect for human rights, peaceful coexistence, nonaggression, noninterference in the internal matters of member states, mutual respect for national sovereignty, and territorial integrity of each state. The declaration would reaffirm members' commitments under article 4.d of the Constitutive Act, and article 3.e of the Protocol Relating to the Establishment of the Peace and Security Council of the African Union, which called for the "establishment of a common defence policy for the African continent."

Members claimed to be motivated by a common political will to strengthen their collective efforts to contribute to peace, security, stability, justice, and development in Africa, as well as to intensify cooperation and integration on the continent in the best interest of African peoples, which they were convinced could only happen if they undertook mutually reinforcing actions in the areas of defense and security. The declaration recalled and integrated the solemn declaration of an earlier 1990s Organization of African Unity (OAU) organ, the Conference on Security, Stability, Development and Cooperation in Africa (CSSDCA), and revived that document's interactive approach to security as an invaluable tool for the Union to pursue and strengthen its agenda in the new millennium. Significantly, members expressed consciousness of the indivisibility of security in Africa, and particularly the fact that the defense and security of one African country is directly linked to that of other African countries, thereby suggesting the need to harmonize member states' activities in these areas.

Developing policy frameworks for collective African security has been riddled with setbacks, stalemates, and continuous challenges to achievement and implementation. As can be seen, the solemn declaration remains exactly that—an aspirational rhetorical pronouncement. Indeed, PSC proposals for a nonaggression act and a concrete common defense pact have failed to materialize due to grave disagreements among member states. By July 2005, sixteen member states had signed a compromised version of the African Union Non-Aggression and Common Defence Pact, but none had ratified it (Khamis 2008).

In pursuance of the AU's security objectives outlined in its Constitutive Act, article 2 of the pact underscored two important security values for Africa that would guide the Union's conflict- resolution initiatives in Libya, Sudan, Somalia, and Côte d'Ivoire. They are defining "a framework under which the Union may intervene or authorise intervention, in preventing or addressing situations of aggression, in conformity with the Constitutive Act, the Protocol and the Common African Defence and Security Policy," and that "any aggression or threat of aggression against any of the Member States shall be deemed to constitute a threat or aggression against all Member States of the Union."

Regarding its intervention to prevent aggression, the AU would articulate the first value guiding AU intervention to address destructive militia wars in member states, the Nonindifference Clause. Nonindifference is an African equivalent of the UN's "responsibility to protect" (R2P) doctrine and it permits Africans (through the AU) to intervene into the political affairs of sovereign African nations undergoing conflict, when certain criteria are met. The AU's Nonindifference Clause is a first step toward the AU's achievement of a self-determined, continent-wide security policy as it makes way for African member states to give up their sovereignty—albeit temporarily—in circumstances of heinous conflict, violence, and war.

R2P is also an important institutional norm that undergirds contemporary global security rules and policies. Its loose policy narrative in the UN Charter vaguely encourages international institutions (such as the UN) to intervene into the internal affairs of civil conflicts in order to protect civilians against regimes alleged to be committing human rights abuses. That is to say, when a state is unwilling or unable to protect its population or is targeting its citizens with aggression, the responsibility to protect is transferred to the international community, which has an obligation to act or intervene even without the consent of the target state (Powell and Tieku 2005). Criteria for intervention include a large- scale loss of life (actual or apprehended) with genocidal intent or not, which is the product of either deliberate state action or state neglect or inability to act, or a failed state situation, or large- scale ethnic cleansing, whether carried out by killing, forced expulsion, acts of terror, or rape (Powell and Tieku 2005).

Four important elements define the distinctiveness of the AU's Nonintervention Clause, which stands starkly apart from its predecessor OAU's prosovereignty, nonintervention policy (Kioko 2003). The AU's aggressive mission to eradicate conflict from the continent in a self-determined manner persuaded African nations to accept their own African version of R2P that the AU Constitutive Act names its Nonindifference Clause. In adopting nonindifference, the AU became the only intergovernmental organization—regional or international—that officially subscribes to such a policy for its members. Nonintervention is the official policy adopted by UN member states despite the organization's rhetorical support for R2P principles. However, the policy represents a norm but does not constitute international law. The AU's Nonindifference Clause is unique in this respect; no other international organization, including the UN and the European Union (EU), support such an antisovereignty, military intervention clause as a matter of law (Bogland, Egnell, and Lagerström 2008).

Be that as it may, the AU's Nonindifference Clause is contradictorily stated in its Constitutive Act and PSC Protocol, as the PSC's rules may be interpreted vaguely as supporting both prosovereignty and antisovereignty stances. For example, article 4.h of the Constitutive Act states that the AU has the right to intervene in a member state pursuant to a decision of the Assembly in respect of grave circumstances, namely: war crimes, genocide and crimes against humanity. They may also intervene in situations that pose a serious threat to legitimate order to restore peace and stability in the Member State of the Union upon the recommendation of the PSC. Yet the document contains some prosovereignty clauses that contradict the AU's intervention rights. Article 4. f of the PSC Protocol still states that the AU will adhere to the principle of "non-interference by any Member State into the internal affairs of another," while article 3. b of the Constitutive Act states that one of the objectives of the Union is to "defend the sovereignty, territorial integrity and independence of its Member States."

What's more, while the AU adheres to its own R2P regime for the continent through its Nonindifference Clause, the Union and its members have been very critical of the UN's R2P norm. African leaders have argued that the UN's norm has been disproportionately applied to African countries. In 2008, then AU Commission chairperson Jean Ping delivered a speech to an AU Commission Roundtable on Responsibility to Protect. Ping articulated the concerns that African nations had with the clause:

> the concerns that were expressed by many States during the consideration of the Declaration [2007 UN Outcomes Document] are still valid and cannot be ignored. In short, the concern of States was and still is about the possibility of abuse of the principle of responsibility to protect.
>
> The sense of ownership that AU Member States have in their own institutions is not replicated in respect of UN Member States *vis-à-vis* the UN Security Council because of the right of veto and the role of the P5. (Murithi 2009)

Citing problems with the role of the UNSC, the human rights council, the theory of human security, and the abuse of superpower authority, Ping raised a number of questions that needed to be resolved if Africans and the developing world would accept the doctrine. Among them are two important factors that inform the AU's and Africans' tensions with the international security arena—UNSC, ICC, and NATO. First, Ping asked the forum to consider what needs to be done to overcome the fears of African states that this principle could be the object of abuse or double standards.

Second, referring to the instrumental interests defined by a realist agenda behind the new international interventionism, Ping inquired why the world community had not reacted concerning Somalia, a country that has been without the protection of state authority for over twenty years, in spite of the killings, the terrorism, and piracy. Ping's thesis illustrates the reality that Africa's security agenda is underpinned by the values of *Pax Africana* Pan-Africanism and not merely an intergovernmental body's desire to resolve conflicts in its region. The AU's Non-Aggression and Common Defence Pact's second criterion, to protect member states from aggression, reflects Ping's uneasiness with the UN's RP2 interventionist principles targeted at Africa (practiced through the UNSC, ICC, and NATO). The pact's narrative infers that a threat against one member represents a threat against all. Here, Africans are expressive of *Pax Africana*.

INSTITUTIONAL ARCHITECTURE: APSA, PSC, AND PSD

The AU's African Peace and Security Architecture (APSA), made up of the Peace and Security Council (PSC), an organ of the AU, and the AU Commission's Peace and Security Department (PSD), should be seen as institutional vehicles that facilitate the continent's goal to integrate its security structures to achieve long-lasting, sustainable peace and development in Africa. Seven organs and quasi-institutions within the Union make up the APSA, including the PSC, the Panel of the Wise, the Military Staff Committee (MSC), the Special Peace Fund, the African Standby Force (ASF), the Continental Early Warning System (CEWS), and the Committee of Intelligence and Security Services of Africa (CISSA). These security organs operate in conjunction with the AU Commission's PSD whose Peace and Security Directorate implements the Assembly and the PSC's decisions.

As the AU's standing decision-making organ for the prevention, management and resolution of conflicts and modelled around the ECOWAS Mediation and Security Council, the PSC is the AU security architecture's most important organ (Franke 2009). The PSC represents the AU's mandate to promote peace, security, and stability, anticipate and prevent conflicts, promote peacemaking and peace building, develop a common defense police for the Union, and encourage democratic practices, good governance, the rule of law, and human rights. African leaders attending the 2003 Maputo Summit offered wide support for the establishment of the PSC as a priority to allow the continent to solve its own conflicts. The AU's Executive Council elects fifteen PSC members (five of them for three-year terms and ten for two- year terms). The PSC holds formal meetings, briefing sessions where it is updated, and consultations with experts. Approximately to date, the PSC has held 360 meetings, published 100 communiqués, and run 4 peacekeeping missions.

Also part of the AU's APSA, the Commission's PSD supports the PSC in carrying out its responsibilities as provided for under the protocol. The PSD also supports the Commission in its activities, which are aimed at supporting the promotion of peace and security on the continent. The PSD organizes its activities in three divisions: the Conflict Management Division, which includes a Border Program, the CEWS, the Panel of the Wise, and the Post-Conflict Reconstruction and Development Unit; the Defence and Security Division includes Counter-Terrorism, Disarmament, Arms Control, Nonproliferation, and Security Sector Reform units; and the Peace Support Operations Division (PSOD) supports policy development, plans and operations, capability development, and mission support units. Security affiliates to the AU also include CISSA and the African Centre for Studies and Research on Terrorism (ACSRT), whose discreet name does not mention that it also provides counterterrorism training.

Other APSA PSC institutions—the Panel of the Wise, MSC, and CEWS—have not evolved their structures as elaborately as the PSC at this time, though each provides an important appendage, complement, and checks-and-balance for the PSC in ways that foster a strengthened security agenda for the Union. This cannot, however, be said for the ASF that, while also supporting PSC and PSD decisions, has evolved into a foremost security organ for the AU that again—aside from the UN and NATO—has few equals where other international organizations are concerned. The ASF is accountable to the PSD and is headed by Nigerian Major General Ishaya Hassan. It consists of five brigades from each continental region and is being established in five stages, phase 1 (2005) and phase 2 (2010) having been completed. So far, not the ASF brigades formally, but ad hoc missions of peacekeepers, peacemakers, military advisors, and observers have grown to over twenty-three thousand boots on the ground, mostly in the Sudan and Somalia.

The AU's ad hoc military missions and the ASF are the current equivalent of the African army that *Pax Africana* envisions. The institution is built around a standby arrangement whereby African states earmark and train specific military units (troops) from respective volunteer member nations for joint operations and then keep these units ready for rapid deployment to conflict zones at appropriate notice (Franke 2009). The ASF is modelled around a five- brigade, UN-style force ready to police the continent's trouble spots. In its final establishment, it will consist of six regionally based brigades, with the sixth unit headquartered in Addis Ababa (AU headquarters). Phase 1 of the roll out of the ASF should have the organ be ready and able to offer military advice to a political mission (scenario

1), establish an observer mission codeployed with a UN mission (scenario 2), establish a stand-alone observer mission (scenario 3), and develop the capacity to use a standby reinforcement system to manage its missions (scenario 4). Phase 2 of the ASF plan should have the AU able to develop the capacity to manage a regional peacekeeping force for complex multidimensional missions (Solomon and Swart 2004).

In 2012, the PSC has achieved some of the ASF goals—albeit not in the linear chronological order that it envisioned. After all, the de facto ASF does not consist of troops on standby in five regions, but rather its boots on the ground have seen continuous action since 2003 with missions in Burundi (AMIB), Sudan (AMIS I and II), Sudan-Darfur (joint UN/AU Mission in Darfur—UNAMID), Comoros (AMISEC), and Somalia (AMISOM) (P. Williams 2006). Table 5.1 chronicles and maps out the AU security agenda and initiatives to date.

TABLE 5.1. TIMELINE OF THE AFRICAN PEACE AND SECURITY ARCHITECTURE

1958:	Nkrumah proposes an African Legion and African High Command
1963:	OAU Defense Commission, 1st meeting, Accra
	OAU founds Liberation Committee, with Defense Committee
1965:	OAU Defense Commission, 2nd meeting, Freetown
1970:	OAU Defense Commission, 3rd and 4th meetings, Addis Ababa, Lagos
1971:	OAU Defense Commission, 5th meeting, Addis Ababa
1979:	OAU Defense Commission, 6th meeting, Addis Ababa
1981–82:	OAU 1st military peacekeeping, Chad, December 1981–June 1982
1990:	ECOMOG peacemaking in Liberia
1991:	OAU, National Military Observer Group (NMOG) in Rwanda, 55 observers
1993:	OAU Mechanism on Conflict Prevention, Management and Resolution founded
1994–95:	OAU, OAU Mission in Burundi (OMIB) in Burundi, 52 observers
1995:	OAU Peace Fund established; decision to set up peacekeeping brigades in each of five regions
1996:	OAU 1st Chiefs of Staff meeting
1997:	OAU 2nd Chiefs of Staff meeting, Harare

1998:	SADC peacemaking in Lesotho
	ECOMOG peacemaking in Sierra Leone, almost 15,000 at peak
	ECOMOG peacemaking in Guinea-Bissau
	OAU sets up Situation Room in its Conflict Management Centre
	OAU, OAU Mission in Comoros (OMIC) in Comoros, 29 observers
2002:	Protocol Relating to the Establishment of the Peace and Security Council of the African Union signed
2003:	3rd Chiefs of Staff meeting; AU 3,000 peacekeepers in Burundi
2004:	4th African Chiefs of Defense Staff (ACDS) meeting
	1st meeting of African Ministers of Defence
	AU PSC inaugurated
	ASF de facto operational in Darfur, Sudan
	EU Peace Facility account founded
	CISSA founded
	ACSRT founded
2005:	Algerian, Egyptian, Libyan, Mauritanian, SADR, and Tunisian Chiefs of Defense Staff meeting in Tripoli: memorandum of understanding for North African Regional Capability (NARC), African Union Non-Aggression and Common Defense Pact signed, including Article 4.d: "As part of the vision of building a strong and united Africa, State Parties undertake to establish an African Army at the final stage of the political and economic integration of the Continent."
2007:	CEWS set up
	Panel of the Wise set up
	Memorandum of understanding on Cooperation in the Area of Peace and Security between the AU, the RECs, and the Coordinating Mechanisms of the Regional Standby Brigades of Eastern Africa and Northern Africa
2008:	5th ACDS and Heads of Security and Safety Services meeting
2009:	6th ACDS and Heads of Security and Safety Services meeting
2010:	ASF Military Staff Committee founded, meets monthly, only advisory
	ECOWAS sets up in Abuja Observation and Monitoring System, with four subsystems
	SADC sets up Early Warning System, HQ Gaberone
	IGAD sets up Conflict Early Warning and Response Mechanism, Addis Ababa
2011:	7th ACDS and Heads of Security and Safety Services Meeting
2012:	Current peacekeeping and peacemaking operational strength of 23,000 military and police personnel
2013:	Emergency Crisis Prevention Capacity Mechanism

THE AU'S SECURITY IMPACT: SOMALIA AND SUDAN VERSUS LIBYA

The AU's New International Security Dirigsme

In practicing its global security politics, the AU experiences a paradoxical, love-hate relationship with the international community in the security domain. The relationship fosters tensions as well as cooperation with competing global governance bodies—the UNSC, NATO, ICC, USAFRICOM. Both circumstances inhibit as well as enable the AU's ability to achieve its collective security and conflict-resolution goals for Africa. Conflicts in the Sudan, Somalia, Libya, and Côte d'Ivoire occurring since 2008 present case studies illuminating a range of tensions between the AU and the UN as the institution seeks to embody the role of global *Pax Africana*. Be that as it may, the tensions that the AU's PSC encounters in achieving its goals also signify and illustrate significant inroads that the Union is making in the area of African security in international law with regards to war and peace.

As an example, at its January 2012 Eighteenth Session, the Assembly of the Union, while reiterating its commitment to fight international impunity in conformity with the provisions of the Constitutive Act of the AU, additionally stressed the need to explore ways and means that would ensure that the Union's request to the UNSC to defer the ICC warrant on an AU sitting member (Sudan's President Omar al-Bashir). The Assembly expressed the need for its members to support its member states (Malawi, Djibouti, Chad, and Kenya), who in receiving the Sudanese president had appropriately conformed to the Union's noncooperation with the ICC on President Bashir's arrest and surrender. The AU's Decision (Assembly/AU/Dec. 404 XVIII) was premised on its argument that the ICC is not capable of removing an immunity that international law grants to the officials of states that are not parties to the Rome Statute.

As well, when the ICC issued an arrest warrant for the late Muammar Gaddafi in 2011, then AU Commissioner Jean Ping accused the court of being "discriminatory" because it only went after crimes committed in Africa while ignoring crimes committed by Western powers in Iraq, Afghanistan, and Pakistan (Voice of America 2011). The tension was illustrated best at a January 2012 speech that South Africa's President Jacob Zuma gave at the UN. Zuma remarked,

> Critical to building a stronger relationship will be to avoid the situation such as that which transpired during the conflict in Libya last year. As

everybody is aware, the AU developed a political roadmap that would have assisted in resolving the political conflict in that country. That AU's plan was completely ignored in favour of bombing Libya by NATO forces. (United Nations Radio 2012)

Zuma's concerns reflected a long-standing criticism by Africans against the UN. Representing this ideological stance through the vehicle of the AU demonstrated the growing competition between the two suprastate institutions, particularly between the UNSC and the AU's equivalent PSC.

At the heart of Zuma's criticism of the UN are three issues. First, in the global arena, Africans have no voice, no agency, and no power. This is because the UN founding charter of 1945 was ratified at a time when Africans were colonized. As such, this was a period that did not include the voice and representation of Africans. Yet, presently, 70 percent of the issues brought to the UNSC are on Africa while no African country has permanent representation on the world's premiere security institution. Divergent strategies over questions of war and peace in Africa, as well as jurisdictional turf tussles, are reasons for the disagreements between the AU and the UN. Each institution claims overlapping jurisdictional scope in determining who oversees peace and security matters on the African continent.

The AU's UNSC-equivalent security organ, the PSC, states in one article (16.1) of its protocol that the AU "has the primary responsibility for promoting peace, security and stability in Africa," but in another (17.1) that the UN has the "primary responsibility for the maintenance of international peace and security." On the other hand, the UN Charter claims that the UNSC possesses universal jurisdiction over international conflict, including conflicts in Africa. Therefore, the UN's policies imply that the AU's jurisdiction in global affairs is subsumed under the UN's. The UN Charter's Chapter 8 classifies the AU as a regional organization that must seek permission to act from the UNSC (African Union 2011). However, the current principle of subsidiarity practiced by regional organizations could tilt international law and custom in the AU's favor. The tussle over international law is reflected in the AU's capacity to carry out security functions for the continent. In 2011, both the Côte d'Ivoire and Libyan conflicts underscored the realpolitik significance of these new fissures between the AU and the UN.

Nonetheless, the UN and AU relations are not always contentious as the two international governmental organizations have forged successful cooperation in African affairs on most occasions. As seen from the AU's peace keeping operations in the Sudan-Darfur (UNAMID) and in Somalia (AMISOM), in both cases the

AU-UN relationship can be described in terms of multilateral cooperation. For example, in November 2006, the then secretary-general of the UN, Kofi Annan, and the former chairperson of the AU Commission, Alpha Oumar Konaré, signed a joint declaration titled, "Enhancing UN-AU Cooperation: Framework for the Ten-Year Capacity Building Programme for the AU."

The agreement sought to increase cooperation between the two organizations by enhancing UN system engagement with the AU and other regional organizations in Africa, particularly in the area of peace and security. In its own words, the objective of the framework was to "enhance the capacity of the AU Commission and subregional organizations to act as effective UN partners in addressing the challenges to human security in Africa."

Asymmetrical Multilateral Cooperation in Somalia and the Sudan

The first real test of the Union's peacekeeping capacity occurred in the Sudan. AMIS was established in 2006 when the AU deployed a peacekeeping mission to Sudan. The action was precipitated by an AU Abuja Treaty, which oversaw the signing of the Humanitarian Ceasefire Agreement on April 8, 2005 by the government of Sudan, the Sudan People's Liberation Movement/Army (SPLM/A), and the Justice and Equality Movement (JEM). AMIS was deployed with a mandate to monitor and observe compliance with the Humanitarian Ceasefire Agreement, assist in the process of confidence building, and contribute to securing the environment for the delivery of humanitarian relief and, beyond that, the return of internally displaced persons and refugees. In its three-year heyday, AMIS has deployed a force of 3,320 personnel with 1,647 soldiers as part of the protection force in AMIS I from Nigeria (587), Rwanda (392), Gambia (196), Senegal (196), Kenya (35), and South Africa (241); and 6,171 in AMIS II (the strengthened peacekeeping force) with increased troops from Nigeria (2,040), Rwanda (1,756), and Senegal (538). There are also new troops that have been deployed from Chad and Gambia.

For AMIS II, the second stage of the mission, the AU received financial assistance from the EU and turned to NATO for more resources to improve the mission's capacity. The almost collaboration with NATO, however, divided the AU member states and especially angered the Sudan, introducing greater internationalized tensions into the Sudan conflict, which certainly undermined its resolution. Moreover, while AMIS had set up to address the Darfur conflict, the UN established its Mission in Sudan (UNMIS) at the same time as AMIS to implement the resolution of the Global Peace Agreement for Southern Sudan, a different Sudan conflict (the long-standing north-south war that culminated in the country's division into two in 2011 and the establishment of Africa's fifty-sixth state, South Sudan).

Given AMIS's resource and capacity limitations in Darfur with only about five thousand troops, the AU requested its replacement with a UN peacekeeping force. Rather than establish a second mission in the Sudan, the UN decided to extend UNMIS's mandated to Darfur authorizing twenty thousand soldiers. Using the AU as vehicle, the Sudan rejected the UN mission and refused to allow UN troops into Darfur. It was amid this global power play among the UN, the AU, and the government of Sudan that in 2008 the unprecedented joint AU/UN hybrid operation in Darfur (UNAMID) was born, currently with 23,466 uniformed personnel on the ground, the largest peacekeeping mission in the world. The government of Sudan would also use its influence as an AU member state to shape Africanization of the hybrid operation by insisting on the African composition of the forces (Mubiala 2012, 370). As a result, the UNAMID leadership command consists of AU-UN high-level representatives from Nigeria, Ghana, Somalia, Rwanda, and Niger. Violence has dramatically fallen in Darfur from its 2003 level.

The AU set up AMISOM in 2007 in accordance with the UN Charter's Chapter 8 on "Regional Arrangements," which declared that the AU's peacekeeping mission would create conditions for a UN follow-up mission. Africa's mission had its roots in the Horn of Africa's Intergovernmental Authority on Development (IGAD, made up of Djibouti, Eritrea, Ethiopia, Somalia, Sudan, South Sudan, Kenya, Uganda) Peace Support Mission in Somalia (IGASOM), a peacekeeping mission of an African Regional Economic Community (REC) that was established to support the reconciliation process in Somalia and the security and ceasefire monitoring activities of the country's transition federal authorities. Its goal had also been to replace it by an AU support mission.

The African mission was deployed on March 6, 2007, with Ugandan troops following Ethiopia's military intervention in December 2006 into neighboring Somalia to make it possible for the transitional government to take back control of the capital. For the AU, the deployment of AMISOM represented an initial phase of the stabilization of Somalia, in support of the political process. It would contribute to creating the conditions for the deployment of a UN operation for long- term stabilization and post conflict resolution in Somalia (Tehindrazanarivelo 2012, 400). AMISOM is mandated to conduct Peace Support Operations in Somalia to stabilize the situation in the country in order to create conditions for the conduct of humanitarian activities and an immediate take over by the UN.

The mission consists of four divisions: police, humanitarian, military, and political affairs. The military component is the largest of the four, currently comprising just over 9,500 troops. The AMISOM military provides protection to the country's Transitional Federal Institutions as they carry out their functions and guard key infrastructure including the Adden Adde International Airport and the State House (Villa Somalia). The Political Affairs Unit aids Somalia's Transitional Federal Government in the search for an inclusive political process, the reestablishment of functioning state institutions, and the implementation of a clear national vision and road map for the transition in accordance with the terms of the Djibouti Agreement. In support of efforts to stabilize the situation in the country, the unit monitors, interprets, and reports on political and other developments throughout Somalia, as well as provides advice on political processes. The unit is responsible for the implementation of political decisions on Somalia taken by the AUPSC and is helping build up the capacity of the nation's public service.

AMISOM is the AU's longest peacekeeping operation, and to date, over five years after its launching, a UN mission has not replaced AMISOM despite both an AU PSC and UNSC mandate to do so. Nonetheless, for the AU, Somalia represents an African national, local, and people environment through which the institution is realizing its goals. Despite challenges, the mission's military operation has succeeded in pushing back al-Shabaab (the extremist successor to the Islamic Courts Union), the Islamic militia group that had overrun the country since the mid-2000s. The military mission has taken back control of 70 percent of the country, especially securing much more substantively the Somali capital at Mogadishu. Nevertheless, the operation continues to undergo crucial challenges in terms of troops shortage. Whereas 8,000 troops were pledged initially in 2007, only 3,500 were actually assigned for over three years, notwithstanding the current 17,500 troops; however, compared to NATO's 150,000 troops in Afghanistan, AMISOM's troop level in Somalia is still very limited.

AMISOM's political mission in Somalia must be commended. While setbacks occur often in the stabilization and hand over of the transitional national government to a formal constitutional process and government for the country, the AU succeeds in facilitating that process with a political solution to the ongoing Somali crisis. There are many challenges to this process as well, as AMISOM experiences mandate problems. Its support for the Transitional Federal Government and Ethiopian military intervention have created a bias perception that the militant Islamic Courts Union, and later al-Shabaab, has exploited to challenge the AU's legitimacy in peacemaking in the country. Be that as it may, AMISOM attempts to influence the hearts and minds of Somali people whose resistance to AU troops and the larger mission has substantially declined as they value the legitimacy of the African conflict- resolution process and the gradual return of peace to the country (see *AMISOM Magazine*).

Finally, there are challenges in AMISOM's operational cooperation with the UN in Somalia despite the fact that the African mission is operated solely by the AU. The UN cooperates with the AU mission in boosting capacity in terms of logistical and intelligence support; however, after two failed peacekeeping missions in Somalia itself—UMOSOM I and II— international cooperation in Somalia has led to international competition with the AU. UN and AU military technocrats squabble over command, strategy, personnel, and resources, which are crucial factors that undermine the mission.

Hegemonic Global Tensions and the Case of Libya

The conflict in Libya (2011) perhaps drew some of the sorest international legitimacy challenges for the AU. This occurred not only because of Libya's geopolitical strategic influence as an Organization of Petroleum Exporting Countries (OPEC) state and its previous conflicts with the West (UK Lockerbie and the US) as a pariah state in the international scene; it also occurred as a result of the fact that the violence and war in the country was ushered in on the trails of the Arab Spring. Libya's conflict began as a prodemocracy opposition movement that degenerated to civil war. Of course, like the Sudan, for the AU, Libya represents a big state, and its fallen leader, the late Muammar Gaddafi, was an even huger influence in shaping the orientation and establishment of a strengthened AU.

All of these interconnected, multilayered factors contributed to the PSC's extremely challenged conflict- resolution agenda for the Libyan conflict of 2011. The AU's initiatives and policies toward the country in this regard were laced with various iterations and layers of hegemonic power jockeying for influence, interests, and stakes within the country as well as outside, especially emanating from the UNSC and NATO, as well as French, British, and US foreign policy.

As did the Northern African Arab Spring, especially in Tunisia and Egypt, Libya's conflict fostered an intensive debate within the AU Assembly about the chicken-and-egg conundrum that the cases presented in terms of dictatorship versus imperialism. Was Benghazi a prodemocracy movement that should have been supported by the Union's nonindifference aggression clause for peacekeeping intervention? Or should external NATO aggression in Libya have been coun-teracted in Libya by the Union's protection of member states' aggression pact? Former President Mbeki would ask, "The stark choice we faced was—should we side with the demonstrators or with the governments they demanded should resign!" (*Guardian* 2011). The principles of *Pax Africana*, nonindifference, and responsibility to protect would be tested through the Libyan case on the one hand; but so would Africa's common defense policy and nonaggression act against external imperialism.

In spite of vitriolic contentious debates over deciding how to intervene in Libya, the AU's PSC did formulate an intervention policy. The Union's first position was an ideological one allied to its values embedded in *Pax Africana*. Significantly in this regard, unlike the Arab League, the AU unequivocally rejected UN Resolution 1973 (2011) and the ultimate NATO attack on Libya launched as Operation Odyssey, while simultaneously condemning the Gaddafi regime's suppression of the uprising. The AU's PSC proceeded to convene a high-level meeting on March 26, 2011, calling for an immediate ceasefire and initiation of a dialogue between the warring parties, and proceeded to draw up a road map to resolve the crisis, including the formation of a transitional government, the holding of elections, and the building of democratic institutions to meet the aspirations of all Libyans.

The AU could not have treated the Libyan crisis in the same way that it addressed Sudan-Darfur or Somalia. The Libyan civil war erupted quickly in a matter of months (December 2010 to March 2011 when it crystallized into outright war). Moreover, the Arab Spring nature of the conflict and Gaddafi's response of aggression invited immediate responses for intervention from the UN, Britain, France, and the United States. As a result, rather than a peacekeeping mission in Libya, the AU's PSC embarked upon a conflict- resolution framework embodied by the establishment a PSC High-Level Ad Hoc Committee on the Situation in Libya on March 10, 2011 and a road map that underscored a political solution to the crisis.

A political solution to conflict resolution in Libya would use the AU as a broker for negotiations among international and domestic partners in conflict on a ceasefire and the establishment of an inclusive transitional period, during which the necessary reforms to address the causes of the crisis would be under-taken. The transition would culminate in democratic elections to enable the Libyan people to freely choose their leaders and make it possible to promote, in a sustainable way, the legitimate aspirations of the Libyan people for reform, democracy, good governance, and the rule of law. For the AU, such a verifiable and internationally monitored ceasefire would be key, both to creating conducive conditions for successful negotiations among the Libyan parties and also to ensuring the protection of the civilian population in accordance with UN Resolution 1973.

As such, while willing to cooperate with the UN, the Arab League, and other multilateral organizations in solving the crisis in Libya, the AU had a number of disagreements that it would not concede to. First, it claimed supremacy over jurisdiction to settle the Libyan crisis. In one resolution, the PSC announced that it welcomed the steps taken and efforts made to interact with AU international partners, in particular the UN, the League of Arab States, the Organization of Islamic Cooperation (OIC), and the EU, as well as the Libya Contact Group, the BRICS, and bilateral partners. However, it also urged the ad hoc committee and the AU Commission to continue to request the said partners to extend the necessary cooperation to the AU's efforts, bearing in mind the provisions of Chapter 8 of the UN Charter on the role of regional arrangements in the settlement of disputes among and within their member states (African Union Peace and Security Council 2011). In this regard, the AU was invoking its jurisdiction to settle the conflict on behalf of the African region.

The AU PSC also disagreed with the international community on using a military solution to settle the conflict—especially one that targeted regime change. Its resolutions would stress the need for all countries and organizations involved in the implementation of UNSC Resolution 1973 to act in a manner fully consistent with international legality and the resolution's provisions, whose objective is solely to ensure the protection of the civilian population. The PSC urged implementers of Resolution 1973 to refrain from actions, including military operations targeting Libyan senior officials and socioeconomic infrastructure, that would further compound the situation and make it more difficult to achieve international consensus on the best way forward.

An AU delegate addressed the UNSC on the PSC's disagreements. Referring to the AU's Non-Aggression and Common Defence Pact, he proclaimed that an attack on Libya or any other member of the AU without express agreement by the AU would be a dangerous provocation on Africa. He warned that careless assaults on the sovereignty of African countries were tantamount to inflicting fresh wounds on the destiny of Africans whereby foreign invasions, meddling, and interventions had caused Africa to become more disadvantaged on account of foreign meddling. The delegate accused the UN of ignoring the AU for three months so that it could sustain bombings on the "sacred land of Africa." He accused the UN of being high-handed, arrogant, and provocative and presented an alternative mandate to the UNSC:

It is essential that the UN Security Council works with the African Union to ensure that a ceasefire is immediately established with an effective and verifiable monitoring mechanism and dialogue embarked upon, leading to a political process including transitional arrangements and the necessary reforms. The crisis in Libya requires a political solution and not a military one; and the AU Road Map is the most viable option (Rugunda 2011).

Libya was not the first time that the AU had recommended its political solution to resolve African conflict. It had done so in the 2002–7 Zimbabwe crisis and disagreed with the international community (specifically the United Kingdom, the Commonwealth, and the United States) on its preference for a military option and regime change as well. A political solution was also the AU's preferred conflict-resolution policy for Sudan-Darfur before AMIS and for Côte d'Ivoire in its 2011 civil war over an election crisis. For the AU, a political solution to conflict resolution in Africa was consistent with Africans' consensus values whereby the legitimate aspirations of all parties to the conflicts would be met.

CONCLUSION: INTERDEPENDENT *PAX AFRICANA*

As it expands the development of its security architecture, the AU's capacity to eradicate conflict on the continent and influence a security agenda for Africa is growing stronger, despite what Benedict Franke describes as the emerging suprastate's ambition-resource gap, whereby the AU's ambitious goals for the continent surpass the Union's ability to pay for and implement its programs in the arenas of peacekeeping operations (Franke 2009). The Sudan, Somali, and Libyan cases illustrate the paradoxical love-hate relationship between the two organizations' security councils. The UN will exercise its right to overpower the AU in intervening in cases of geopolitical power, significance, and interest (Libya) while it will cooperate with the AU in unstrategic cases (Somalia) while it assures that it exercises its supremacy. In the Sudan, for example, the AU-UN hybrid partnership has been described as a hybrid form of paternalism where AU troops and personnel do the basic and dangerous work on the ground and are guided by the all-wise and fatherly coterie of UN advisors.

In the arena of global governance, the AU-UN relationship remains an asymmetrical one given that the UN enjoys universal global membership including its core super power members and is a much older institution with more resources and peacekeeping experience compared to the AU. Rather than a partnership, because the advice and resources are unidirectional—flowing from the UN to the AU (Murithi 2007)—the UN is positioned in a hegemonic position in relation to the AU. Nonetheless, by fostering genuine partnership between the UNSC and the AU to work together in finding a lasting solution to the crisis in Libya, the AU established a moral standard for the international community to follow. The Libyan case demonstrates the dynamism and strengthening of the AU's ideological posture vis-à-vis its engagement with global governance in the security arena. The Union's alternative intervention into the Libyan conflict enlivened its moral mandate of *Pax Africana* Pan-Africanism and high-level diplomatic peacemaking.

At the close of the Seventeenth AU Summit in July 2011, the then chairperson of the AU, President Obiang Nguema Mbagoso of Equatorial Guinea, noted the concerns of the AU's security agenda in a global era. He affirmed that the ideological underpinning behind the Union's strategy had been to defend all of the people involved in the crisis in Libya as well as to defend the integrity of the African continent. He added that the members' declaration in support of a road map and a political solution had strengthened the unity of Africa because the majority of delegations at the summit had reaffirmed their commitment to the map prepared by the AU. The message to the international community was that the AU was garnering greater respect in regard to issues concerning the continent.

The AU's assertiveness regarding Libya may not have concluded with the outcomes that an authentic application of *Pax Africana* would have expected—that the AU (Africa) resolved the conflict in Libya rather than imperialistic external forces. Nevertheless, the AU's diplomatic persistence in presenting a moral and legal challenge to the UN may have fostered a model of *Pax Africana* that can be described as interdependent. UN Resolution 2085 and the African-led International Support Mission in Mali (AFISMA) serve as pointers to this interdependence. The positive outcome of the AU's diplomatic assertiveness regarding Libya and the Sudan and its relative success in Somalia has fostered the quadripartite cooperation among nation-state (Mali), subregion (ECOWAS), continental/regional (AU), and global (UN) that has culminated in Mali 2012.

While initial tensions existed between the AU and ECOWAS over which organization had jurisdiction over resolution of the conflict in Mali, the vague issue of subsidiarity (REC acts first if it has capacity) was set aside with the AU delegating authoritative leadership to—and in cooperation with—ECOWAS. Both organizations played a significant role in pushing out the Malian junta and restoring partial civilian rule, which they would use to leverage global support for the intervention. Once this had occurred, speaking in Addis Ababa, the Ethiopian capital, Ramtane Lamamra, AU Peace and Security Commissioner, said that the PSC would lift the suspension of Mali from the activities of the AU so that the country could participate in the conflict resolution in the north. All three institutions (including the Malian democratic regime) played a role in designing and lobbying for the UNSC resolution. Because the resolution was not funded, not only does the AU coordinate the hybrid force, it also is forced to mobilize critical funds and resources for the hybrid.

As a consequence of encroaching internationalization of conflict in Africa— Somalia, Côte d'Ivoire, Libya, and Mali directly, and the Sudan and Kenya indirectly—the AU Assembly agreed to establish an emergency intervention force to quell such conflicts across the continent. The new force would be an interim measure until the long-planned ASF becomes fully operational. The AU viewed the ICC's act against elected Kenyan leaders as a violation of sovereignty that it would protect for its member country whose public have just showed their confidence in their leaders and systems. Hence, the AU should send a clear message to the ICC that this is not tolerated. "'Kenya's request has strongly been supported at the level of heads state,' AU Peace and Security Commissioner Ramtane Lamamara told journalists. '. . . it's not for the court of the north to try leaders in the south'" (Redi 2013, 22).

Kwame Nkrumah's vision of a *Pax Africana* is nascent in the contemporary geopolitical maneuvers that the AU embarks upon to achieve the continent's CADSP and eliminate conflict and violence in its weak states. Pan-Africanist self-determination remains a foremost objective for African union in this regard. For Africa's many security problems, African intelligence and home-grown resolutions (African solutions) designed, formulated, and managed by African institutions, drawn from local and national African contexts and scenarios, and designed to improve the livelihoods of African peoples, characterize the most valuable elements of the continent's CADSP and striving for *Pax Africana*.

Driving the Pan-African Economic Agenda: Ideology and Institutionalism

In reflecting on the African Union's (AU's) first ten years of achievements and challenges, founding AU chairperson Thabo Mbeki revealed the foremost rationale for the institution's establishment. It would transform and modernize the African economies to end the unequal and exploitative economic relations between Africa and the West. It would end Africa's economic marginalization and the continent's unequal access to the claimed benefits of globalization (Mbeki 2012b).

The agenda that Mbeki refers to was presented in more practical detail at the Union's January 2012 Eighteenth Summit, "Boosting Intra-African Trade." The Assembly members who convened for the annual meeting of heads of states reaffirmed the provisions of the Accra Declaration of December 2011 asserting the ultimate objective of African integration and its resultant effect of achieving development and a renaissance for the continent. The Assembly invited other member states to join hands to map out more resilient regional and continental integration policies between the continent's Regional Economic Communities (RECs) and the AU organs with focus on priority actions capable of leading, in the shortest possible time, to the free movement of persons, goods, and services and the building of various intra- and intercommunity infrastructures required to speed up the process.

The January 2012 Summit underscored the importance of the Union in working closely with the continent's RECs to develop recommendations on currency convertibility as a crucial factor of economic and commercial integration. As well, it called upon its member states to take the necessary steps to involve the peoples of Africa and the diaspora in the integration process, which it claimed would be the sole guarantee of African renaissance and the affirmation of Africa in the concert of nations.

Striving for ownership and operation of Africa's economic future has deep historical roots in Pan-Africanism. Kwame Nkrumah's mantra, "Africa must unite," had economics as its strategy and politics as its goal. Already conscious of the way that colonial balkanization would lead to the neocolonialism of Africa, particularly as most of Africa's new nations were too small to avert economic dependency in a then globalizing economy, Nkrumah advocated African union with specific economic goals. It would be a means for African independent nations to establish independent currency and financial institutions, to break the pattern of economic exploitation established through colonialism, and to reconstruct African economics to achieve higher living standards for all African nations—big or small (Marah 2007, 24).

Nkrumah's vision evolved as an idea through several historical phases of African union. The Organization of African Unity (OAU) and United Nations Economic Commission for Africa (UNECA) authored the 1980 Lagos Plan of Africa (LPA) that first outlined a Pan-Africanist integration plan through the continent's existing RECs. In 1994, the OAU members ratified the establishment of the African Economic Community (AEC), also known as the Abuja Treaty. The AEC would achieve a continent-wide economic and monetary union and a Pan-African Parliament (PAP) between 2028 and 2034 after completing five phases: creation of regional blocs (by 1999), strengthening intra-REC integration (2007), establishing free trade areas and customs unions in each bloc (2017), establishing a continent-wide free trade area and customs union (2019), and establishing a continent-wide African Common Market (2023). Most recently, the AU's Minimum Integration Program revised the penultimate stages of this sequence. The RECs, after each becomes a free trade area, should aim at harmonizing into a continental free trade area before attempting the next stage of becoming a customs union. Of course, within the RECs, Africa already has four customs unions:

- Communauté Économique et Monétaire de l'Afrique Centrale (CEMAC)
- East African Community (EAC)

- Southern African Customs Union (SACU)
- Union Économique et Monétaire Ouest-Africaine (UEMOA)

In new postcolonial scholarly interpretations attempting to explain the dynamic and direction of African international political-economies, the Eighteenth Summit's decisions and ratifications would have been described as an ideological regime known as "African owned and operated development" whereby a cadre of postapartheid African leaders—many of whom were founders of the new AU—referred to a self-reliant path to African development (Edozie 2004). Recognizing transformations in the post–Cold War global environment in the early twenty-first century, African leaders would seek to redefine the continent's role vis-à-vis the millennial global agenda by shifting the burden of global engagement back to Africa (Khadiagala and Lyons 2001). Mbeki again articulated this position best when he wrote, "A balance between our rights and duties as Africans to protest against an unjust world order and our need to practically engage our development partners with a partnership that breaks the old relationship between hapless African recipients of aid and benevolent donors must be created" (Mbeki 2002b).

The AU's economic agenda aspires to engage with the new global economy in distinctive ways that would break with the past as Mbeki asserts. It would establish a continent-wide economic community by engaging strategically in international political economic structures of regional economic integration, international trade, and foreign direct investment, aid, and development. Each sector overlaps, intersects, and reinforces each other while undergirding the dirigisme of the Union's economic suborganizations: the AEC program, the African Central Bank (ACB), the African Investment Bank (AIB), the African Monetary Fund (AMF and its all-Africa currency, the Gold Mandela), and the New Partnership for Africa's Development (NEPAD).

The AEC treaty is a key norm driver of all these institutions. In 2002, all signatories to the AU's Constitutive Act also pledged to establish the AEC, initially established ten years earlier by the OAU as the historic 1991 Abuja Treaty, to promote the socioeconomic development of Africa, and they declared that the provisions of the Constitutive Act would take precedence over and supersede any inconsistent or contrary provisions of the treaty establishing the AEC. In this regard, through Africa's AEC, the AU would establish on a continental scale a framework for the development, mobilization, and utilization of the human and material resources of Africa in order to achieve self-reliant development (El-Agraa 2004). Upon its establishment in 2002, the AU took immediate steps to incorporate and revitalize the goal of African economic integration into its Constitutive Act and its new agenda for Africa in the twenty-first century.

With the establishment of the AEC agenda, Africa's economic agenda in the new millennium has been incorporated into the fabric of the Union's architecture. Of fourteen subarticles that make up the Constitutive Act's article 3, "Objectives," five (arts. 3.i–m), outline the organization's political-economic objectives. They are to

(i) establish the necessary conditions which enable the continent to play its rightful role in the global economy and in international negotiations;

(j) promote sustainable development at the economic, social and cultural levels as well as the integration of African economies;

(k) promote co-operation in all fields of human activity to raise the living standards of African peoples;

(l) coordinate and harmonize the policies between the existing and future Regional Economic Communities for the gradual attainment of the objectives of the Union; [and]

(m) advance the development of the continent by promoting research in all fields, especially in science and technology.

Subarticles (j), (k), and (m) are economic outcomes and thus follow from subarticle (i), which is a goal. That is to say, the AU's raison d'etre is to enable fifty-five African countries and a billion African people to have a productive role in the contemporary global economy that promotes sustainable development for them, raises living standards for them, and gives them access to science and technology. Subarticle (l) is a strategy, and its integrationist narrative perhaps speaks to the core existence and advancement of Africa's Pan-African union.

NEPAD, an important suborgan of the AU, has been its most prominent economic institutional innovation. Established independently from the AU in 2001—though fully, officially, and comprehensively incorporated into the AU as the NEPAD Planning and Coordination Agency (NPCA) suborgan in 2010—NEPAD was founded to navigate for Africans new parameters of the international political economy. Unlike the AU's ACB, AIB, and AMF, whose goals are to advance continental economic regionalism, NPCA is an economic organization of the AU that serves to consolidate national economic arenas and reintegrate them into global development opportunities. It achieves its goals through a range of global policy initiatives and pacts such as public-private partnerships.

Another set of economic institutions are the AU's RECs, which are loose affiliations of the Union, today with incrementally closer articulation because they are critical to its integration goal. In addition to further advancing and in many ways reinforcing Africans' integrationist goal to create an economic community covering the whole of the African continent (Oppong 2010), the OAU-AEC Abuja Treaty would seek to endow RECs with supranational authority that would sanction noncompliance with regional arrangements, as well as establish a transparent link between the institution of the AEC and African member states (Ikome 2007). Thus, while Africa's RECs are not members of the AEC or the AU, they are its geographic building blocks (Oppong 2010, 92–103). The Economic Community of West African States (ECOWAS), the Southern African Development Community (SADC), the Common Market for Eastern and Southern Africa (COMESA), and the East African Community (EAC) are four of the most viable of the continent's fourteen RECs. The AU's goal, in relation to these multiple miniregional economic organizations, nonetheless, is to coordinate their activities, harmonize their economic policies, and foster their progressive integration into a single AU-AEC economic and political union.

This chapter examines the AU's economic agenda analyzing the norms, values, and strategies that the institution uses to achieve its objectives and posits the following thesis. We argue that the AU's economic agenda builds on the AEC whereby Pan-Africanist member states resolved to fully erase intra-African trade barriers and create a single African economy of scale to compete in the global economy and achieve a 2034 vision for Africa to become a suprapolitical institution that governs such an economy. The AEC has acted as ideological bedrock as well as institutional rubric, and thus a vehicle for integration that the AU uses to aspire to a continent-wide economic community. A consequence of this is that the AU's economic agenda remains in contestation with the neoliberal global governance international arena.

The AU Commission's suborgans and the AU Assembly's ministerial Specialized Technical Committees (STCs) imbibe the AEC ideology to carry forth the AU's objectives; while the AU's financial institutions are innovations that it has created to more comprehensively implement its economic agenda, they remain to be implemented as this book goes to press. On the other hand, the continent's RECs—ECOWAS, SADC, EAC, COMESA—continue to present mesolevel models and experiments of what a continent-wide economic union would look like and that the AU engages in to achieve its economic goals.

How one evaluates this framework in relation to Africa's Pan-Africanist economic objectives, achievements, challenges, and our own key insights is the main objective of the current chapter. We examine the AU's goals to achieve regional economic integration, development, and greater, more dynamic inclusion and participation in a new global economy. In the process, we analyze and assess the AU's institutional economic organs, activities, and trajectories in the context of economic globalization, while asking several important questions: What are Africans' economic aspirations in this era, and what role is the AU playing in achieving these goals? How do African member states participate in AU economic initiatives through its suborgans and RECs, and why do they participate? What measurable gains has the AU achieved in eradicating African underdevelopment and integrating the continent into the global economy? The chapter illustrates the supranational agency of the Union in this respect by examining the regional and international organization's creation and facilitation of new economic principles, strategies, and institutions that would better navigate the complexities of the millennial global economy (see table 6.1).

We use this thesis and our research questions to assess the AU's progress in making an impact on Africans' economic agenda and developmental prospects. The chapter will demonstrate that with regard to impact in the African economy, it is unclear whether the AU has made much progress in terms of measurable development outcomes or whether the AU has made substantial enough progress toward its own goals toward economic integration and union; however, the chapter reveals that there has been observable progress made in the areas of strengthening the ideology of economic self-reliance and self-determination among Africans. The AU appears to be gradually increasing and deepening cross- and intraregional institutional relationships among member states through the proliferation of the number of development initiatives and projects while consolidating development operations across the continent.

Subsequent subsections will present a more detailed analysis of the AU's economic goals in relation to current trends in the global economy and Africa's positionality. This will be followed by a description and analysis of the AU's economic organs or suborganizations that it uses to drive various aspects of its economic goals. The section will examine AU activities, events, and initiatives in the areas of integration, intracontinental trade, foreign direct investment, and aid. Final and concluding sections will assess the impact of the AU's economic agenda in the national and global arenas while considering the possibilities and implications of an African political-economic union by 2034.

TABLE 6.1. AFRICA'S ECONOMIC AGENDA

AFRICAN ECONOMIC COMMUNITY (AEC)

THE IDEOLOGICAL BEDROCK OF THE AU'S ECONOMIC AGENDA: The 1991 Abuja Treaty called for OAU (now AU) member states to create favorable conditions for the actualization of integration and to establish harmonizing national economic policies in accordance with the Treaty's integrationist agenda.

AU FINANCIAL INSTITUTIONS

ACB, Johannesburg	ACB is aimed at building a common monetary policy and creating an African currency.
AIB, Tripoli	AIB will ideally promote investment activities of the public and private sectors intended to advance regional integration of the member states of the AU.
AMF, Abuja	The main objective of the AMF is to facilitate the integration of African economies through the elimination of trade restrictions and by enhancing greater monetary integration.

AU COMMISSION ORGANS AND MINISTERIAL TECHNICAL COMMITTEES

Infrastructure and Energy Trade and Industry Rural Economy and Agriculture Economic Affairs	The AU Commission is charged with the key day-to-day management of the Union, among many other responsibilities. It is also charged with elaborating, promoting, coordinating, and harmonizing the programs and policies of the Union with those of the RECs. Four of eight of the commission's portfolios are dedicated to the Union's economic agenda.
The Committee on Rural Economy and Agricultural Matters The Committee on Monetary and Financial Affairs The Committee on Trade, Customs, and Immigration Matters The Committee on Industry, Science and Technology, Energy, Natural Resources and Environment The Committee on Transport, Communications, and Tourism.	At the AU Assembly's ministerial level, five of the AU's STCs are strategically oriented toward the sectoral strengthening and harmonization initiatives.

AU REGIONAL ECONOMIC COMMUNITIES AND NEPAD

REGIONAL ECONOMIC COMMUNITIES	The Abuja Treaty of 1991 specifies that the regional economic communities are the cornerstones "to establishing a Customs Union at the continental level" (art. 6.2.d). The Constitutive Act of the African Union in 2002 commits the states to "coordinate and harmonize the policies between . . . Regional Economic Communities for the gradual attainment of the objectives of the Union" (art. 3.l).
ECOWAS	ECOWAS is a customs union but not a free trade area, though the REC does foster aggressive monetary cooperation with a goal of establishing a common currency, the "eco," by 2020.
COMESA-SADC-EAC	The supra-REC's main objective is the strengthening and deepening economic integration of the southern and eastern Africa region achieved through harmonizing policies and programs of the three RECs in the areas of trade, customs, and infrastructure development.
CFA	Dominant in West Africa although extending to cover central Africa as well, the CFA has been a monetary union for twenty-five years encompassing 123 million people in fourteen different Francophone African countries in two separate monetary unions— UEMOA and UDEAC.
NEW PARTNERSHIP FOR AFRICAN DEVELOPMENT (NEPAD)	An organ of the AU based in Midrand, South Africa, NEPAD is the AU's socioeconomic development program with diplomatic benefits and immunities.

VISION 2063 AFRICAN UNION GOVERNMENT AND ECONOMY—NKRUMAH'S DREAM

The AEC would achieve a continent-wide economic and monetary union and Pan-African Parliament by 2028 after completing five phases: creation of regional blocs (by 1999), strengthening intra-REC integration (2007), establishing free trade areas and customs unions in each bloc (2017), establishing continent-wide free trade area and customs union (2019); and establishing a continent-wide Africa Common Market (2023).

The Political Economy of the AU's Owned and Operated Development Ideology

In the new millennium, the African economic agenda is ideological; it has to be if it is to persuade fifty-five sovereign economies to participate. This is how it goes: economic unity or continent-wide regionalism, realized through Africans' self-determined efforts is Africa's means to an end to achieve economic parity for Africans vis-à-vis a postmodern global economy. Ownership and operation of the African economic agenda is a value that is rooted in the Pan-African discourse whose objective has long-standing roots in facilitating collective African political renewal, in reversing marginalization and downward trends of socioeconomic decline that are common to Africa, and in interjecting African economies into the mainstream global political economy to foster greater production, trade, and thus development and wealth creation for the continent (Adejumobi and Olukoshi 2008, 4).

Even the wealthier African countries—South Africa, Egypt, and Nigeria— share in the reality that their respective nations overdepend on former colonizers and economic superpowers, and in the tragedy that, despite laden resource and human potential, neither they nor other Africans have been able to develop their material human potential relative to the rest of the world. The fact of history—colonialism—the postindependent struggle against neocolonialism, and the yearnings for poverty reduction and development continue to unite African nations and peoples around economic union (Adejumobi and Olukoshi 2008, 4).

In 2002, the AU's reason for its establishment was to leverage African underdevelopment realities. Caused by a colonial legacy, the balkanization of Africa's economic space was for AU architects a commonplace theory. The continent consists of the world's smallest states with more than thirty states having populations of less than ten million. Only eleven of the fifty-five states have populations exceeding twenty-five million people; however, this minority of states accounts for 64 percent of the continent's population and over two-thirds of the continent's output (Ikome 2007).

By way of its establishment in the AU predecessor, the OAU, Africans' ownership economic agenda has had time to evolve ideologically as the continent laid out numerous blueprints for several decades. The LPA, established in 1980, was the first continent-wide effort by Africans to forge a comprehensive, unified approach to the continent's economic development. LPA has been described as Africa's fourth stage of economic regionalism and modeled around a collective self-reliance approach (Ikome 2007). In the words of the African heads of government, the preamble of the LPA read,

> The effect of unfulfilled promises of global development strategies has been more sharply felt in Africa than in other continents in the world. . . . Faced with this situation [the devastating effects of global economic crisis on

Africa], and determined to undertake measures for the basic restructuring of the economic base of our continent, we resolved to adopt a far-reaching regional approach based primarily on collective self-reliance. (OAU preamble, para. 1 in Shaw, 1981)

Because LPA was merely a pledge and a blueprint to guide Africa's separate national economies, its most important value was the ideological grounding for the 1991 AEC. The AEC or Abuja Treaty (as it is often referred to) incorporated LPA's principles of collective self-reliance while establishing new institutional mechanisms for African states and peoples to achieve economic integration and to mobilize their skills and financial support (Asante, Nwonwu, and Muzvidziwa 2001). Two important principles were articulated. First is the AEC's first-time establishment of institutional parameters and a framework to implement integration. The treaty called for member states to undertake to create favorable conditions for the actualization of integration and to establish harmonizing national economic policies in accordance with the treaty's integrationist agenda.

A second important principle established by the AEC demonstrates the gradualist ideological longevity of the African economic integration agenda. As with the 2012 Eighteenth Summit, "Boosting Intra-African Trade," the 1991 Abuja Treaty Summit two decades earlier would emphasize a break with the neoliberal market approach to integration recommended by the Washington Consensus at the time, and instead emphasize the development of the continent's productive capacity as a prerequisite for increased intra-African trade (Asante, Nwonwu, and Muzvidziwa 2001). The AEC Treaty called on member states to focus on agriculture, mining, and industry as well as on the development and diversification of Africa's productive base. The goal then was to increase locally produced goods and services, which would give rise to more intra-African trade flows (Asante, Nwonwu, and Muzvidziwa 2001).

The Abuja Treaty was a building block for the AU whose goal by 2034 is to achieve political and economic integration and union. Despite the ambiguity of the AU/AEC relationship—after all, the Abuja Treaty of 1991 called for the establishment of three Africa regional organizations (AU, AEC, and PAP)—the AU has been able to establish its supremacy over the PAP and the AEC. Replacing the OAU Charter, which brokered the AEC, the AU's Constitutive Act resolved AU members to accelerate the process of implementing the Abuja Treaty to promote the socioeconomic development of Africa. Legally superimposing its own legal personality and authority over the AEC, the Constitutive Act dissolved the OAU/AEC and absorbed it as a framework for the continental-scale development, mobilization, and utilization of the human and material resources of Africa (El-Agraa 2004).

Of its eighteen annual heads of assembly summits, the themes of six have been strategically dedicated to the topic of economic integration and development.

18th (2012) "Boosting Intra-African Trade"
13th (2009) "Investing in Agriculture for Economic Growth and
    Food Security"
12th (2009) "Infrastructure Development in Africa"
10th (2008) "Industrial Development of Africa"
8th (2007) "Science, Technology and Scientific Research for Development"
7th (2006) "Rationalisation of RECS and Regional Integration"

Similar to previous summits, the Eighteenth Summit acted as a forum for African representatives to reinforce their commitment to the AEC principles, as well as inch forward the five-phase agenda. Yet twenty years after Abuja/AEC and ten years after the AU establishment, while the 2012 Summit spelled out the parameters of the AEC integrationist ideology that has now become enshrined in the AU political-economic agenda, the summit's actual practice appeared to merely reiterate decisions made in the past.

The AU pledged to achieve the AEC agenda as members resolved to consolidate the gains made from the continent's 2011 6 percent growth rate by pooling continent-wide material and human resources. It pledged to continue to ensure that African leadership take the helm of the development process and to focus on boosting intra-African trade by 25–30 percent, underscoring the strategic targeting of foreign investment, trade, and aid. The AU's AEC coordinating body, the AU Commission, would push its members to fast- track regional economic integration through the establishment of a continental free trade area while targeting market integration in sectors of agriculture and food security, information and communications technology, energy, finance, tourism, and trade in services. The continent's RECs, such as the then recently formed COMESA-EAC-SADC Tripartite Arrangement, would continue to be seen as building blocks of this agenda, as well as present successful mesolevel models of existing integration (*AU Echo* 2012b).

DRIVING THE AEC IDEAL AND THE AU's ECONOMIC ORGANS:
AU COMMISSION PORTFOLIOS, STC, AND PROPOSED FINANCIAL
INSTITUTIONS

To assess the African economic agenda—integration and development—beyond
the numerous declarations of intent articulated in the Union's many meetings
and forums over the past ten years, the Union's economic organs provide an
occasion to evaluate more actionable assessment. AU economic organs have been
established to advance the AEC stages. Of the six stages outlined in article 6 of the
Abuja Treaty, stages 1 and 3 (strengthening existing RECs and creating new ones
where needed; and the establishment of a free trade area and a customs union
at the level of each REC) are perhaps the only stages that have so far produced
observable measurable outcomes.

To advance its four other stages, which has a common goal to implement
union by 2034, stages 2 (stabilization of tariff and other barriers to regional trade
and the strengthening of sectoral integration, particularly in the fields of trade,
agriculture, finance, transport and communication, industry, and energy, as well
as coordination and harmonization of the activities of the RECs), 4 (coordination
and harmonization of tariff and nontariff systems among RECs, with a view
to establishing a continental customs union), 5 (establishment of an African
Common Market and the adoption of common policies), and 6 (integration of
all sectors, establishment of an ACB and a single African currency, setting up of
an African Economic and Monetary Union, and creating and direct elections for
the first PAP) all require the specialized and coordinated actions and outcomes
of the AU's economic organs (AEC).

To achieve stages 1, 2, and 4, the AU Commission, charged with the key
day-to-day management of the Union, among many other responsibilities, is
also charged with elaborating, promoting, coordinating, and harmonizing the
programs and policies of the Union with those of the RECs. Four of eight of the
commission's portfolios—Infrastructure and Energy, Trade and Industry, Rural
Economy and Agriculture, and Economic Affairs (which is singularly dedicated to
economic integration, monetary affairs, private sector development, investment,
and resource mobilization)—are also dedicated to the Union's economic agenda.
Additionally, at the ministerial level, five of the AU's STCs are strategically oriented toward the sectoral strengthening and harmonization of initiatives required
in stage 2. These STCs are the Committee on Rural Economy and Agricultural
Matters; the Committee on Monetary and Financial Affairs; the Committee on

Trade, Customs and Immigration Matters; the Committee on Industry, Science and Technology, Energy, Natural Resources and Environment; and the Committee on Transport, Communications and Tourism.

The AU's RECs are critical for AEC stages 1 thru 4. While not forming legal entities of the AU's Constitutive Act, RECs' role as loosely affiliated bodies of the Union is critical for advancing Africa's economic agenda. The 2007 Protocol on the Relations between the African Union and the Regional Economic Communities addresses the AEC's challenge of integration in relation to the multiple regional economic integration organizations, which themselves have overlapping memberships and need clear principles of coordination among them (Oppong 2010). Without the formal establishment of the AU's own international financial institutions (AU-IFIs)—ACB, AIB, and AMF/currency—beyond blueprints, it is easy to see why stages 4, 5, and 6 of the Union remain in stasis for so long.

Since there is no single administrative overseer of the AEC, the AU's existing organs are ill-equipped to meet the current challenges of integration (Oppong 2010). The AU's three proposed financial organs have critical roles in advancing the integration agenda; nonetheless, of the three, none are functional and only one—the AIB—is even established and ratified by the member states. The AU will ideally:

i)   Promote investment activities of the public and private sector intended to advance regional integration of the member States of the African Union;

ii) Utilize available resources for the implementation of investment projects contributing to the strengthening of the private sector and the modernization of rural sector activities and infrastructures;

iii) Mobilize resources from capital markets inside and outside Africa for the financing of investment projects in African countries; and

iv) Provide technical assistance as may be needed in African countries for the study, preparation, financing and execution of investment projects. (African Union "The Financial Institutions")

Currently, the African Development Bank (AfDB), which is not an organ or office of the AU, performs these functions alongside and sometimes in collaboration with the AU, as do thirteen regional financial quangos. So the main objective of the AMF is to facilitate the integration of African economies through the elimination of trade restrictions and thus enhance monetary integration. When operational, it will provide financial assistance to AU member states, act as a clearing house as well as undertake macroeconomic purveyance within the continent, coordinate the monetary policies of member states and promote cooperation between the monetary authorities in these states, and encourage capital movements between member states, among others. The AU Commission is currently performing these functions.

The ACB has similar laudable but unrealized goals; it was proposed in the 1991 Abuja Treaty and reiterated by the 1999 Sirte Declaration that called for the speeding up of the implementation process. The ACB, just like the other African financial institutions, is aimed at building a common monetary policy and creating a single African currency as a way for accelerating economic integration in Africa. The more specific objectives of the ACB would be to:

a) Promote international monetary cooperation through a permanent institution;
b) Promote exchange stability and avoid competitive exchange rates depreciation;
c) Assist in the establishment of a multilateral system of payments in respect of current transactions between members, and eliminate foreign exchange restrictions which hamper the growth of world trade.

However, it wasn't the AU-IFIs but the AU's eminent person's panel that in 2010 announced the AU's plans to float an all-Africa currency—the Gold Mandela. Currently, there are two regional central banks and a continental association of central banks, plus regular meetings of the governors of central banks at both the continental level and in some regional communities such as ECOWAS, EAC, and SADC.

In 2012, on the heels of the Eighteenth Summit, the AU Commission's Economic Affairs Department had begun to recommend alternative strategies for establishing AEC integration goals prior to the launch of the AU-IFIs. In the interim, following an ECOWAS precedent, an AU Monetary Institute will be set up to study policies that need to be put in place before an ACB and a single currency can be created. The African Monetary Institute would be able to spearhead studies on AEC benchmarks and work with member states to draw up a road map for the common currency and the ACB. The institute will serve as a forum to agree on economic convergence criteria, a budget-deficit ratio of 3 percent inflation targets to be accepted, and the free movement of people, goods, and capital.

To discern the real vibrancy of the Union's economic and development agenda, RECs demonstrate the best modeling for economic integration and thus hope for the realization of an African Common Market, while NEPAD provides the best illustration of the possibilities of harmonized and collaborative continent-wide development initiatives. AEC ideological values—intra-African trade, deepening into a free trade area, then customs union, and later common currency and economic union—are already manifest in different dimensions in ECOWAS, COMESA-EAC-SADC, and the two Communauté Financière Africaine (CFA) monetary unions, and there exists a growing array of initiatives embarked upon by the NPCA to reveal that African-led collaborative development initiatives are taking hold on the continent.

DRIVING THE INTEGRATION AGENDA: THE AU'S RECs

The Abuja Treaty of 1991 specifies that Africa's RECs are the cornerstones "to establishing a Customs Union at the continental level" (art. 6.2.d; see also art. 4.2.a and b). The Constitutive Act of the AU in 2002 commits the states to "coordinate and harmonize policies between . . . regional economic communities for the gradual attainment of the objectives of the Union" (art. 3.l).

In addition to its Constitutive Act, the AU's Peace and Security Council (PSC) Protocol of 2002 bluntly states that "the Regional Mechanisms are part of the overall security architecture of the Union" (art. 16; see also article 7.j). The 2007 Memorandum of Understanding on Cooperation in the Area of Peace and Security between the African Union, the Regional Economic Communities and the Coordinating Mechanisms of the Regional Standby Brigades of Eastern Africa and Northern Africa, which includes ECOWAS, SADC, the Eastern Africa Standby Brigade Coordinating Mechanism (EASBRICOM), and the North African Regional Capacity (NARC), institutionalizes them within the AU (arts. I and III). The regional organizations agree to submit reports every six months to the AU Commission chair; the AU Commission chair will have annual meetings with the regional organizations' chief executives and open liaison offices in the regional organizations' headquarters, with reciprocal arrangements also encouraged (arts. VI, XVII.3, 5, 6, and XVIII).

Africa's RECs are both inspired and encouraged by the AU and are unique in their multiplicity of overlapping structural schema represented in every region of the continent (El-Agraa 2004). Established in 1975 and with 29 percent of Africa's population, at an estimated three hundred million people, West Africa's fifteen-member ECOWAS is the most populous REC in Africa. The REC's most significant accomplishment is its protocol on the free movement of people. With the establishment of the ECOWAS passport, members of the ECOWAS market integration do not require visas or customs restrictions to travel within the region. ECOWAS aims to become a customs union; the REC does foster monetary cooperation with a goal of establishing a common currency, the "eco," by 2020.

Also dominant in West Africa although extending to cover central Africa as well, the CFA has been two monetary unions for sixty-seven years. Encompassing 123 million people, the RECs consist of fourteen different countries that represent two separate monetary unions, UEMOA and the Customs and Economic Union of Central Africa (UDEAC—Union Douanière et Économique de l'Afrique Centrale). In each of these two areas there is a single currency and a single central bank. In addition to monetary union and common currency, CFA countries pool foreign exchange reserves and provide their members with a free intrazone capital mobility and common trade policies (Wane, Burkett, and Guell 1996).

Representing East and Southern Africa, the objective of three of Africa's largest and most institutionalized RECs is the Tripartite COMESA-EAC-SADC, with a political lineage arguably dating back to the Pan-African Freedom Movement of Eastern, Central and Southern Africa (PAFMECSA) founded in 1958. The supra-REC's main objective is the strengthening and deepening economic integration of the southern and eastern African regions, to be achieved through harmonizing policies and programs of the three RECs in the areas of trade, customs, and infrastructure development. The twenty-three-member REC is the only subregional body that has consciously pledged to model its structure toward AEC goals. In June 2012, the Tripartite resolved to harmonize the three trading blocs into a single REC with the objective of fast-tracking the attainment of the AEC.

Onetime SADC chairperson and former South African president Kgalema Motlanthe stated that the time has come for COMESA, EAC, and SADC to bring together members' respective regional integration programs in order to further enlarge markets, unlock productive potential, increase the levels of intra-Africa trade, and enhance southern Africa's developmental prospects (Madakufamba 2008). With 527 million people, the Tripartite's North–South Corridor is a flagship model "aid for trade" program, and the region hopes to generate a gross domestic product of up to $629 billion.

The AU dedicated its Seventh Annual Summit held in Banjul, Gambia, in 2006 to the theme "Rationalisation of RECS and Regional Integration." At the

meeting, AU Assembly members took note of the recommendations of the special committee African Ministers on Integration to rationalize Africa's RECs in
relation to the AEC agenda. The body decided to suspend the recognition of
new RECs outside of the existing eight—the Arab Maghreb Union (AMU), the
Community of Sahel-Saharan States (CEN-SAD), COMESA, EAC, the Economic
Community of Central African States (ECCAS), ECOWAS, the Intergovernmental
Authority on Development (IGAD), and SADC)—and strongly urged these existing RECs to coordinate and harmonize their policies among themselves and with
the Commission with the view to accelerating Africa's integration process.

DRIVING THE DEVELOPMENT AGENDA: THE AU'S NEPAD

Two factors in the development of the AU economic agenda distinguish NEPAD's
role from, on the one hand, the AU Commission up until 2010 at least, and on the
other, the RECs' subregional integrationist agenda. With regard to the former, in
2001, NEPAD was established as an autonomous organization before the AU was
established; only recently was it appropriated by the Union and structured into
the international organization as the NPCA, a significant organ of the Union. As
a result, the relationship between the AU and NEPAD remains controversial, a
fact that may explain NEPAD's success. Some scholars have dubbed NEPAD the
new AEC (Ndayi 2009). Notwithstanding, the AU-NEPAD ambiguity, emerging
from separate institutional origins has produced challenges for both institutions
regarding the economic agenda. The latter factor—integration versus development—does not present the same kind of challenge except if one sees the two
agendas as following from each other: integration fosters development. Through
NEPAD, the AU treats the two economic objectives as separate, though as simultaneously occurring projects and initiatives, and it charges NEPAD to perform
the latter objective—development.

NEPAD was first established as the New Africa Initiative (NAI) in association
with the transformation of the OAU to the AU; on October 23, 2001, the NAI was
renamed NEPAD and pledged as its main objective to direct,

> a common vision and a firm and shared conviction of African leaders to
> anchor a development program in the determination of Africans to extricate
> themselves and the Continent from the malaise of underdevelopment in a
> globalizing world. (NEPAD 2010–12)

For seven years, until 2006 when the AU Assembly ratified its decision to integrate NEPAD into the structure and the processes of the AU, NEPAD operated as Africa's new (post-LPA) development blueprint and implementation organization in a global era. In 2001, the NEPAD blueprint included seven detailed parts, a three-tiered program of action (conditions for sustainable development), and 207 articles (Edozie 2004). The organization ran an ideological mission across Africa, outlined in its preface consistent with Africa's owned and operated development agenda established in the early years of the millennium. African ownership and leadership and anchoring of the redevelopment of the continent on the resources and resourcefulness of the African people would be the NEPAD philosophy. The document would encourage Africans not to be wards of benevolent guardians but to be architects of their own progress" (Melber et al. 2002).

In this regard, NEPAD represents an ideological successor of the LPA in that it emphasizes collective self-reliance and acknowledges regional integration as part of the strategy for an African economic renaissance (Ndayi 2009). Nonetheless, differently from the inward-thinking and structuralist ideological underpinnings of the LPA, through the advocacy of its more distinct leadership cohort (Mbeki, Olusegun Obasanjo, Abdoulaye Wade, and Abdelaziz Bouteflika), NEPAD was somewhat of a departure from Lagos in its embrace of market globalism and the neoliberal hegemony of the day. NEPAD's embrace of economic globalization also underscored its important adherence to a core strategy that defines it—global partnerships. The AU recommends global partnerships and interdependency in the economic arena as a route to African development. NEPAD's architects do not, however, view self-reliance and interdependency as mutually exclusive. African-led partnerships, drawn from African knowledge contexts and collaboratively controlled by Africans, are at the heart of NEPAD's developmental pragmatism (Ndayi 2009).

NEPAD originated from an African leadership diplomatic cohort and agenda that combined both the inward-looking structuralism of the AEC with new externally oriented global market principles and partners, a fact that is NEPAD's genius (Ikome 2007). Nonetheless, there is no doubt that NEPAD's ideological dialectics (regionalism and globalism) and the organization's autonomy giving rise to its vulnerability (global hegemonic co-option rather than partnership) led to the decision by the AU in 2006 to formally, fully, and conclusively incorporate and subsume NEPAD to its authority.

As early as 2002, the tussle between the AU and NEPAD's so-called global partners was apparent when the Canadian government threatened to pull support from the organization. There had been differences between former president

Mbeki and former Canadian prime minister Jean Chrétien over the implementation of a NEPAD program—the African Peer Review Mechanism (APRM). The Canadian donor government was eager to implement its good governance ideology in nurturing African democracy and thus impose its direct control and supervision over the program through the NEPAD Secretariat. Mbeki reminded the Canadians that NEPAD had been established through the AU and that given its governance, rather than development agenda, the APRM would best be supervised through the Union. Comparing the AU-NEPAD relationship to Europe's European Union (EU) and its programs, Mbeki stated, "The AU is the primary organization that unites the people of Africa: NEPAD is its (AU) socio-economic development program" (*Herald* 2002b). Prime Minister Jean Chrétien's reply laid bare the concerns of NEPAD's African critics regarding partnership. "NEPAD and its Secretariat—who we do trust—is distinct and separate politically and institutionally from the African Union—which we do not trust, because it is too soon to say whether it will be any different from its predecessor, the Organization of African Union" (Eno 2008, 266).

The year 2010 saw the successful finalization of the five-year process that fully structured NEPAD into the AU. The key institutional change was the transformation of the NEPAD Secretariat into the NPCA. The restructuring gave NEPAD additional tools for a more diligent management of its projects and programs, which had important administrative and programmatic implications for NEPAD. At the administrative level, NPCA became an organ of the AU, based in Midrand, South Africa, with diplomatic benefits and immunities. At the level of programs, NEPAD has embarked on a strategic reorientation that is based on themes in the areas of regional integration and infrastructure development, agriculture and food security, economic and corporate governance, climate change and natural resources management, human development, and other cross-cutting issues, in particular gender, capacity building, and the use of information and communications technology applications (NEPAD 2010–12).

NEPAD's restructuring underscores its goals more succinctly in relation to the AU Pan-African economic agenda. Its seven most important aims are to achieve and sustain a continent-wide annual growth rate of 7 percent over fifteen years, attract $64 billion a year in foreign direct investment to Africa, increase investment in human resource development, promote the role of women in the development process, reduce poverty by half by 2015 in line with Millennium Development Goals (MDGs), reduce the gap between the industrialized countries of the North and those of Africa, and foster Africa's meaningful participation in the global economy (Ikome 2007, 99).

NEPAD's impact on the AU development agenda is most apparent when one assesses the array of projects and initiatives that the organization has established, brokered, and is in collaboration with in Africa's name. As discerned from table 6.2, the organization divides its activities into six thematic areas ranging from agriculture, climate change, regional integration, human development, gender and capacity building, to economic and corporate governance. NEPAD's signature projects and initiatives are worth examining in detail.

TABLE 6.2. NEPAD AGENDA AND PROJECTS

AGRICULTURE AND FOOD SECURITY	CLIMATE CHANGE AND NATURAL RESOURCES	REGIONAL INTEGRATION AND INFRA- STRUCTURE	HUMAN DEVELOPMENT	CROSS- CUTTING ISSUES AND GENDER	ECONOMIC AND CORPORATE GOVERNANCE
• CAADP • ABI • Partnership for African Fisheries (PAF) • TerrAfrica	• Environment Initiative • Energy Program • African Water Vision Framework	• e-Africa • e-Schools Africa • ICT Broadband Framework • PIDA • AAP	• Consolidated Plan of Action (CPA) • ABI • ASTII	• Gender and Women Empowerment Program • Capacity Development Strategic Framework (CDSF)	• APRM

The Comprehensive Africa Agriculture Development Programme (CAADP) focuses on improving and promoting agriculture across Africa while aiming to eliminate hunger and reduce poverty. The program brings together key players at the continental, regional, and national levels to promote joint and separate efforts to achieve the CAADP goals. As of May 2011, twenty-six countries had signed the CAADP Compact and incorporated it into their agricultural agenda to foster dynamic agricultural markets within and between countries and regions in Africa. The program was successful in assisting farmers in being active in the market economy and in the continent becoming a net exporter of agricultural products. The program sought to produce a more equitable distribution of wealth for rural populations by helping the continent become a strategic player in agricultural science and technology. CAADP helps to foster environmentally sound agricultural production and a culture of sustainable management of natural resources in Africa.

NEPAD's Regional Integration and Infrastructure thematic area houses several programs and initiatives including eighty flagship programs and projects for regional and continental integration in Africa, particularly infrastructure. The regional integration and infrastructure thematic area launched the AU-NEPAD African Action Plan (AAP) 2010–15 and is noted for four projects of significance. One important program is the Short Term Action Plan (STAP), established in 2002 to address specific infrastructure development problems including facilitation, capacity building, physical and capital projects, and studies required to prepare future projects. STAP feeds into the Programme for Infrastructure Development in Africa (PIDA), which is aimed at developing regional and continental infrastructure policies and establishing prioritized development programs. Another program is the NEPAD Infrastructure Project Preparation Facility (IPPF), a fund set up to assist in developing high-quality infrastructure proposals. Managed by the AfDB the 2007/8 IPPF pipeline had up to thirty projects valued at US$50 million, of which the energy and transport sectors accounted for 80 percent.

Also part of NEPAD's Regional Integration and Infrastructure thematic initiatives is the e-Africa Programme, which pursues cross-sector initiatives so that information and communications technology is entrenched in all social sectors, e-services are developed, and Africa is digitally competitive. As well, NEPAD's Broadband Infrastructure Network for Africa (BINA) is one of the key initiatives of the e-Africa program, and it aims to connect all African countries to one another and to the rest of the world through existing and planned submarine (Uhurunet) and terrestrial (Umojanet) cable systems. There is also a NEPAD's e-Schools Initiative, which harnesses information and communications technology to improve the quality of teaching and learning in African primary and secondary schools.

Through the work of five sector-program initiatives, NEPAD also conducts the continent's human development work, which is aimed at a range of ventures to improve education and training, health, and science education for Africans. Significant initiatives and projects include NEPAD's Africa Day Celebrations, which have culminated in the adoption of a legacy project. The project aims to promote indigenous musical and literacy arts and encourages research, documentation, and publication of indigenous approaches to arts, literacy, and development. NEPAD's African Science, Technology and Innovation Indicators (ASTII) program establishes, promotes, and monitors science, technology, and innovation indicators for Africa's scientific and technological development. These indicators assist Africans in formulating, adjusting, and implementing technology and innovation policies and strategies, as well as in monitoring global technological trends, conducting foresight exercises, and determining specific areas of investment. Relatedly, NEPAD's African Biosciences Initiative (ABI) is a cluster of three of the twelve NEPAD Science and Technology flagship program areas, namely biodiversity science and technology, biotechnology, and indigenous knowledge systems.

Significantly, gender is one of three of NEPAD's thematic initiatives, made evident by NEPAD's Gender and Women Empowerment Program. Through projects such as the Spanish Fund for African Women Empowerment, NEPAD aims to contribute to the eradication of poverty and the economic empowerment of women through financial and technical assistance to projects that support gender equality and the improvement of women's economic, political, and social empowerment. The concern by critics of the AU takeover of NEPAD was that the Union's bureaucracy would decelerate a program that had initially been launched by African heads of government, who had wanted to accelerate the pace of change in a voluntary way not constrained by the politics and strict rules of a multilateral institution such as the AU (Venter and Neuland 2005, 494). Contrarily, the rich and dynamic network of initiatives and projects that NEPAD is involved with in advancing the Pan-African economic agenda has been beneficial for NEPAD, for the AU, and for Africans, as seen by the AU-NEPAD AAP 2010–15, which has become a defining statement of Africa's current priority initiatives related to the promotion of regional and continental integration, together with the AU, as its rightful subsidiary.

In adopting the premise that it is critical that African development and regional cooperation programs take place in the context of good economic and political governance, NEPAD now places its flagship APRM under its Economic and Corporate Governance sector. APRM is a mutually agreed program, voluntarily adopted by the member states of the AU, to promote and reinforce high standards of governance. The APRM, a self-monitoring mechanism, ensures that the policies and practices of participating countries conform to the agreed values in the following four focus areas: democracy and political governance, economic governance, corporate governance, and socioeconomic development.

NEPAD covers a wide range of economic sectors and has evolved a wide array of projects and programs, in which it seeks investment for and financing both internationally and from African sources. With each thematic initiative, sector, and program, NEPAD deepens, builds upon, and expands the objectives, challenges, and opportunities of its programming to advance the goals of regional and continental integration in Africa. For example, under its banner, NEPAD works collaboratively and ideologically contiguously with the AU Commission, NPCA, AfDB, and the eight RECs.

THE POLITICAL-ECONOMIC MATRIX THAT DRIVES THE AU'S AEC AGENDA: ASSESSING PROGRESS

To assess the progress of the Pan-African economic agenda led by the AU regime, one must look through three prisms: the advance of the AEC's ideological agenda, the strengthening of AU institutional relationships with member states, sub-regions, and peoples through nonstate actor organizations, and measurable outcomes leading to livelihood improvement among African peoples, communities, and nations. From the point of view of the first two prisms—ideology and relationships—the AU appears to be making dynamic progress. However, measurable outcomes in terms of full economic integration and concrete continent-wide measurable income enlargement, increase in productivity and gross national product, and increase in socioeconomic indicators such as educational attainment and access to health are more difficult to ascertain.

The AU makes a greater difference in the active procurement of African development initiatives compared to its predecessor, the OAU, and compared to the actions of individual nations. In collaboration with other important Africa economic institutions—UNECA and the AfDB—as well as through its organs assigned to the economy (AU Commission, STCs, NPCA, and RECs), the AU orchestrates and directs the Pan-African economic agenda. Ideology—translated as the shared belief in values, premises, and principles that ground action—has been an important factor in the AU's facilitation of its agenda.

Self-reliance, economic union, and reversing underdevelopment have been values enshrined in the African ontology since Nkrumah introduced them. Nkrumah's foundational ideas have been mainstreamed into the fabric of the AU's institutional evolution via the LPA and the AEC Abuja Treaty. As such, through the activities of the AU-NEPAD and the AU's organs and STCs, the Pan-African ideology, focused on African owned and operated development, is sustained, proliferated, and even expanded upon to facilitate the realization of Africans' collective economic interests.

Notwithstanding this ideological crystallization, because the LPA and the AEC remained blueprints that are merely pledged to by African leaders, under them, Africa's Pan-African economic agenda rightly suffered the criticism of not advancing beyond mere rhetorical statements imbued in the many documents and speeches of African leaders. By institutionalizing the Pan-African economic agenda and assigning its values to separate functional organs, the AU agenda has been transformed from mere rhetoric to action in the form of a network of continent-wide institutional arrangements that identify and establish goals, initiatives, and projects. This action culminates in the formulation of effective economic and public policy for the continent.

For the AU, institutionalization has furthered the important value held by Africans for ownership of their developmental agenda. Africans own and direct the economic agenda; they use and draw from national and community knowledge and talent; and through numerous projects continent-wide, they are forced to regularly come together to implement policy decisions that they have collectively devised. One sees an illustration of this kind of activity in the AU's energy development activities. Through NEPAD, the AU works in cooperation with a number of specialized continental and regional organizations to promote regional integration in energy in Africa. Its partners are continental, regional, and global and include the African Energy Commission (AFREC), the Forum of Energy Ministers in Africa (FEMA), the Union of Producers, Transporters and Distributors of Electric Power in Africa (UPDEA), and Africa's RECs. Together, three of the coalition's five important strategic objectives are to promote intra-African trade in energy, to pay attention to building regional power pools to leverage economic and social development of the regions, and to promote global exports in energy by developing energy resources (water, oil, and gas in particular) and their exports for intra-African trade and to the rest of the world. In chronological order of starting operations, the Comité Maghrébin de l'Electricité, Southern African Power Pool, and West African Power Pool enable twenty-one countries to minimize power failures and rationing by interconnecting their national power grids, so they can import and export electricity when needed.

The AU-NEPAD and ECOWAS West African Gas Pipeline (WAGP) represents another example of how the AU's institutional relationships manifest in this respect. The objective of the WAGP is to optimize the energy resources of West Africa by promoting the utilization of natural gas by industries, oil-field power plants, and domestic consumers in Nigeria, Benin, Togo, and Ghana (S. Asante 2007). The project has built a pipeline that supplies clean and affordable energy from Nigeria to Benin, Togo, and Ghana. It was launched in 2004, and Chevron, Texaco, Nigeria National Petroleum Corporation, Shell, and Takoradi Power Company committed more than $500 million toward its construction.

This regime of AU institutional relationships is replicated across the continent and is leading to gradual albeit actionable contributions to African development. Other projects carried out in the same way include the Kariba-North and Itezhi Tezhi Hydropower Expansion Project, the Sambangalou Kaleta Hydropower and OMVG Interconnection, the Nigeria-Algeria Gas Network Connection, the Kenya-Uganda Oil Pipeline Project, the Senegal River Basin Water and Environmental Management Project, the Water Resources Planning and Management in the Nile River Basin, AfricaRail, and the Improvement of Maritime Ports for African Island Countries.

Measurable outcomes in the areas of the AU's progress in economic and development indicators are more difficult to assess. In terms of regional integration, the AU has not yet achieved its goal of establishing a continental free trade area. The Minimum Integration Program hails the start of negotiations toward the Tripartite COMESA-EAC-SADC free trade area and holds this up as a template for ECOWAS to absorb the ECCAS, the AMU, and CEN-SAD. Intra-African trade still stands at only 10 percent in volume compared to 40 percent with Europe/the United States. Moreover, African exports represent only 4 percent of world trade; and despite a 2011 average growth rate of 5–6 percent, the continent remains at the bottom of MDG socioeconomic development indicators.

Of course, ten years of AU longevity is a short evaluation period to discern dramatic economic change. It is more important to ascertain whether the AU is moving in the right direction to the extent that it will eventually meet its goals. Is rhetoric equivalent to action and thereby progress? There is evidence to suggest an affirmative answer to this question. Regional integration and economic union has long been a high priority in the development agenda of African countries. Drawn from the principles of the AEC, currently the AU is much more assertively promoting the continent as a grouping of fifty-five countries that trade goods manufactured or originating within the countries of a proposed continental free trade area.

AU leaders and peoples are aware of the economic benefits that a continental free trade area would bring to African peoples as surely as it did to the thirteen US colonies in 1791: boost employment opportunities in the public and private sectors, increase food security by consolidating trade in agricultural production among African countries, increase competitiveness of Africa's industrial products by harnessing the economies of scale of a large continental market of an estimated one billion people, increase rate of diversification and transformation of Africa's economy by assuring that the continent supplies its import needs from its own resources, better allocate resources through improved competition and reduced price differentials, grow intraindustry trade and develop geographically based specialization in Africa, reduce African countries' vulnerability to external trade shocks, enhance participation of Africa in global trade, and reduce dependency of the continent on aid and external borrowing (*AU Echo* 2012a).

This knowledge was formulated and is being promoted by an AU STC—the AU Conference of Ministers of Trade—at its Sixth Ordinary Session meeting. The knowledge of the benefits of economic integration inspired African country representatives of the meeting to fast-track the creation of a continental free trade area, and the trade ministers' report further inspired the Assembly to focus its January 2012 meeting on the theme "Boosting Intra-African Trade." Deliberations and debates on the topic at the 2012 meeting led to the publication and dissemination of several issue papers and action plans that identified and articulated future African economic policy required to reverse the existing levels of low performance of intra-African trade and integration.

What should be obvious to AU economic leaders and to Africans is the actual realization of the gains from integration that are already being realized through Africa's RECs. The creation of the COMESA free trade area led to a sixfold increase in intraregional trade among southern and eastern African countries. A consolidation of the free trade areas of at least two RECs could simultaneously reduce Africa's global protection by 68.7 percent and consequently reduce intra-African average trade protection from 8.7 percent to 2.7 percent (*AU Echo* 2012a).

CONCLUSION

Should Africa pursue economic union and political union separately (Oppong 2010)? Is the NEPAD Planning and Coordination Agency (NPCA) or the AU Commission a more effective driver for African integration and development? Further, will African economic integration ever be achieved? What are its major challenges? And what has it accomplished for African peoples thus far? These interrelated questions have underlain the current chapter, and they appropriately capture the challenge of the Pan-African economic agenda of the AU by way of conclusion.

As with other aspects of African affairs—cultural identity, democratic identity, security relations—one can't help concluding that in the economic realm as well, the AU's economic agenda relies on its various encounters with the international global economy. In this regard, through the AU, the African economic agenda sustains a long-standing struggle to mitigate the new rules of the neoliberal global economy and Western economic interests that Africans experience as imperialistic. Of the AU's economic organs that exhibit this globally interactive paradox, the most expressive is the AU-NEPAD, which is at its best when achieving intergovernmental development goals, but due to its own ties with global market liberalism, is unable to authoritatively foster the continent's much-needed economic and political integration.

As well, the chapter reveals that pursuing political union at the same time as economic integration does indeed represent a major challenge for the AU with its uneven national economies and weak fledgling insecure states. Nonetheless, the extent to which the integration process is complicated and thereby hampered by the broader AU political agenda may be a self-defeating question for the institution whose foremost goal is to achieve union. A thorough discussion of these challenges will be addressed in the concluding chapters. The current chapter has merely scratched the surface in presenting evidence of the AU economic agenda as both a phenomenon as well as a problem.

What we mean is that as the AU members pragmatically compromise their lofty ideals, especially in achieving political union, they seem to be more enthusiastic about the economic integration agenda. Rendering more authority to the AU's economic organs, NEPAD and the AU Commission, to advance and accelerate integration suggests that members see the benefits and thus value economic integration and the faster achievement of economic development. While the AU Commission creates a continent-wide environment for its nation-state economies to harmonize their economic policies, pool their economies together, and benefit from intracontinental production and trade, AU-NEPAD embarks upon demonstrable, on the ground development initiatives that target poverty reduction, infrastructural development, and education and research.

PART 3

The Prospective and the Prescriptive

The African Union's *Africa*: Its Prospects and Its Challenges

In *No One's World*, Charles Kupchan predicts a global world that will no longer be dominated by the West (Western Europe, the United States, and the geopolitically West, Japan). In twenty years, the Western share of global gross domestic product has fallen from 75 percent to 50 percent and is rapidly still falling as emerging markets—China, India, Russia, Saudi Arabia, and Brazil to name a few, countries he refers to as the "Rest"—are growing exponentially. As a result of these countries' growing economic influence, in the short-term future, argues Kupchan, the international system will be much more plural and inclusive of a political economy that he claims will be dominated by multiple modernities. These will be the different models of political and economic development (state capitalism, sovereign democracy) that these new leading developing world countries bring to bear on the international system (Kupchan 2012).

If not Western superstates, what central institutions will manage this new world order?—a commentator of the book asked during a C-Span book talk promoting the book. Kupchan replied: a parallel reformed United Nations (UN) that is inclusive of these emerging powers and *regional* organizations—like (Kupchan says) the European Union (EU) and the Association of Southeast Asian Nations (ASEAN), and (we say) possibly Africa's African Union (AU). While certainly relevant and interesting, yet in describing the phenomenon from a we versus they approach, Kupchan's book is Eurocentric. Also like similar discourses on the topic, concentrating on China and BRICS (Brazil, Russia, India, China, South Africa), not much attention—or belief in prospects—is given to Africa in this regard as global innovation is represented by the dynamics occurring in China and, to a lesser extent, Russia.

Be that as it may, the constructivist concept and notion of multiple modernities (also see Appadurai's alternative modernities) in an era of globalization represents an intriguing way to examine the real prospects for growth and development in Africa as well as for assessing the AU's role in providing a continent-wide institutional framework for carrying forward such an agenda for Africa. Why can't the AU, through the platform of Pan-Africanism, be seen to present an alternative or multiple modernity through which it strives to attain political and economic development for Africa?

The AU is certainly not the equivalent of China or Russia—mere nation-states—but the institution does parallel the EU as a variable and yet ambiguous institutional configuration and model of neofunctional, collective nation-state action. The Union is classified by conventional wisdom as a regional organization, but closer observation of the AU dynamic reveals that the Union strives to function as more than a regional organization that will manage the global change that Kupchan suggests. A regional organization serves to primarily foster economic integration among members to consolidate economies of scale in trade. Nonetheless, in addition to this goal, the AU seeks to develop Africa in order to eradicate its chronic conflict and insecurity, alleviate its endemic poverty and underdevelopment, and foster health access, educational attainment, and employment for African peoples. In this regard, the AU operates as an intergovernmental development organization similar to the UN.

The AU's function as a cultural reservoir and mobilizer of a Pan-African identity and a facilitator of a political-economically integrated continental free trade area that will be encapsulated in a future political union called the Union Government perhaps is much more ambitious than the institutional objectives of the UN, where in reality, one-world government or world-state is not a desirable goal. When the AU strives for such a goal, it represents itself as more than either a regional organization or an intergovernmental organization (IGO). The AU acts more like a suprastate in the act of supranation building. It functions as a vehicle to achieve an integrated, interdependent Africa imbued with the ideals of justice and peace and underpinned by political, economic, social, and cultural integration that would enable the continent to make the best of its human and material resources. As a suprastate the AU ensures the progress and prosperity of its citizens by taking advantage of the opportunities offered by a globalized world.

The reality is that it is among these three institutional parameters that the AU functions in order to transform African politics and contribute African initiatives to the complex terrain of global governance and globalization. In thus determining the Union's real impact on African affairs and its prospects to achieve its goals, closer attention to each institutional configuration's behavior is necessary. The AU's variable institutional configuration also sheds light on the complexity of the AU's many challenges that it encounters in its attempts to facilitate positive change for Africa.

For instance, the challenge of integration reveals that while the continent's Regional Economic Communities (RECs) have been more successful at fostering economic integration, the AU remains active and purposeful in advancing its goal to achieve continent-wide regional economic integration. We see how this objective is assigned as a core goal of the AU Commission where five of the Commission's eight departments are dedicated to economic integration issues. Integration is a means to an end for the AU; economic union will accelerate development and facilitate Africa's greater global-economic enmeshment (positive wealth gains garnered from interdependence rather than the exploitation and poverty increase that is characteristic of economic marginalization and dependence).

Similarly, while we can see from the dedication to its policy commitments and initiatives that achieving its goal of political and economic development is a significant challenge for the AU, assessing it as an IGO reveals some insights to help understand the problems that it encounters. The AU is aware that while symptoms of underdevelopment—insecurity, conflict, disease, poverty, and inaccessibility to health and education—are also impediments to economic integration and development, they can be tackled in the short term through concerted governance effort. As an IGO, the AU achieves more success for Africa than its mere function as a regional organization. Its departments of Peace and Security, Political Affairs, and Social Affairs successfully develop continent-wide public policy frameworks, agendas, initiatives, programs, projects, and rules in the areas of each department's respective portfolio.

It is admirable that a range of African politicians, bureaucrats, and professionals—the human resource leadership of the AU—dedicate their skills, expertise, and service to African development. However, the biggest challenge in this enterprise is the reality that, while the African development operation run by the AU is conducted by Africans, it is not funded by them. Ninety percent of the AU's development projects are funded by the AU's so-called partners. Given this reality, is the AU too dependent on its former colonizers, on the Western international community that it claims it will free Africa from? Is the AU a product and an enabler of the new neocolonialism?

Another challenge concerns the AU's supranationality, which affects the organization's poor implementation of its agenda. In this regard, the AU's polycentric sovereignty (referring to its layers of authority over multiple sovereign nations) may be seen to be tenuous. Member states ratify the policies that they devise but do little to implement these policies in their national arenas, unless it is one that that state is enthusiastic about. Member states must consider whether establishing a union government and Pan-African identity is a vehicle to advance development for Africa or an endgame to achieve a new form of state formation for Africans. If the aspiring suprastate configuration realizes its goal of union by 2034, its realization is challenged by the uncertainty of whether African member states will ever fully give up their sovereignty to achieve Nkrumah's vision for a United African States (UAS). Do Africa's fifty-six nation-states share common values and ideals? Do its peoples see themselves as African? Do they believe in the compulsion of socioeconomic integration, political union, and a singular historical and cultural identity?

A final challenge involves the international legitimacy of the AU and whether the modern world system and its hegemons will ever let it achieve a suprastate status. That is to say, international organizations like the EU and UN and superpower states like the United States may prefer the AU's institutional status as an IGO over any of the two other forms. Regional organization is of little interest to the international community, whose interests in reality serve their own regions' economic nationalism, and the AU's suprastate status could be a stark threat to those interests. Addressing the aforementioned questions in relation to the challenges that the AU encounters while assessing the institution's evolving architecture and variable structure as an institutional format that it uses to achieve its goals is the objective of our final section of *The African Union's Africa*.

Through previous sections of the book, we have seen how the AU's political objectives are intricately connected with the major issues that influence the dynamics of African politics in the areas of conflict and security, economic development, democracy and politics, and sociocultural identity. This chapter begins our discussion of proscriptive and prescriptive conclusions about the AU's institutional and structural challenges, opportunities, and future with respect to its performance and continued impact on the politics of Africa and the world. Navigating a matrix that we have formulated to more clearly illustrate this assessment—varied institutional structure against challenges and impact assessment—the chapter examines the AU's and Africa's future as determined by the prospects that it can accomplish its goals in three important areas: resources, organizational capacity, and legitimacy. These variables are qualified by understanding specific empirical dimensions of the Union drawn from the AU's own self-evaluation; they are political will, budget, and human resources and are indisputably the three major challenges faced by the AU and its family of associated institutions.

Organizational capacity and human resources refer to the AU's chameleon-like evolving institutional structures—regional organization, IGO, and suprastate—and the ability of the organization to move beyond a talking shop. Resources and budget assess whether Africa is too poor to support and sustain an agenda of Pan-African magnitude. Legitimacy and political will concern the AU's interactions and engagement with a hegemonic international community committed to rule of the world, as well as with African national member states' implementation of the AU agenda and their real commitment to a penultimate Pan-African union (see table 7.1).

Revealing this contradictory terrain upon which the AU attempts to achieve its goals for Africa, through the aforementioned variables, this chapter, while continuing our analytical induction method of thoroughly interpreting and analyzing secondary-sourced materials and archival data, will be complemented with a quasi-ethnographic study. Our inspiration for this was the 2012 AU first-time branding campaign launched to raise awareness of the organization's visual identity—its AU flag, colors, and visions. The campaign would aim to foster more direct linkages between the AU and its people to show that African people are the drivers of the success of the continent. Significantly, the branding campaign was first launched internally within the AU organization on AU employees whom the branding campaign designers described as the organization's most critical stakeholders and who originated from the diverse spectrum of Africa.

Through observation of—and some brief participation in and attendance of—some of its meetings, workshops, and summits, we too have leveraged that campaign and conducted an interview survey of these critical stakeholders. For our concluding study, we used their responses on a range of topics on the organization that they work for to provide first-order discursive voice from the Union that thereby provides supplementary contributed knowledge for our thesis and objective. Representative of the AU's Africans, AU employees—elected commissioners, directors, program officers, analysts, advisors, consultants, and affiliates—present a verisimilitude through which to reveal and assess the prospects of the organization, its accomplishments, challenges, and futures.

TABLE 7.1. ASSESSING AFRICAN UNION IMPACT: A MATRIX

	RESOURCES (Budget)	CAPACITY (Human Resources and Technical Logistics)	LEGITIMACY (National— Relations among Member States))	LEGITIMACY (International— Relations with the West and Powers of International Community)
REGIONAL ORGANIZATION	Member State procurements	Underdevelopment	Strong commitment at subregional level—RECs	Indifferent commitment by international community— sometimes undermined due to trade interests EU, US
INTER-GOVERNMENTAL ORGANIZATION	90% funded by international community	Strong capacity due to partnerships	Moderate commitment— except if a grant recipient country to receive aid	Strong commitment by international community to advance its development initiatives
SUPRASTATE	Need to consolidate intrastate resources— discussion just beginning	Weak pragmatic capacity and undermined by neofunctionalist structure and sovereign realpolitik	Strong symbolic will and commitment to Pan-Africanism, self-determination, desire to develop	Antagonistic to notion of suprastate; undermines Western imperialist interest

Twenty of these employees were surveyed on a range of questions that would solicit their views, and respondents were drawn from a range of AU departments and offices. They included the AU Liaison Office in South Sudan (AU-LOSS), Gender Coordination and Outreach Division, Social Affairs Department, Conflict Management Division, Border Program, Bureau of the Chairperson, Economic Affairs Department, Office of Legal Counsel, Citizens and Diaspora Directorate (CIDO), New Partnership for Africa's Development (NEPAD) Planning and Coordination Agency (NPCA), Peace and Security Department, Peace and Security Directorate (Panel of the Wise), Defense and Security, Political Affairs Department, Democracy and Electoral Assistance Unit, and an ambassadorial office—the Special UN Office to the AU.

Respondents had country origins in Kenya, Tanzania, Nigeria, Libya, Ghana, Guinea, Cameroon, Mauritania, the Democratic Republic of the Congo, Ethiopia, South Africa, Côte d'Ivoire, Central African Republic, and Malawi. They are men and women and represent Africa's regions, official lingua francas, and diverse nationalities and ethnicities. They were surveyed on a range of questions, including their motivation for working with the AU, their knowledge of the Union's Pan-Africanist history, culture, and politics, the Union's impact in key areas of African affairs, and the Union's prospects in achieving integration, unity, and development for Africa.

Most could be described as Pan-Africanists, committed to a vision to build and unite Africa. Their Pan-Africanist ideals had originated from their local, country-level upbringing. One respondent described his long-standing desire to work for the AU as "a calling." This revelation provided support for the reality that Pan-Africanism is rooted in local African environments and contexts and is shaping Africans' public attitudes. When asked to assess the AU's practices in the context of globalization and regionalism and predict the institution's prospects in advancing democracy and development for Africa, respondents described the AU variably as an IGO, a suprastate, and a regional organization. In response to their assessment of the AU in terms of its accomplishments and challenges in the areas of security, political-economy, social issues, and culture, and in explaining these challenges in relation to global and national legitimacy, respondents provided detailed, though varied, evidence of the AU's luster as well as its huge problems.

Despite acknowledging sometimes hair-raising challenges—ranging from a lack of resources (and especially independent resources), foreign intervention, reluctance of national regimes to implement AU policies, lack of AU institutional and legal authority to enforce its policies, and weak commitment to the AU's economic integration and political union goals—respondents were relatively confident of the AU's prospects for economic integration, though less so for the prospects of political union by 2034.

In drawing upon the short-term observation, subsequent sections of this chapter will reaffirm our book's thesis that the AU's performance and impact and thereby necessity for Africa, is evidenced by the institution's gradualist, nuanced, variable, and fluid fostering of political change in and of Africa. Of course, just as big a thesis is the fact that this mild accomplishment and sustained vision is certainly challenged by international and continental realpolitik. This concluding thesis begins by presenting the AU's challenges as laid out above—organization, resources, and legitimacy—and concludes by restating these challenges in separate subsections that demonstrate the AU's impact on African politics and affairs.

The AU's Three Heads: Regional Organization, Intergovernmental Organization (IGO), and Suprastate

The EU Commission requires twenty-three thousand staff members to service its twenty-seven states with five hundred million citizens (European Commission 2013). By that standard, the AU, which services fifty-five states with one billion citizens, needs to establish a minimum of forty-six thousand posts for its Commission in Addis Ababa. The reality is that the AU Commission currently has filled about 1 percent of the EU posts on a per capita basis. By 2007, the AU Commission had approved 912 posts on its establishment, but had only filled 617 posts, including 349 professionals (African Union 2008). Even if one adds to these numbers the combined secretariats of all AU organs plus the Common Market for Eastern and Southern Africa (COMESA), the East African Community (EAC), the Economic Community of West African States (ECOWAS), and the Southern African Development Community (SADC), the full-time number would still only total around 1,100 current Afrocrats versus the 23,000 Eurocrats in Brussels, Strasbourg, and Luxembourg.

In reflecting on the aforementioned challenge of institutional design and human resources and their effect on AU capacity, one of our respondents representing the AU's Office of Legal Council spoke to the criticality of the question of the AU's institutional structure in relation to its ability to achieve its goals. He reaffirmed a public pronouncement that he had made in 2011 regarding the AU Commission's institutional reconfiguration into an Authority. The (to date) three-year deliberations regarding the transformation is aimed at strengthening the institutional framework of the Union with the purpose of revitalizing the continental organization so that it can play a more active role in the governance of Africa. The measure had been proposed and approved by member states in a 2009 protocol amending the Constitutive Act and the Statute of the Authority.

Key to the amendment is the fact that the new Authority shall exercise its functions on the basis of the principle of subsidiarity with regards to member states and RECs. Doing so gives the current Commission legal capacity to implement its development goals, including poverty reduction and peace and security. It would allow the AU to establish a *Pax Africana* common defense and foreign policy that it supervises. Economically, it will accelerate the African Economic Community (AEC) in fostering the free movement of persons and goods. Essentially, by strengthening the function of the Commission and streamlining its functions while at the same time specializing them in relation to other AU power bases, an AU Authority might address the organization's tripartite institutional dilemma where it functions as a regional organization, an IGO, and a suprastate.

In affirming the need for a strengthened Commission—renamed an Authority—another respondent attributed inadequate organs and institutional framework as the major constraint on the Union's effectiveness. While its institutional structure hampered the AU's predecessor, the Organization of African Unity (OAU), restricting it to a status of what most agreed was inaction—hence the organization's dictator's club image—the new AU would supposedly have to innovate its structure to overcome these obstacles. In documenting his own ideas in a book that he wrote on the topic, this AU employee argued that the problem was the fact that the main organs that the African leaders opted to use for running the OAU—the Assembly of Heads of State, the Council of Ministers, and the Specialized Commissions and Technical Committees, especially—were comprised of member states' governmental officials who had other pressing commitments at home limiting their time. "As a result, the organs developed such weaknesses as deficient structures and resources, improper representations, absenteeism, as well as insufficient time for in-depth deliberation of issues during their sessions and follow up thereafter. They could hardly perform well" (Khamis 2008, 7).

The current AU governing institutions emerged from their OAU counterparts: the Assembly of Heads of State and Government is now the Assembly, the Council of Ministers is the Executive Council, and the Committee of Ambassadors has become the Permanent Representatives Committee (Adejumobi and Olukoshi 2008). There are two issues that concern this transformation. First, the new bodies do not appear very different from those of their predecessors because the core organs, especially the Assembly, are still comprised of member states and their representatives. In this regard, African countries treat the AU like a multilateral regional organization that is comprised of sovereign African states. The problem here is that in the Assembly, where the AU's greatest authority lies, decisions are ratified and become Constitutive Act law by way of one-week deliberations at biannual summits. When this happens, the main summit deliberations and debates are merely rhetorical and do not pay sufficient attention to the real practical implications of summit decisions. As a result, member states fail to implement at the country level these complex—and many times controversial—new AU public policies, and the AU body has little capacity to enforce its rules.

The second concern speaks to member states' support for the transition from the AU Commission to the AU Authority. The decision was ratified by a majority at a summit in Sirte, Libya, in 2009. Interestingly, by providing the AU responsibilities and powers that are substantially greater than the OAU, and in acknowledging the need to confer more institutional power and authority to the AU Commission, African member states exhibit their desire for the AU to invoke supranational powers. This follows the precedent of ECOWAS, whose reforms already confer certain supranational authority on its secretariat. Nonetheless, what is behind this apparent contradiction whereby member states guard and protect their sovereign powers while conferring supranational powers to the Union? Perhaps African member states are not being blindly contradictory but instead are willing to delegate the Commission to assume supranational authority in some key areas. For example, many respondents felt that member states are proud of the AU's accomplishments in peacekeeping in Somalia, and thus feel that the AU Commission should have greater powers to reduce conflict in certain member states—as long as it is not their country!

Members' competing support for the AU as an IGO, a regional organization, and a suprastate couldn't be more apparent than when examining the reality of the Somalia case. Most regional organizations merely mediate conflict in their regions. The Arab League does so in Syria (2012), while ASEAN does so in Burma. It is expected that the AU do so in Somalia, the world's most sustained post–Cold War conflict. But respondents admitted that the AU's initiatives in Somalia far extended the pro forma mediation activities of the aforementioned regional organizations. The AU's peacemaking operation in Somalia has the authority to intervene in the country with troops, prosecute a war against the militant opposition, and facilitate conflict resolution and state building. This way, the AU functions like the UN, an IGO.

In Africa and the larger developing world, conflict resolution is a development objective. Achieving security is a foremost developmental goal for the AU. Insofar as the Union keeps the peace for Africa in Somalia, member states are happy to utilize the institution as a development organization. However, ratifying a Common African Defence and Security Policy (CADSP), which would require member states to pool their security apparatuses under the authority of the AU, is another matter. To date, members have not ratified the pact with a majority vote. Respondents suggested reasons for members' reluctance. African regimes, regardless of their democracy credentials, are militarized regimes that cherish their sovereignty and guard their militaries very closely. As such, in this case, the AU Commission and the Peace and Security Council (PSC), are heralded for its multilateral development initiatives but resisted for their supranational assertions.

These institutional bottlenecks are reflected in the economic domain as well, although respondents suggested that member states are more willing to defer to or are simply desirous of the AU's supranational capacity in this respect. Nonetheless, in this realm too, institutional contradictions prevent greater capacity for the AU to meet its objective to achieve economic integration. That problem, according to one respondent, is explained by the vibrancy of Africa's RECs, which have perhaps been more successful in the economic integration realm than the AU has been so far, despite its ambitious mandate to achieve a continental free trade area for Africa by 2034.

The AU would have to be a supranational economic institution like the EU's European Economic Community (EEC) to achieve such a feat of economic integration. However, contradictorily again, at its founding establishment to upgrade the OAU to the AU, members provided for three separate institutions that would facilitate its integrationist goals: an AEC, a Pan-African Parliament (PAP), and an AU. While the PAP was structurally absorbed—responders say subsumed—into the new AU as a new organ, the AEC was not. That institution remained as a quasi-autonomous development objective. It is as a development initiative—suggesting again the AU's greater success as an IGO —that AEC objectives are best realized through the AU's NEPAD.

While with its many development projects across the continent, through for example its organ the NPCA, the AU functions as a successful multilateral or intergovernmental development organization (IGO) for Africa, it is a problem that the institution's suprastate organs—the African Central Bank (ACB), the African Monetary Fund (AMF), and the African Investment Bank (AIB), which are key institutions to facilitate the integration agenda—remain to be established, barring the fact that the AIB's mandate is currently implemented by the African Development Bank (AfDB). Respondents felt that it is probably much more convenient for members to rely on the AU to assist them in select development initiatives that they are unable to operate alone. As an IGO, the AU assists member states with resources mobilization, knowledge and expertise, and fostering at least subregional collaboration on key development initiatives that the member would not have access to otherwise.

Yet Africa's RECs compete with the AU for the realization of economic integration gains. ECOWAS, COMESA, SADC, and EAC are more successful than the AU at economic integration and intraregional trade. As a result, respondents say that there is little incentive for members to rely on the AU for this function. Structurally and institutionally, the AU attempts to counter REC autonomy by claiming the subregional organizations as affiliate organs of the AU. The AU certainly works closely, cooperatively, and rather successfully with Africa's RECs; however, the relationship exhibits the AU's intergovernmental and regional cooperation functions best. Supranationalism—required for achieving a continental free trade area—is muted.

The way that the AU is structured as an organization of politics also influences its divergent statuses. Leadership, citizenship, and democratization are all political factors through which the institution advances its objectives. The AU has provided important posts for its leaders: the AU Commission chairperson, the one-year rotating chair of the Assembly, the elected AU commissioners and their directors. The AU chairperson, deputy chairperson, and eight commissioners are nominated by member states and regions and then elected by the Assembly. Some respondents have complained that this process leads to the politics of identity rather than the emergence of leaders with integrity and competence to facilitate the AU's achievement of its goals.

The 2012 election for the AU Commission chairperson was riddled with vitriolic factionalism, camps, and personal attacks between the two candidates. The contest fostered a Francophone versus Anglophone rift, a subregional rift, and a gender rift (the candidate who won was a woman) across the Continent. However, a few respondents argued that the 2012 AU chairperson election reflected the characteristics of African democratic politics (Edozie 2008). It was important, for example, that the AU chair of the Assembly, President Thomas Boni Yayi, was a West African Francophone, the new AU Commission chairperson, Nkosazana Dlamini-Zuma, a Southern African Anglophone woman (who also speaks French), and the deputy chairperson, Erastus Mwencha, an East African Anglophone. It is also significant that the AU commissioners operate on a gender quota. A male commissioner must match a female commissioner. Regardless of the AU's diversity, political, social, and cultural integration is much more difficult to achieve.

Political union means that identities are harmonized into a single African identity, in the famous EU phrase, "ever closer union." Strongly holding onto linguistic, regional, and national identities reinforces separate identities making the African political union ever more elusive. One respondent was highly critical of the Anglo/Franco divide arguing that both languages are imperial impositions. "I am Yorubaphone," she announced in making the larger point that Africans should hold on to their ethnic identities but also move faster toward adopting an African citizenship. Nothing in the AU's Constitutive Act or even its Diaspora Clause confers to African citizens the political rights of African citizenship. Instead, also within this sphere, the AU functions as a regional organization in mediating diplomatic (political) relations among member states.

Internationally in its relations with the Black diaspora and its efforts to persuade their inclusion, the AU confers citizenship on Africans in the diaspora, but does so only rhetorically. In engaging the diaspora, the AU functions as an IGO, deploying one of its Commission directorates, CIDO, to work with diaspora governments and people. Yet the organization has done little structurally and institutionally to assume suprastate status in this regard. Respondents believe that achieving African political union requires more supranational authority of the AU to provide opportunities for substantive citizen participation in the AU.

Similar structural concerns are expressed in the AU organs the Economic, Social and Cultural Council (ECOSOCC) and PAP, whose strengths lie in their functions as citizen advisory mechanisms to the AU. Here, the concern is that the AU organs are structured in such a way that they are institutionally asymmetrically authoritative and lead to a democratic deficit for the AU when it comes to the quality of leadership in relation to societal participation and representation. ECOSOCC is seen as being offered as a platform and space for the community and civil societal groups—though on AU terms rather than the other way around. The advisory role, rather than independent, autonomous status of a real parliamentary body, that the PAP holds also augers well for the AU's intergovernmental status but not its integrative capabilities. As the head of an organ of the AU, the PAP's president plays an important role in the summits of the Assembly in representing the national parliaments that have nominated its steering committee.

Nonetheless, the PAP also has a mandate to take views on issues of critical importance to African affairs and to communicate them publicly to generate debate throughout Africa. While this is still an IGO initiative, if the PAP were conferred with its rightful autonomous-to-the-AU role, direct elections plus true legislative powers of citizen representation, the organ would foster greater gains for AU supranationalism. Failure to ratify the full implementation of the PAP so that the organ can fulfill its original mandate to represent African citizens in this manner may have more to do with the internal democracy dynamics of member states than the reluctance of member states to commit to Pan-African integration.

FINANCING DEVELOPMENT, RESOURCES, AND THE SHADOW OF NEOCOLONIALISM

On assuming office as chairperson in September 2012, AU commissioner Dr. Nkosazana Dlamini-Zuma was shocked to learn that western donors funded over 97 percent of AU programs. The first female AU Commission chairperson asserted, "No liberated mind can think their development agenda can be funded by donors. . . . We should be more self-reliant. Our governments must put money there [in the AU]" (*African Globe* 2012). Dlamini-Zuma refers to a major contradiction concerning the AU's goals and objectives to free Africans from imperialism, neocolonialism, and global control. If its agenda is not funded by Africans, but by the very forces from which it seeks freedom, how will it in effect realize its integrationist and union agenda? This is not an easy question for the AU at all, which relies on external funding from the wealthy capitalist world because its own continent—Africa—is income poor. Former South African president Thabo Mbeki asked: can a country be called sovereign if half its budget comes from its former colonial powers?

The AU confronts this additional challenge of self-sufficiency that is not shared by the EU, ASEAN, Arab League, or the Organization of American States (OAS). A vast majority of its members are so poor that they are unable to pay basic member dues; how much more can they fund expensive development projects? Only during the OAU's inaugural year were its membership fees essentially paid up, after which over twenty states were in arrears (Wolfers 1976). Throughout the thirty-nine years of the OAU, and the first four years of the AU, the majority of member governments defaulted on paying their annual assessments, and those who paid usually paid late and only in part. AU members had developed the habit of claiming that there was an administrative budget that was compulsory and an operational budget that was voluntary, but as the first female AU Commission chair remarked, "What is the use of paying salaries if you do not pay them to do anything?" (Dlamini-Zuma 2006).

Each of the twenty survey respondents cited lack of resources that led to overdependence for funding of the AU on international donors as the main factor contributing to the constraints on the AU's capacity to achieve its goals. Most are aware of the stark reality that the AU is a product of the least developed, poorest continent in the current international system, and thus realized that there should be little surprise to know that a poor continent would reflect weak institutions. Nonetheless, as one respondent wailed, that the AU's development projects and initiatives are funded by international donors is a serious problem! In this case, he pondered whether or not the AU was enabling the imperialism of Africa rather than eliminating it.

One respondent argued that it was not enough for member states' annual membership fees to support operational costs of the Union. Members' annual dues support the AU to exist as a bureaucratic institution, "so we get to be here and draft important policies and agendas for Africa," he complained. Nonetheless, he continued, "It is our so-called international partners who fund the initiatives of the Union and their implementation on the ground." The respondent complained further that when this happened, the AU's self-determined Pan-Africanist agenda is put aside for an external one—especially one that is controlled by the UN, EU, and US state-development agencies and by international nongovernmental organizations (NGOs), usually headquartered in the West.

There exists an acute awareness among AU employees regarding the problem of financing African development and global capital as they reflected on the way that they believed that the International Monetary Fund (IMF)/World Bank market-led economic agenda had fostered African deindustrialization and greater dependence on international donor aid. Separate African countries watched it happen but could do nothing to arrest the process except share knowledge to address the problem in OAU platforms—and now in AU platforms—which they hoped would collectively implement common economic agendas to address the issue. A staff writer for the *Economist* articulated the AU's economic dilemma more tactlessly. In an article that he titled "African Union: Short of Cash and Teeth," the writer underscored the challenges as follows:

> A big problem is money. The combined size of the economies of all the AU's countries is still on a par with the Netherlands' at an official exchange rate. This year's AU budget is $260m, compared with the $1.8 billion the UN spends just on its contribution to the Darfur peacekeeping mission. And African countries pay for only about 40% of the AU's budget. Algeria, Egypt, Libya, Nigeria and South Africa give $15m each. Malawi, whose president, Bingu wa Mutharika, holds the AU's annual chair, puts in $160,000; some countries pay as little as $20,000. China, the European Union and America pay for the rest. A new AU headquarters, to be built by the Chinese, is due to open next year beside the existing one. African stinginess, sighs Mr Ping, "does not do honour to the African cause." (*Economist* 2011)

There are several issues to parse out in order to understand the challenge of financing AU-led African development. One is the relative poverty of the AU's budget compared to its counterparts. The AU's 2011 annual budget was $260 million. Compare this to the annual budget of the AU's counterpart, the EU, that in 2011 was about $170 billion. What's more, with expensive peacekeeping operations and development agendas to stimulate production and economic growth for the world's poorest continent, compared to the EU, the AU's budget really should be much more. Another issue, of course, is the uneven advancement of AU member states' economies; some are relatively wealthy while most are very poor. Unlike the EU, the AU did not restrict its membership to economic standards and criterion. The AU was founded differently; but of course, the consequence is that the wealthier countries will be tasked with the burden of funding Africa's initiatives.

A more critical issue that explains the Africa-AU financing development dilemma is found in the structure of the developing world political economy and is a problem exhibited by the African contemporary circumstance the most. This concerns the issue of global-economic dependency whereby external powers, now including China, finance African development, a reality that has also become both a characteristic and a limitation for the AU. The issue represents a sore reality but a huge challenge for the AU, particularly as it concerns the terms that Africans choose to embark upon in order to achieve their economic progress. Characterized by an ideological prism that the late scholar Claude Ake referred to as "contending visions," through the AU (and former OAU), African countries have always struggled for self-determination in economic and development policy implementation (Ake 1996).

As soon as the Lagos Plan of Action (LPA) and the Final Act of Lagos were adopted, the Bretton Woods Institutions placed pressure on the countries of Africa to abandon the commitments they had just made to achieve economic integration and instead favor the Washington Consensus of individually negotiated structural adjustment programs that in design were ideologically hostile to the very notion of integration. The AU 2008 report acknowledged the toll that the issue of dependency was having on Africa and noted that the African integration project had been subject to competing pressures from outside the continent that pulled it in different directions and sought to lock it into binding agreements that facilitated a new scramble for the continent (African Union 2008).

The continual financial crisis facing the AU not only gravely inhibits its capacity to act effectively, but also renders it vulnerable to financial politics played by both member states and external powers (Khamis 2008, 65). The African Commission on Human and Peoples' Rights (ACHPR) depends on foreign donors for one-third of its budget, including depending on a Danish institute to write its documents. This caused the 2008 AU audit reviewers to recommend for the AU moving forward that "a strategic plan is the operational plan of the Mandate of an Organization and cannot be outsourced to a foreign interest" (African Union 2007, 85). The same donor dependency is evidenced in many NGOs in Africa. Over 90 percent of their funding may come not from membership fees, but from foreign donors, typically a single donor. That is why one criterion for admitting NGOs into the AU's ECOSOCC is that more than 50 percent of their funding should come from Africa (Statutes of the ECOSOCC of the AU, art. 6.6).

The fact that five of eight of the departments of the AU Commission are dedicated to economic development and growth emphasizes the importance of resolving the financial dependency problem for the Union and for Africa. Integration has been no accidental ideology of economic and development policy for Africans and their union. Nkrumah eloquently articulated the African dilemma during decolonization, whereby he would argue that a continent without unity would fragment economically and suffer the fate of insignificantly populated, landlocked, economically unviable states. This has been one of the most persuasive arguments for African integration and unity. For African nations, pooling the resources of their small, underdeveloped economies into an enlarged single one through which they would mutually benefit from their comparatively endowed neighbor is a very good idea. But even this agenda could not be advanced by commitment alone.

As such, already historically and structurally tied to economic networks connected to their wealthy former colonizers whose political-economic interest favored the status quo, continental economic integration would entail the institutional savvy of an enlarged, collective, and more strategic practice of African politics—the AU—to achieve an outcome. Significantly, former colonizers and contemporary capital-intensive international communities—whether multinational corporations, international finance institutions, or their wealthy host nations, especially the G8—have certainly been willing to help finance African development and have jumped at the chance to do this through the AU. However, the economic support has been delivered through charitable donor aid, which is riddled with political and economic conditionality and given on strict terms in contrast to Africa's self-determined agenda.

In contrast to Western donor economic policies that focus on laissez-faire markets, raw material comparative advantage, export trade, poverty reduction, and good governance and anticorruption policy, as well as on other social development indicators, the AU is primarily interested in increasing Africa's productive forces through greater continent-wide industrialization and in building the transcontinental infrastructure that will support this venture. The AU's Committee on Trade, Customs and Immigration Matters—one of the AU's seven Specialized Technical Committees (STC)—recognizes that among the fundamental drivers of trade are the development of productive capacity and industrial sophistication, trade-related infrastructure and services, and flawless operation of Africa's transport and transit corridors. Availability of trade information and trade finance are equally important for unleashing the potential of trade within Africa. Given the imbalances in the levels of development in African countries, the T&I STC also ensures equitable outcomes for member states through compensation mechanisms to address adjustment costs to greater trade opening, which helps smaller and weaker countries build their production and trade capacities.

The AU seeks to facilitate continental intraregional trade, seeing such a measure becoming an opportunity, on the one hand, for Africans to realize gains from trade while, on the other, for Africa to foster greater gains from collective continental export to the global gross domestic product. They understand that when African nations trade with each other, total African output is increased. Companies will produce for intra-African as well as domestic national markets. The AU's integration and continental free trade area goals for Africa are noble. However, if the West tends to fund Africa's peacekeeping operations and development projects, but not its economic integration agenda, the AU agenda needs to be funded all the same. In lieu of the unfortunate reality that the AU has not launched its three international financial institutions to achieve its economic agenda, there has been a lot of talk about launching new, short-term initiatives to raise funds. Respondents spoke positively about some of the initiatives that they had been involved with directly to help address the issue.

One example is the themed, "Africans Helping Africans" African Solidarity Initiative (ASI) that was established with a call to encourage, motivate, and empower African countries to assist in the AU's development initiatives, including in peacekeeping/building and in economic development projects across the continent. Targeting and soliciting African countries for the financing of African development, through measures like the ASI, has presented important opportunities for the AU to address the funding and resource challenge.

Pan-Africanism and National-International Legitimacy

While the ASI initiative addresses one of the AU's key challenges, respondents were more excited about the initiative's capacity to address other key challenges for the Union, namely the forging of a more close-knit relationship among member states. The initiative deliberately used the term "solidarity" to achieve this purpose. The integration of Africa, which respondents reminded was at the heart of the objectives of the AU, could not be achieved without a feeling of solidarity among Africans. Solidarity, in this formula, could take many forms beyond financial contributions, including various in-kind contributions by African countries to each other, such as experience sharing, best practices, provision of expertise, and capacity building (African Union 2012b).

The solidarity initiative speaks to the major challenge that respondents say faces the contemporary AU and follows from the challenges of organization and lack of resources. This is the national legitimacy question. Do member states believe in African union? Are they willing to share sovereignty with the AU? Respondents couched the national legitimacy challenge in various ways; they discussed issues pertaining to political will, national implementation, and Pan-African vision or commitment. They believed that the ASI would at least cultivate member states' commitment and conviction for Africa causes.

International legitimacy (respect of Africa in the international arena) would flow from this, many claimed. While Africa may be poor and thereby lack power and luster on the international stage, in a democratic world where humans were perceived as equal and where subjects were citizens with voice and agency, political will, couched with shared ideas, was more important than economic capacity. A continent that was united on its objectives could not be maneuvered by international interests.

As such, the legitimacy challenge for the AU engages both a national and international phenomenon. It refers to the AU's capacity to achieve its supranational objectives continent-wide and regionally, as well as globally and internationally. Every respondent attributed this challenge as the AU's most critical obstacle. The continental Pan-African congresses of the 1950s and 1960s—more than fifty years ago—laid bare the reality that the Pan-African vision of union was a contested idea among African member states. The ideological camps that formed fifty years ago between the unionist Casablanca group and the gradualist Monrovia group shifted over time but remain intact (see table 7.2). However, between 1999 and 2002 (the transition period from the OAU to the AU), the unionist position, reinvigorated by Libya and supported by Senegal, was overwhelmed yet again by the gradualists' position, which has become the mainstream approach to integration and union by member states of the AU.

The gradualist commitment to Pan-African unity was debated at a conference in Abuja, Nigeria, in 2005, under the theme "Desirability of a Union Government in Africa." Convened by the then four-year-old AU, the conference was attended by a wide spectrum of participants including members of the Union, academics, technical experts, representatives of the African diaspora, civil society organizations, as well as executives of the RECs and media practitioners from different parts of Africa. The gradualist position was again reinforced with the conference's conclusions:

The "necessity for Union Government is not in doubt."
It must be a "Union of the African people and not merely a Union of states and governments."
Its formation must be "based on a multi-layered approach" and on the principle of "gradual incrementalism."
The role of the RECs should be highlighted as building blocks for the continental framework. (African Union Commission 2007)

TABLE 7.2. CRITICAL MOMENTS IN THE DEBATE ABOUT AFRICAN UNION GOVERNMENT SINCE 1957

1957: Ghanaian independence

1963: Formation of the OAU

1980: LPA and the Final Act of Lagos

1981: African Charter on Human and Peoples' Rights

1990: Treaty Establishing the AEC, a.k.a. the Abuja Treaty

1990: Charter on Popular Participation in Development and Transformation

1991: Kampala CSSDCA

1995: Relaunching Africa's Economic and Social Development: The Cairo Agenda for Action

1998: Protocol to the African Charter on Human and Peoples' Rights on the Establishment of an African Court on Human and Peoples' Rights

2000: OAU Declaration on Unconstitutional Changes of Government

2000: Solemn Declaration on the CSSDCA

2000: Constitutive Act of the AU

2002: Establishment of NEPAD

2003: AU Convention on Preventing and Combating Corruption

2003: Memorandum of Understanding on the APRM

2003: Protocol to the African Charter on Human and Peoples' Rights on the Rights of Women in Africa

2006: Grand Debate on Union Government

2007: African Charter on Democracy, Elections and Governance

2013: Declaration of Pan-Africanism and African Renaissance—Vision 2063

As a follow-up to the January 2007 conference, the AU Assembly planned for the theme at its Ninth Ordinary Session in July 2007 to be a "Grand Debate on the Union Government," which reaffirmed that the ultimate goal of the AU is full political and economic integration leading to a united African government (African Union Commission, 2007). Member states accepted the UAS as a common and desirable goal but acknowledged that differences existed over the modalities and time frame for achieving this goal and the appropriate pace of integration. The debate over Pan-Africanism is certainly different fifty years after the founding of the OAU. In a global geopolity and economy, historic ideological positions have been transformed. It is the so-called satellite African states—the more successful economies with more active civil societies and new breed renaissance leaders—that tend to support the gradualist position and the smaller countries that support more rapid trajectories toward unionism (Wanyeki 2007). Whatever the rationale, most respondents felt that, aside from rhetorical lip-service, the general weakness of member states to commit to Pan-Africanist unionism has contributed to the Union's very slow progress toward economic integration and political unity. Aside from lack of political will in support of Pan-Africanist unionism, other reasons that member states—and African peoples—are circumspect of the AU's assertive supranationalism are their differences in national values and that states are uneven in their capacities to implement AU policies.

According to its 2011 Sixteenth Annual Summit, shared values of the AU are conceived as those norms, principles, and practices that provide the basis for collective actions and solutions in addressing Africa's political, economic, and social challenges. These values are anchored in the belief that Africans must work collectively for their common destiny. Furthermore, shared or collective values have always been a feature of African integration efforts and have been an important subject of dialogue during interactions within the AU. It is not clear, however, whether African member states hold shared values. There are differences in the ideology of Pan-Africanism. Some African countries are democracies while others are not. Moreover, while each African country has its share of ethnic, linguistic, and religious pluralism within its national borders, intracontinental pluralism is particularly underscored by lingua-franca pluralism, which also divides the AU among the Anglophone and Francophone countries.

Many of our respondents cited these differences as reasons why member states of the AU fail to own, imbibe, and passionately implement the AU's many valuable collectively ratified Africa public policies. Member states treat summits as public showcases whereby decisions are ratified by them in a lot of fanfare, yet are not devolved down to national political cultures and environments once annual summits are over. One respondent suggested that the AU's democracy initiatives had little impact in fostering democratic development for the many nondemocratic countries. Those countries were trapped in historic structural arenas that inhibited democratization, despite their fraternizing with democratic countries of the Union through AU membership and peer review mechanisms. In this respondent's opinion, democratic African countries had a greater vision toward integration and they possessed the knowledge (technical and civil society) to advance the Union and its vision. With equitable decision-making power in the Union (each member state has equal vote in decisions), nondemocratic countries had no incentive to domestically reform. An unintended consequence of the AU was to have given them an opportunity to wax their undemocratic power.

Others see the issue differently, however. One respondent thought that the AU's gender initiatives (e.g., the commissioner gender quota) have demonstrably provided models for facilitating gender equity within member states' nations. In compelling 50 percent gender membership for its eight commissioners, the AU Commission quota provides member states with a strong incentive to foster gender equity within their countries. As well, because the commissioner elections are based on regional representation, female commissioners have come from a range of countries, not only from the more democratic countries. Female commissioners from countries that are not advanced in their democratic credentials function as important vehicles for engendered democratic development in their countries. The respondent suggests that they also function as facilitators of intracontinental values, of which gender equity was an important value, that countries sought help and assistance from the AU in integrating across the continent.

The fact and value of sovereignty—the fact that African nation-states are recognized as lowest denominator legal entities by international law—is another reason why AU member states may not support the AU's economic integration and political union objective in the immediate, short-term future. While there are clear advantages to economic and political community, like regimes everywhere in the international system, most African regimes cherish their right to statehood and hold on dearly to all the powers that are derived from such a status. If this weren't the case, Africa's two newest states, Eritrea and the South Sudan, would never have been founded. Prior to their current statuses as nation-states, these states were minority communities within sovereign states. Now, with equal membership rights with member states that they consider hegemonic, majority states that no longer had legitimate rights to govern them, they see too well the benefits of self-determined sovereign rule of smaller, more relatively homogeneous communities. It is difficult for AU members from these countries to value the supranational pan-sovereignty that Africa's AU aspires to.

On the issue of international legitimacy, one respondent put it this way: International legitimacy for the AU stems from the continent's disunity. That is to say, Africans will not garner much luster in an international community where there is only muted allegiance to a Pan-African unity that is easily expressed through voice and pronouncements, but that is loosely structured, variably implemented, and vaguely institutionalized. In such a scenario, international powers and institutions are much more inclined to bypass the AU to embark upon bilateral interstate relations in Africa where interests are more easily brokered one-on-one directly. In a post–Cold War international system, neorealism explains why states cherish their sovereignty and continue to compete in an international arena structured by hierarchies of power and interest. Although most of the African continent is at the bottom of that hierarchy, as fifty-five individual states, African states act in accordance with their own interests.

> Osman Kargbo, editor of the *MarketPlace Business* newspaper in the Gambia, has argued that trade can be boosted in Africa only when "we have leaders that are politically willing and also have economic know-how of intelligibly controlling the micro- and macroeconomic systems of their countries."
>
> [Kargbo] said the present crop of African leaders, some of whom might have the know-how to boost trade and real economic integration within Africa, are not willing to commit themselves to achieve it because most of them are stooges of Western powers and multinational organisations, some of which are not dedicated to Africa's economic liberation and development. (Jahateh 2012)

The AU international legitimacy dilemma is manifest in international security governance. We have already seen how donor dependency, which for the AU's peacekeeping operation units is probably around nine-tenths of its optimal funding, incapacitates the Union and weakens its suprasovereignty. Where there is consensus between AU members and global powers, this results in the AU's largest peacekeeping and peacemaking operations to date, as in the Sudan and Somalia. But where western powers and many AU members hold divergent views, as over the 2011 Libyan civil war, the AU finds its authority marginalized by North Atlantic Treaty Organization (NATO) powers.

The reinforcement of Africans' marginalization in the global security hierarchy is manifest through the hegemonic power play of international security organizations and institutions that compete with the AU's own security organization, the PSC. For example, the US African Command (USAFRICOM) persists in its agenda for Africa, despite African and AU protestations. Ambiguity is deepened when many AU member states request antiterrorism training missions from USAFRICOM. NATO and the UN Security Council (UNSC) exercise military power in Libya and in Côte d'Ivoire despite the AU's alternative security agenda for the continent. While the United States cites sovereignty to justify its nonsignatory to the International Criminal Court (ICC), African countries are targeted for ICC arrests and war crimes despite the AU's attempts to negotiate fairness in the distribution of ICC justice. To underscore this lack of legitimacy that the top-tier international system has for the AU is the example of the United Kingdom, which has, in the recent past, threatened a resource- and income-poor AU member, Malawi, with withdrawal of aid if it didn't adhere to ICC rules to arrest sitting AU member, President Omar al-Bashir, at the AU summit that it would have held. This demand was insisted upon by the United Kingdom even though the AU does not observe the ICC warrant for African countries.

The *Malawi Voice* referred to the incident as a new form of imperialism, faulting Britain's cruel persistent need over three hundred years to control Malawi and subvert the African vision through bullying tactics. The *Voice* also faulted the AU for remaining silent and its inability to stand up for countries like Malawi when it was victimized this way (Nyondo 2012). In such a scenario, AU Pan-Africanism operates at the periphery of global power; it is no wonder that the multiple affronts to its authority—from the national to the international—will severely constrain the Union's legitimacy as a viable suprastate, whose ability to achieve its integration and unity objectives for Africa will need a long haul to be realized.

ACCOMPLISHMENTS, IMPACT, AND FUTURE

Despite the AU's many challenges, which sometime seem insurmountable, dooming the institution to criticisms of failure, there was not a respondent to our survey who did not have confidence in the AU's accomplishments, its impact on transforming African politics and affairs, and its likely prospects for achieving its economic integration and unity goals in the future, regardless of how far flung into a *longue-durée* future, according to one respondent. This respondent put it this way: In a global era, no one African country can handle globalization's huge problems alone. African governments realize that they need help from an organization that they have designed and established—and that they can especially trust. That organization is the AU. Furthermore, the AU is a developmental statist institution much like African political regimes. What we mean is that there is no doubt that the Union has not stayed in one place over fifty years. It has grown and continues to evolve. The AU draws continuous lessons from its interaction with member states, African peoples, and international communities.

Recognizing, nonetheless, more challenges than opportunities in the status of the AU's supranationality, especially in achieving immediate or near-term sociocultural economic integration and political union, most respondents observed the AU's accomplishment and immediate future impact as being drawn from its status as an African IGO and as a regional organization. As an IGO, it is in the arenas of conflict resolution and economic development that the AU finds its greatest successes and prospects. Looking at the AU phenomenon this way, respondents suggested that, combined with an ideology of gradualist supranationalism, the intergovernmental agency of the AU also addresses its economic dependency problem and ultimately the dilemmas in AU national and international legitimacy.

One may find evidence for this thesis in the area of political development where the AU's intergovernmental success in Somalia is comparable only to NATO's success—or not—in Afghanistan. Of course for both chronic conflict-prone countries, success can only be measured minimally whereby both peacemaking operations—AMISOM for Somalia and the International Security Assistance Force (ISAF) for Afghanistan—have been able to push back violent opposition militias to the margins of the country, control at least the capital cities and seats of government, and establish a governing political process for the warring parties that facilitates long-term stability. It is the differences in each operation that mark the AU's operation a success and representative of an institutional model for other regions.

NATO's ISAF operation constitutes a global international force led by and funded by wealthy Western countries and supported through these countries' will by way of the UN. ISAF comprises approximately 129,000 troops with huge air support from fifty different countries deployed throughout Afghanistan, while AMISOM comprises 16,383 troops with scant air support from eight African countries. In a given year, NATO's Afghanistan budget is $4.1 billion (2009 estimates), while AMISOM's budget was $1.7 billion (2008 estimates). Afghanistan, in the Central Asian region, has no homegrown regional organization that can intervene on behalf of it as the AU has achieved for Somalia. As such, in Afghanistan, NATO's liberal agenda for postconflict resolution is pushed despite the alternative cultural context of the country. In Somalia, by engaging fellow Africans in a familiar sociocultural context such as the revival of Somali indigenous institutions, the AU is able to infuse core principles of engaging grass roots in the conflict resolution process (see Intergovernmental Authority on Development [IGAD] principles and Conference on Security, Stability, Development and Cooperation in Africa [CSSDCA]), and as a result, garners more respectability in the peacemaking process.

As an intergovernmental agency representing the region of continental Africa, compared to other multilateral institutions in an era of globalization, Africa's AU realizes some of its best gains for the continent economically. Importantly as well, it is through this institutional structure that, while it might appear to enable external control of the continent through the solicitation of foreign direct investment, AU mediation of the process may indeed be the reason why, despite the fact that most of the AU's initiatives are funded by external donors, this fact does not foster imperialism.

By interjecting itself into every aspect of a diverse global economy and negotiating economic transactions—albeit asymmetrically—with global partners, the AU is at least actively engaged in what Anthony McGrew termed as "enmeshment," which it mobilizes on its own terms (McGrew 2004). This is a form of international economic interdependence where, while gains among parties may not be absolutely mutual, they are at least relatively mutual. Table 7.3 shows that, at least in the earlier years (2004–7) of the AU establishment, due to its many fundraising activities, especially through the NPCA, the Union anticipated a large share of external budget, and by the end of most years, the Union received much less from its member states, and certainly a lot less than was pledged. Nevertheless, the AU has for the first time, for Africa, established a mechanism for raising funds for development and thereby operating as a viable donor for the continent's projects.

An example is the African Union for Housing Finance (AUHF), which is an association of mortgage banks, building societies, housing corporations, and other organizations involved in the mobilization of funds for shelter and housing on the continent of Africa. Given that the regulatory environments in many African countries are not appropriate for mortgage finance, the AUHF actively seeks ways to incorporate and assist, among others, informal sector lenders, such as community banks, peoples' banks, saving associations, and credit unions to participate in the housing finance market.

Another example is the fact that the AU's NPCA, the AU Department of Agriculture, and the RECs, together with a number of donors and African gov-

TABLE 7.3. SUMMARY OF THE AU APPROVED BUDGET (SOURCED FROM AFRICAN UNION 2008) IN US$ '000S

YEAR	APPROVED BUDGET	ASSESSED BUDGET TO MEMBER STATES	BUDGET REQUEST-ED FROM EXTERNAL PARTNERS	INCOME RECEIVED FROM MEMBER STATES	INCOME RECEIVED FROM EXTERNAL PARTNERS	TOTAL ANNUAL INCOME
2004	43,000	40,422	2,578	25,632	10,560	36,192
2005	149,223	60,228	88,995	48,822	25,542	74,364
2006	136,004	69,389	66,615	73,890	15,003	88,893
2007	132,988	96,449	36,539	63,773	10,101	73,874
TOTAL	461,215	266,488	194,727	212,117	61,206	273,323

ernments, collaborate in raising funds for the Multi-donor Trust Fund of the Comprehensive Africa Agricultural Development Programme (CAADP, a program of AU-NEPAD), hosted at the World Bank. The fund will channel financial support to fostering common African agricultural standards in the areas of extending the area under sustainable land management, improving rural infrastructure and trade-related capacities for market access, increasing food supply and reducing hunger, agricultural research, and technology dissemination and adoption. Again, in April 2012 responding to its own chronic food crisis in the Horn of Africa, in collaboration with the AfDB, the AU raised $380 million to help famine-hit families during a donor conference. African nations pledged $28.8 million. Fundraising initiatives such as these increase the AU's international legitimacy, as evidenced by this US State Department website posting:

> The African Union has been using the phrase, "African Solutions for African Problems," to mean that Africa as a continent must endeavor to be full partners in addressing African problems. The African Union has never suggested that it wants to solve its problems in isolation from the international community rather it has consistently asserted that it wants to insert African partnership, plans, and proposals into the dynamic of the discovery of solutions to African problems.

By taking leadership, in concert with the United Nations and African Union Partner Group Nations, the African Union has demonstrated commendable leadership and has put into action the proverbial statement of "putting your money where your mouth is." (U.S. State Department Official Blog 2011).

Essentially then, optimists of the AU understand the reality of a postcolonial world where subverted and weak power can be asserted through negotiations as well as maneuverings. Given its focus on idealism and multilateral cooperation, international liberalism certainly partially explains the AU's success as Africa's manifestation of an institution in this regard. Nonetheless, liberalism doesn't go far enough.

It is through a consideration of the way that the international constructivist framework operates that the AU finds its greatest accomplishment and hope for Africa. International constructivism reveals more comprehensive aspects of the AU-Africa phenomenon—the relationship between identity and global politics and the subtext and subjectivity behind political behavior that reveals the more nuanced psychoanalytical understandings, agencies, and rationales involved in the political process and the exercise of power. William Zartman's famous adage that ideologies not only rationalize and explain the reasons for one's present situation, they also provide strategies toward future goals (Zartman 1966, 38) rings so true.

So be it with the idea of Pan-Africanism in prophesying a suprastate vision for Africa and its diaspora carried forth in the contemporary international arena by Africa's AU. It is in this status—as an emerging suprastate—that the institution embodies the constructivist method. With it, the Pan-African AU brings along a diaspora history that straddles the globe cross-generationally, through diverse political regimes and diverse civil societies, communities, and social movements across the continent and its own new institutions, innovations, public policies, and ideas toward a vision for an integrated Africa in union.

It is this vision (diaspora suprastatism), voice and discourse (its numerous communiqués by its leaders, representatives, and staff), and agency (its self-determined actions in resolutions, policy enactments, institution building)—all also important methodologies that characterize the constructivist method—that explains the AU's sustenance and relevance. In viewing the AU through a constructivist lens, we know that the institution's successful status as an international organization and regional organization is not enough for it (in terms of the institution's self-proclaimed objectives) or for African peoples who desire a stronger, more united leadership that can effectively represent Africa in the world. Yet, contradictorily, constructivism helps us to see both challenges and future opportunities for Africa's AU.

Constructivism also addresses the notion of the external funding results in imperialism dilemma that many are concerned with regarding the AU's viability. Reliance on international funding may not subvert the self-determined African agenda as it would appear to do so. There are a few reasons why this is the case. The institutional structure of the Union, especially its suprastate that embeds the ontological imprints of Pan-Africanism for its members, leaders, and agent actors, guides AU actions and decisions in a manner that is determinative on an African-owned ideological vision. In the case of international finance capital, for example, ideally it is AU actors who initiate the solicitation of funding for projects they deem fit to be assigned to needs that they prioritize. As agents, these Africans direct the projects according to their will. This is what African solutions for African problems looks like. In the long run, the hope is that as Africa develops (hopefully through the AU's many development projects), the continent will have the increasing ability to self-finance its development and growth.

Moreover, the AU's three-tiered structure deflates the inclination toward old-style imperialism whereby foreign donors fund to control the continent politically and militarily. After all, the fact that 97 percent of the continent's development projects are funded by the international community did not stop the AU from taking a decision against the UN and against NATO in the 2011 Libyan conflict. This is because it is the AU IGO that solicits funding for the development of Africa, while it is the AU suprastate (through its Assembly and its PSC) that makes decisions and enacts policies on war and peace.

The savvy and complex institutional structure—based on an internal democracy—of the AU's numerous suborgan decision-making procedures assures decision outcomes that are made by member states on behalf of their country constituencies deliberated against the Union's objectives and vision for Africa. There is no space for foreign representation or intervention here. The AU's multilateralism—its ability to operate from multiple platforms with multiple actors—is at play here. As such, whereas foreign actors will try to influence African politics to achieve their own interests, it is much more difficult to do so through Africa assembled and united.

CONCLUSION

Ironically, outside of the organizational culture of the AU, many are not confident that the Pan-African vision that the AU has made its core mission will ever realize.

A recent publication on the AU edited by African judges from Somalia (Yusuf) and Algeria (Ouguergouz) entitled *The African Union: Legal and Institutional Framework* began its 576-page manual of the institution as follows:

> "African Unity" is evidently not a powerful uniting force and Pan-Africanism must continue to overcome many recurrent obstacles such as linguistic and cultural differences, the weight of multifarious links with the former colonial masters, the reluctance of countries when it comes to pooling their wealth, the attachment to a brand new national sovereignty. . . . At present, the construction of African continentalism seems an arduous task. (Yusuf and Ouguergouz 2012, 22–23)

Alternatively, the current research study of the AU sees the glass half full rather than half empty with constructivism as our wheel. The AU faces challenges and obstacles in achieving its goals for Africa, but it has been navigating these challenges for thirty-nine (OAU) plus eleven (AU) years, thus fifty years. That the institution has sustained as well as reinvented itself over the years is testimony to its success and the will of Africans for its presence. Like all statecraft in human histories, the AU builds upon its setbacks and stalemates, finding new avenues to function and perform.

It is as a result of these Africa challenges that the AU has been created and established in the first place—by Africans. The AU's vision for Africa is for the continent to become a unified continent that is a single federated country and a conglomerate of Africa's cultural unity in diversity worldwide. Such a country secures and polices its borders. Significantly, the AU's Africa wishes to be an economically integrated and rapidly modernizing continent that is on par with the growth and development of China and India. In achieving such a goal, the AU's Africa will engage freely in the global arena projecting on the world scale the human integrity, professional dignity, and cultural aesthetic of the African identity.

The (Pan) African Union Phenomenon: Mali as Exemplar

T he African Union (AU) held its Twentieth Ordinary Session in Addis Ababa, Ethiopia, on January 27 and 28, 2013, and significantly, Ethiopia, the country site of the AU's headquarters, assumed the leadership of the international organization. In accepting the leadership mantel from Benin's President Thomas Boni Yayi, President Hailemariam Desalegn, Ethiopia's new prime minister at the time, expressed commitment to Africa's founding fathers for laying a solid foundation for the unity and solidarity of Africa when they met in Addis Ababa fifty years prior to establish the AU's mother—the Organization of African Unity (OAU). The new leader of Africa cited Emperor Haile Selassie in a statement that he had delivered at the founding Addis Ababa Conference on May 25, 1963.

> What we require is a single African organization through which Africa's single voice may be heard, within which Africa's problems may be studied and resolved. . . . Let us, at this Conference, create a single institution to which we will all belong, based on principles to which we all subscribe, confident that in its councils our voices will carry their proper weight, secure in the knowledge that the decision there will be dictated by Africans and only by Africans and that they will take full account of all vital African considerations. (Daviso 2013)

With Selassie's statement Desalegn reminisced fifty years of OAU-AU achievements in successfully contributing in a significant way to the liberation of Africa from colonialism and apartheid. He noted how the organization had served as a common platform for Africa's collective efforts in its interaction with the rest of the world. Yet Desalegn couldn't help but also note the sustained challenges for the AU as new conflicts, such as the crisis in Mali, threatened African peace and security. In this regard, the 2013 AU chairperson led the rest of the continent in pledging to do everything possible to help restore constitutional order in Mali, safeguard the sovereignty and territorial integrity of the country, and address the humanitarian crisis in collaboration with the Economic Community of West African States (ECOWAS), the United Nations (UN), and other international partners (Federal Democratic Republic of Ethiopia 2013).

With the new Ethiopian leader dedicating its January meeting to both Pan-African renaissance and the conflict in Mali, the AU proceeded with its adoption of the Resolution on Mali. The resolution claimed that on behalf of Africa, the AU reiterated its firm commitment to the national unity and territorial integrity of the Republic of Mali, noting that the continued occupation of the northern part of Mali by various armed, criminal, and terrorist groups was a serious threat to peace, security, and stability in Mali, in the region, and beyond. The AU went on to reaffirm Africa's deep solidarity with Mali, a founding member whose commitment to Pan-Africanism and the causes of the continent had never wavered in half a century of independence. The resolution expressed the collective will of Africans' determination to pool their efforts together to help their sisterly country to overcome its challenges.

The AU Mali Resolution brings to bear key elements of the current book's major research questions, its core thesis, and its key themes. In bringing with it the unraveling of the associative content on the Mali crisis of 2012–13, the resolution acts as an important occasion for concluding the current book, *The African Union's Africa*. Our conclusion is titled, "The (Pan) African Union Phenomenon: Mali as Exemplar" to reaffirm the book's research objective in this respect. In addressing the manner in which the AU addresses the problems of one of its members, and in assessing the impact that such actions have on the continent and in the world, both the 2013 Mali Resolution and the objective of our concluding chapter are integrally tied.

Note that we began our book with the following questions: Why does the AU still stand fifty years after its original emergence as the OAU? How has the organization institutionally evolved, strengthened, and expanded from the OAU regional to the AU global? Why do all countries in Africa (ergo Mali)—except one

(Morocco)—continue to participate in the organization's collective action? How do African nations and peoples use the AU for their collective interests on behalf of Africa and in the service of Africa vis-à-vis the contemporary global governing order? Our study formulated these questions to examine the AU's impact on African politics and affairs and used them to consider further questions: Is the AU relevant to Africa? Does it matter to African politics? Is it making change in key areas of African affairs: cultural and social identity, democracy and human rights, security and conflict resolution, and economic development?

By way of formulating a core thesis response to these questions, the book's Introduction proposed the African Union phenomenon as a theoretical lens and an ideological standpoint that we as authors would use as a guide to reveal research insights regarding the AU institution's political behavior in the contemporary global hierarchy. We defined the AU phenomenon as the AU's evolving institutional efforts, capacities, style, and prospects to address the continent's myriad challenges. The term "phenomenon" would especially refer to the international organization's distinctive efforts to transform the national politics of Africa, as well as globalize the practice of African politics utilizing key institutions that it claims are rooted in African self-determined, international norms and values. These cultural institutions are Pan-Africanism, African solutions for African problems, hybrid democracy, *Pax Africana*, and the African Economic Community (AEC). Their construction, establishment, implementation, and interactive engagement with Africa and the world are representative of the manner in which Africans are expressing and practicing diverse values and agencies. They are building and evolving practices, leaders, and social forces that are—through the continent's AU—contributing to the advancement of contemporary global development.

Significantly as well, we presented the aforementioned thesis and thematic about Africa's AU as important new ways to examine international relations and political science in relation to the study of Africa that we claimed must do more to examine the dynamism, complexity, nuance, and vibrancy of African agent-led practices in transforming national politics comparatively that is contributing an impact on global affairs. In this regard, we have been especially attentive to the concept of agency, whereby Africans exercise autonomy through institutions that they establish, develop, own, control, and lead regarding issues that affect them. We assessed scholar Tom Tieku's nascent conceptualization of the notion of agency in the international relations of Africa in this regard to discover ways that the AU has enhanced African agency, particularly in the international arena, by making the African voice louder in a crowded global governance arena (Tieku 2011).

For our conclusion, using the Malian crisis, we reaffirm the ways that ideology, institutionalism, and African internationalism underpin the AU's capacity to engage in a more expansive and assertive Pan-Africanism. We treated the topic of ideology in the Introduction by presenting African solutions for African problems as an important norm and value that undergird and guided our core thesis, captured by what we have referred to throughout the book and now use as a concluding chapter title in the AU phenomenon. African solutions for African problems would inform the cultural politics that the AU would use to mobilize Africans to the establishment of a new global AU out of an old regional OAU. It would refer to African autonomy and the imperative to develop capacities indigenous to African cultures and contexts and public policy solutions for continental affairs. It would connote and invoke a genre of pan-nationalism, pride, and a can-do attitude, as well as evidence of Africa's new global engagement. African solutions for African problems would mark a new acceptance of division of labor and sharing of responsibilities with the international community by Africans, and thereby reflect the complexity of Africa's problems, which requires a collective and collaborative approach premised on a range of partnerships that should seek to establish coordination on both the international and continental levels.

We developed our thematic on institutionalism first in chapter 2 where we described the AU's complex architecture. We extended our theme about institutionalism to collective security matters in Africa in chapter 5 where we began with the question of whether, given the pervasive conflict on the continent, the AU could achieve its goals of economic integration and cultural as well as political union. In this regard, we pondered over whether the continent's weak states and regions need to unify first and galvanize their institutional resources to address the continent's challenges with conflict and insecurity. *Pax Africana* would represent the institutional vision through which this could be achieved: the peace of Africa would have to be assured by the exertions of Africans themselves, in Ali Mazrui's words, a call for Africans to police their own continent (Mazrui 1969).

With regard to internationalism, in presenting our opening theoretical framework about Africa's AU in relation to globalism, the notion of the AU phenomenon would also reveal how the Union fostered participation in and advancement of the complex project called globalization in the context of globalization's underlying structures—politics, culture, and economics—which are employed as intersecting precipitators of transformation. We argued that it is in this globalized context that the AU represents African regions, nation-states, communities, and peoples and fosters their agency and collective action in a global arena. It is the AU phenomenon that provides Africans with institutional capacity and agency to project African voice in proscribing its own self-determined policy solutions on important African global affairs and issues. As such, the AU allows Africa to exercise independent authority on a continent that has been historically dependent on the international community in decision making regarding issues that affect the continent.

For the current conclusion, as such, we will apply the book's thesis about the AU phenomenon in relation to ideology, institutionalism, and internationalism to Mali, an AU member state that underwent a crisis from 2012 to 2013. The AU's Mali Resolution represents what has now become a standard approach employed by Africa's AU to address Africa's political affairs in this regard. Several resolutions have been similarly styled for conflicts in the Democratic Republic of the Congo (DRC), Guinea, Somalia, the South Sudan and Sudan, Mauritania, and Mauritius. In 2012–13, Mali was a member state undergoing dire crisis whose elements dovetail areas of AU impact that our book sought to examine, including cultural identity, democracy and society, economic development, and conflict and security.

In the area of cultural identity, we see how Mali's history represents the ideals of Pan-Africanism and refers back to many of Africa's greatest empires and cultures such as Ghana, Mali, and Songhai. Like most African countries, the country is socially stratified in terms of ethnicity and religion that, given the continent's regional expansiveness and diversity, is sometimes ethnicized, racialized, and neocolonialized. Mali also reveals the challenges of Africa in the area of development and democracy. For a twenty-year period, the country was heralded by Western liberal rankings as a beacon of democracy; but this assessment ignored the stark underdevelopment and poverty of the country that would do little to foster a sustainable democracy.

In the area of conflict and security, we examine how Mali imploded into a collapsed state practically overnight. The democratic government was unable to stave off a coup from lowly junior mutinous officers and the numerous rebel groups that had easily become animated in the country's north. By 2013, Mali illuminated the conflict and security challenge of Africa in the context of global insecurity that unleashed a war on terror in the country and in Africa since 2001. With Operation Serval (January 13 French military intervention), Mali also resuscitated debates about neocolonialism in Africa, crystallizing and magnifying to the news headlines our thesis about the AU phenomenon and its relevance in the context of geopolitical global power.

In our conclusion, we will see how the AU realizes its objectives and practices its geopolitical behavior,—defined in this text as the global politics of Pan-Africanism—through its response to the Mali crisis. The AU's attempt to address the Mali crisis illustrates for the Union a given paradox of challenge and opportunity in its attempt to address some of the continent's most critical dilemmas in the areas of integration, security, democracy, and development. As a case study for the current book on the AU, Mali reveals the continent's dire challenges from which one can glean prospects for resolution when AU Pan-African institutional agency is deployed. The AU's Pan-Africanism is manifest in the areas of African countries' common and shared vulnerability, their shared nation-building, and the region's collective security. We will refer to this as greater Pan-Africanism whose core values and imprint are reflected in the AU's 2013 Mali Resolution.

Common and shared Mali vulnerability refers to Mali's collapse as a signal for other African countries that share similar prospects for breakdown. The internal dimensions of Mali's 2013 crisis were not very different from where other African countries had been before Mali—Côte-d'Ivoire, Libya, Guinea, Mauritania, the DRC, and Somalia—and where others could go: Nigeria, Senegal, Kenya, or Tanzania. Like Mali, much of Africa possesses similar contextual national terrains that include ethnic and religious pluralism and deep divisions, a democracy and development conundrum, and global terrorist networks attracting foreign regional and international wars.

Shared nation-state building refers to the prowess of the collective AU state as a Pan-African institutional actor that lends its collective will and institutional support to African countries' political and economic development. As a Pan-African regional state actor, the AU had been working with the Malian state to support it with conflict resolution before the crisis. After the coup, the AU deployed its institutional mechanisms to ensure that the Malian state adhered to the rules of its Constitutive Act. To uphold its policy that its states would be democracies, the AU suspended Mali from the Union to force its coup leaders to step down. It assisted the Malian state in reestablishing an interim civilian regime as well as organized postconflict democratic transition and national sovereignty and cohesion. With regard to the crucial area of collective security, in addressing the Malian conflict as a transborder regional one with both domestic and international nexuses and thus implications for global Africa, the AU lobbied the international community to adopt UN Resolution 2085 and supported France's military intervention, Operation Serval, and deployed the African-led International Support Mission in Mali (AFISMA) to resolve Mali's conflict and keep the peace.

Our conclusion, then, attempts to illustrate and reaffirm our thesis throughout the book that the AU's response to the Mali crisis reflects the international organization's style of governance representative of a geopolitical dirigisme used to continually evolve the Union's institutional structure and deploy its codes, public policies, projects, programs, human capital, and initiatives to assert its supremacy over Africa and on behalf of it in a global world. This is the AU's Pan-Africanism. In subsequent subsections, we will review the previous chapters, first presenting the Malian crisis and then presenting details of the AU's response. We conclude our book with a final discussion about the AU's impact on the continent and the world.

The Malian Crisis: A Historical, Regional, and Global Survey

The 2012–13 Malian crisis can be characterized in four dimensions. It was a coup, a democratic reversal, a collapse of the state and government, and the eruption of a civil war. The crisis began in March 2012 when a military coup led by Captain Amadou Sanogo deposed a second-term, and voluntarily term-limited, President Amadou Toumani Touré, which ended the twenty-year democratic regime. Soon after the coup in the same year, Mali deteriorated to an intractable civil war, whereby Tuareg militants seceded from the country's northern region renaming it the state of Azawad, which became a haven for warring Islamic extremist militants and other secessionists.

In January 2013 the crisis made another turn when France militarily intervened into the country by way of Operation Serval, which served to take back the north and its key cities (Gao, Timbuktu, and Kidal) from the Islamic militants. By January 17, 2013, Mali's crisis crystallized as an African problem for an African solution when Africa formally and militarily intervened in Mali through the deployment of AFISMA, whose troops were drawn from twenty-one African countries.

Mali's four-tiered crisis had not been expected and thus plunged the world into debates about an explanation for the crisis. After all, from 1992 to March 2012, Mali had been considered a blossoming democracy by international freedom ratings. There are three prisms through which one may explain the 2012–13 Malian crisis: Africa's cultural pluralism that leads to deep divisions, the democracy-development conundrum, and the intensification of the war on terror facilitated by a growing internationalism, militarism, and interventionism in the region. Each prism presented below exposits complex dimensions of Mali's state-society. The dilemma of Mali's cultural diversity refers to the continent's deep precolonial subnational pluralism and the problems that have arisen as a result of a colonially imposed nation-state heritage manifest in a postcolonial state of affairs.

As with other African countries, at the national level, Malian symbols reinforce central aspects of pan-national African culture through the struggle against colonization, the celebration of Mali's rich history dating back to the Malian Empire, and its long multicultural tradition. For example, contemporary Mali is the site of three of Africa's most magnificent empires: Ghana (eighth to twelfth centuries), Mali (thirteenth to fourteenth centuries), and Songhai (fifteenth century). And from 1600 to 1800, present-day Mali was also the site for a number of famous African kingdoms and city-states, including Jaara, Segu, Macina, and Tukulor.

Before taking on the name Mali, a name of a precolonial civilization that symbolizes Pan-Africanism when it signifies Africa's glorious contribution to world history, Mali was part of the colony of French Sudan; it was later part of the Mali Federation (Senegal, Mali, and Guinea), and then the Ghana-Guinea-Mali Union of African States in 1961–63. Given this history, the establishment of the independent Mali Republic as we know it today embodies the deep precepts of the aforementioned *longue durée* and expansive regional and internationalist history in its postnational identity. As such, it is no accident that Mali's flag uses the color symbolism of the Pan-African unity movement: green (hope), gold (a reference to one of Mali's natural resources), and red (the blood sacrificed in the struggle against colonization).

Mali's contemporary postnational cultural pluralism reflects this *longue-durée* African history that spans linguistic, cultural, and social influences from North Africa, West Africa, and Mali's former colonizer, France. Today's major ethnic group in Mali is the Mande (e.g., Bamana, Jula, Malinke), who comprise 50 percent of the population and who were the populace of the ancient Malian Empire. There are also the Peul or Fulbe, who represent 17 percent and whose ancestry stretches across the Fulani jihadist routes spanning old migration routes from northern Nigeria to Senegal. The Voltaic (e.g., Bobo, Senufo, Minyanka) are 12 percent; the Tuareg and Arabs spanning the Maghreb are 10 percent. The Soninke of the old Songhai are 6 percent, and the Dogon are 5 percent. There are Christian minorities that make up about 5 percent of the population and those who follow traditional African beliefs. However, over 90 percent of people generally follow Sufi Islam.

Unmanaged cultural and religious pluralism is an important explanation for Mali's crisis. Deep ethnic divisions and conflict manifest in the unresolved Tuareg national-ethnic question that began with rebellions and state subversions in 1963, again in the 1990s, and resumption in 2011. Constituting much of the population of the north, Malian Tuareg have dominated the northern region and lived as pastoralist nomads. At independence in 1960, the bulk of the Tuareg community remained outside the web of political relationships and material benefits of the new state. This status caused Tuareg to view the southern Malian leadership with resentment and discontent from the onset (Keita 1998).

Tuareg nationalism would result in an independent state comprised of Tuareg populations from northern Mali, northern Niger, and southern Algeria. The Azawad Republic, the end product of Tuareg nationalism, has been an aspiration for Tuareg populations since Malian independence. Reacting against both social and cultural discrimination as well as to their perceived structural discrimination whereby the Tuareg have been neglected in the distribution of state benefits and state representation, Tuareg began to wage wars against the state as early as 1962.

Thirty years of intense military repression, resource discrimination, including drought, and alienation from what would become a hegemonic south caused the Tuareg to launch their second rebellion against the Malian state in 1990. In response, on January 6, 1991, the government of Mali and Tuareg military leaders signed the Tamanrasset Accords in Algeria to address the deep-seated roots of Tuareg dissatisfaction. Features of the agreement included a cease-fire and exchange of prisoners. Taureg military leaders would withdraw insurgent forces to cantonments. The Malian government would reduce its army presence in the north, especially in Kidal, and disengage the army from civil administration in the north. It would also eliminate selected military posts in the north considered threatening to the Tuareg communities and would integrate insurgent combatants into the Malian army. Finally, the Malian government would accelerate the ongoing processes of administrative decentralization in Mali as well as guarantee a fixed proportion of Mali's national infrastructural investment funding (47.3 percent) to northern regions 6, 7, and 8 (Keita 1998).

Supposedly, the Tamanrasset Accords would neutralize the armed threat on both sides and repatriate refugees from within Mali and those who had been displaced to Algeria and Mauritania, and in decentralizing state control in the region, the agreement called for cultural representation, respect, and value to Tuareg cultural identity. Nonetheless, this sustained state of affairs was complicated by identity fissures that have emerged from the global and regional resurgence of political Islam, especially in northern Mali.

The deep structural underbelly of Mali's unmanaged cultural pluralism is political (democracy) and economic (development) since Tuareg complained about inequality, uneven development, and exclusion from the Malian democracy. Adam Przeworski contends that democracies with a per capita income indicator of less than $1,000 are not sustainable and are subject to democratic breakdown (Przeworski et al. 2000). At a per capita income of $1,100 by the time of the 2012 coup, in relating Przeworski's democracy-development conundrum to Mali, the country's collapse begs the question as to whether there can be democracy without development.

A land-locked country twice the size of its colonizer, France, by 1960 when Mali would attain independence, the country embodied both the dilemma of democracy and development, as well as the promise of its own attempts to resolve this paradox. We know that Mali still has mineral resources such as the gold that built its great empires as the country's largest exports are gold, cotton, and livestock. Yet, after more than a century as a province in a larger expanse of the French West African colony of which it, given its hinterland status, was not a hub, by its independence, Mali was a poor and underdeveloped country with little potential to regain the wealth of its previous empires. At independence, the majority of Malians were subsistence farmers or pastoral nomads. Life expectancy was forty-five years. Access to modern education was restricted to a small minority in the south, and infrastructure had not significantly been developed.

Neither Mali's founding President Modibo Keita's socialist modernization plans nor the liberal market French modernization efforts of Moussa Traoré helped much to reverse the dire economic statistics of this country. Mali could advance little production, little wealth creation, little growth, little individual income, little equitable income distribution, and lots of inequality, poverty, and exploitative neocolonial resource extraction. By 2011 estimates, with a per capita income of $1,100 for a fifteen million population size and a Human Development Index (HDI) ranking of 159, Mali remained one of the poorest countries in the world.

However, Mali's democratic development was more successful. The distinctiveness of Modibo Keita's democratic nationalism had begun through his and other French Sudanese leaders' participation in the Rassemblement Démocratique Africain (RDA) in their struggle against French colonialism. It produced a socialist brand of democracy consistent with the hybridized and experimental forms of democracy practiced in much of Africa at the time. Liberal democracy came to Mali in 1992 through a third-wave post–Cold War era movement. Surprisingly differently from other countries in Africa, Mali's democracy was qualitatively rich with sustained steep political, civil, and human rights through 2012. Significantly, the first AU chair, Alpha Konaré (2003–8) also served as Mali's first liberal democratically elected leader from 1992 to 2002. A member of the Alliance for Democracy in Mali–African Party for Solidarity and Justice (ADEMA-PASJ—Alliance pour la Démocratie en Mali–Parti Africain pour la Solidarité et la Justice), this prodemocracy movement that had begun in 1989 established a democratic era for Mali that Freedom House would rank as the only Muslim majority country with a democracy. Mali's democracy was celebrated as a deliberative democracy (Wing 2008) combining the historical legacies of its cooperative-village style socialist democracy with the National Conference style 1990s transition to democracy that would attempt to convene Mali's multiethnic constituents to build and formulate the new democracy. A participant of the conference reflected Mali's deep history and diversity in democracy building when he said, "In 1236, in Kouloukagonga, after the fall of Soso, Sundiata and King Aliou created a constitution in 4 days that defined the state and external influence. Today, we are in the same situation" (Wing 2008, 76). Mali's national conference represented many sectors of society that came together to debate how to create a more legitimate system of government that would foster the growth of a plural and free press, as well as a governmental regime that was open to dialogue and popular participation. ADEMA-PASJ ruled with Konaré at the helm until the 2002 election of the former 1991 coup leader from Mopti, Amadou Toumani Touré, who had run as an independent candidate.

Regrettably, northerners, and mostly rural citizens, felt excluded from the Malian democracy (Wing 2008). As well, the institutional dimensions of democracy in Mali may not have matched the country's deliberative democratic vibrancy. One red flag was that Konaré's second-term election was a one-party victory, as supposedly all sixteen opposition parties boycotted the election in protest against perceived ADEMA-PASJ party dominance. Amadou Touré was also elected as a single no-party candidate, supported variably by a number of party coalitions from which Touré did not derive his political authority. This fact weakened the democratic state significantly in the new millennium and led to his ousting by a sergeant's coup claiming the Touré regime's ineffectiveness in dealing with yet a third Tuareg rebellion.

The weakness of Mali's institutional democratic regime by the start of the war on terror in 2002 coupled with the fact that 80 percent of Mali's economy consists of rural citizens who have been left out of the foreign aid–supported neo-liberal market-led economic growth are the factors that explain Mali's ultimate collapse of democracy in 2012. The crisis can be seen as products of unmanaged deep divisions and the democracy-development conundrum. Nevertheless, two additional key factors explain Mali's fast-paced resort to outright war by 2013. One was the unresolved Tuareg nationalist question that fostered the arrival of political Islam into the region in the 1990s. This change led, after 9/11, to the other: a US war on terror military operation called the Pan-Sahel Initiative (PSI) to fight political Islam in northern Mali.

Since 2006, with most Tuareg feeling that the Tamanrasset Accords commitments had never fully been met by the Malian state, a third Tuareg rebellion led by Ibrahim Ag Bahanga had taken place and lasted until 2009. Thereafter, Mali became one of four West African Sahelian countries (others are Niger, Mauritania, and Chad) that are targeted for the US PSI. The US government marked the Sahel as the second most vulnerable site for terrorist insurgencies. The PSI would target Mauritania, Mali, Niger, and Chad as vulnerable to penetration by foreign extremists from border states in Algeria, Libya, and the Sudan. Algeria's Salafist Group for Call and Combat (GSPC— Groupe Salafiste pour la Prédication et le Combat) was seen to be the biggest threat to spreading political Islam in the region, and it was believed that the GSPC had a presence in northern Mali. The PSI was initially funded at $7.75 million, with more than half of its funds channeled to support for defense and security forces in Mali. The initiative's purpose was to train government troops in the Sahelian countries to resist terrorist activity in the Sahara (Harmon 2008).

The war on terror targeted the entire region as a site for insecurity and violence that involved simultaneous ethnic wars by militias against the state, and state war against nonstate militias. PSI initiatives began to conflate so called Islamic missionaries of Bamako and Kidal (Jama'at al-Tabligh)—whom Americans claimed held Wahhabi beliefs—and the political Islam promoted by Tuareg notables such as the mayor of Kidal, the traditional ruler of Kidal, and the former head of the Tuareg rebellion, Bahanga, who had become the spiritual leader of Mali's Tablighis (Harmon in Jalloh and Falola 2008). The 2011 North Atlantic Treaty Organization (NATO) war on Libya further fanned the flames of an already volatile northern region when both armed Tuareg militia fighting with the then Libyan leader Colonel Muammar Gaddafi and Islamic jihadist militias fighting against the Libyan regime siphoned off their newly acquired cache of arms proliferated from the West and East and travelled through familiar cross-border routes back into Mali. Using a military option again in an era of the war on terror, in 2009, Mali dispatched troops to stop Bahanga, who was exiled to Libya until his return in the summer of 2011. During his time in Libya, Ibrahim Ag Bahanga made contact with Tuareg who served in Muammar Gaddafi's military including Mohamed Ag Najem, commander of Gaddafi's elite desert units. In a 2011 interview with the Algerian newspaper *El Watan*, Bahanga said, "The disappearance of Al-Qaddafi is good news for all the Tuareg in the region. . . . His departure from Libya opens the way for a better future and helps to advance our political demands. Now he's gone, we can move forward in our struggle" (Gunaratna 2012). Bahanga was killed in a mysterious car accident, but his mobilization is attributed to the uprising to gain control of northern Mali that took root among many Tuareg. On the heels of the collapse of the Gaddafi regime in September 2011, Tuareg fighters began to cross into Mali after emptying several Libyan arms depots to form the Mouvement National pour la Libération de l'Azawad (MNLA). In a short period, the MNLA took control over northern Mali and named it Azawad. The MNLA faced the immediate challenge of the threat of militant Islamist dominance with some Tuareg joining both Ansar Al Dine and the violent regional Salafist group linked to Al-Qaeda in the Islamic Maghreb (AQIM) (Stewart 2012).

Climaxing with the 2013 French military intervention, at the request of the Malian government and with the support of the AU, the war that began in Mali in 2012 consisted of a similar array of domestic, regional, and global actors that reflect Mali's deep history. There was the south represented by 80 percent of Mali's population, who are primarily Bamana speaking. Culturally, the south exhibited the ideals of the Malian postcolonial, national state first nurtured by the modernizing socialist, anti-French Pan-Africanist aspirations of the country's leader, Modibo Keita.

In the north, in addition to the Tuareg, there had developed a number of rebel and ethnic groups opposed to the Malian state. From the Maghreb north, there was Ansar Dine, which sought to impose Islamic law across the country and which drew from Tuareg militants who returned from Libya after fighting alongside Muammar Gaddafi's troops. The northern Mali based AQIM belonged to a network of Al-Qaeda's North African wing, with roots in Algeria. The Movement for Oneness and Jihad in West Africa (MUJAO— Mouvement pour le Tawhîd et du Jihad en Afrique de l'Ouest) was an AQIM splinter group whose aim is to spread jihad to the whole of West Africa. MUJAO advocates Islamic law and in the past had waged a campaign of violence against Tuareg separatists. The MNLA was the secular Tuareg group that sought independence for a homeland they call Azawad.

International and regional actors involved in the conflict included ECOWAS, convening an array of former Malian Empire cultures, communities, and identities from Senegal, Mauritania, Côte d'Ivoire, Burkina Faso, Northern Nigeria, and Niger, who officially supported the Malian government and state. The Arab Maghreb Union (AMU), convening Algeria, Morocco, Tunisia, and Libya, includes nomadic Tuareg and other Amazigh (Berber) identities and cultures that are also in opposition to their states. While not necessarily supporting the Malian state, they supported security in the region.

The United States (a new actor) and France (an old and deeply familiar actor) were both key participants in the conflict. Since 2011, the United States has earmarked the African Western Sahel as a war on terror region and has funneled millions of dollars into covert military operations to achieve its ends in this respect. France, Mali's former colonial power, while possessing resource interests in the Sahelian region, also still maintained symbolic interests and objectives of French Empire in Africa aligned intricately with the Malian south especially, which itself has developed a hybrid Francophone Afrique transnational identity.

Much of Africa possesses contextual national terrains similar to Mali whereby ethnic and religious pluralism and deep divisions, a democracy and development conundrum, and global terrorist networks attracting foreign regional and international wars inform the core elements of their state-societies. What's more, given the cross-border regional proliferation of the conflict (Algeria and Libya to the north; the West African Sahelian states, Niger, Chad, and Mauritania; and the West African southern region, Senegal and Guinea), a Pan-African response to Mali by Africa's AU was required.

Given the global context of the Malian crisis, the AU behaved like a suprastate actor for Mali that on behalf of Africa mediated the actors involved in the crisis while also collaborating with them as well as introducing initiatives of its own.

GREATER PAN-AFRICANISM WITH AFRICAN SOLUTIONS

The AU Mali Resolution adopted in January 2013 is drawn from previous templates used by the organization to address African conflicts such as Mali. Through its Mali Resolution, for example, the AU articulated the Pan-African standpoint, considered the ideological reaffirmation of Africa's deep solidarity with Mali to commit African solutions to the Malian crisis. In doing so, the members expressed their determination to pool their efforts together to help their sisterly country to overcome its challenges. For AU members, restoration of sovereignty seen as the commitment to national unity and territorial integrity was an important rallying point. The Union resolved to restore security and bring peace to Mali by putting down armed militia, criminal, and terrorist groups, and members would engage in efforts to restore democracy and economic development in the country. The AU's response in Mali provides deeper understanding of the AU's global governance of Africa dirigisme vis-à-vis the continent's larger security and development challenges.

The AU would both compete and collaborate with ECOWAS in mediating the Malian crisis, and significantly had developed pre-2012 programs with the Malian government and President Touré that were designed to solve the Tuareg conflict. Post-2012, the AU suspended Mali from the Union as an incentive to oust the coup leaders and restore a civilian government. It assisted Mali in restoring the interim civilian government led by President Traoré and Prime Minister Django Sissoko to lead the peace plan and prepare for a postconflict transition. As suprastate, the AU acted as Mali's chief arbiter at the UN. In December of 2012, with ECOWAS and Mali's partially restored interim government of national unity, the AU facilitated the successful, collaborative, and joint international diplomatically achieved establishment of UN Resolution 2085 authorizing the 3,500-man AFISMA.

To achieve this feat, previously, at the regional level, the AU and ECOWAS had both separately and jointly on occasion deployed their institutional prowess to pressure the military junta to hand back power to the elected democratic regime. The pressure forced the military to retreat and allowed for a new government of national unity to be formed in August 2012, with interim president Dioncounda Traoré and Cheick Modibo Diarra, who led the interim government as prime minister until he was forced to resign. Interim President Traoré named Django Sissoko, a former senior official in the president's office, to replace Diarra. Sissoko's first diplomatic moves further illustrate AU legitimacy as he visited President Yayi, 2012–13 chairman of the AU, stating,

> I came to Cotonou, not only to deliver a message of goodwill from the Malian people through their leaders to the sub-region, the Economic Community of West African States (ECOWAS) and the AU, but also to get the opinion of president Yayi on what has been achieved so far, and what remains to be done to resolve the Malian crisis. (*Global Times* 2012)

UN Security Council (UNSC) Resolution 2085 was built on African solutions for African problems and was inspired by the AU's own plan for Mali. This included the AU's Strategic Concept for the Resolution of the Crises in Mali, and the harmonized Concept of Operations developed under the auspices—and with the support—of the AU, which covered various aspects of the multidimensional crisis facing Mali. As such, in adopting UNSC 2085, the UN took note of the final communiqué of the extraordinary session of the authority of ECOWAS Heads of State and Government held in Abuja on November 11, 2012, and of the subsequent communiqué of the AU Peace and Security Council (PSC) on November 13, 2012, endorsing the Joint Strategic Concept of Operations for the International Military Force and the Malian Defense and Security forces.

The AU's ideology of African solutions for African problems would be underscored in the UNSC resolution when it significantly tackled Mali's conflict by drawing on African values, knowledge, policies, and precedents. It would authorize African efforts in Mali (AU and ECOWAS) in continuing negotiations between diverse Malian groups, in ensuring an inclusive redemocratic transition in Mali, and in the deployment of AFISMA to assist the Malian interim government in recovering occupied regions in the north and dismantling the terrorist and criminal networks there.

In deploying AFISMA, the AU would be exercising a light version of *Pax Africana*. Collective security and policing the continent in a self-determined manner occurred as the AU mobilized its membership to contribute troops to peacekeeping efforts in Mali. Militarily, while AFISMA would not be an exclusive AU force like the AU Mission in Somalia (AMISOM), it did end up looking more like the evolved hybrid force of the joint UN/AU Mission in Darfur (UNAMID) with Africans in charge. African agency was exerted as UNSC 2085 mandated that the AU would be in charge of a multiplicity of military functions through AFISMA, including the European mission to Mali, the African-led mission to Mali, the participation of ECOWAS, and the participation of other regional states and other regional and international organizations.

Illuminating again the Union's suprastate role in addressing the Malian crisis on behalf of Africa, AU ambassador to the Office of the UN, Mr. Téte António, responded to the adoption of Resolution 2085. He acclaimed its emergence as a further step in the evolution of the partnership between the UN and the AU. António celebrated the resolution's enactment as marking a defining moment in the coordinated international efforts to assist Mali in reestablishing her unity and territorial integrity, in dismantling terrorism and criminality in the north, and in restoring full constitutional order through free, fair, and transparent elections.

Incorporating the Malian conflict into the fulcrum of its deliberations at its Twentieth Annual Summit in January 2013, the AU's governance style of addressing Africa's myriad security, development, cultural, and social challenges was reinforced and reaffirmed. Pan-Africanist values—African solutions for African problems and *Pax Africana*—would be used as cultural signifiers to remind and rally member states around Africa's key objectives. The summit's theme, "Pan-Africanism and African Renaissance," suggested a renewal and resurgence of African solutions for African problems by working hand in hand with a select group of partners who would assist in restoring Mali.

NEOCOLONIALISM VERSUS ASYMMETRICAL DEPENDENCY

The AU's response in Mali has come with many challenges that underscore key questions about the international Pan-African actor's relevance, capacity, and national and international legitimacy. With AU-backed French intervention, for example, the resolution of the Malian conflict seemed far away from such ideals as African solutions for African problems or *Pax Africana*. Alternatively, the response reflected capacity limitations as well as legitimacy tensions with both contending subregional actors such as ECOWAS as well as international actors like France and the UN.

As far as capacity is concerned, again at its January 2013 Summit, presided over by the new Pan-Africanist leadership of the first female AU Commission chair, Dr. Dlamini-Zuma, the then AU President Yayi self-criticized the AU's institutional response in Mali. He complained that peacekeepers took too long to arrive despite the stark reality that as a result of the crisis Africa had been faced with a danger that threatened its very foundations. Yayi claimed that though the AU had the means to defend itself, it continued to wait. African troops galvanized by the AU's solicitation and mobilization arrived only after the French had intervened.

In terms of regional limitations as well, initial tensions existed between the AU and ECOWAS over which organization had jurisdiction over resolution of the conflict in Mali. This caused a delay in the AU's more assertive military intervention. The initial squabbling over which regional organization had jurisdiction over the conflict resolution of Mali—defined as "subsidiarity" (regional economic actor acts first if it has capacity)—was eventually set aside with the AU delegating authoritative leadership to, and in collaboration with, ECOWAS. Capacity and jurisdictional tensions also emerged as a result of the AU's global partnering. In not funding Resolution 2085 and AFISMA, the international community—convened in the UN—disabled AU capacity in Mali as it would not be able to raise the resources to fund a military operation despite UN authorization. It is no surprise that the AU was forced to rely on its wealthy international donors.

With France's gross domestic product of $2.77 trillion dollars (2011 estimates) and a $35,000 per capita income, compared to Africa's combined $1.8 trillion gross domestic product (2009 estimates) and $1,800 per capita income, the AU's desire to organize fifty-four countries to collectively contribute a military force and intervention in Mali outmatched the Union's ability to pull off such a project. The capital-intensive West, which is also the globe's primary arms and weaponry manufacturer, maintains the monopoly over military resources and thereby possesses control over global security. Africa's reliance on Western military resources to maintain the peace on the continent presents the paradox of neocolonialism.

With French intervention in Mali in 2013, much of the leftist press characterized the French action as neocolonial; but the AU's diplomatic persistence in presenting a moral and legal challenge to the international community may have fostered a model of *Pax Africana* that can alternatively be described as asymmetrical interdependence. Given the Union's ambition–resource gap, *Pax Africana* would continue to compete with *Pax Americana*'s and *Pax Europa*'s global hegemonic agendas exercised through and embodied in the UNSC. Thus, rather than viewing the Mali crisis merely as a recurrence of neocolonialism, it may be more valuable to see how interdependent *Pax Africana* indicates the AU's dirigisme in asserting African agency over the collective security policing of Africa with other actors—including subregional and international—to ensure that African goals, interests, and outcomes are achieved. Indeed, the AU may be Africa's most appropriate vehicle to combat neocolonialism.

Two factors explain why it is reasonable to be cautiously optimistic rather than pessimistic about the AU's prospects as a relevant suprastate actor for Africa and the world evidenced by the case of Mali. First is evidence that the AU's power exists in its institutionalization of sustained agency and voice. A second factor explains the AU's global governance style in terms of asymmetrical interdependence rather than merely a sidekick to an increasing neocolonialism of the continent.

With the Mali 2012–13 crisis, the AU demonstrated its sustained voice and agency at its January 2013 Summit when, despite France's Operation Serval, the AU committed to the organization of a Mali Donor's conference to galvanize

African states to pledge 7,700 troops in the realization of AFISMA to support French and Malian forces. Moreover, regardless of Mali's crisis, in commemorating fifty years of African cooperation, the AU continued to map out a vision for political and economic union by 2063. Launching Vision 2063 would allow Africans to reflect on half a century of independence and chart a course for the future.

The 2013 January Summit demonstrated how sustained institutionalized agency and voice has led to the AU's simultaneous and overlapping ability to address the Malian conflict while pursuing Africa's own strategic goals of economic and political union. The Union's style of addressing Africa's myriad security, development, cultural, and social challenges remains resilient as discussed at its Twentieth Summit and indicated by its conference themes. Pan-Africanism is constantly used as a cultural signifier to remind and rally the summit's participants around Africa's key objectives. Renaissance suggested a renewal and resurgence of African solutions for African problems by working hand in hand with a select group of partners who would assist in the process.

Regarding neocolonialism and the French factor in Africa and Mali in 2013, it is fair to consider whether the reality of French intervention in Mali rendered the AU a subordinate partner in the security role of the continent, an act that opens up the continent to becoming a vulnerable site for a continuing—and increased—practice of neocolonialism. Africa's own founding Pan-Africanist, Kwame Nkrumah, first coined the term "neocolonialism" and used it to describe ways in which socioeconomic and political control can be exercised economically, linguistically, and culturally among formerly colonized peoples. Nkrumah defined it as follows: "The essence of neo-colonialism is that the State which is subject to it is, in theory, independent and has all the outward trappings of international sovereignty. In reality, its economic system and thus its political policy is directed from outside" (Nkrumah 1965, ix). It is the practice of granting a sort of independence with the concealed intention of making the liberated country a client state and controlling it effectively by means other than political ones (Legum 1962, 118). Internationally, the term describes the domination-praxis (social, economic, cultural) of countries from the developed world in the respective internal affairs of the countries of the developing world; that, despite the decolonization that occurred in the aftermath of the Second World War (1939–45), the former colonial powers continue to apply existing and past international economic arrangements with their former colony countries, and so maintain colonial control (Sartre 2001).

While it is true that France and other Western powers remain neocolonial in their foreign policy pursuits toward Africa as they continue to be deeply engaged in Africa's affairs in order to preserve a high international profile that assures access to strategic resources that further continue highly favorable economic relationships that benefit them more than they do Africa, the question is whether or not Africa's AU facilitates this process or combats it. In Mali, given France's own resource and mining interests—including oil prospects—and the United States's imperial interests in the war on terror in the Maghrebian and West African Sahelian regions, neocolonialism explains Western powers' high-profile surveillance of Mali. Indeed, one might argue as well that Mali's 2012 collapse occurred as a casualty of Western imperial interests in the country.

That being said, in 2013, the AU remains caught in a paradox between the neocolonialist interests of global governance actors such as France and its own interest to achieve *Pax Africana* hegemony and control over Mali. Unlike the 2011 intervention by NATO of Libya, undergird by a UNSC resolution that the AU vehemently rejected as illicit, in Mali, it was the AU that lobbied for and formulated the legal language for the UNSC resolution authorizing international use of force in Mali, Resolution 2085. AU president at the time, Thomas Boni Yayi, praised what he claimed had been the remarkable work of the French military in Mali, saying its troops were practically saving Africa. However, for the AU, with the secession of the north and the threat by militants to take the south in Mali, the military option was the policy of last resource. Moreover, at the time, a military solution could only occur by way of Africa's dependence on the resource-laden West—in this case, Mali's former colonizer, France. With ECOWAS headed by a Francophone close French client, the president of Côte d'Ivoire, and the AU led by Francophone Yayi of Benin, regrettably, these regional leaders of Africa would lobby France to support their institutions' efforts to enjoin what they considered a motherly nation's assistance to their sisterly nation.

Nonetheless, asymmetrical interdependence with France and the UN allowed the AU to provide Mali with concerted and sustained support of Africa's collective institutional resources and solidarity to assist it in addressing the country's problems. Moreover, while the AU collaborated with France on the security end, the institution continued its proactive support for an African country in the broader goal of African development, peace, and political-economic union. Noteworthy, for example, is the fact that, despite its occurrence a day before the 2012 Malian coup, the AU PSC's Support and Follow-up Group (SFG) had held a meeting in Bamako on March 20, 2012. The meeting had been organized to facilitate coordinated international action with respect to the situation in northern Mali. This and the February 8, 2013 SFG meeting on Mali in Brussels a year later provides a semblance of the AU's sustained and intertwined, albeit asymmetrical, global power model in relation to hegemonic actors in the West.

That is to say that while the SFG is an organ of the AU, with the AU's permission, the Malian crisis solution group's third meeting was hosted in Brussels by the European Union (EU), and cochaired by the AU's PSC as well as the UN's Political Affairs Commission, and ECOWAS. In designating former Burundi president Pierre Buyoya as the AU High Representative for Mali and the Sahel and Special Representative and Head of AFISMA, who also attended the meeting, the AU's global governance dirigisme on behalf of Africa for Mali affords Africans an opportunity to collaborate with the Malian government on solutions to the country's conflict while also facilitating the support of the international community for Mali. Especially, this style of institutional forum that the AU has established enables African and Malian stakeholders to take ownership of the efforts to find lasting solutions to the multidimensional crisis facing their country and the continent.

Nevertheless, asymmetrical dependence is not an ideal status for Africa's AU. Global power play between the AU and the UN continues to characterize both institutions' collaborative and competitive engagement with Mali. In April 2013, the UNSC established Resolution 2100 launching the UN Multidimensional Integrated Stabilization Mission in Mali (MINUSMA—Mission multidimensionnelle intégrée des Nations Unies pour la stabilisation au Mali). While MINUSMA would claim to support the political process in Mali, in close coordination with the AU and ECOWAS, its initial establishment stated that it would take over from AFISMA to help the Malian authorities to implement the transitional road map toward the full restoration of constitutional order, democratic governance, and national unity, which included the holding of elections, confidence building, and facilitation of reconciliation at the national and local levels.

As a result of MINUSMA's establishment, AFISMA's mission struggles to avoid being subjugated by the presence of the UN. In its own revised agenda, the AU claimed that AFISMA is not to limit its activities in Mali as per its requests to the UN through MINUSMA, but that it could spread it to the neighboring states (with their consent) as per its Africa mandate. In an article titled, "'Operation Mali': United Nations Complicit in Recolonization of Africa," one journalist put it this way:

> The Africans are made to refuse the idea of tackling the conflict themselves.
> The African Mission—AFISMA has failed. One of the reasons—it never got
> the funds it needed. The United Nations and the donor-states have refused

to finance an African mission. But they agree to reverse their stand in case
the UN would be a decision maker. At that, the very same AFISMA forces
would do the job, but under the command of "international community."
(Mezyaev 2013)

Recolonization seems rather extreme to describe what should instead be viewed
as the assertiveness of the international community (through the UN) in desir-
ing domination and control of Africa's problems through the establishment of
its own mission in Mali only after France and AFISMA have brought the peace
to the country.

Perhaps alternatively to recolonization, in revealing the complex and nuanced
iterations of the way that we have characterized the AU as an international organization delicately navigating a globalized world, using the case of Mali we see
postcolonialism and even gradual decolonization despite Meyaev's observations.
The Mali crisis and the AU's intervention supports such a contention. The case
reveals key elements of the AU's institutional behavior by examining the AU
as a regional organization, a suprastate, and an international intergovernmental governance body, depending on the context of its activities. The Union is
reinventing Pan-Africanism as greater Pan-Africanism in Mali. Shared solidarity
and collective nation building facilitates African unity as fellow Africans solve
tensions among southern and northern as well as culturally diverse Malians and
their regional neighbors. The AU's participation enables the reconstruction of a
universal African identity among the geographically and socioculturally diverse
arena of peoples of Africa and its diaspora who are already linked historically,
socially, and culturally through complex networks.

The AU phenomenon thesis applied to Mali reveals and assesses how it is
that Africa's AU is increasingly sculpting a prominent place for itself and for
Africans in today's global era by advancing Africa's political, security, cultural, and
economic integration and development in global governance. From its relations
with France and the UN over Mali, we see how the AU attempts to delicately
navigate global power hierarchies and negotiate with powerful global institutions
in order to attain its own ends in Africa. As a result, however, while asserting
the Pan-Africanist principles of anti-neocolonialism, self-determination, plural
inclusion, and freedom from global marginalization and structural poverty on
behalf of Africa and Africans, we see how the institution creates reluctant, though
strategic and asymmetrical, partnerships with more powerful global forces and
institutions as it attempts to address the continent's complex challenges.

FINALE

In presenting the complex layers of what we have termed the AU phenomenon in our introduction, we began the current monograph by identifying three takeaway for readers that we hoped would illustrate our book's key objectives through the current conclusion. Throughout the book, we have sought to reveal the dynamics of the phenomenon by elucidating these takeaways and by presenting them as distinct insights that we claim make the book an important contribution to the topic and discussion of African affairs.

First is the claim that *The African Union's Africa* should be used as an applied African case study for the constructivist international relations turn. Self-determined African voices—be they those of leaders, regimes, movements, or individuals—represent and speak on behalf of Africans' self-determined desires, ideas, and contexts. We have taken care to demonstrate that, through Africa's AU, Africans *are* contributing to contemporary global development and governance in distinct ways. As the Malian case and other instances that we have documented throughout the book demonstrate, the AU is relevant to Africa and to the world. Through the institutional expression of the AU, Africans exhibit agency—and thus freedom despite structural constraints.

Second, we have argued that Pan-Africanism still lives in a suprastatist third phase institutional configuration that is intricately tied to contemporary globalization and international relations processes. That Pan-Africanism is understood as a practice of international relations is a related insight. Extending from both observations (Pan-Africanism lives and is an international relations practice), we conclude that Africa's millennial engagement with the world is neither colonialist nor neocolonialist. On the contrary, we have demonstrated that Africa's global governance dirigsme is postcolonialist. "Post" indicates that Africans have agency and use it even though they may not always produce successful outcomes.

While deep-seated political and economic global structures that were established during Africa's period of colonization still exist, and thereby continue to mitigate African progress while privileging Western superpower interests, Africans are conscious of these structures and sustain a complex, collective struggle to overcome them. This contention is evidenced by the insights that we have revealed in presenting the AU phenomenon throughout this book. Through its intergovernmental organization, the AU provides Africans with an institutional vehicle to exercise a delicate navigation of globalization and a dirigisme engagement with global governance with gains that are mutually reinforcing for both Africa and the world despite their asymmetry.

Former AU Commission chair and president of Mali Alpha Konaré's affirmation of our Pan-Africanist method and its usage by the AU as a global culture reinforces the contribution of Pan-African institutionalism to international relations and African affairs. Konaré believed that the AU is anchored by the foundations of Pan-Africanism, which is celebrated by all Africans as a historic opportunity to renew the Pan-Africanism that was born at the close of the nineteenth century. Pan-Africanism would endow Africa with the requisite capacities to take up the challenges of the twenty-first century, including rapid and sustainable development, poverty eradication, and effective integration of the continent into the global economy and society. The former chairperson reiterated the ideas of Pan-Africanists who had built Africa before him, restating that

> Pan-Africanism's objectives were, inter alia, to build African unity through establishment of a United States of Africa, had the ultimate goal of not only eliminating colonial borders and frontiers but also eradicating the differences arising from ethnic, racial or linguistic pluralism. However, this Pan-Africanism had only limited impact on the process of building African Unity due to the fact that the OAU had espoused the principle of respect for the boundaries inherited from colonialism, and also due to lack of political will. (Konaré 2004, 20)

In referring to the distinct presentation of the inner workings of the AU's institutional global governance operation within a three-tier configuration of power and impact agenda to achieve its Africa objectives—we referred to this as the AU phenomenon—Konaré underscores the book's third unique contribution in this respect. We have described the AU's institutional evolution and dynamism according to a three-tiered intergovernmental/regional integration/suprastate trajectory that we have used to explain the AU phenomenon. In contrasting the AU with the old OAU, which Konaré described as merely an intergovernmental cooperation organization, he argued that the new AU had made significant accomplishments to underscore the continent's long struggle toward integration.

Speaking to the way that institutional structures had contributed to the facilitation of this evolution, Konaré demonstrated how the AU now consists of multiple sources of authority that, while still respecting national authority, had added the right to intervene, contained a provision to suspend governments coming to power by unconstitutional means, and through the New Partnership for Africa's Development (NEPAD) and the Conference on Security, Stability, Development and Cooperation in Africa (CSSDCA) provided for peer review mechanisms and public monitoring of its actions. The integration organization has authority and the power of initiatives with a team of elected commissioners with a fully recognized mandate.

All three themes defining and characterizing the AU that we have tried to elucidate in the current book are evidenced by considering the way that the Pan-African idea and its power to mobilize African member states and peoples alike has been one of the most consistent vehicles through which the AU continues to be relevant for the continent and through which it achieves its impact. In his 2006 study on the prospects of a United States of Africa, former AU chairperson Olusegun Obasanjo outlined sixteen strategic areas that an African Union Government should focus on: continental integration; education, training, skills development, science, and technology; energy; environment; external relations; food, agriculture, and water resources; gender and youth; governance and human rights; health; industry and mineral resources; finance; peace and security; social affairs and solidarity; sport and culture; trade and customs union; and infrastructure, information technology, and biotechnology (Murithi 2007).

Notwithstanding the tough challenges ahead for the AU, our book has documented how the AU family of organizations has already outperformed all contemporary regional organizations except the vastly better resourced EU. What makes this reality remarkable is that to negotiate common interests between the fifty-four AU members is a far more challenging task than to negotiate a Union of South American Nations (UNASUR— Unión de Naciones Suramericanas) between merely twelve governments. Be that as it may, the AU is well ahead of UNASUR, which still awaits operationalization. What's more, in one aspect, the AU is ahead of the EU, where the AU's Constitutive Act permits supranational military intervention in grave circumstances. Similarly, African peer review is broader than that of the Organisation for Economic Co-operation and Development (OECD) since it includes political governance, and not merely corporate governance. AU institutions also have intrinsic as well as performative importance: "The supranational organs of the Community with their implications for the Members' sovereignty can . . . be viewed in this context. They are symbols of certain values that still enchant Pan-Africanists within the Community. They exist not because of what they can or will do, but rather for what they are or what they represent" (Kufuor 2006, 45).

In Africa, Afro-realists would observe that deadlines tend to be guidelines. We can confidently predict that by 2063, the new nominal end year of the AEC treaty, Africa will witness, alongside continuing aspirational rhetoric, continuing substantial progress toward the institutions, practices, and prerogatives of a hybrid intergovernmental and supranational ever closer union. In our view, the AU is already entering an epoch of polycentric shared sovereignty, with some national prerogatives and some supranational continental or regional prerogatives. This is what we mean by the AU phenomenon. What better way to conclude the current treatise that has been *The African Union's Africa* than with a reflection of the aspirations of the AU summary in events that occurred within the organization as we laid our pens to rest. As we have argued, the promise of Africa's AU rests in the institution's sustained agency and voice, its Pan-Africanist resilience, consciousness of, and commitment to African solidarity, and its institutional dirigsme that allows the institution to innovate while evolving and leading Africans in global partnerships.

A major outcome of the Pan-African/African Renaissance summit was the adoption of the Declaration of the OAU/AU fiftieth anniversary, in which the leaders committed themselves to achieve the AU goals of an integrated and prosperous Africa by 2063 and especially translate the African vision into action in their different countries. The summit reinvited Africans to provide inputs and contributions toward the elaboration of a development agenda that would support, promote, own, and build alliances for an African common position on African affairs and development and that would enable Africa to speak with one voice in global governance forums. The summit also adopted a financing plan to consider alternative sources of funding the AU to ensure that Africa takes ownership of its Pan-African strategies.

Concrete outcomes of the sustained one voice and ownership principles that Africans attempt to underscore through the AU were evidenced in the AU's Mali Donor Conference held in Addis Ababa on January 28, 2013. In a historic first action (where the AU would spend a majority of its budget on a peacekeeping operation), the Union pledged a total of $50 million to help fund the military intervention in Mali, as well as drum up support for AFISMA. The AU-led donors' conference on Mali galvanized and solicited African and international matching funds for the operation that it budgeted at an estimated cost of $406 million. Algerian Ramtane Lamamra, the AU's Peace and Security Commissioner, told reporters. "For the first time in the history of the African Union, the budget will be used to support a peace operation. . . . It represents around ten percent of the overall budget of AFISMA, [which is] unprecedented" (*France 24* 2013).

The donation by African countries to Mali came six months after the AU Commission chair, Dr. Dlamini-Zuma, invoked Pan-Africanism to call for African unity and African accomplishments, and as the first female AC chair pledged to use the AU to take the continent in the same direction that we as authors have similarly tried to take you throughout the current book on *The African Union's Africa*.

Such a direction leads us to President John Mahama of Ghana, who at the fifty-year golden jubilee AU summit in January 2013 paid tribute to Pan-Africanist founder Dr. Kwame Nkrumah. In underscoring the evolving African suprastate, the emerging Pan-African identity, and the gradually deepening socioeconomy and socioculture, Mahama put it best by recognizing that, despite Ghana having been his birthplace, his desire for African unity made him a citizen of Africa.

Finally, if you thought that we have been provocative in positing the AU in an oppositional role that resuscitates radical discourses protesting antiracism in a global world that continues to subvert African freedom, the first six-month chairmanship of Ethiopia's Desalegn offers more testimony that our thesis about the AU's dynamic dirigisme in the contemporary global arena is supported in the real world. Desalegn's radical Pan-Africanist discourse in rallying Africans in support of a new leader at the time, Kenya's Uhuru Kenyatta (son of Jomo), against the race-hunting International Criminal Court (ICC) is a case in point (Solemn Declaration 2004). More than the AU's previous chairpersons who were also outspoken regarding their own self-determined stances against the ICC's indictment of sitting president of Sudan, Omar al-Bashir, distinctively, Ethiopia's 2013 chairperson actually rallied up African nations in threatening a mass withdrawal of the continent from the ICC membership and Rome Statute.

African Union: Provenance and Derivation of Organs and Institutions in Comparative Context

EU (Established 1957)	ECOWAS (Established 1975)	OAU (Established 1963)	AFRICAN UNION (AU) Treaty of Abuja, 1991 and Constitutive Act, 2000	
European Council	Authority of Heads of State and Government (AHSG)	Assembly of Heads of State and Government	Assembly of Heads of State and Government A 7 and 8, A 6 and 9	
Council of Ministers		Council of Ministers	Executive Council A 7–11, A 10–13	
Commission	Executive Secretariat	Secretariat	Commission A 7 and 21, A 20	
Comité des représentants permanents (COREPER)			Permanent Representatives Committee (PRC) A 21	
European Court of Justice European Court of Human Rights	Tribunal of Community (1993) Community Court of Justice		Court of Justice A 7 and 8, A 18	(2009) African Court of Justice and Human Rights (ACJHR)

EU (Established 1957)	ECOWAS (Established 1975)	OAU (Established 1963)	**AFRICAN UNION (AU)** Treaty of Abuja, 1991 and Constitutive Act, 2000	
European Parliament	(1993) Community Parliament		Pan-African Parliament (PAP) A 7 and 14, A 17	
	(1993) Mediation and Conciliation Council	Commission of Mediation, Conciliation and Arbitration (1993) Mechanism for Conflict Prevention, Management and Resolution		(2004) Peace and Security Council (PSC)
	(1993) Council of Elders			(2010) Panel of the Wise
(2000) European Union Military Committee (EUMC) and European Union Military Staff (EUMS)	(1981) Defense Council Defense Commission	Defense Commission		(2010) Military Staff Committee
(2003) European Union Force (EUFOR)	(1990) Economic Community of West African States Monitoring Group (ECOMOG)			(2003) African Standby Force (ASF)
Economic and Social Committee	(1993) Economic and Social Committee	(Specialized Commission) Economic and Social	Economic, Social and Cultural Council (ECOSOCC) A 22, A 7, 15, 90	
	Technical and Specialized Commissions (TSC)		Specialized Technical Commissions (STCs) A 7 and 2, A 14–15	

EU (Established 1957)	ECOWAS (Established 1975)	OAU (Established 1963)	**AFRICAN UNION (AU)** Treaty of Abuja, 1991 and Constitutive Act, 2000	
European Central Bank (ECB) European Investment Bank (EIB) European Investment Fund (EIF)	(1999) ECOWAS Bank for Investment and Development (EBID)	(1964) African Development Bank (AfDB)* (1994) Afreximbank*	African Central Bank (ACB) African Investment Bank (AIB) African Monetary Fund (AMF) A 19	
	Ecobank†			(2008) Pan-African Infrastructure Development Fund*
(1962) European Space Research Organisation (ESRO) (merged into European Space Agency [ESA], 1975)		(1993) Regional African Satellite Communications Organization* (RASCOM)	(1994) Committee of Intelligence and Security Services of Africa (CISSA)	
			(1994) Committee of Intelligence and Security Services of Africa (CISSA)	
				(2004) African Centre for Studies and Research on Terrorism (ACSRT)
				(2006) African Academy of Languages (ACALAN)
				(2002, 2009) Afro-Arab Institute for Cultural and Strategic Studies

EU (Established 1957)	ECOWAS (Established 1975)	OAU (Established 1963)	**AFRICAN UNION (AU)** Treaty of Abuja, 1991 and Constitutive Act, 2000
European Social Fund	(1979–99) ECOWAS Fund for Cooperation, Compensation, and Development (then becomes EBID)		Solidarity, Development, and Compensation Fund A 80 (never established)	
(1951) European Coal and Steel Community (ECSC)				(2008) African Energy Commission
Euratom				(2010) African Commission on Nuclear Energy

Note: "A" followed by a number in this table represents an article number of the AU Constitutive Act of 2000.

*Quangos

†Corporate sector

Notes

Foreword

1. On the slave trade, see generally Horne 2007a. On an analogous commerce, see, e.g., Horne 2007b.

Preface

1. Course offerings in political science and international relations departments are increasingly being designed to reflect the transformations in political practice as a result of globalization. Michigan State University (James Madison College of Public Affairs) calls its African Politics course "Regional Cooperation, Politics, and Conflict in Africa." The University of Delaware named its graduate program in political science the Global Governance program. With the proliferation of international relations programs, polisci departments are increasingly throwing up courses entitled "States and Societies in Transition," "Comparative Foreign Policy," "Special Topics in International Security, Politics, and Change," "The Changing Developing World," and "Politics and Conflict." All of these courses would be designed to reflect the precepts and methods of the current book. Moreover, the University of Maryland has developed a computer-assisted, multimedia software course on African politics that simulates the organization and events of the AU. As with the popular model of Model United Nations, Model African Union presents a new and innovative way to teach and learn about transformations in African politics.

Chapter 2. The Evolving "African" Suprastate: Histories, Anatomies, and Comparisons

1. Assembly/AU/Dec.287(XIV), http://www.au.int viewed 15 March 2010.
2. India comes closest with its annual Pravasi Bharatiya Divas; these are only forums.
3. In the matter of African Commission of Human and Peoples' Rights v. the Great Socialist Libyan People's Arab Jamahiriya, order 004/2011.

4. Tesfaye Gebre Egzy was provisional secretary-general at the founding conference of the OAU. He was among the sixty-nine persons shot on November 23, 1974 after a creeping coup d'etat.

Chapter 3. Pan-Africanist Globalization and Cultural Politics: Promoting the African World View

1. The geographical distribution of the five regions is currently as follows:
    1. West Africa, Sixteen Member States:
    Benin, Burkina Faso, Cape Verde, Côte d'Ivoire, Gambia, Ghana, Guinea, Guinea-Bissau, Liberia, Mali, Niger, Nigeria, Senegal, Sierra Leone, and Togo.
    2. East Africa, Thirteen Member States:
    Comoros, Djibouti, Eritrea, Ethiopia, Kenya, Madagascar, Mauritius, Rwanda, Seychelles, Somalia, Sudan, Tanzania, and Uganda.
3. Southern Africa, Ten Member States:
    Angola, Botswana, Lesotho, Malawi, Mozambique, Namibia, South Africa, Swaziland, Zambia, and Zimbabwe.
4. Central Africa, Nine Member States:
    Burundi, Cameroon, Central African Republic, Chad, Congo, Democratic Republic of the Congo, Equatorial Guinea, Gabon, and São Tomé and Principe.
5. Northern Africa, Six Member States:
    Algeria, Egypt, Libya, Mauritania, Tunisia, and Saharawi Arab Democratic Republic.
    2. Cultural quangos
    African Academy of Languages (ACALAN), Bamako
    Afro-Arab Institute for Cultural and Strategic Studies, Bamako
    Centre d'Études Linguistiques et Historiques par Tradition Orale (CELHTO) (Centre for Linguistic and Historical Studies through Oral Traditions), Niamey
    Pan-African News Agency (PANA), Dakar

Chapter 5. *Pax Africana* versus International Security: New Routes to Conflict Resolution

1. Al-Shabaab twitter announcement—Al-Jazeera, June 19, 2013, "Gun battle at UN compound in Mogadishu end Somali and African Union forces regain control of compound in Somali capital after attack kills at least 15 people."

Bibliography

Books and Articles

Abrahamsen, Rita. 2000. *Disciplining Democracy: Development Discourse and Good Governance in Africa*. London: Zed Books.

Adebajo, Adekeye. 2010. *The Curse of Berlin: Africa after the Cold War*. New York: Columbia University Press.

———. 2011 "Tale of Two Visionary Men Who Became Cassandras." *Business Day* (Johannesburg). March 17.

Adejumobi, Said, and Adebayo O. Olukoshi. 2008. *The African Union and New Strategies for Development in Africa*. Amherst: Cambria Press.

Africa Village. 2011. "AU Elects Obiang Nguema Mbasogo, Président de la République." February 11. http://www.africaglobalvillage.com/west-africa/215-guinea-bissau/615-de -guinee-equatoriale.html?device=xhtml.

African Globe. 2012. "Dlamini-Zuma Shocked That 97% of African Union Is Funded by Western World." October 30. http://www.africanglobe.net/africa/dlamini-zuma-shocked -97-african-union-funded-western-world-1/.

African Union. "AU in a Nutshell." Accessed March 1, 2014. http://www.au.int/en/about /nutshell.

African Union. "The Financial Institutions." Accessed February 25, 2014. http://www.au.int /en/organs/fi.

———. "Organs." http://www.au.int/en/organs.

African Union. 2005. "Meeting of Experts on the Definition of the African Diaspora." 11–12 April. Addis Ababa, Ethiopia.

———. 2010. African Charter on Democracy, Elections and Governance. http://www.au.int /en/sites/default/files/AFRICAN_CHARTER_ON_DEMOCRACY_ELECTIONS_AND_ GOVERNANCE.pdf.

————. 2011. "African Union Calls for an End to Bombing and a Political, Not Military Solution in Libya." June 15. http://www.normangirvan.info/wp-content/uploads/2010/05 /african-union-calls-for-end-to-bombing-and-a-political-solution-in-libya.pdf.

————. 2006. "Décision sur le Gouvernement de l'Union—Doc.Assembly/AU/2 (VII)." Assembly/AU/Dec.123 (VII). Seventh Ordinary Session, July 1–2, Banjul, The Gambia. http://www.au.int/en/sites/default/files/ASSEMBLY_FR_01_JULY_03_JULY_2006 _AUC_SEVENTH_ORDINARY_SESSION_DECISIONS_DECLARATIONS.pdf.

————. 2007. *Audit of the African Union.*

————. 2011. "The AU Intensifies Its Efforts towards a Political Solution in Libya and Stresses the Importance of the Respect of the Letter and Spirit of Resolution 1973(2011). http://www.au.int/en/sites/default/files/Press%20release%20on%20Libya%203%20 05%2011.pdf.

————. 2012a African Solidarity Initiative in Support for Post-Conflict Reconstruction and Development in Africa. http://www.peaceau.org/uploads/asi-concept-note.pdf.

v. 2012b. "Boosting Intra African Trade: Q&A." January. http://summits.au.int/en/sites /default/files/REVISED%20QA%20-%20Final%20_3_%20underlined.pdf.

————. 2013. "African Leaders Sign Declaration of OAU/AU 50th Anniversary." May 27. http://summits.au.int/en/21stsummit/events/african-leaders-sign-declaration -oauau-50th-anniversary.

African Union, Assembly of the Union. 2007. "Decisions and Declarations." Assembly/AU/Dec. 134–164(VIII). Eighth Ordinary Session, January 29–30. Addis Ababa, Ethiopia.

African Union, Assembly of the Union. 2012. "Decision on 'Integration as a Factor for African Renaissance'—Assembly/AU/14(XVIII) Add.4." Assembly/AU/Dec.404(XVIII). Eighteenth Ordinary Session, January 29–30. Addis Ababa, Ethiopia. http://www.au.int/en/sites /default/files/ASSEMBLY%20AU%20DEC%20391%20-%20415%20(XVIII)%20_E.pdf.

African Union, Executive Council. 2005a. "The Common African Position on the Proposed Reform of The United Nations: 'The Ezulwini Consensus.'" Ext/EX.CL/2 (VII). 7th Extraordinary Session, March 7–8, Addis Ababa, Ethiopia. http://www.africa-union.org /News_Events/Calendar_of_%20Events/7th%20extra%20ordinary%20session%20ECL /Ext%20EXCL2%20VII%20Report.pdf.

————. 2005b. "Decision on the Definition of the African Diaspora." Doc. EX.CL/164 (VI). Sixth Ordinary Session, January 24–28, Abuja, Nigeria. http://www.au.int/en/sites/defaul t/files/COUNCIL_EN_24_28_JANUARY_2005_%20EXECUTIVE_COUNCIL_SIXTH _ORDINARY_SESSION_SESSION.pdf.

African Union, Peace and Security Council. 2011. "Communique." PSC/MIN/COMM.2 (CCLXXV). 275th Meeting, April 26, Addis Ababa, Ethiopia. http://www.peaceau.org /uploads/communiquelibyaeng.pdf.

Afrikanunityofharlem (blog). 2010. "First Consultation of the African Diaspora to the African Union." November 25. http://afrikanunityofharlem.wordpress.com/2010/11/25/first -consultation -of-the-african-diaspora-to-the-african-union.

————. 2011. "Second Consultative AU meeting with the African Diaspora 2/27/011." May 4. http://afrikanunityofharlem.wordpress.com/2011/05/04-second-consultative -au -meeting-with-the- african-diaspora-227011/

Ajala, Adekunle. 1973. *Pan-Africanism: Evolution, Progress, and Prospects.* London: Andre Deutsch.

Ake, Claude. 1996. *Democracy and Development in Africa.* Washington, DC: Brookings Institution Press.

Akokpari, John, Angela Ndinga-Muvumba, and Tim Murithi, eds. 2008. *The African Union and Its Institutions.* Cape Town: Fanele-Jacana and Centre for Conflict Resolution.

Akukwe, Chinua. 2006. "Ghana: Growing Momentum for Africa." *allAfrica*. August 16. http://allafrica.com/stories/200608160832.html.

American Opinion Publishing. 2002. *First Europe, Now Africa*. Gale Group. http://www.thefreelibrary.com/First+Europe,+now+Africa.+(Insider+Report).(African+Union+to+be ...-a089812405.

Anderson, Walter Truett. 2001 *All Connected Now: Life in the First Global Civilization*. Colorado: Westview Press.

Appadurai, Arjun. 1996. *Modernity at Large: Cultural Dimensions of Globalization*. Minneapolis: University of Minnesota Press.

Appiah, Kwame. 1993. *In My Father's House: Africa in the Philosophy of Culture*. New York: Oxford University Press.

Apuuli, Kasaija Phillip. 2011. *The Principle of "African Solutions to African Problems" under the Spotlight: The African Union (AU) and the Libya Crisis*. Open Society Institute: Africa Governance Monitoring and Advocacy Project AfriMAP. September, Nairobi, Kenya. http://www.afrimap.org/english/images/paper/AfriMAP_NAfrica_Kasaija_EN.pdf.

Asante, Molefi. 1998. *The Afrocentric Idea*. Rev. ed. Philadelphia: Temple University Press.

Asante, S. K. B. 1997. *Regionalism and Africa's Development: Expectations, Reality, and Challenges*. Basingstoke: Palgrave Macmillan.

———. 2007. *Ghana and the Promotion of Pan-Africanism and Regionalism*. J. B. Danquah Memorial Lectures 40. Accra: Ghana Academy of Arts and Sciences.

Asante, S. K. B., F. O. C. Nwonwu, and V. N. Muzvidziwa. 2001. *Towards an African Economic Community*. Pretoria: Africa Institute of South Africa.

Ashcroft, Bill. 1997. "Globalism, Post-Colonialism and African Studies." In *Post-Colonialism: Culture and Identity in Africa*, ed. Pal Ahluwalia and Paul Nursey-Bray. New York: Nova Science Publishers.

AU Echo. 2012. "Intra African Trade: Perspectives from the 7th Ordinary Session of the AU Conference of Ministers of Trade." January 24. http://summits.au.int/en/sites/default/files/Issue%201%20January%2024%202012_1.pdf.

Bayart, Jean-François. 2009. *The State in Africa: The Politics of the Belly*. 2nd ed. Cambridge: Polity.

Berger, Peter L. 1992. "The Uncertain Triumph of Democratic Capitalism." *Journal of Democracy* 3 (3): 7–16.

Best, Jacqueline, and Matthew Paterson, eds. 2010. *Cultural Political Economy*. New York: Routledge.

Bogland, Karin, Robert Egnell, and Maria Lagerström. 2008. *The African Union: A Study Focusing on Conflict Management*. Stockholm: FOI Swedish Defense Research Agency. http://storage.globalcitizen.net/data/topic/knowledge/uploads/2010051311473 5760.pdf.

Calland, Richard. 2002. "Keeping the Show on the Road." *Mail and Guardian* (Johannesburg). November 7.

Cape Times (Cape Town). 2011. "The Arrogance and Hypocrisy of the West in the Guise of NATO Has Been Amply Demonstrated by Their Handling of the Libyan Situation, Particularly by Their Rudeness and Cavalier Treatment of President Jacob Zuma." June 30.

Cervenka, Zdenek. 1977. *The Unfinished Quest for Unity: Africa and the OAU*. New York: Africana Publishing.

Daniels, Ugo. 2009. "United States of Africa: A Wishful Thinking?" http://www.africanloft.com/united-states-of-africa-a-wishful-thinking/.

Davis, Carole Boyce, and Babacar M'Bow. 2007. "Towards African Diaspora Citizenship: Politicizing an Existing Global Geography." In *Black Geographies and the Politics of Place*, ed. Katherine McKittrick and Clyde Woods. Cambridge, MA: South End Press.

Daviso, William. 2013. "Ethiopia's Hailemariam Desalegn Elected as African Union Chairman." January 27. http://www.meleszenawi.com/ethiopias-hailemariam-desalegn-elected-as -african- union - chairman/.

Diamond, Larry, and Marc F. Plattner, eds. 2010. *Democratization in Africa: Progress and Retreat.* 2nd ed. Baltimore: Johns Hopkins University Press.

Dillon, Karin. 2007. "Prospects for Peace in Northern Mali: The Touareg Rebellion's Causes, Consequences, and Peacebuilding Process." Master's thesis, American University, Washington, DC.

Dlamini-Zuma, Nkosazana. 2006. Question & Answer Breakfast Show. SABC. Cape Town. May 30.

Du Bois, W. E. B. 1979. *The World and Africa: Inquiry into the Part which Africa Has Played in World History.* Rev. ed. New York: International Publishers.

Dunn, Kevin. 2008. "Theory Talk #22: Kevin Dunn on Identity in International Relations, the African Challenge to IR Theory, and the White-Male Bias of the Field." *Theory Talks.* October 28. http://www.theory-talks.org/2008/10/theory-talk-22.html.

Dunn, Kevin C., and Timothy M. Shaw, eds. 2001. *Africa's Challenge to International Relations Theory.* Basingstoke: Palgrave Macmillan.

Economist. 2000. "The Hopeless Continent." May 13.

———. 2011. "The African Union: Short of Cash and Teeth." January 27.

Edozie, Rita Kiki. 2004. "Promoting African 'Owned and Operated' Development: A Reflection on the New Partnership for African Development (NEPAD)." *African and Asian Studies* 3 (2): 145–73.

———. 2008. *Reconstructing the Third Wave of Democracy: Comparative African Democratic Politics.* Lanham, MD: University Press of America.

Edozie, Rita Kiki, and Peyi Soyinka-Airewele, eds. 2010. *Reframing Contemporary Africa: Politics, Economics, and Culture in the Global Era.* Washington DC: CQ Press/SAGE.

El-Agraa, Ali M. 2004. "The Enigma of African Economic Integration." *Journal of Economic Integration* 19 (1): 19–45.

Eno, Robert. 2008. "Human Rights, Human Development, and Peace: Inseparable Ingredients in Africa's Quest for Prosperity." January. PhD diss., University of Witwatersrand, Johannesburg. http://wiredspace.wits.ac.za/bitstream/handle/10539 /6827/PhD%20 Final %20Submissions.pdf?sequence=1.

Esedebe, Olisanwuche. 1982. *Pan-Africanism: The Idea and Movement, 1776–1963.* Washington, DC: Howard University Press.

European Commission. 2011. "Joint Declaration – The 5th College-to-College Meeting of the European Commission and the African Union Commission." June 1, Brussels, Belgium. http://europa.eu/rapid/press-release_MEMO-11-371_en.htm.

———. 2013. "About the European Commission." http://ec.europa.eu/about/index_en.htm.

Federal Democratic Republic of Ethiopia, Ministry of Foreign Affairs. 2013. "Acceptance Statement by H. E. Mr. Hailemariam Dessalegn Prime Minister of the Federal Democratic Republic of Ethiopia and Incoming Chairperson of the African Union at the 20th Ordinary Session of the Assembly of African Heads of State and Government." January. http://www.mfa.gov. et/theminister.php?cpg=3&pg=2.

Finnemore, Martha. 1996. *National Interests in International Society.* Ithaca: Cornell University Press.

Fortin, Jacey. 2013. "The Continent Versus the Court: African Union Deliberates Withdrawal from the ICC." *International Business Times.* October 11. http://www.ibtimes.com/ continent-versus-court-african-union-deliberates-withdrawal-icc-1422434.

France 24. 2013. "African Union Pledges $50 Million for Mali Intervention." January 28. http://www.france24.com/en/20130128-african-union-pledges-50-million-dollars-mali -intervention-france.

Franke, Benedikt. 2009. *Security Cooperation in Africa: A Reappraisal*. Boulder: FirstForumPress.

Freedom House. 2013. *Freedom in the World 2013: Democratic Breakthroughs in the Balance*. Washington, DC: Freedom House. http://www.freedomhouse.org/report/freedom-world/ freedom-world-2013#.Uw9YUM68lGA.

Fukuyama, Francis. 1992. *The End of History and the Last Man*. New York: Free Press.

Gathii, James Thuo. 2011. *African Regional Trade Agreements as Legal Regimes*. Cambridge: Cambridge University Press.

Genge, Manelisi, Francis Kornegay, and Stephen Rule. 2000. "African Union and Pan-African Parliament: Working Papers." http://unpan1.un.org/intradoc/groups/public/documents/ IDEP/UNPAN003885.pdf.

Giddens, Anthony. 2002. *Runaway World: How Globalization Is Reshaping Our Lives*. New York: Routledge.

Gilroy, Paul. 1993. *The Black Atlantic: Modernity and Double Consciousness*. Cambridge, MA: Harvard University Press.

Global Times. 2012. "Malian PM in Benin to Seek Solution to Malian Crisis." December 28. http://www.globaltimes.cn/content/752850.shtml.

Gomez, Michael A. 1998. *Exchanging Our Country Marks: The Transformation of African Identities in the Colonial and Antebellum South*. Chapel Hill: University of North Carolina Press.

Gottschalk, Keith. 2012. "The African Union and Its Sub-regional Structures." *Journal of African Union Studies* 1 (1): 9–39.

Guardian (Manchester). 2011. "Libya and African Self-Determination." April 2.

Hamilton, Ruth Simms. 2006. *Routes of Passage: Rethinking the African Diaspora*. Vol. 1, Part 1. East Lansing: Michigan State University Press.

Harmon, Stephen. 2008. "Radical Islam in the Sahel: Implications for U.S. Policy and Regional Stability." In *The United States and West Africa: Interactions and Relations*, ed. Alusine Jalloh and Toyin Falola. Rochester: University of Rochester Press.

Haynes, Jeffrey. 2005. *Comparative Politics in a Globalizing World*. Cambridge: Polity.

Held, David. 1995. *Democracy and the Global Order: From the Modern State to Cosmopolitan Governance*. Stanford: Stanford University Press.

———, ed. 2004. *A Globalizing World? Culture, Economics, Politics*. 2nd ed. London: Routledge.

Held, David, and Anthony G. McGrew. 2007. *Globalization/Anti-Globalization: Beyond the Great Divide*. Cambridge: Polity.

Herald, The (Harare). 2002a. "Nepad Not Independent of AU." November 19.

———. 2002b. "African Heads of Mission Criticize EU." February 27. http://allafrica.com /stories/200202270317.html.

Herskovits, Melville. 1941. *The Myth of the Negro Past*. Boston: Beacon.

Heyns, Christof H., and Frans Viljoen. 2001. "The Impact of the United Nations Human Rights Treaties on the Domestic Level." *Human Rights Quarterly* 23 (3): 483–535.

Horne, Gerald. 1986. *Black and Red: W. E. B. Du Bois and the Afro-American Response to the Cold War, 1944–1963*. Albany: State University of New York Press.

———. 2000. *Race Woman: The Lives of Shirley Graham Du Bois*. New York: New York University Press.

———. 2007a. *The Deepest South: The United States, Brazil, and the African Slave Trade*. New York: New York University Press.

———. 2007b. *The White Pacific: U.S. Imperialism and Black Slavery in the South Seas after the Civil War.* Honolulu: University of Hawaii Press.

Human Rights Watch. 2011. "African Union: New Plan for Mixed Court to Try Hissène Habré." January 26. http://www.hrw.org/news/2011/01/26/african-union-new-plan-mixed -court-try-hiss-ne-habr.

Huntington, Samuel P. 1991. *The Third Wave: Democratization in the Late Twentieth Century.* Norman: University of Oklahoma Press.

Ikome, Francis Nguendi. 2007. *From the Lagos Plan of Action to the New Partnership for Africa's Development: The Political Economy of African Regional Initiatives.* Midrand: Institute for Global Dialogue.

Independent (Addis Ababa). 2012. "Ethiopians Give Lackluster Welcome to Kwame Nkrumah Statue." February 14.

Inikori, Joseph E. 2002. *Africans and the Industrial Revolution in England: A Study in International Trade and Economic Development.* New York: Cambridge University Press.

Jahateh, Lamin. 2012. "Long Route to Uniting Africa through Trade." *Al Jazeera.* July 22. http:// www.aljazeera.com/indepth/opinion/2012/07/2012719113836485774.html.

Jalloh, Alusine, and Toyin Falola, eds. 2008. *The United States and West Africa: Interactions and Relations.* Rochester, NY: University of Rochester Press.

James, C. L. R. 1963. *The Black Jacobins: Toussaint L'Ouverture and the San Domingo Revolution.* New York: Vintage Books.

Jere, Regina Jane. 2012. "10 Years of the AU: The Hurdles and the Triumphs." *New African.* July.

Jobson, Elissa. 2012. "African Union's Dlamini-Zuma Calls for Political and Economic Unity." *Guardian* (Manchester). July 18. http://www.theguardian.com/global-development/2012 /jul/ 18/african-union-dlamini-zuma-political-economic.

Johnson, Sterling. 1998. *Black Globalism: The International Politics of a Non-state Nation.* Aldershot: Ashgate.

Jowitt, Kenneth. 1993. *New World Disorder: The Leninist Extinction.* Berkeley: University of California Press.

Karenga, Maulana. 1982. *Introduction to Black Studies.* 2nd ed. Los Angeles: University of Sankore Press.

Keita, Kalifa. 1998. *Conflict and Conflict Resolution in the Sahel: The Tuareg Insurgency in Mali.* Darby, PA: Diane Publishing.

Keto, C. Tsehloane. 2001. *Vision and Time: Historical Perspective of an Africa-Centered Paradigm.* Lanham, MD: University Press of America.

Khadiagala, Gilbert M., and Terrence Lyons, eds. 2001. *African Foreign Policies: Power and Process.* Boulder: Lynne Reinner Publishers.

Khamis, Kassim Mohammed. 2008. *Promoting the African Union.* Washington, DC: Lillian Barber Press.

Kioko, Ben. 2003. "The Right of Intervention under the African Union's Constitutive Act: From Non-interference to Non-intervention." *International Review of the Red Cross* 85 (852): 807–24.

Kloman, Erasmus H. 1962. "African Unification Movements." *International Organization* 16 (2): 387–404.

Konaré, Alpha. 2004. *Strategic Plan of the African Union Commission.* Vol. 1: *Vision and Mission of the African Union.* May. Accessed February 2011. http://www.africaunion.org/root/au /AboutAu/Vision/Volume1.pdf.

Kornegay, Francis. 2008. "The AU and Africa's Three Diasporas." In *The African Union and Its Institutions*, ed. John Akokpari, Angela Ndinga-Muvumba, and Tim Murithi. Cape Town: Fanele-Jacana and Centre for Conflict Resolution.

Kouassi, Edmond Kwam. 1984. "The OAU and International Law." In *The OAU after Twenty Years*, ed. Yassin El-Ayouty and I. William Zartman. New York: Praeger.

Kufuor, Kofi Oteng. 2006. *The Institutional Transformation of the Economic Community of West African States*. Aldershot: Ashgate.

Kupchan, Charles A. 2012. *No One's World: The West, the Rising Rest, and the Coming Global Turn*. Oxford: Oxford University Press.

Laporte, Geert, and James Mackie. 2010. *Building the African Union: An Assessment of Past Progress and Future Prospects for the African Union's Institutional Architecture*. Maastricht: Nordiska Afrikainstitutet; European Centre for Development Policy Management.

Legum, Colin. 1962. *Pan-Africanism: A Short Political Guide*. London: Pall Mall Press.

M'bayo, Tamba E. 2007. "Bou El Mogdad Seck, 1826–1880: Interpretation and Mediation of Colonialism in Senegal." In *African Agency and European Colonialism: Latitudes of Negotiations and Containment; Essays in Honor of A. S. Kanya-Forstner*, ed. Femi J. Kolapo and Kwabena O. Akurang-Parry. Lanham, MD: University Press of America.

Mackay, Hugh. 2000. "The Globalization of Culture?" In *A Globalizing World? Culture, Economics, Politics*, ed. David Held. London: Routledge.

Madakufamba, Munetsi. 2008. "Giant Step Toward a Single SADC-COMESA-EAC." *Southern African Development Community Today* 11 (3). http://www.sardc.net/editorial/sadctoday/view.asp?vol=720&pubno=v11n3.

Makinda, Samuel M., and F. Wafula Okumu. 2007. *The African Union: Challenges of Globalization, Security, and Governance*. Hoboken: Taylor and Francis.

Marah, John K. 2007. "Kwame Nkrumah's Continental Africa: A Dream Deferred but Not Forgotten." In *Africa in the 21st Century: Toward a New Future*, ed. Ama Mazama. New York: Routledge.

Martin, Tony. 1976. *Race First: The Ideological and Organizational Struggles of Marcus Garvey and the Universal Negro Improvement Association*. Westport, CT: Greenwood Press.

May, Vivian M. 2007. *Anna Julia Cooper, Visionary Black Feminist: A Critical Introduction*. New York: Routledge.

Mazrui, Ali A. 1967. *Towards a Pax Africana: A Study of Ideology and Ambition*. London: Weidenfeld and Nicolson.

———. 1969. *Towards a Pax Africana: A Study of Ideology and Ambition*. Rev. ed. Worthing: Littlehampton Book Services.

———. 1987. *The Africans: A Triple Heritage*. Boston: Little, Brown and Co.

———. 2001. "Africans and African-Americans in Changing World Trends: Globalizing the Black Experience." In *Issues in Africa and the African Diaspora in the 21st Century*, ed. Seth N. Asumah and Ibipo Johnston-Anumonwo (Binghamton: Binghamton University Global Publications), pp. 3–20.

Mazrui, Ali A., and Michael Tidy. 1984. *Nationalism and New States in Africa*. Portsmouth, NH: Heinemann.

M'Bayo, Tamba. 2011. "Diaspora Paradigms: New Scholarship in Comparative Black History." September. Unpublished paper. Morgantown: West Virginia University.

Mbeki, Thabo. 2002a. "Africa's Moment of Hope." In *Africa: Define Yourself*. Cape Town: Tafelburg and Mafube.

———. 2002b. "Building Africa's Capacity Through Nepad." *New African*, October.

———. 2011a. "Thabo Mbeki Speaks on Libya." *Guardian* (Manchester). April 8.

―――. 2011b. "What the World Got Wrong in Côte d'Ivoire." *Foreign Policy*. April 29. http://www. foreignpolicy.com/articles/2011/04/29/what_the_world_got_wrong_ in_cote _d_ivoire.

―――. 2012. "The African Union at 10 Years Old: A Dream Deferred." *SAFPI* (*South African Foreign Policy Initiative*). October 2. http://www.safpi.org/news/article/2012/thabo mbeki african union 10 years old dream deferred.

McColm, R. Bruce. 1992. *Freedom in the World: Political Rights and Civil Liberties 1991–1992*. New York: Freedom House.

McGrew, Anthony. 2004. "Power Shift: From National Government to Global Governance?" In *A Globalizing World? Culture, Economics, Politics*, ed. David Held. London: Routledge.

McNamara, Kathleen R. 1999. *The Currency of Ideas: Monetary Politics in the European Union*. Ithaca: Cornell University Press.

Mearsheimer, John J. 1994/95. "The False Promise of International Institutions." *International Security* 19 (3): 5–49.

Melber, Henning, Richard Cornwell, Jephthah Gathaka, and Smokin Wanjala. 2002. *The New Partnership for Africa's Development (NEPAD): African Perspectives*. Uppsala: Nordiska Afrikainstitutet.

Mezyaev, Alexander. 2013. "'Operation Mali': United Nations Complicit in Recolonization of Africa." Global Research. April 8. http://www.globalresearch.ca/operation-mali-united-nations-complicit -in-recolonization-of-africa/5330465.

Mkandawire, Thandika. 1994. "Adjustment, Political Conditionality and Democratisation in Africa." In *From Adjustment to Development in Africa: Conflict, Controversy, Convergence, Consensus?*, ed. Giovanni Andrea Cornia and Gerald K. Helleiner. Basingstoke: Macmillan.

Møller, Bjørn. 2009. "The African Union as Security Actor: African Solutions to African Problems?" Crisis States Working Papers, Series 2, no. 57: Regional and Global Axes of Conflict. London: Crisis States Research Center. August. http://eprints.lse.ac .uk/28485/1/ WP57.2Moller.AU.pdf.

Mubiala, Mutoy. 2012. "Peacekeeping Operations: The Examples of Burundi and Sudan." In *The African Union: Legal and Institutional Framework; A Manual on the Pan African Organization*, ed. Abdulqawi A. Yusuf and Fatsah Ouguergouz. Leiden: Martinus Nijhoff Publishers.

Muchie, Mammo, ed. 2003. *The Making of the Africa-Nation: Pan-Africanism and the African Renaissance*. London: Adonis and Abbey.

Mudimbe, V. Y. 1994. *The Idea of Africa*. Bloomington: Indiana University Press.

Murithi, Tim. 2005. *The African Union: Pan-Africanism, Peacebuilding and Development*. Burlington, VT: Ashgate.

―――. 2007. "From Pan-Africanism to the Union of Africa." *Pambazuka News*, no. 309 (July 20). http://pambazuka.org/en/category/comment/42079.

―――. 2009. "The African Union's Transition from Non-Intervention to Non-Indifference: An Ad Hoc Approach to Responsibility to Protect?" http://library.fes.de/pdf-files/ipg /ipg-2009-1/08_a_murithi_us.pdf.

Mwakikagile, Godfrey. 2007. *Relations between Africans and African Americans: Misconceptions, Myths and Realities*. Dar es Salaam: New Africa Press.

Najam, Adil. 2002. "International Environmental Negotiation: A Strategy for the South." In *Transboundary Environmental Negotiation: New Approaches to Global Cooperation*, eds. L. Susskind, W. Moomaw, and Gallagher, 41–81. San Francisco: Jossey-Bass.

Nazret: Ethiopian News Portal. 1994–2014. "H.I.M. Haile Selassie OAU Speech 1963 African Summit." http://www.nazret.com/history/him_oau.php.

Ndayi, Zoleka. 2009. "Contextualising NEPAD: Regionalism, Plurilateralism and Multilateralism." *South African Journal of International Affairs* 16, no. 3: 371–87.

Ndlovu-Gatsheni, Sabelo J. and Ndhlovu, Finex, eds. 2013. *Nationalism and National Projects in Southern Africa: New Critical Reflections*. Pretoria: Africa Institute of South Africa.

Nkrumah, Kwame. 1965. *Neo-Colonialism: The Last Stage of Imperialism*. London: Nelson.

———. 1970. *Africa Must Unite*. New York: International Publishers.

Nweke, G. Aforka. 1987. "The Organization of African Unity and Intra-African Functionalism." *Annals of the American Academy of Political and Social Science* 489 (1): 133–47.

Nyondo, Mbabi. 2012. "British Pressure on Malawi over Al Bashir Is a Form of New Imperialism." *Malawi Voice*. June 11.

O'Donnell, Guillermo A. 1996. "Illusions About Consolidation." *Journal of Democracy* 7 (20): 34–51.

Okpewho, Isidore, Carole Boyce Davies, and Ali A. Mazrui, eds. 2001. *The African Diaspora: African Origins and New World Identities*. Bloomington: Indiana University Press.

Oppong, Richard Frimpong. 2010. "The African Union, the African Economic Community and Africa's Regional Economic Communities: Untangling a Complex Web." *African Journal of International and Comparative Law* 18 (1): 92–103.

Padmore, George, ed. 1947. *Colonial and Coloured Unity: A Programme of Action; History of the Pan-African Congress*. London: The Hammersmith Bookshop.

Patterson, Tiffany Ruby, and Robin D. G. Kelley. 2000. "Unfinished Migrations: Reflections on the African Diaspora and the Making of the Modern World." *African Studies Review* 43 (1): 11–45.

Peters, Wolff-Christian. 2010. *The Quest for an African Economic Community: Regional Integration and Its Role in Achieving African Unity – the Case of SADC*. Frankfurt am Main: Peter Lang.

Pfaff, William. 1995. "A New Colonialism: Europe Must Go Back into Africa." *Foreign Affairs* 74 (1): 2–6.

Pieterse, Jan Nederveen. 2003. *Globalization and Culture: Global Mélange*. Lanham, MD: Rowman and Littlefield.

Poe, Daryl Zizwe. 2003. *Kwame Nkrumah's Contribution to Pan-Africanism: An Afrocentric Analysis*. London: Routledge.

Powell, Kristiana, and Thomas Kwasi Tieku. 2005. "The African Union's New Security Agenda: Is Africa Closer to a Pax Pan-Africana?" *International Journal* 60 (4): 937–52.

Przeworski, Adam, Michael E. Alvarez, José Antonio Cheibub, and Fernando Limongi. 2000. *Democracy and Development: Political Institutions and Well-Being in the World, 1950–1990*. Cambridge: Cambridge University Press.

Redi, Omer. 2013. "ICC under Fire Again as African Leaders Sternly Oppose Its Moves." May 27. Accessed May 30, 2013. http://www.capitalethiopia.com/index.php?view=article&id =3018%3Aicc under fire again as african leaders sternly oppose its moves&format=pdf& option=com_content&Itemid=27.

Riazat, Saba. 2006. "A Closer Look: Professor Seeks Stronger U.N." *Daily Bruin* (Los Angeles). October 17.

Rodney, Walter. 1981. *How Europe Underdeveloped Africa*. Washington, DC: Howard University Press.

Rosenau, James N., David C. Earnest, Yale H. Ferguson, and Ole R. Holsti. 2006. *On the Cutting Edge of Globalization: An Inquiry into American Elites*. Lanham, MD: Rowman and Littlefield.

Rugunda, Ruhakana. 2011. "African Union Statement on the NATO Invasion of Libya: It's Time to End the Bombing and Find a Political Solution in Libya." *Counter Punch*. June 22.

Gunaratna, Rohan. 2012. "Instability Threatens the Sahel." *The National Interest*. April 26.

Sartre, Jean-Paul. 2001. *Colonialism and Neo-colonialism*. London: Routledge.

Schmidt, Siegmar. 2010. "Through the Lens of European Integration Theory: African Peace and Security Architecture as a Framework in Transition." In *Crafting an African Security Architecture: Addressing Regional Peace and Conflict in the Twenty-first Century*, ed. Hany Besada. Burlington, VT: Ashgate.

Schmitter, Philippe C. 2004. "Neo-neofunctionalism." In Antje Wiener and Thomas Diez, *European Integration Theory*. Oxford: Oxford University Press.

Scholte, Jan Aart. 1997. "Global Trade and Finance." In *The Globalization of World Politics: An Introduction to International Relations*, ed. John Baylis and Steve Smith. Oxford: Oxford University Press.

Schulz, Dorothea E. 2012. *Culture and Customs of Mali*. Westport, CT: Greenwood.

Scott, William R. 1993. *The Sons of Sheba's Race: African-Americans and the Italo-Ethiopian War, 1935–1941*. Bloomington: Indiana University Press.

Sehen, Hirpo. 2006. "The Pan-African Parliament: Its Promise for Human Rights and Democracy in Africa." LL.M. diss., Faculty of Law, Centre for Human Rights, University of Pretoria.

Shaw, Timothy M. 1981. *Alternative Futures for Africa*. Boulder: Westview Press.

Sherwood, Marika. 2010. *Origins of Pan-Africanism: Henry Sylvester Williams, Africa, and the African Diaspora*. London: Routledge.

Shivji, Issa. 2011. "Tanzania: Nyerere, Nationalism and Pan-Africanism." *allAfrica*. March 17. http://allafrica.com/stories/201103180842.html.

Solomon, Hussein, and Gerrie Swart. 2004. "Defending African Unity: Can the Peace and Security Council of the African Union Succeed?" In *Perspectives on the OAU/AU and Conflict Management in Africa*, ed. Abdalla Bujra and Hussein Solomon. Tripoli: African Center for Applied Research and Training in Social Development; Addis Ababa: Community of Sahel-Saharan States; Oxford: Development Policy Management Forum.

Steger, Manfred B. 2003. *Globalization: A Very Short Introduction*. Oxford: Oxford University Press.

Tehindrazanarivelo, Djacoba L. 2012. "The African Union's Relationship with the United Nations in the Maintenance of Peace and Security." In *The African Union: Legal and Institutional Framework; A Manual on the Pan-African Organization*, ed. Abdulqawi A. Yusuf and Fatsah Ouguergouz. Leiden: Martinus Nijhoff Publishers.

Thompson, Grahame. 2000. "Economic Globalization?" In *A Globalizing World? Culture, Economics, Politics*, ed. David Held. London: Routledge.

Tieku, Thomas Kwasi. 2011. "African Agency via Multilateral Channels: Opportunities and Challenges." Paper presented at a seminar organized by the British International Studies Association/International Studies Association Africa Working Group, University of Birmingham. April.

Tomaselli, Keyan G. 2003. "Dialectical Intellectuals, Essentialism and the African Renaissance." *Journal of Cultural Studies* (Nigeria) 5 (1): 1–34.

Touray, Omar A. 2005. "The Common African Defence and Security Policy." *African Affairs* 104 (117): 635–56.

Tigroudja, Hélène. 2012. "The African Charter on Democracy, Elections and Governance." In *The African Union: Legal and Institutional Framework*, ed. Abdulqawi A. Yusuf and Fatsah Ouguergouz. Leiden: Martinus Nijhoff Publishers.

Tucker, Philip Thomas. 2012. *Father of the Tuskegee Airmen, John C. Robinson*. Washington, DC: Potomac Books.

United Nations Economic Commission for Africa. 2006. "Ten-Year Capacity Building Programme for the African Union." December 12. www.uneca.org/nepad/pages/ten-year-capacity-building - programme-african-union.

United Nations Radio. 2012. "Stronger Cooperation Needed between UN and African Union." January 12. http://www.unmultimedia.org/radio/english/2012/01/stronger cooperation needed between un and african union/.

U.S. State Department Official Blog. 2011. "African Solutions for African Problems." http://blogs.state.gov/stories/2011/08/31/african-solutions-african-problems.

Valiente, Alexandra. 2011. "The Pan Afrikanist Steering Committee of Namibia against the United Nations Resolution 1973 (PSCNAUNR)." June 6. http://vivalibya.wordpress.com/2011/06/06/the-pan-afrikanist-steering-committee-of-namibia-against-the-united-nations-resolution-1973/.

Venter, Daniel J., and Ernst W. Neuland. 2005. *NEPAD and the African Renaissance*. Johannesburg: Richard Havenga and Associates.

Viljoen, Frans. 2007. *International Human Rights Law in Africa*. Oxford: Oxford University Press.

Vinson, Robert Trent. 2012. *The Americans Are Coming! Dreams of African American Liberation in Segregationist South Africa*. Athens: Ohio University Press.

Vitalis, Robert. 2000. "The Graceful and Generous Liberal Gesture: Making Racism Invisible in American International Relations." *Millennium—Journal of International Studies* 29: 331–56.

Voice of America. 2011. "African Union Says ICC Prosecutions Are Discriminatory." July 4. http://www.voanews.com/content/article african union says icc prosecutions are discriminatory 125012734/158424.html.

Walraven, Klaas van. 2004. "From Union of Tyrants to Power to the People? The Significance of the Pan-African Parliament for the African Union." *Afrika Spectrum* 39 (2): 197–221.

Walters, Ronald W. 1993. *Pan-Africanism in the African Diaspora: An Analysis of Modern Afrocentric Political Movements*. Detroit: Wayne State University Press.

Wane, Mamadou, Paul Burkett, and Robert C. Guell. 1996. "Economic Growth and Monetary Union in Sub-Saharan Africa: New Evidence on the Effects of CFA-Zone Membership." *Applied Economics Letters* 3 (12): 769–73.

Wanyeki, L. Muthoni. 2007. *Africa Unite*. Open Society Institute, AfriMap. May. http://www.afrimap.org/english/images/paper/AU_Wanyeki.pdf.

Waterfield, Bruno. 2010. "More than 50 EU Embassies Open across the World." *The Telegraph*. (London). January 22.

Weiss, Thomas G., David P. Forsythe, Roger A. Coate, and Kelly Kate-Pease. 2007. *The United Nations and Changing World Politics*. 5th ed. Boulder: Westview Press.

Welz, Martin. 2013. *Integrating Africa: Decolonization's Legacies, Sovereignty and the African Union*. Abingdon: Routledge.

Wendt, Alexander. 1992. "Anarchy Is What States Make of It: The Social Construction of Power Politics." *International Organization* 46 (2): 391–425.

———. 1999. *Social Theory of International Politics*. Cambridge: Cambridge University Press.

———. 2008. "Theory Talk #3: UFO's, Black Swans and Constructivist International Relations Theory." http://www.theory-talks.org/2008/04/theory-talk-3.html.

Williams, Eric. 1994. *Capitalism and Slavery*. Chapel Hill: University of North Carolina Press.

Williams, Paul. 2006. "The African Union: Prospects for Regional Peacekeeping after Burundi and Sudan." *Review of African Political Economy* 33, no. 108: 353–57.

Wing, Susanna D. 2008. *Constructing Democracy in Transitioning Societies of Africa: Constitutionalism and Deliberation in Mali*. Basingstoke: Palgrave Macmillan.

Wiredu, Kwasi. 1996. *Cultural Universals and Particulars: An African Perspective*. Bloomington: Indiana University Press.

Wolfers, Michael. 1976. *Politics in the Organization of African Unity*. Studies in African History 18. London: Methuen.

Yusuf, Abdulqawi A., and Fatsah Ouguergouz, eds. 2012. *The African Union: Legal and Institutional Framework; A Manual on the Pan-African Organization*. Leiden: Martinus Nijhoff Publishers.

Zahorka, Hans-Jürgen. 2002. *The Foundation of the African Union: International Internet Press Clippings (with the Constitutive Act of the African Union), 08th/09th July, 2002*. European Centre for Transnational Integration Studies: Dossier no. 1. Sindelfingen: Libertas.

Zartman, I. William. 1966. *International Relations in the New Africa*. Englewood Cliffe, NJ: Prentice Hall.

Statutes and Treaties

African Union Non-Aggression and Common Defence Pact. 2005. http://www.au.int/en/sites/default/files/AFRICAN_UNION_NON_AGGRESSION_AND_COMMON_DEFENCE_PACT.pdf.

Charter of the Organization of African Unity. http://www.au.int/en/sites/default/files/OAU_Charter_1963.pdf.

Constitutive Act of the African Union. 2000. http://www.au.int/en/sites/default/files/Constitutive_Act_en_0.htm.

Memorandum of Understanding on Cooperation in the Area of Peace and Security between the African Union, the Regional Economic Communities and the Coordinating Mechanisms of the Regional Standby Brigades of Eastern Africa and Northern Africa.

http://www.paxafrica.org/areas-of-work/peace-and-security -architecture/peace -and-security-architecture-documents/mou-in-the-area-of-peace-and-security -between-the-au-and-the-recs.

Protocol to the African Charter on Human and Peoples' Rights on the Establishment of an African Court on Human and Peoples' Rights. http://www.au.int/en/sites/default/files/PROTOCOL_AFRICAN_CHARTER_HUMAN_PEOPLES_RIGHTS_ESTABLISHMENT_AFRICAN_COURT_HUMAN_PEOPLES_RIGHTS_1.pdf.

Protocol on the Statute of the African Court of Justice and Human Rights. http://www.au.int/en/sites/default/files/PROTOCOL_STATUTE_AFRICAN_COURT_JUSTICE_AND_HUMAN_RIGHTS.pdf.

Protocol Relating to the Establishment of the Peace and Security Council of the African Union. http://www.au.int/en/sites/default/files/Protocol_peace_and_security.pdf.

Protocol to the Treaty Establishing the African Economic Community Relating to the Pan-African Parliament. http://www.au.int/en/sites/default/files/PROTOCOL_TREATY_ESTABLISHING_THE_AFRICAN_ECONOMIC_COMMUNITY_RELATING_PAN_AFRICAN_PARLIAMENT.pdf.

Statutes of the Economic, Social and Cultural Council of the African Union. http://pages.au.int/sites/default/files/ECOSOCC%20STATUTES-English.pdf.

Solemn Declaration on a Common African Defence and Security Policy. 2004. http://www.peaceau.org/uploads/declaration-cadsp-en.pdf.

Treaty Establishing the African Economic Community (Abuja Treaty). http://www.au.int/en/sites/default/files/TREATY_ESTABLISHING_THE_AFRICAN_ECONOMIC_COMMUNITY.pdf.

Legal Cases

African Commission of Human and Peoples' Rights v. the Great Socialist Libyan People's Arab Jamahiriya, Order 004/2011.

Campbell and Another v. Republic of Zimbabwe, SADC (T) 03/2009.

Chief Ebrahim Manneh v. Republic of the Gambia, ECW/CCJ/APP/04/07.

Hadijatou Mani Koraou v. Republic of Niger, ECW/CCJ/JUD/06/08.

James Katabazi and 21 Others v. Secretary General of the East African Community and Others, Judgement Ref. No.1 of 2007.

Mike Campbell (Pvt) Ltd and 78 Others v. The Republic of Zimbabwe, SADC (T) 02/2007.

Socio-Economic Rights and Accountability Project (SERAP) v. the President of the Federal Republic of Nigeria, ECW/CCJ/APP/08/08.

Websites

AACC (All Africa Conference of Churches). 2012. http://www.aacc-ceta.org.

AAG (All Africa Games). 1998. "AAG Background." http://www.aag.org.za/background/index.shtml.

AAU (Association of African Universities). 2011. Accessed August 1. http://www.aau.org.

ACALAN (African Academy of Languages). 2012. "About ACALAN." Accessed March 15. http://www.acalan.org/eng/about_acalan/about_acalan.php.

AfMA (Africa Medical Association). 2011. Accessed August 1. http://www.africama.net.

AFRAA (African Airlines Association). 2011. Accessed August 1. http://www.afraa.org.

African Court of Human and Peoples' Rights. 2011. "African Court in Brief." Accessed July 21. http://www.african-court.org/en/index.php/about-the-court/brief-history.

African Press Organization / Organisation de la Presse Africaine. 2011. "17th AU Summit /Final Session of African Union Announces That Talks on Libya Are Near." http://appablog.wordpress.com/2011/07/04/17th-au-summit-final-session-of-african-union-announces-that-talks-on-libya-are-near.

African Union Commission. 2007. "Concept Note." *Public Consultation on the Grand Debate on an African Union Government*. http://www.africa-union.org/augovernment.htm.

AIPA (ASEAN Inter-Parliamentary Assembly). 2013. "The Statutes of the ASEAN Inter-Parliamentary Assembly (AIPA)." http://www.aipasecretariat.org//about/statutes.

AMISOM Magazine. Accessed December 2013. http://amisom-au.org/amisom-magazine.

APCOF (African Policing Civilian Oversight Forum). 2013. http://www.apcof.org.za/home/default.asp.

ASEA (African Securities Exchanges Association). 2011. Accessed August 3. http://www.africansea.org.

Avalon Project. 2008. "A Decade of American Foreign Policy 1941–1949: Bogota Conference of American States, Charter of the Organization of American States; March 30–May 2, 1948." http://avalon.law.yale.edu/20th_century/decad062.asp.

CODESRIA (Council for the Development of Social Science Research in Africa). 2011. Accessed August 1. http://www.codesria.org.

Department of International Relations and Cooperation, Republic of South Africa. 2003. "African Economic Community (AEC)." http://www.dfa.gov.za/foreign/Multilateral/africa/aec.htm

ECOSOCC-SA (Economic, Social and Cultural Council–South Africa Chapter). "Background." Accessed December 2012. http://www.nacf.org.za/civil-society/ECOSOCC_background.pdf.

ECOWAS Parliament. 2013. http://www.parl.ecowas.int.

European Parliament. 2011. Accessed July 23. http://www.europarl.europa.eu/portal/en.

Freedom in the World. 2013.http://www.freedomhouse.org/.

IIP Digital. 2011. "Fact Sheet: United States and African Union." April 19. http://iipdigital.usembassy.gov/st/english/texttrans/2011/04/20110419173722su0.9427105.html#ixzz1Robqiyiz.

G8 Africa Action Plan. 2002. Kananaskis Summit. http://www.g8.utoronto.ca/summit/2002 kananaskis/africaplan.html.

NEPAD. 2010–12. http://www.NEPAD.org.

OOPAU (Organization of Pan African Unity). Accessed, February 2014. http://www.oopau.org /index.html.

PAAZAB (African Association of Zoos and Aquaria). 2006. http://www.zoosafrica.com.

PAP (Pan-African Parliament). 2006. http://www.pan-africanparliament.org.

Parlamento Centroamericano. 2013. www.parlacen.int.

Report on the New York Town Hall Meeting. 2007. January 15. http://au6ny.tripod.com /id16.html.

United Nations. 2011. "Charter of the United Nations." Accessed July 16. http://www.un.org /en/documents/charter/index.shtml.

Index

A

African contributionism, xiii
African crisis, 100
African development, 7
African Economic Community (AEC), 154, 157, 159–64, 166, 175–78, 190, 215
African identity, xxii, xl, 107, 108, 123, 234
African institutionalism, xiii, 9
African nationalism, 67–68, 74, 80, 83
African politics, xxxiv, xxxviii, xlix, 3–5, 8, 11, 22, 25, 184, 199, 206, 211, 215
African renaissance, xi, 21, 26, 71, 104–9, 154, 230, 238
African solutions for African problems, xxii, xxxi–xxxviii, 12, 72, 131, 133, 209, 211, 215, 216, 227, 228
African Standby Force, 120, 137
Agency, xiii, xxvi, xxxii, xxxiii, 7, 18, 26, 142, 215, 216, 230, 235, 238
Area studies, xxxii
"AU phenomenon, the" xii, xlviii, 8, 25, 209, 213, 215–18, 234–38

C

Civil society organizations, 51, 72, 85, 90, 93, 107, 113, 114
Colonization, xx

Comparative politics, xxx, xxxii, 5, 22
Conflict resolution, xlv, 39, 41, 116, 120, 127, 128, 130, 131, 137, 141, 146–48, 185, 190, 192, 207, 210, 214, 217, 218
Constitutive Act, xxxix, xliv, xlv, xlviii, 5–7, 11, 16, 30, 32, 43–45, 47, 50–52, 61, 62, 100, 101, 104, 107, 109, 110, 116, 131–35, 141, 155, 156, 163, 167, 190, 191, 194, 202, 218, 237
Constructivism, xxxv, xxxviii, xlix, 7, 8, 13–16, 19, 98, 184, 189, 209–11, 235
Cultural identity, xii, xxv, xxxviii, 7, 15, 215, 221

D

Democracy, xii, xxv, xxxviii, xli, xlii, xliii, 15, 23, 38, 43, 50, 66, 97, 98, 100–106, 108–11, 116–25, 128, 137, 146, 147, 171, 178, 188, 192, 195, 217, 221, 222, 226, 228; hybrid, 102–5, 108, 109, 116, 117, 119, 123, 215
Democratic capitalism, 106
diaspora: African, xxix, xxxvii, 6, 25, 35, 50, 54, 55, 61–66, 69, 77–84, 95, 97, 113, 201; Black, 193; Pan-African, 24, 27, 84–93, 95, 210

Diaspora Clause (sixth region), xxix, xxxvi, xlix, 55, 61, 62, 68, 72, 75, 80, 82, 84, 89, 92–95, 97
Du Bois, W. E. B., xxviii, 64, 66, 73, 75, 90

E
Economic development, xii, xxv, 103, 105, 118
Ethiopianism, xx, xxiii, xxvi, xxvii, 79, 86

G
Gaddafi, Muammar, 17, 71, 81, 86, 98, 102, 110, 122, 141, 146, 147
Gender, 89, 174, 188, 204, 237
Global development, xii, xxv, xlix, 162, 215, 235
Global governance, xi, xxiv, xxiv, xxv, xxxviii, xliii, xlviii, xlix, 3–5, 7, 8, 10–12, 16, 21, 27, 52–56, 124, 125–26, 129, 130–32, 149, 153, 155, 157, 185, 186, 218, 227, 232, 235–37
Globalization, xiii, xiv, xxv, xxvi, xxx, xxxii, xxxiii, xxxviii, xxxix, xl, xlix, 4–9, 11, 12, 16, 17, 21, 23, 26, 30, 41, 62, 64, 100, 105, 123, 153, 157, 170, 184, 189, 207, 216, 218, 228, 235, 236

H
Hegemony, xiii, 19, 21, 34, 83, 109, 121, 146, 150, 170, 187, 204, 205, 221, 230, 232

I
Imperialism, xxviii, 17, 68, 206, 210, 232
Integration (political, economic, social), xi, xxxiv, xlvi–xlviii, 8, 19, 26, 42, 44, 47, 56, 57, 63, 70, 71, 133, 153, 154, 157, 159, 162, 163–65, 169, 174, 178, 179, 185, 189, 193, 194, 196, 198, 199, 203, 205–6, 216, 221, 231, 234–38
Intergovernmental organizations, xlviii, 24, 44, 45, 48, 55, 56, 63, 71, 85, 94, 123, 129, 135, 137, 143, 179, 184, 186, 190–95, 196, 200, 201, 207, 209, 227, 238
International community, xxx, xlv, 12, 24, 52, 98, 100, 121, 123, 129, 141, 148–50, 209, 217, 226, 234
International Criminal Court (ICC), xxiv, 127, 136, 141, 151, 205, 206, 239
International organizations, 34, 57, 75, 123, 129, 210, 213, 218, 228, 234, 236, 237

International partnerships, 51, 147, 169, 170, 197, 214
International relations, xiii, xxx, xxxii–xxxiv, 5, 22, 61, 216

L
Lagos Plan, 41, 154, 161–62, 170, 175, 176, 198, 201
League of Nations, xiii, xx, xxi
Legitimacy, xlvii, 10, 98, 102, 122, 132, 146, 200–206, 228

M
Marginalization, xxii, xxxiii, xxxix, xl, xlv, 7, 19, 122, 131, 154, 156, 161, 164, 185, 191, 205, 234
Mbeki, Thabo, xxii, xxviii, xxxv, 21, 22, 32, 43, 71, 72, 105, 108, 110, 130, 147, 153–55, 171, 196

N
Nation state, 22, 183, 216
Neocolonialism, 12, 24, 31, 132, 161, 217, 218, 229–34, 235
Neofunctionalism, 7, 8, 10, 11, 31, 35, 37, 42, 131, 184, 185, 195, 228
Neoliberalism, 97, 100, 106, 157, 162, 170, 179
New Partnership for African Development (NEPAD), 156, 160, 169, 170, 173, 174, 178, 179
Nkosazana, Dlamini-Zuma, xxx, 127, 194, 195, 229, 238–39
Nkrumah, Kwame, vii, xxviii, xxxv, xliv, xlviii, 5, 17, 20, 29, 30, 32, 38, 41, 42, 64, 67, 68, 69, 71–72, 73, 77, 86, 90, 108, 129, 131, 151, 154, 160, 175, 186, 198, 231, 239
Nonindifference, 5, 25, 37, 133, 135, 136, 146

P
Pan-Africanism, xi–xiii, xxiv, xxii, xxii, xxvi–xxix, xxxv–xxxvii, xl, xli, xliv, xlv, xlvi, xlix, 3, 6, 7, 15, 17–19, 24, 27, 30, 31, 35, 40, 42, 43, 50, 57, 62–73, 78, 79, 81, 84, 85, 90, 91, 94, 95, 104, 105, 111, 113, 129, 130, 133, 137, 153, 154, 156, 160, 171, 174, 175, 178, 184–87, 189, 195, 197, 200, 202–4, 206, 210, 214–18, 220, 225, 226, 229, 231, 234–39

Pan-nationalism, xx, xxxviii, 5, 15
Pax Africana, xii, xliv, 5, 12, 31, 127, 129–33,
    137, 139, 141, 147, 150–52, 190, 215,
    216, 226, 229, 230, 232
Peacekeeping, 48
Ping, Jean, xliv, 136, 141, 197
Postcolonialism, xxxv, 12, 20, 24, 132, 154,
    209, 234

R
Regional Economic Communities (RECs),
    xxxiv, xlix, 33, 34, 40, 57, 75, 153, 156,
    160, 163, 165, 167–69, 178, 185, 206
Regional organization (institution), xlvii, 4,
    5, 184, 191, 192, 194, 215, 237
Responsibility to protect, 47, 132–36, 147

S
Security, xii, xxv, xxxviii, xliv, xlv, 5, 20, 22,
    26, 31, 47, 127–29, 131–35, 137, 141,
    142, 149, 151, 178, 192, 205, 214, 215,
    217, 218, 226, 230

Self-determination, xxvii, xxviii, xlv, 8, 20,
    21, 66, 74, 100, 103–5, 107, 125, 130,
    134, 135, 158, 198, 200, 204, 207, 210,
    215, 216, 234, 239
Sovereignty, 4, 5, 10, 12, 15, 20, 26, 30, 35,
    36, 42–44, 55, 57, 70, 73, 80, 95, 109,
    114, 134, 136, 151, 186, 191, 192, 196,
    200, 204, 205, 214, 226, 231, 237
Suprastate, xi, xxii, xxiv, xxv, xl, xliii, xlvii,
    6–8, 10, 16, 22, 25, 31, 32, 62, 85, 101,
    129, 131, 149, 183, 190–92, 200, 206,
    210, 211, 226, 229, 236

T
Transformational globalization, xxx, xxxv,
    xxxviii, xl, 5, 9, 10, 13, 17, 25
Treaty of Abuja, 33, 40, 42, 43

U
Union government, 6, 8, 128, 184, 201, 202